SLEEPY PRINCESS IN THE DEMON CASTLE

6

Story & Art by
KAGIJI KUMANOMATA

NIGHTS

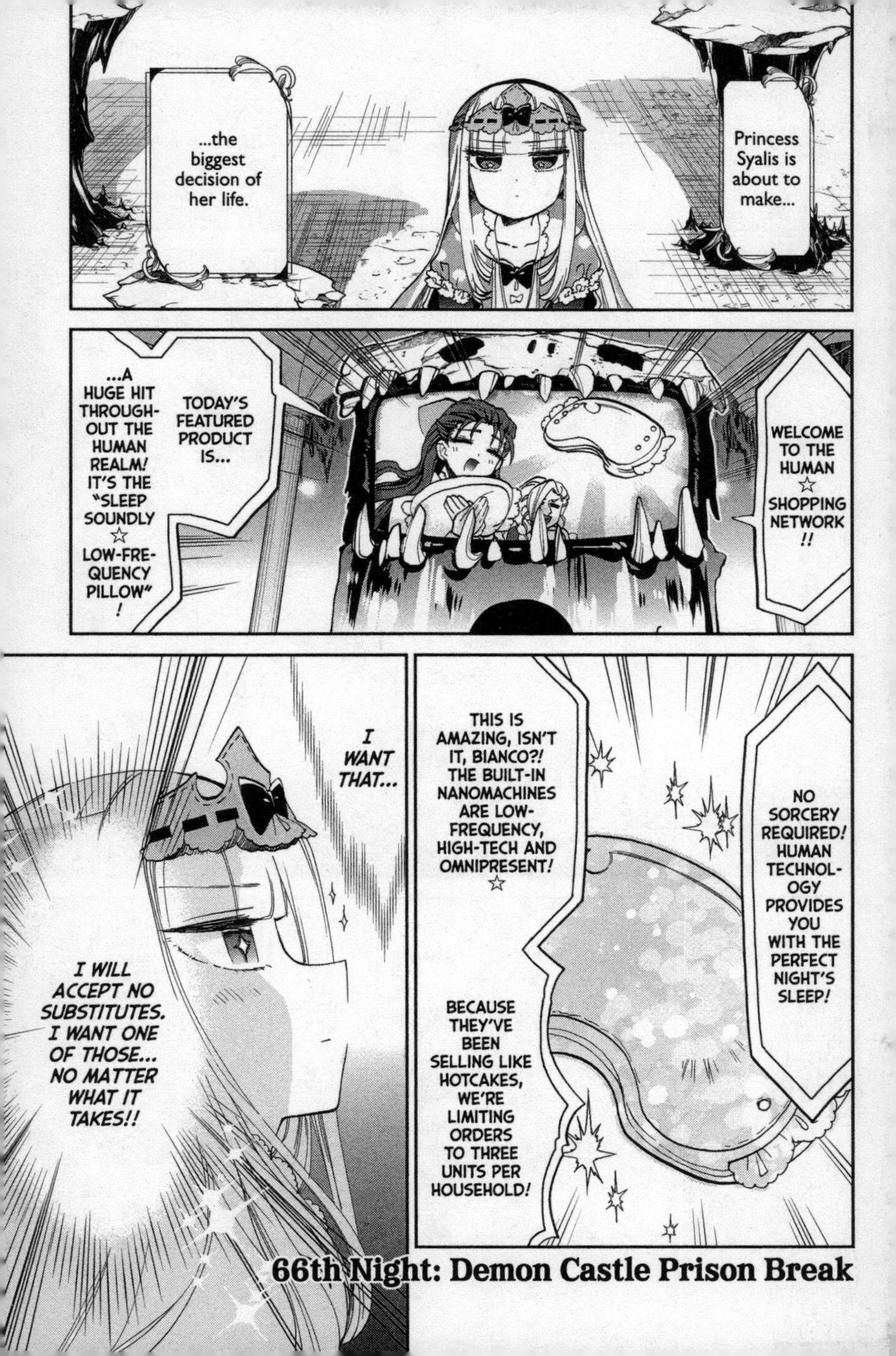
Princess Syalis is about to make...
...the biggest decision of her life.
WELCOME TO THE HUMAN ☆ SHOPPING NETWORK!!
TODAY'S FEATURED PRODUCT IS...
...A HUGE HIT THROUGHOUT THE HUMAN REALM! IT'S THE "SLEEP SOUNDLY ☆ LOW-FREQUENCY PILLOW"!
NO SORCERY REQUIRED! HUMAN TECHNOLOGY PROVIDES YOU WITH THE PERFECT NIGHT'S SLEEP!
THIS IS AMAZING, ISN'T IT, BIANCO?! THE BUILT-IN NANOMACHINES ARE LOW-FREQUENCY, HIGH-TECH AND OMNIPRESENT! ☆
BECAUSE THEY'VE BEEN SELLING LIKE HOTCAKES, WE'RE LIMITING ORDERS TO THREE UNITS PER HOUSEHOLD!
I WANT THAT...
I WILL ACCEPT NO SUBSTITUTES. I WANT ONE OF THOSE... NO MATTER WHAT IT TAKES!!
66th Night: Demon Castle Prison Break

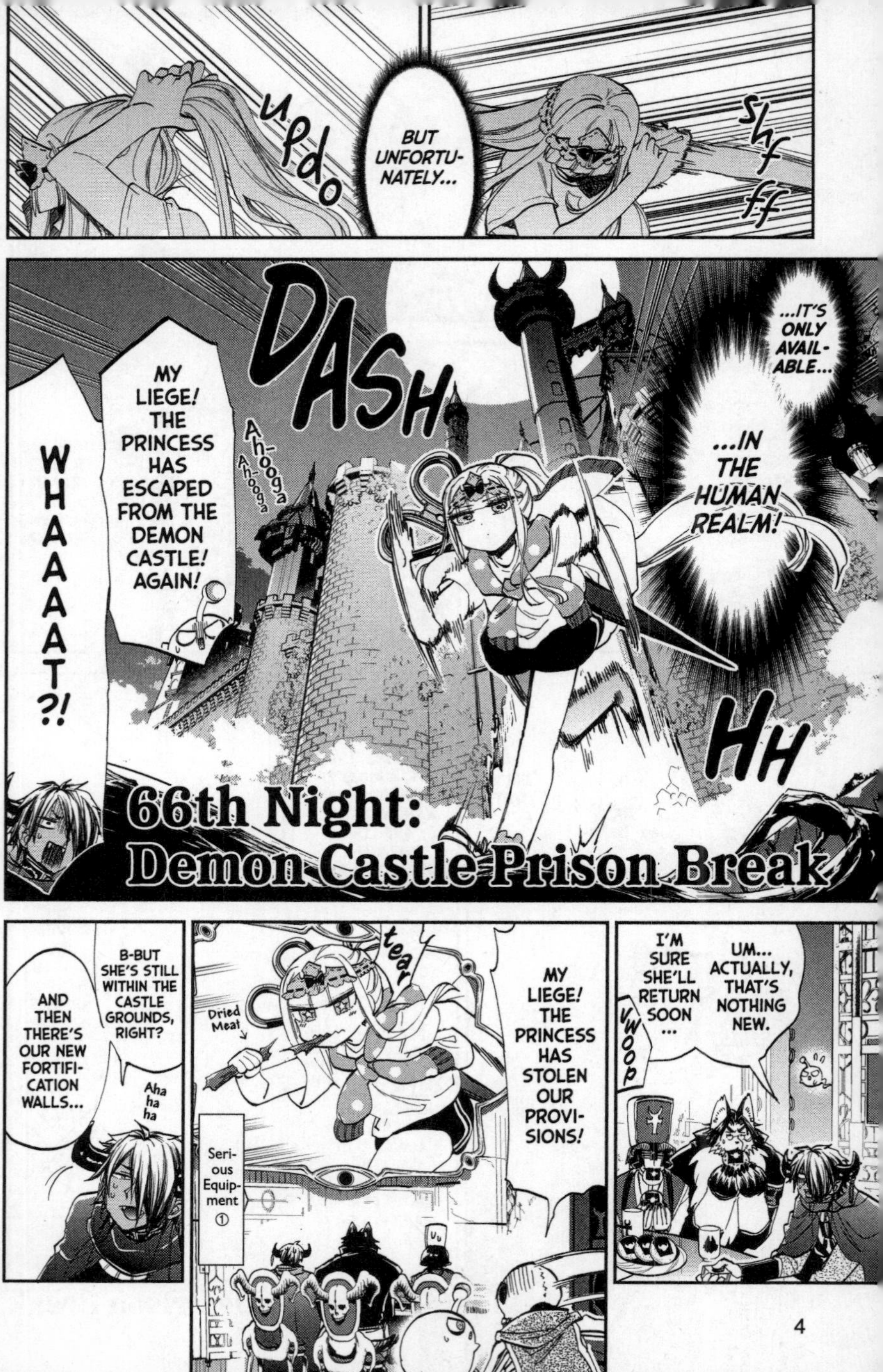
shfff
BUT UNFORTUNATELY...
updo
...IT'S ONLY AVAILABLE...
...IN THE HUMAN REALM!
DASH
HH
MY LIEGE! THE PRINCESS HAS ESCAPED FROM THE DEMON CASTLE! AGAIN!
Ahooga Ahooga
WHAAAAAT?!
66th Night: Demon Castle Prison Break
UM... ACTUALLY, THAT'S NOTHING NEW.
I'M SURE SHE'LL RETURN SOON ...
VWOOP
MY LIEGE! THE PRINCESS HAS STOLEN OUR PROVISIONS!
tear
Dried Meat
Serious Equipment ①
B-BUT SHE'S STILL WITHIN THE CASTLE GROUNDS, RIGHT?
AND THEN THERE'S OUR NEW FORTIFICATION WALLS...
Aha ha ha

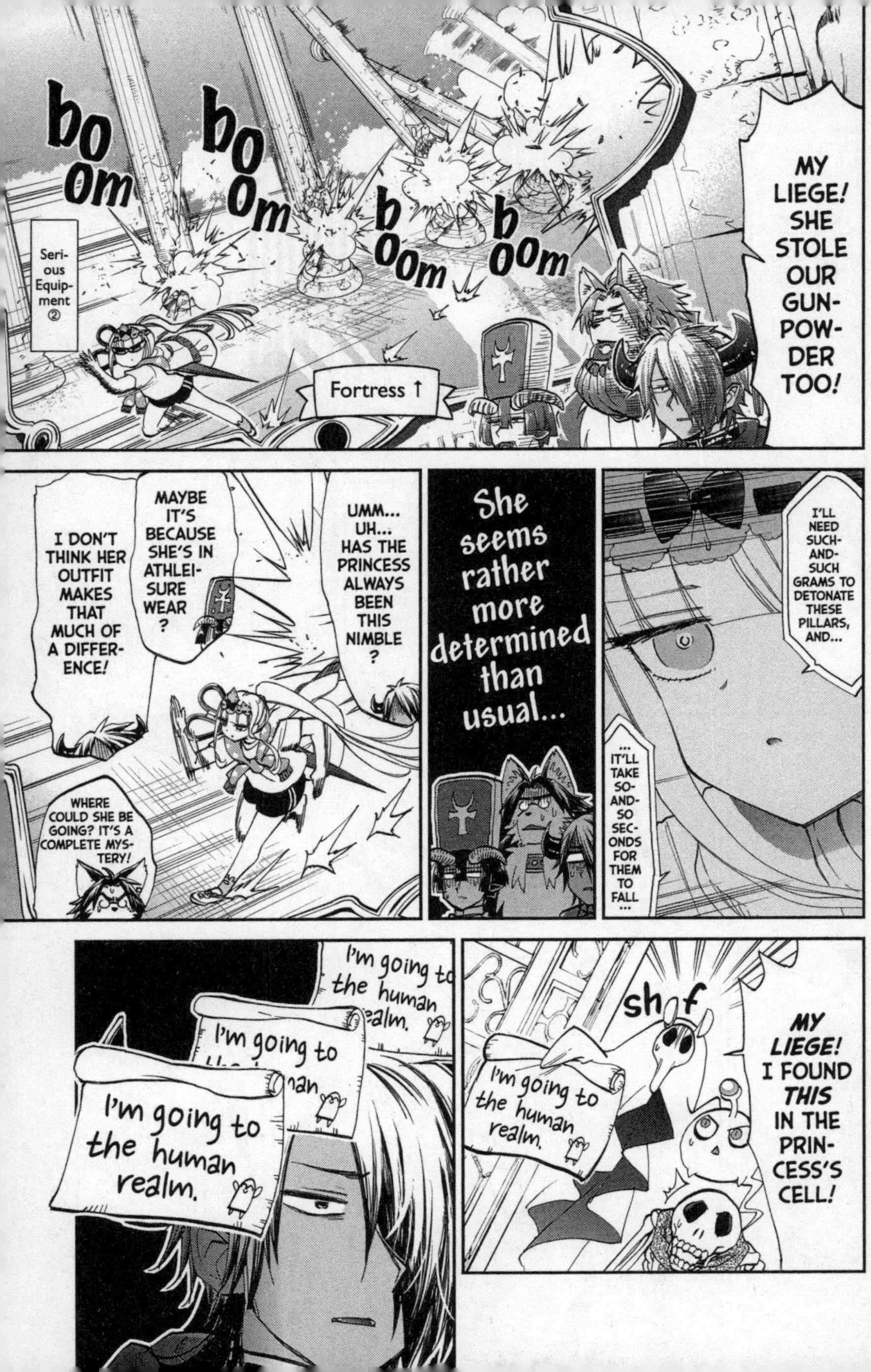

MY LIEGE! SHE STOLE OUR GUNPOWDER TOO!
boom
boom
boom
boom
Fortress ↑
Serious Equipment ②
I'LL NEED SUCH-AND-SUCH GRAMS TO DETONATE THESE PILLARS, AND...
... IT'LL TAKE SO-AND-SO SECONDS FOR THEM TO FALL...
She seems rather more determined than usual...
UMM... UH... HAS THE PRINCESS ALWAYS BEEN THIS NIMBLE?
MAYBE IT'S BECAUSE SHE'S IN ATHLEISURE WEAR?
I DON'T THINK HER OUTFIT MAKES THAT MUCH OF A DIFFERENCE!
WHERE COULD SHE BE GOING? IT'S A COMPLETE MYSTERY!
MY LIEGE! I FOUND THIS IN THE PRINCESS'S CELL!
shf
I'm going to the human realm.
I'm going to the human realm.
I'm going to the human realm.
I'm going to the human realm.

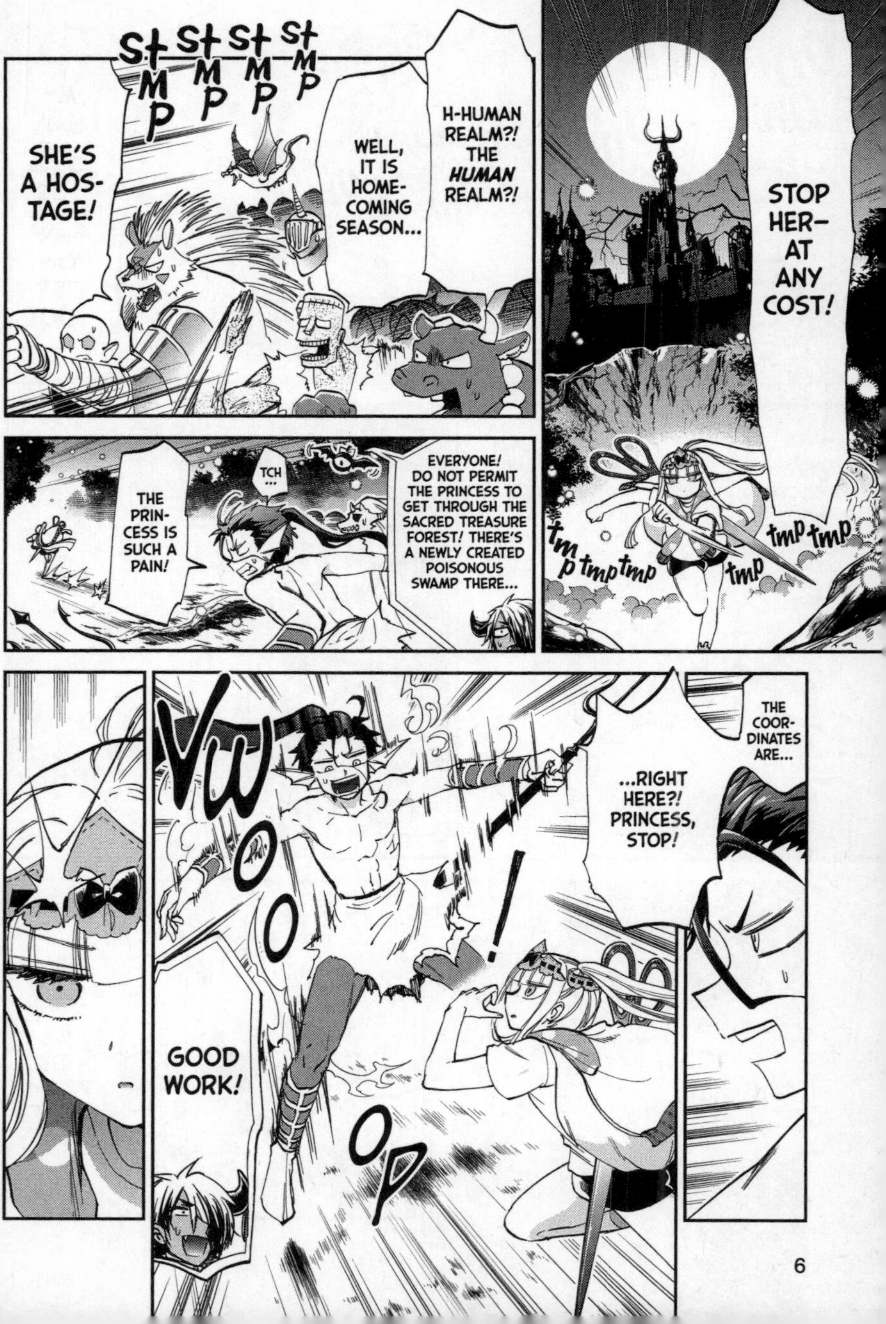
STOP HER—AT ANY COST!
tmp tmp tmp tmp tmp tmp
H-HUMAN REALM?! THE *HUMAN* REALM?!
WELL, IT IS HOME-COMING SEASON...
SHE'S A HOS-TAGE!
STMP STMP STMP STMP
EVERYONE! DO NOT PERMIT THE PRINCESS TO GET THROUGH THE SACRED TREASURE FOREST! THERE'S A NEWLY CREATED POISONOUS SWAMP THERE...
TCH...
THE PRIN-CESS IS SUCH A PAIN!
THE COOR-DINATES ARE...
...RIGHT HERE?! PRINCESS, STOP!
VWOOOOP
!
GOOD WORK!

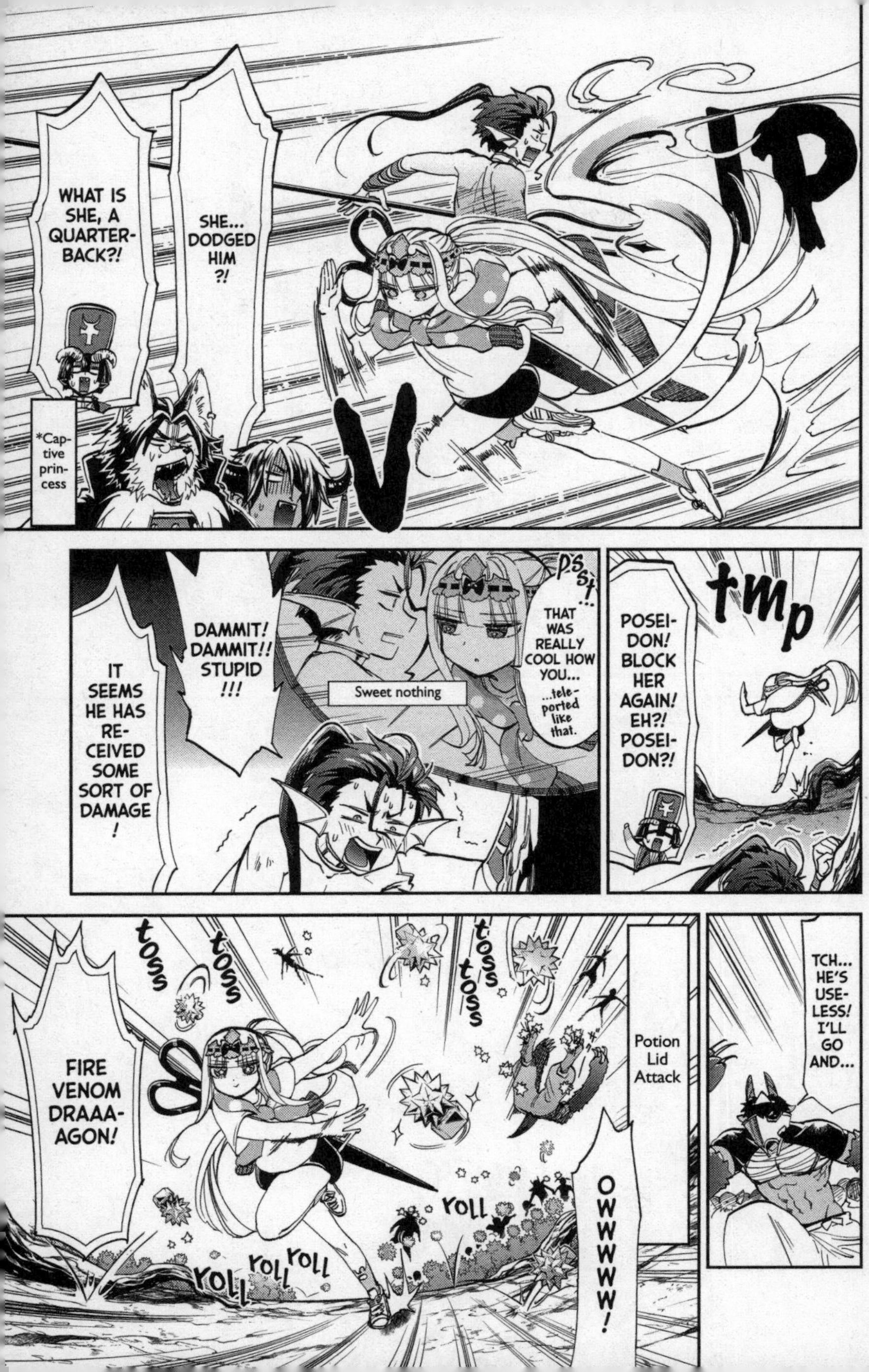

IP
SHE... DODGED HIM ?!
WHAT IS SHE, A QUARTER-BACK?!
*Captive prin-cess
tmp
POSEI-DON! BLOCK HER AGAIN! EH?! POSEI-DON?!
psst...
THAT WAS REALLY COOL HOW YOU... ...tele-ported like that.
Sweet nothing
DAMMIT! DAMMIT!! STUPID !!!
IT SEEMS HE HAS RE-CEIVED SOME SORT OF DAMAGE !
TCH... HE'S USE-LESS! I'LL GO AND...
Potion Lid Attack
toss toss
toss toss
OWWWWWW!
FIRE VENOM DRAAA-AGON!
roll
roll roll roll

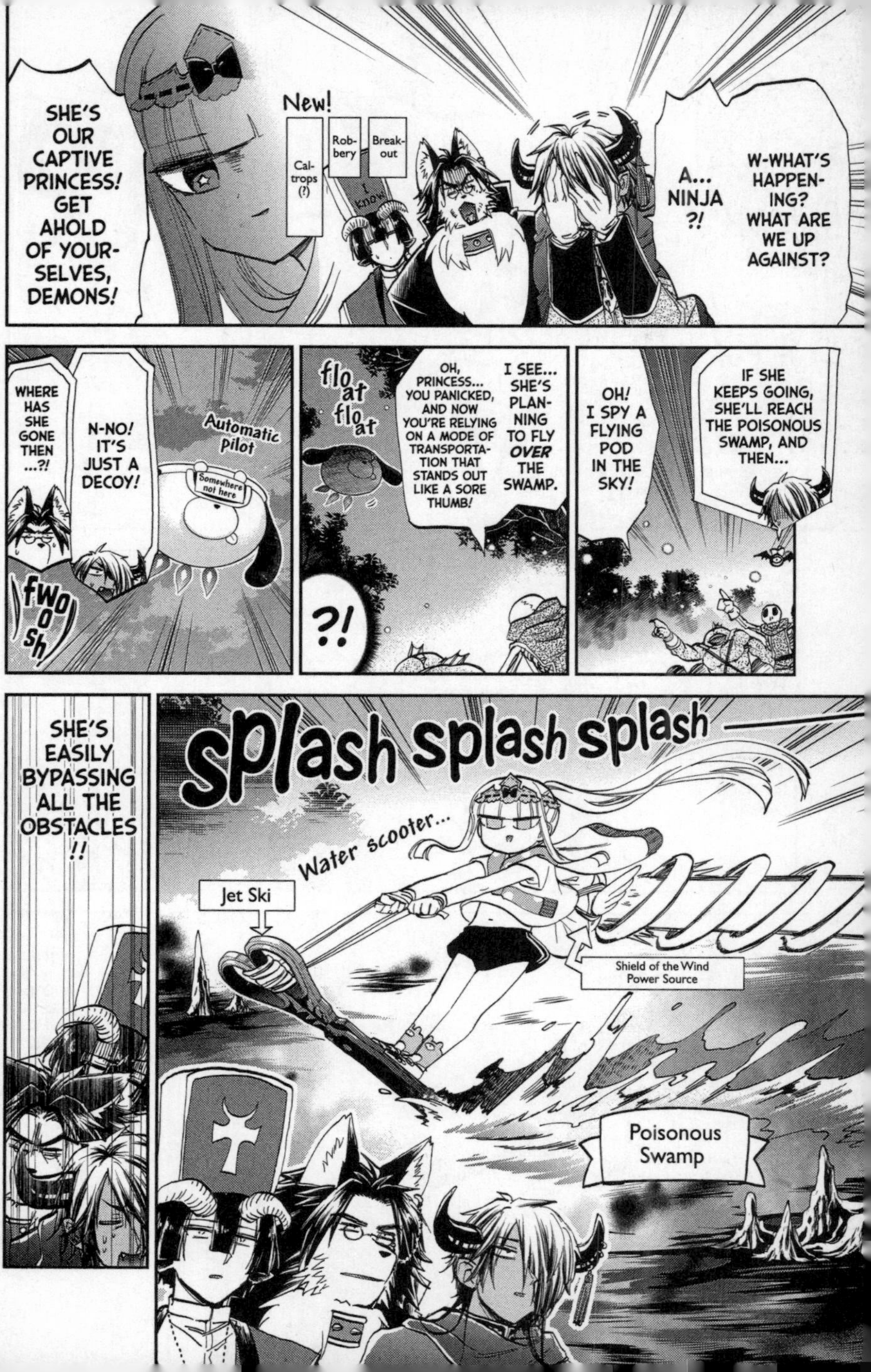

W-WHAT'S HAPPENING? WHAT ARE WE UP AGAINST?
A... NINJA?!
New!
Break-out
Robbery
Caltrops (?)
I know
SHE'S OUR CAPTIVE PRINCESS! GET AHOLD OF YOURSELVES, DEMONS!
IF SHE KEEPS GOING, SHE'LL REACH THE POISONOUS SWAMP, AND THEN...
OH! I SPY A FLYING POD IN THE SKY!
I SEE... SHE'S PLANNING TO FLY OVER THE SWAMP.
OH, PRINCESS... YOU PANICKED, AND NOW YOU'RE RELYING ON A MODE OF TRANSPORTATION THAT STANDS OUT LIKE A SORE THUMB!
floaat floaat
?!
N-NO! IT'S JUST A DECOY!
WHERE HAS SHE GONE THEN...?!
Automatic pilot
Somewhere not here
fwoosh
splash splash splash
Water scooter...
Jet Ski
Shield of the Wind Power Source
Poisonous Swamp
SHE'S EASILY BYPASSING ALL THE OBSTACLES!!

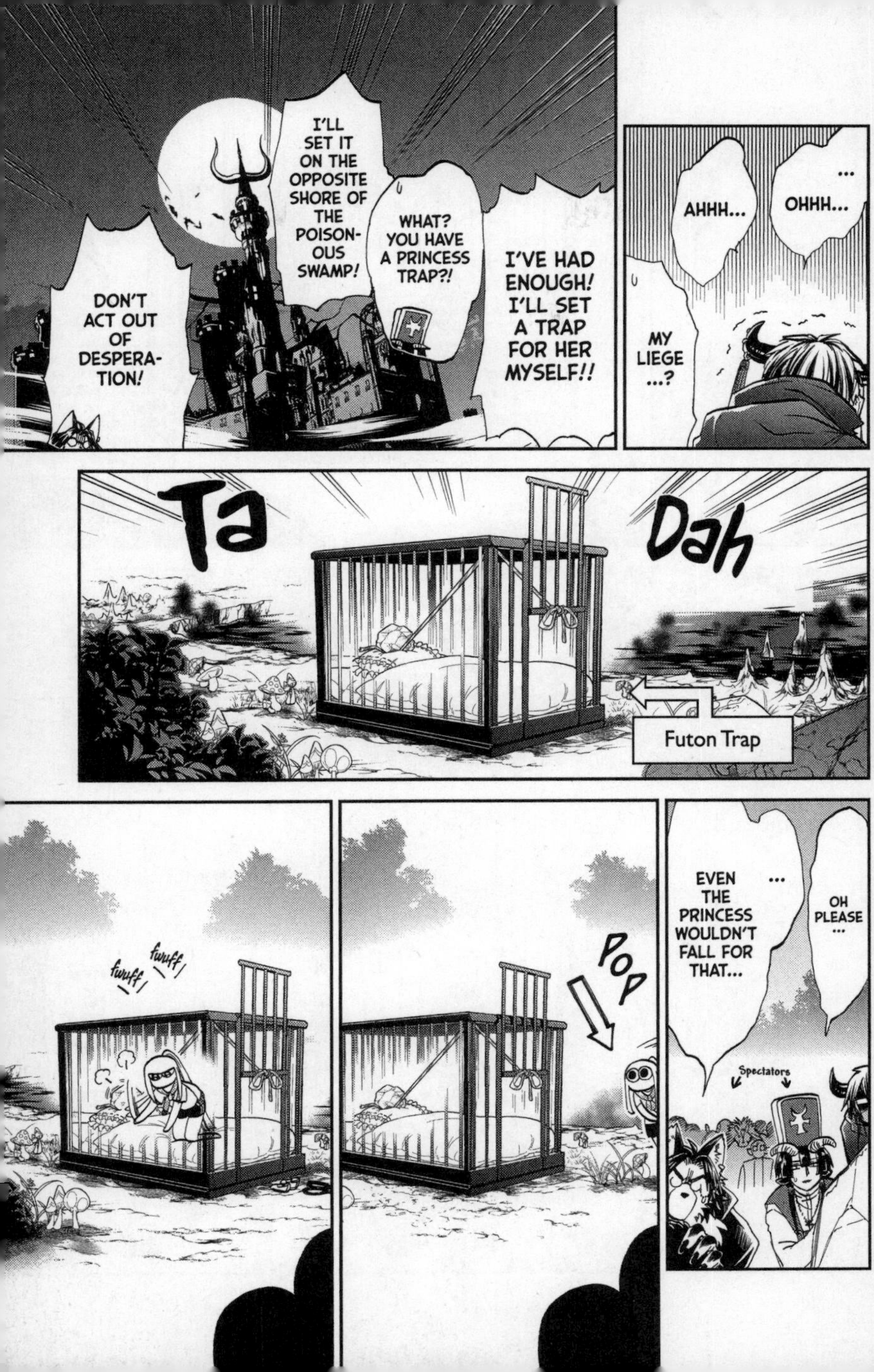
...
OHHH...
AHHH...
MY LIEGE ...?
I'VE HAD ENOUGH! I'LL SET A TRAP FOR HER MYSELF!!
WHAT? YOU HAVE A PRINCESS TRAP?!
I'LL SET IT ON THE OPPOSITE SHORE OF THE POISONOUS SWAMP!
DON'T ACT OUT OF DESPERATION!
Ta Dah
Futon Trap
OH PLEASE ...
EVEN THE PRINCESS WOULDN'T FALL FOR THAT... ...
Spectators
POP
fwuff fwuff

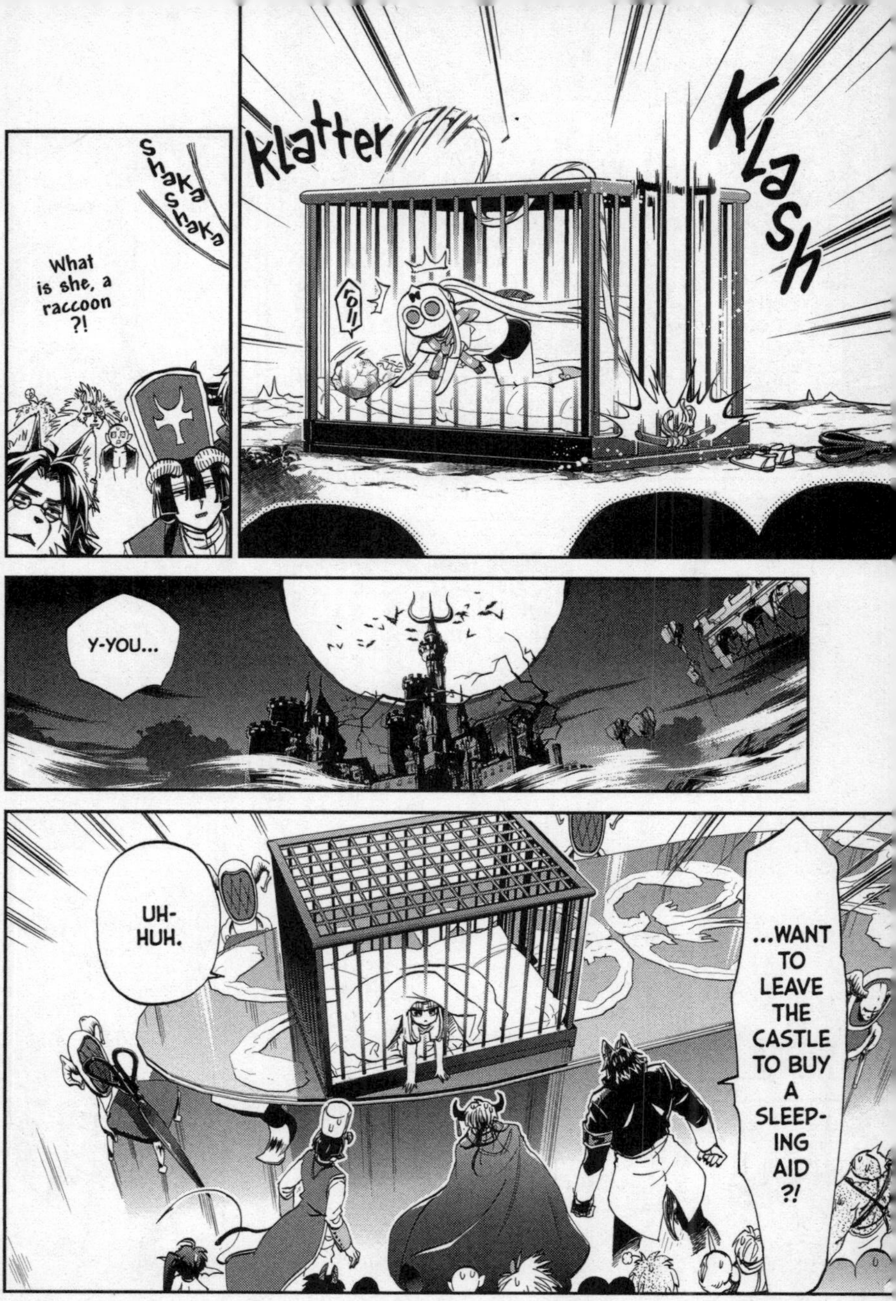
Klatter
Klash
roll
Shaka shaka
What is she, a raccoon?!
Y-YOU...
...WANT TO LEAVE THE CASTLE TO BUY A SLEEPING AID?!
UH-HUH.

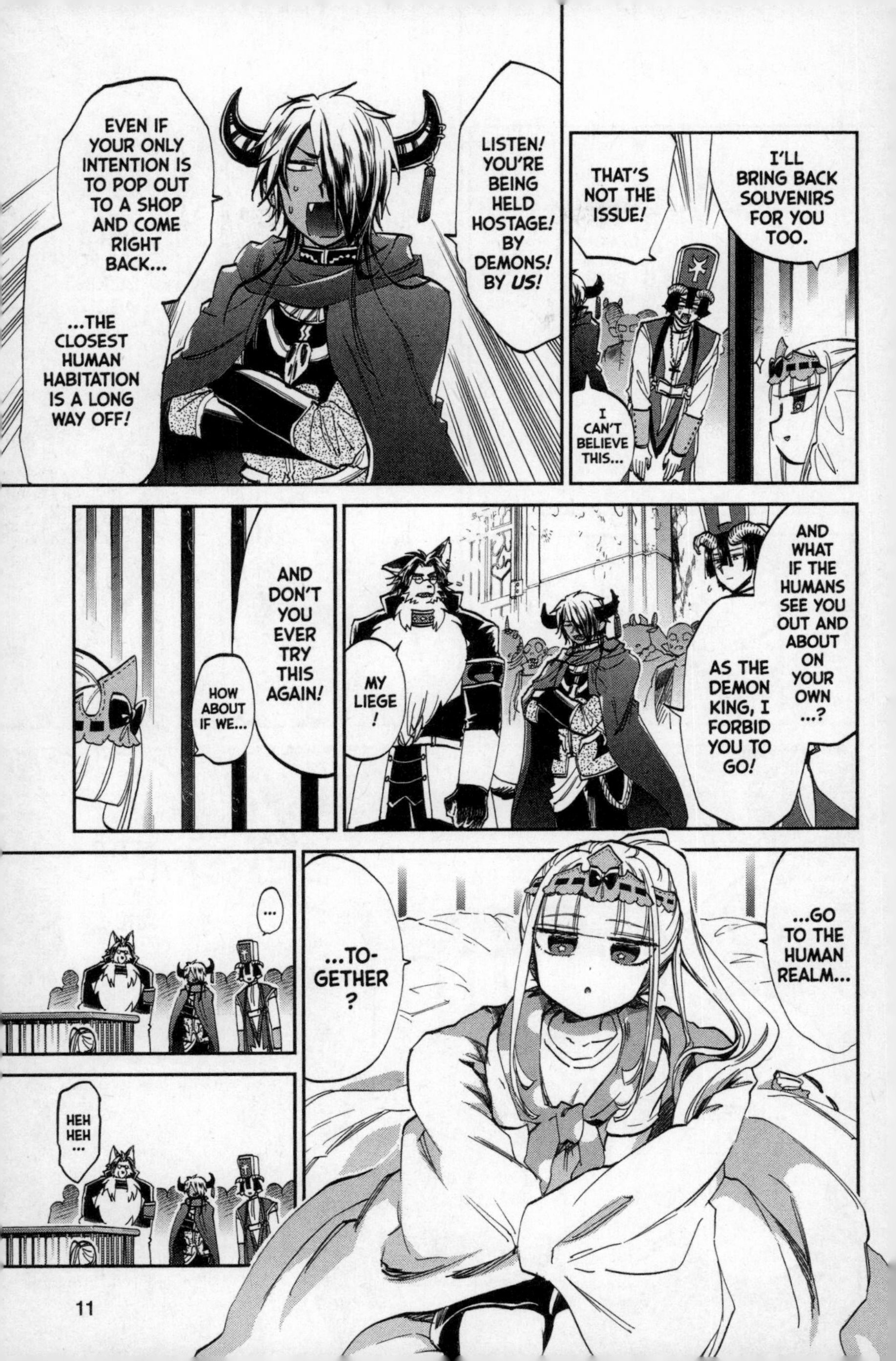
I'LL BRING BACK SOUVENIRS FOR YOU TOO.
THAT'S NOT THE ISSUE!
I CAN'T BELIEVE THIS...
LISTEN! YOU'RE BEING HELD HOSTAGE! BY DEMONS! BY US!
EVEN IF YOUR ONLY INTENTION IS TO POP OUT TO A SHOP AND COME RIGHT BACK...
...THE CLOSEST HUMAN HABITATION IS A LONG WAY OFF!
AND WHAT IF THE HUMANS SEE YOU OUT AND ABOUT ON YOUR OWN ...?
AS THE DEMON KING, I FORBID YOU TO GO!
MY LIEGE!
AND DON'T YOU EVER TRY THIS AGAIN!
HOW ABOUT IF WE...
...GO TO THE HUMAN REALM...
...TO-GETHER?
...
HEH HEH ...

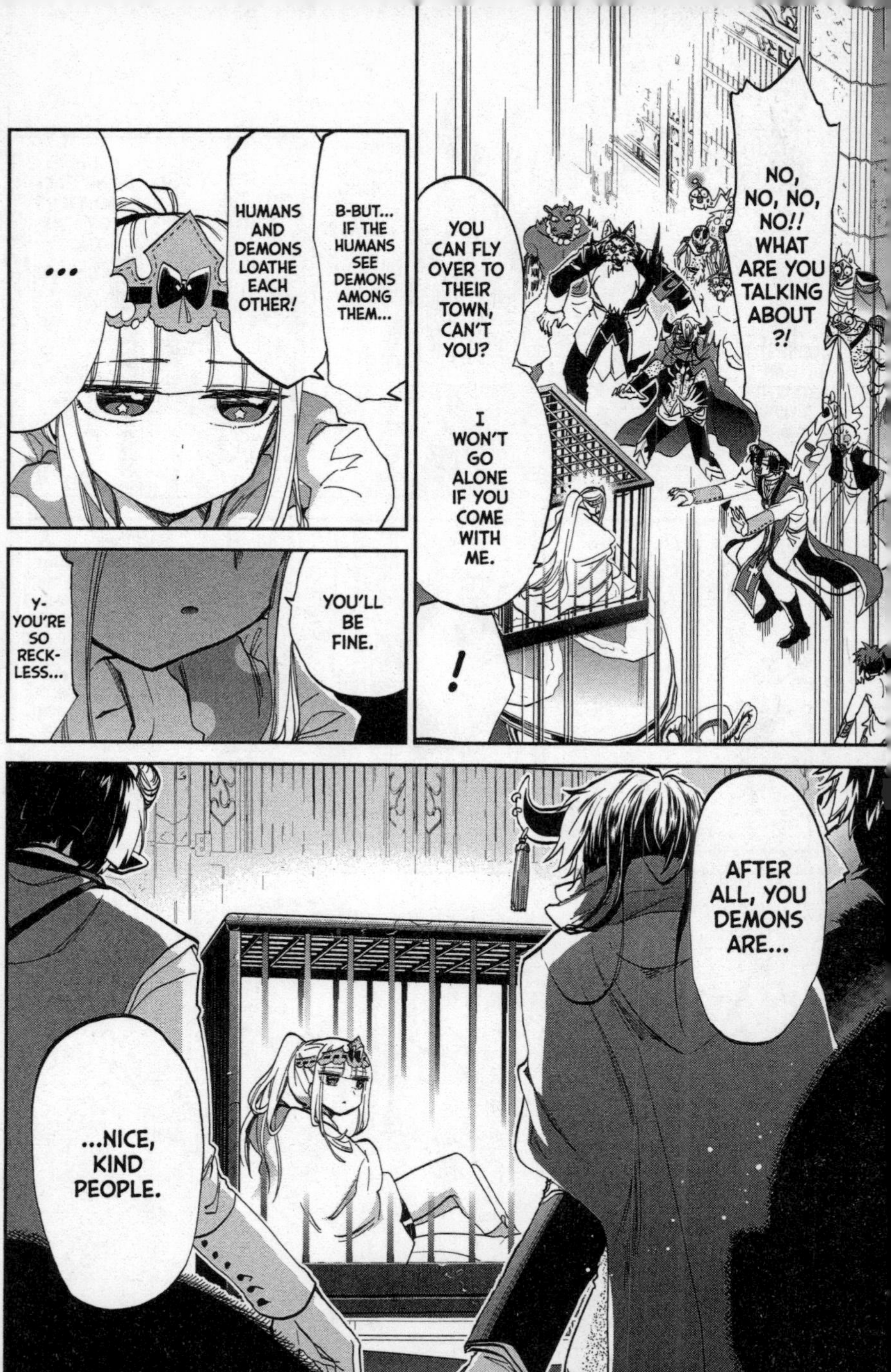
NO, NO, NO, NO!! WHAT ARE YOU TALKING ABOUT ?!
YOU CAN FLY OVER TO THEIR TOWN, CAN'T YOU?
I WON'T GO ALONE IF YOU COME WITH ME.
!
B-BUT... IF THE HUMANS SEE DEMONS AMONG THEM...
HUMANS AND DEMONS LOATHE EACH OTHER!
...
YOU'LL BE FINE.
Y-YOU'RE SO RECK-LESS...
AFTER ALL, YOU DEMONS ARE...
...NICE, KIND PEOPLE.

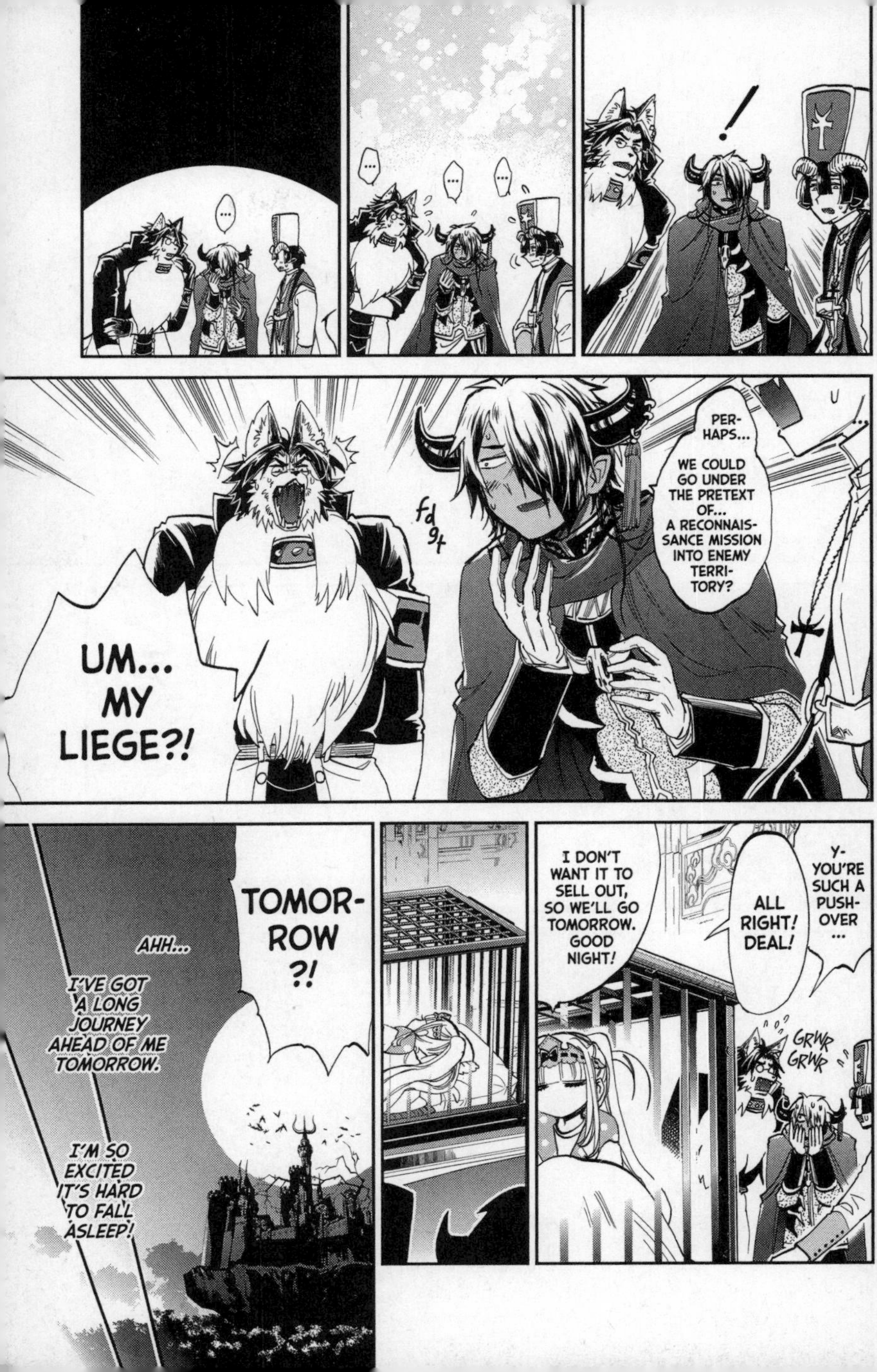
!
...
...
...
...
PER-HAPS... WE COULD GO UNDER THE PRETEXT OF... A RECONNAIS-SANCE MISSION INTO ENEMY TERRI-TORY?
fdgt
UM... MY LIEGE?!
Y-YOU'RE SUCH A PUSH-OVER...
ALL RIGHT! DEAL!
I DON'T WANT IT TO SELL OUT, SO WE'LL GO TOMORROW. GOOD NIGHT!
GRWR GRWR
TOMOR-ROW?!
AHH...
I'VE GOT A LONG JOURNEY AHEAD OF ME TOMORROW.
I'M SO EXCITED IT'S HARD TO FALL ASLEEP!

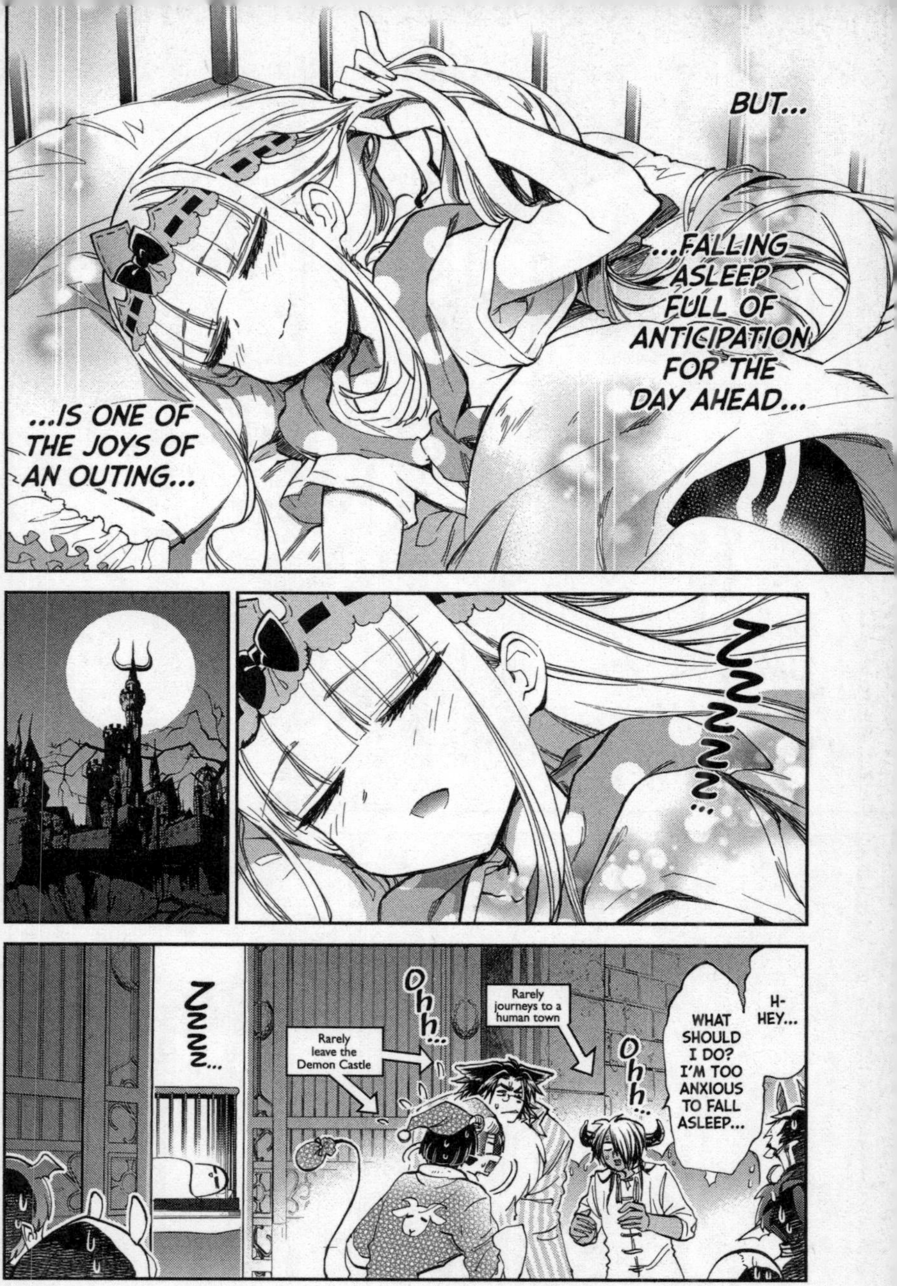
BUT...
...FALLING ASLEEP FULL OF ANTICIPATION FOR THE DAY AHEAD...
...IS ONE OF THE JOYS OF AN OUTING...
ZZZZZ...
H-HEY...
WHAT SHOULD I DO? I'M TOO ANXIOUS TO FALL ASLEEP...
Ohh...
Rarely journeys to a human town
Ohh...
Rarely leave the Demon Castle
ZZZZ...

Demon King's Handcrafted Trap Set

Chagrin: ☆☆☆☆☆☆☆☆☆
Futon: ☆☆☆☆☆☆☆☆☆☆☆

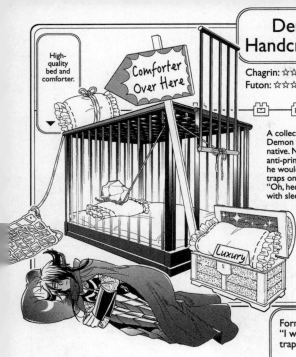

High-quality bed and comforter.

Comforter Over Here
Luxury

A collection of primitive traps that the Demon King uses when he has no alternative. Nowadays most of his traps are anti-princess comforter traps. Actually, he would like to try out various demonic traps on her, but ultimately he thinks, "Oh, heck! I can probably just bait her with sleep aids!" And the fact is, she easily falls for them all. This seems rather pathetic (to the Demon King). Other than the princess, he tried to use these traps on siblings Hades and Poseidon, but all he caught was a puppy. Subsequently, Hades broke open the cage and took the canine home with him.

Former problem:
"I want to invent more demonic traps..."

Current problem:
"In the end it all comes down to sleep aids anyway..."

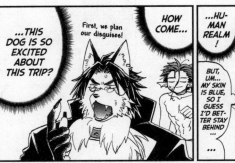

TH-THE...
...HU-MAN REALM!
BUT, UM... MY SKIN IS BLUE, SO I GUESS I'D BETTER STAY BEHIND... ...
HOW COME...
First, we plan our disguises!
...THIS DOG IS SO EXCITED ABOUT THIS TRIP?

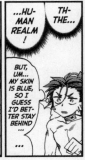

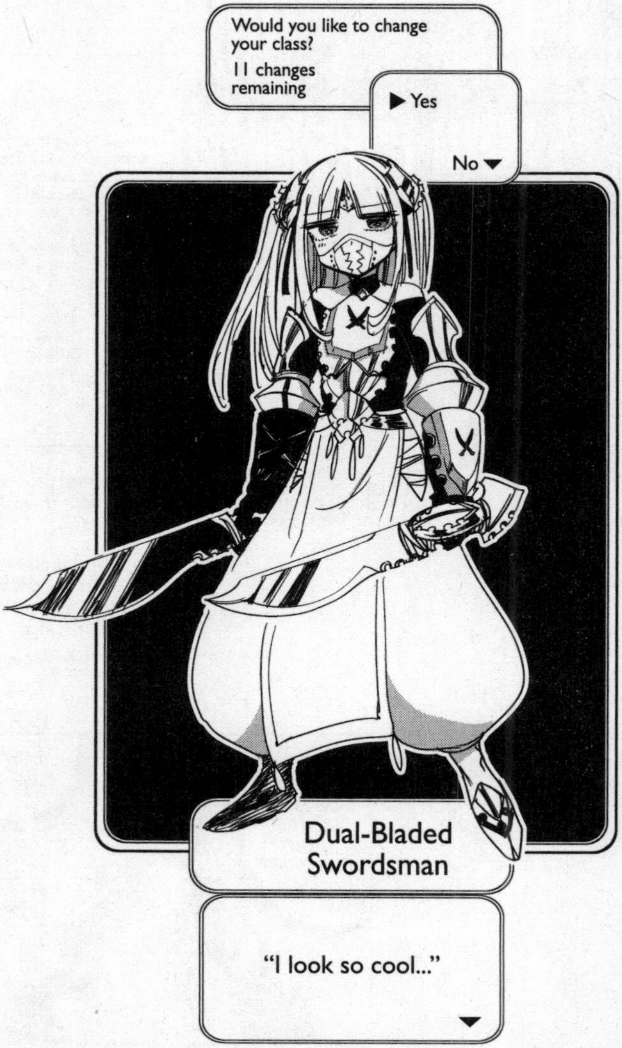
Would you like to change your class?
11 changes remaining
▶ Yes
No
Dual-Bladed Swordsman
"I look so cool..."

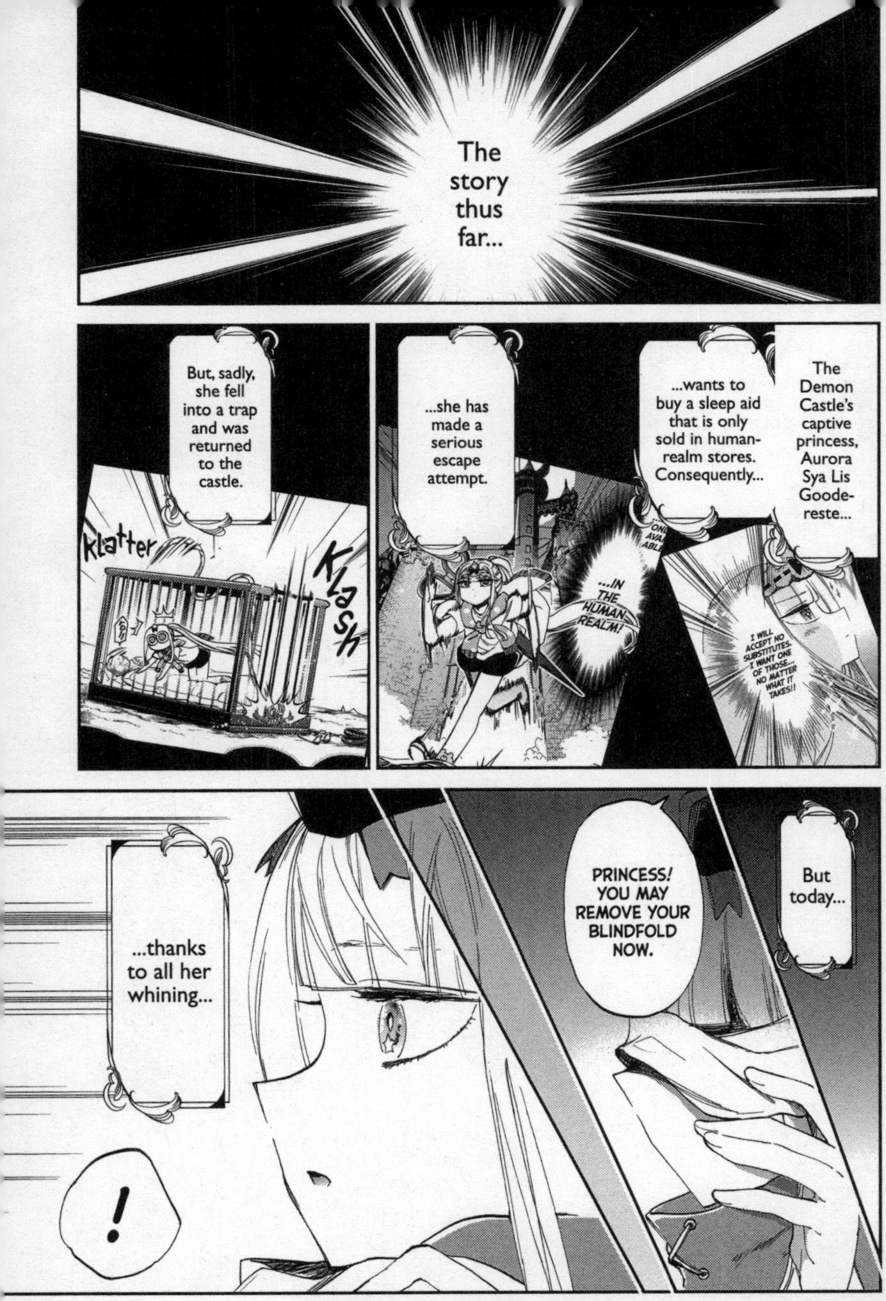
The story thus far...
The Demon Castle's captive princess, Aurora Sya Lis Goodereste...
I WILL ACCEPT NO SUBSTITUTES. I WANT ONE OF THOSE... NO MATTER WHAT IT TAKES!!
...wants to buy a sleep aid that is only sold in human-realm stores. Consequently...
...IN THE HUMAN REALM!
...she has made a serious escape attempt.
But, sadly, she fell into a trap and was returned to the castle.
Klash
Klatter
But today...
PRINCESS! YOU MAY REMOVE YOUR BLINDFOLD NOW.
...thanks to all her whining...
!

67th Night: Demons Are Pale and Tired

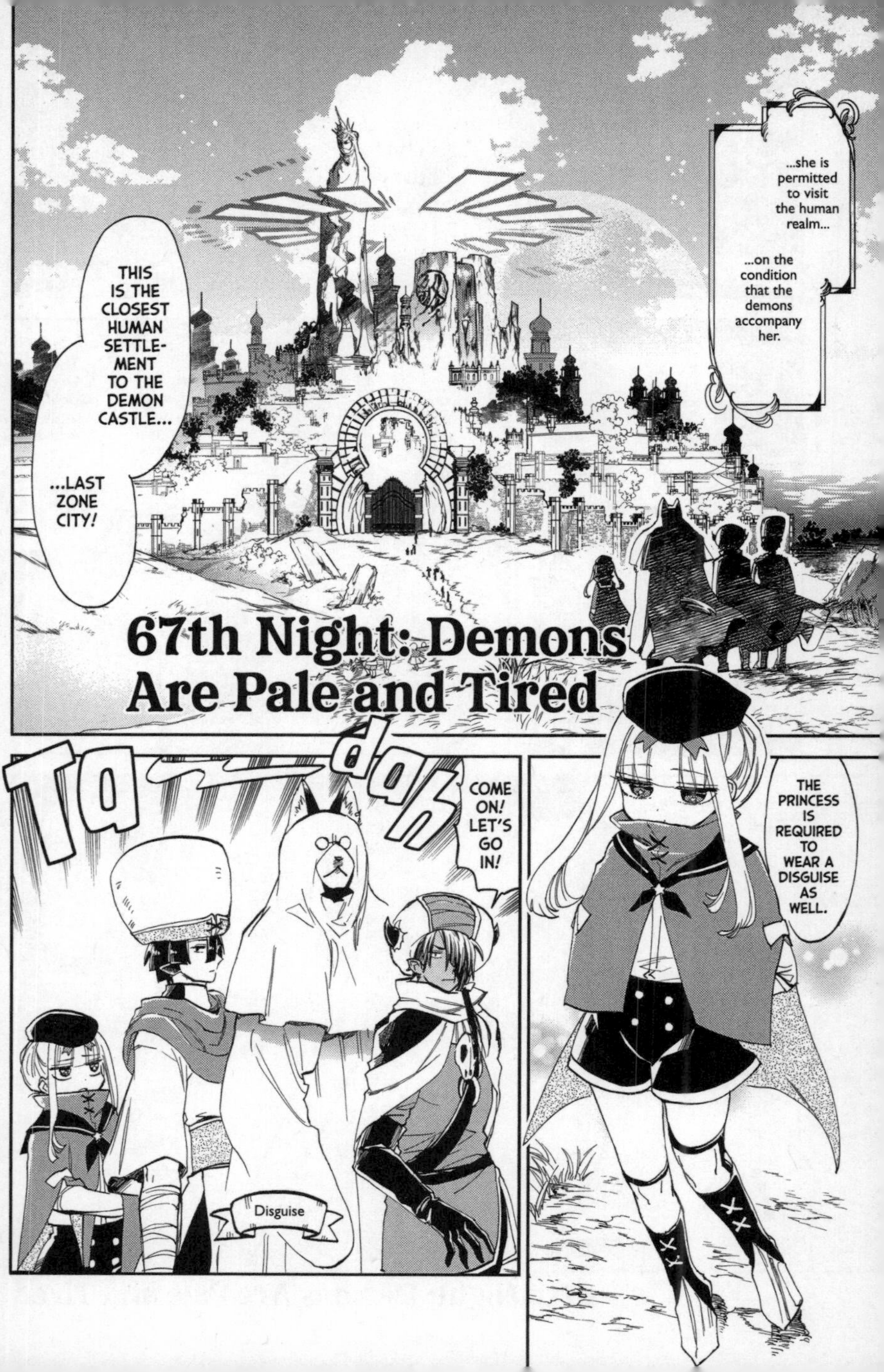
...she is permitted to visit the human realm...
...on the condition that the demons accompany her.
THIS IS THE CLOSEST HUMAN SETTLEMENT TO THE DEMON CASTLE...
...LAST ZONE CITY!
67th Night: Demons Are Pale and Tired
THE PRINCESS IS REQUIRED TO WEAR A DISGUISE AS WELL.
Ta-dah
COME ON! LET'S GO IN!
Disguise

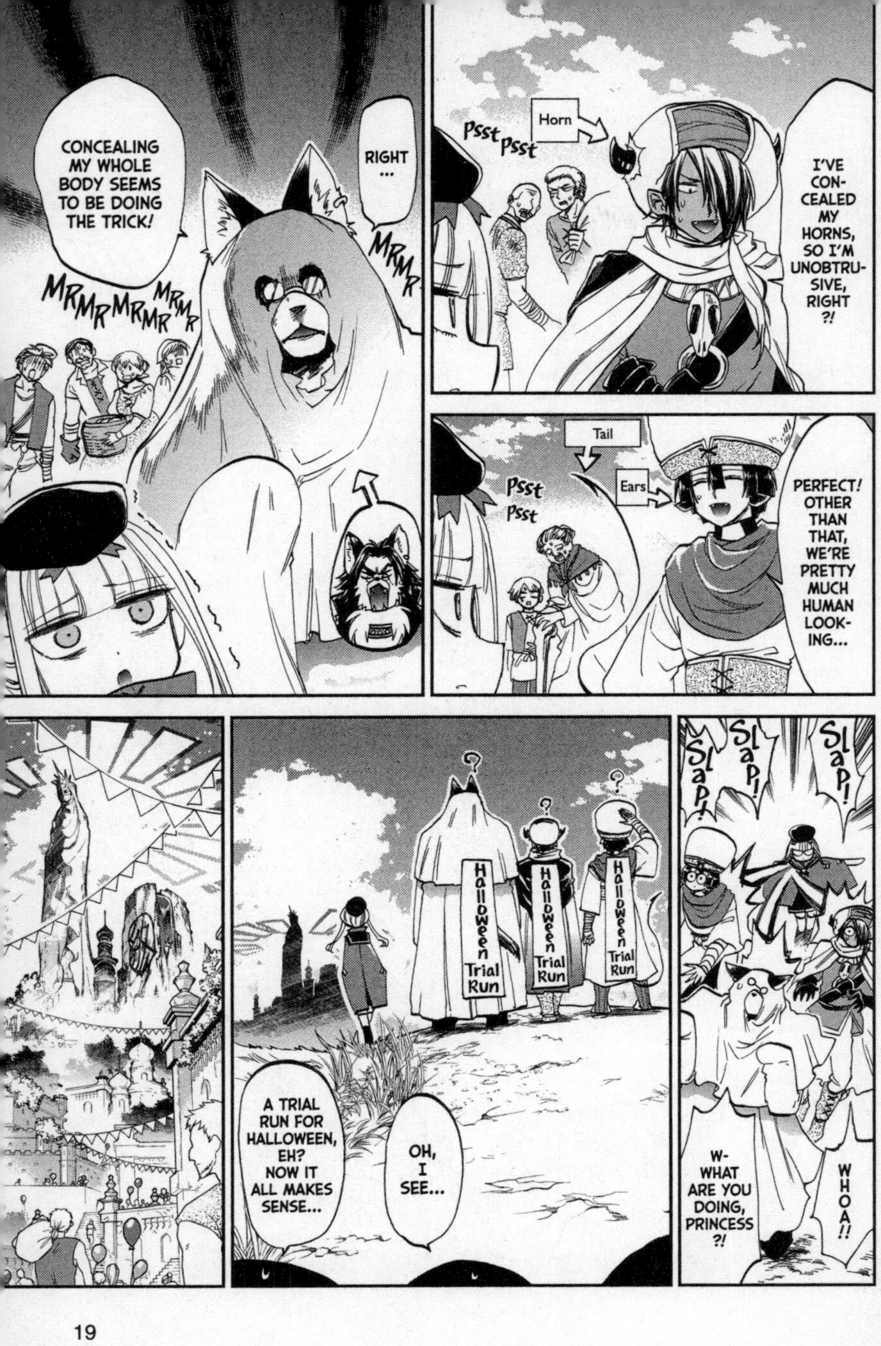
Horn
Psst Psst
I'VE CONCEALED MY HORNS, SO I'M UNOBTRUSIVE, RIGHT?!
Tail
Ears
Psst Psst
PERFECT! OTHER THAN THAT, WE'RE PRETTY MUCH HUMAN LOOKING...
RIGHT...
CONCEALING MY WHOLE BODY SEEMS TO BE DOING THE TRICK!
MRMR
MRMR MRMR MRMR
MRMR
Slap!
Slap!
Slap!
WHOA!!
W-WHAT ARE YOU DOING, PRINCESS?!
Halloween Trial Run
Halloween Trial Run
Halloween Trial Run
OH, I SEE...
A TRIAL RUN FOR HALLOWEEN, EH? NOW IT ALL MAKES SENSE...

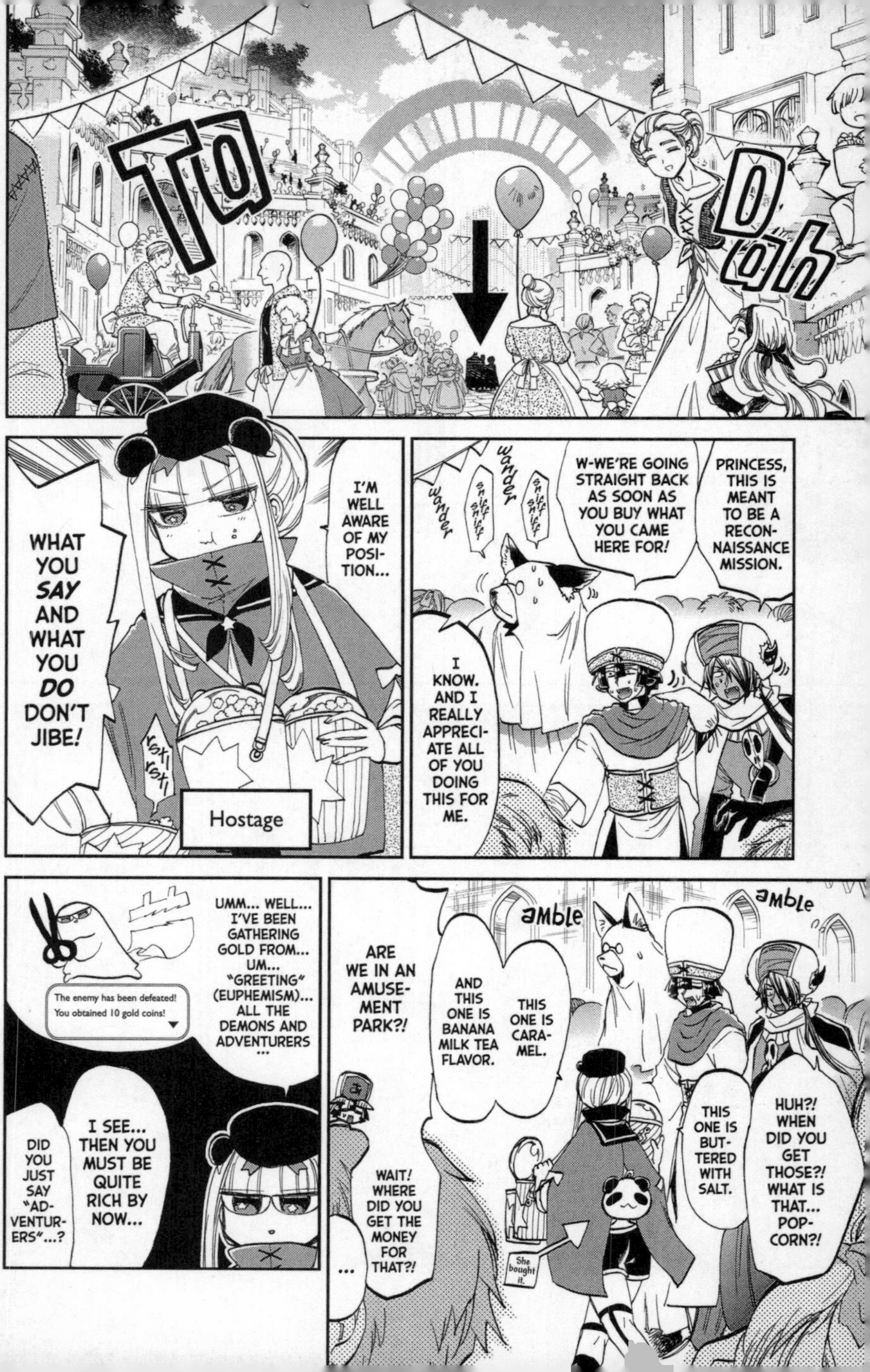
Ta
Dah
PRINCESS, THIS IS MEANT TO BE A RECONNAISSANCE MISSION.
W-WE'RE GOING STRAIGHT BACK AS SOON AS YOU BUY WHAT YOU CAME HERE FOR!
wander
sniff sniff
wander
sniff sniff
I KNOW. AND I REALLY APPRECIATE ALL OF YOU DOING THIS FOR ME.
I'M WELL AWARE OF MY POSITION...
WHAT YOU *SAY* AND WHAT YOU *DO* DON'T JIBE!
rsxl rsxl
Hostage
amble
amble
HUH?! WHEN DID YOU GET THOSE?! WHAT IS THAT... POPCORN?!
THIS ONE IS BUTTERED WITH SALT.
THIS ONE IS CARAMEL.
AND THIS ONE IS BANANA MILK TEA FLAVOR.
ARE WE IN AN AMUSEMENT PARK?!
WAIT! WHERE DID YOU GET THE MONEY FOR THAT?!
...
She bought it.
UMM... WELL... I'VE BEEN GATHERING GOLD FROM... UM... "GREETING" (EUPHEMISM)... ALL THE DEMONS AND ADVENTURERS...
The enemy has been defeated! You obtained 10 gold coins!
I SEE... THEN YOU MUST BE QUITE RICH BY NOW...
DID YOU JUST SAY "ADVENTURERS"...?

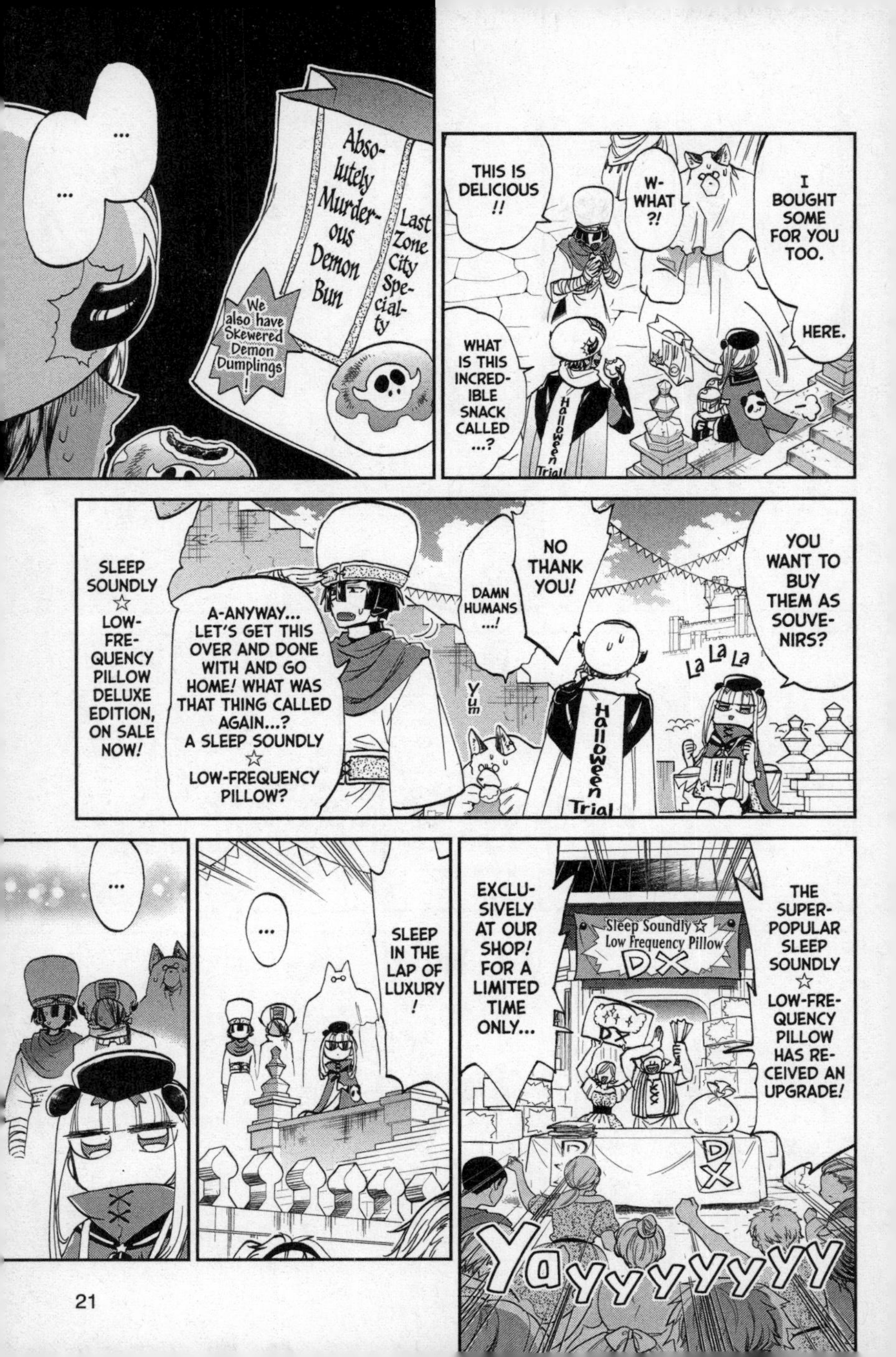
I BOUGHT SOME FOR YOU TOO.
W-WHAT?!
THIS IS DELICIOUS!!
HERE.
WHAT IS THIS INCREDIBLE SNACK CALLED...?
Halloween Trial
Absolutely Murderous Demon Bun
Last Zone City Specialty
We also have Skewered Demon Dumplings!
...
...
YOU WANT TO BUY THEM AS SOUVENIRS?
La La La
NO THANK YOU!
DAMN HUMANS...!
Halloween Trial
Yum
A-ANYWAY... LET'S GET THIS OVER AND DONE WITH AND GO HOME! WHAT WAS THAT THING CALLED AGAIN...? A SLEEP SOUNDLY ☆ LOW-FREQUENCY PILLOW?
SLEEP SOUNDLY ☆ LOW-FREQUENCY PILLOW DELUXE EDITION, ON SALE NOW!
THE SUPER-POPULAR SLEEP SOUNDLY ☆ LOW-FREQUENCY PILLOW HAS RECEIVED AN UPGRADE!
Sleep Soundly☆ Low Frequency Pillow DX
EXCLUSIVELY AT OUR SHOP! FOR A LIMITED TIME ONLY...
DX
DX
YayyyyyYY
SLEEP IN THE LAP OF LUXURY!
...
...

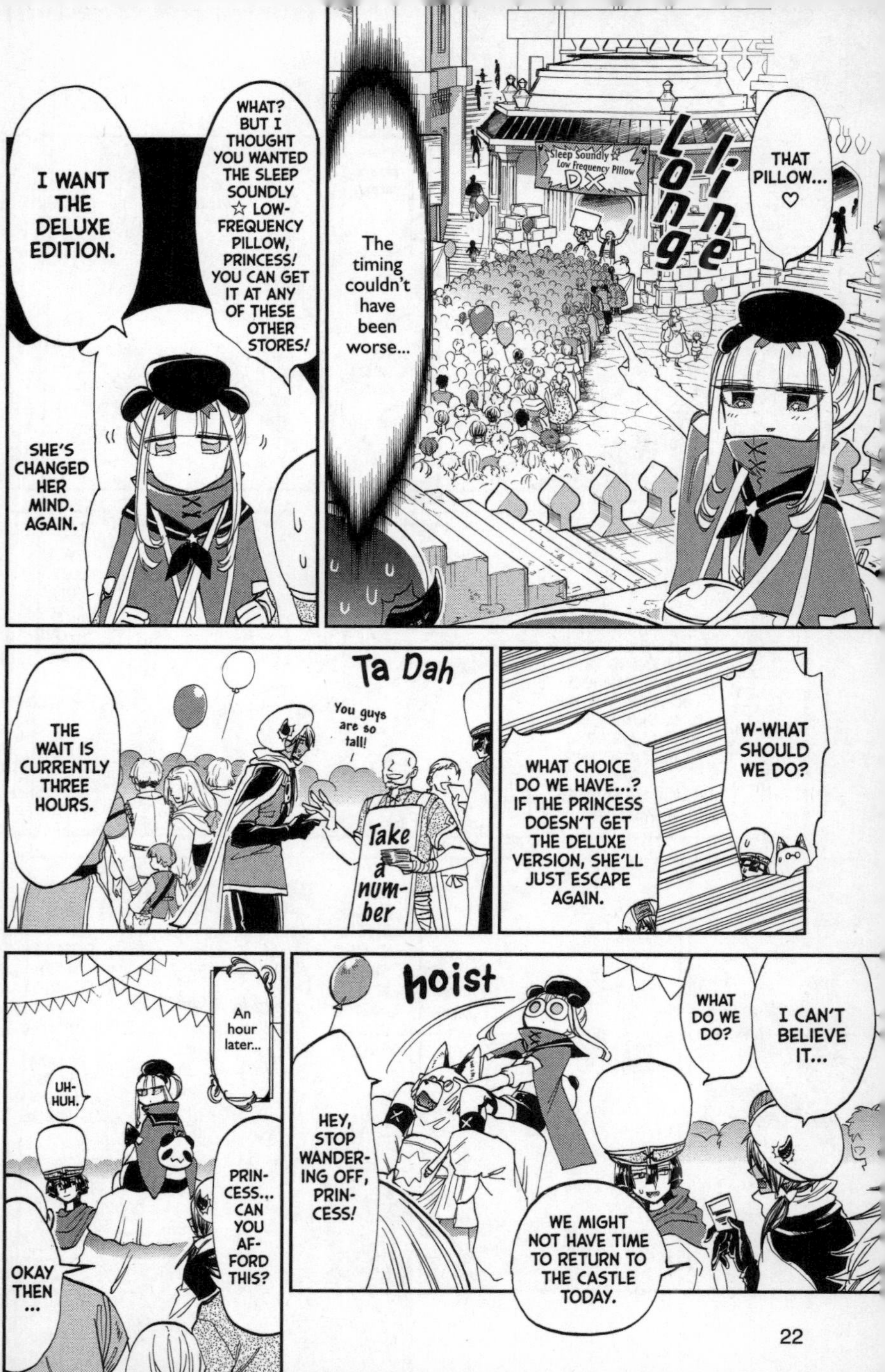
THAT PILLOW... ♡
Long line
Sleep Soundly ☆ Low Frequency Pillow DX
The timing couldn't have been worse...
WHAT? BUT I THOUGHT YOU WANTED THE SLEEP SOUNDLY ☆ LOW-FREQUENCY PILLOW, PRINCESS! YOU CAN GET IT AT ANY OF THESE OTHER STORES!
I WANT THE DELUXE EDITION.
SHE'S CHANGED HER MIND. AGAIN.
W-WHAT SHOULD WE DO?
WHAT CHOICE DO WE HAVE...? IF THE PRINCESS DOESN'T GET THE DELUXE VERSION, SHE'LL JUST ESCAPE AGAIN.
Ta Dah
You guys are so tall!
Take a number
THE WAIT IS CURRENTLY THREE HOURS.
I CAN'T BELIEVE IT...
WHAT DO WE DO?
hoist
WE MIGHT NOT HAVE TIME TO RETURN TO THE CASTLE TODAY.
HEY, STOP WANDERING OFF, PRINCESS!
An hour later...
PRINCESS... CAN YOU AFFORD THIS?
UH-HUH.
OKAY THEN...

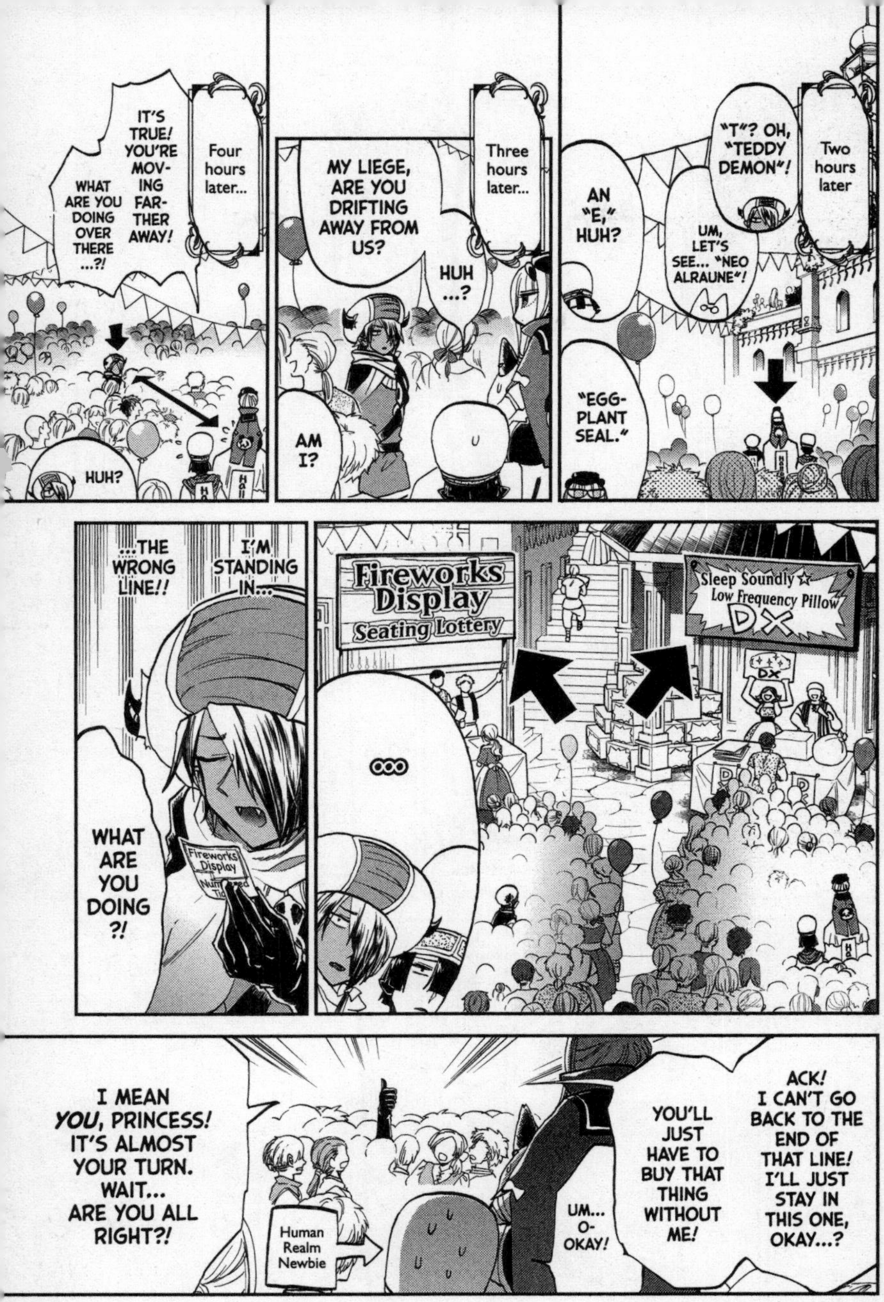
Two hours later
"T"? OH, "TEDDY DEMON"!
UM, LET'S SEE... "NEO ALRAUNE"!
AN "E," HUH?
"EGG-PLANT SEAL."
Three hours later...
MY LIEGE, ARE YOU DRIFTING AWAY FROM US?
HUH ...?
AM I?
Four hours later...
IT'S TRUE! YOU'RE MOV-ING FAR-THER AWAY!
WHAT ARE YOU DOING OVER THERE ...?!
HUH?
Fireworks Display Seating Lottery
Sleep Soundly ☆ Low Frequency Pillow DX
DX
I'M STANDING IN...
...THE WRONG LINE!!
WHAT ARE YOU DOING ?!
Fireworks Display
ACK! I CAN'T GO BACK TO THE END OF THAT LINE! I'LL JUST STAY IN THIS ONE, OKAY...?
YOU'LL JUST HAVE TO BUY THAT THING WITHOUT ME!
UM... O-OKAY!
I MEAN *YOU*, PRINCESS! IT'S ALMOST YOUR TURN. WAIT... ARE YOU ALL RIGHT?!
Human Realm Newbie

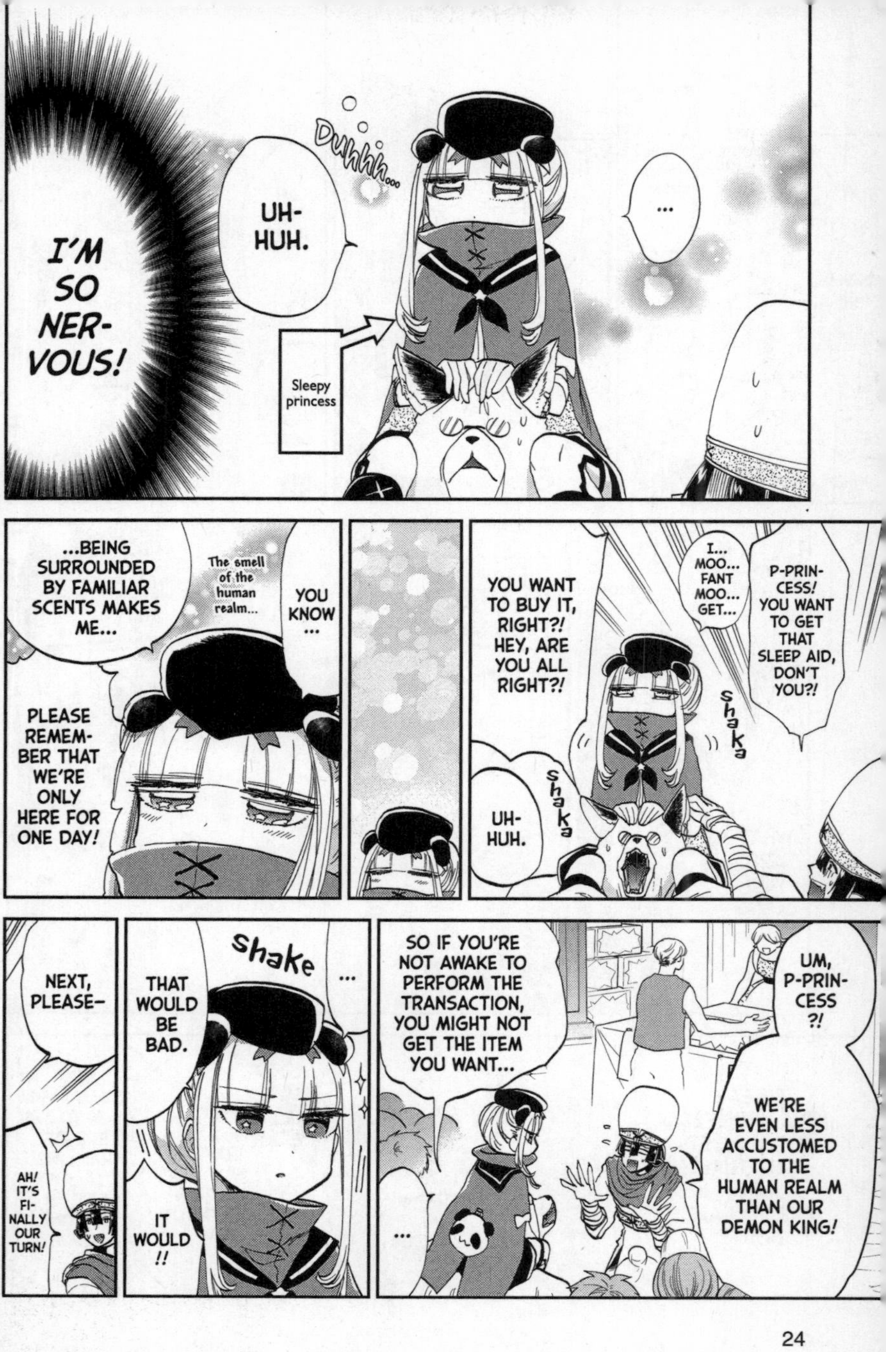
...
Duhhh...
UH-HUH.
Sleepy princess
I'M SO NERVOUS!
P-PRINCESS! YOU WANT TO GET THAT SLEEP AID, DON'T YOU?!
I... MOO... FANT MOO... GET...
shaka
YOU WANT TO BUY IT, RIGHT?! HEY, ARE YOU ALL RIGHT?!
shaka
UH-HUH.
YOU KNOW ...
The smell of the human realm...
...BEING SURROUNDED BY FAMILIAR SCENTS MAKES ME...
PLEASE REMEMBER THAT WE'RE ONLY HERE FOR ONE DAY!
UM, P-PRINCESS?!
WE'RE EVEN LESS ACCUSTOMED TO THE HUMAN REALM THAN OUR DEMON KING!
SO IF YOU'RE NOT AWAKE TO PERFORM THE TRANSACTION, YOU MIGHT NOT GET THE ITEM YOU WANT...
...
...
Shake
THAT WOULD BE BAD.
IT WOULD!!
NEXT, PLEASE—
AH! IT'S FINALLY OUR TURN!

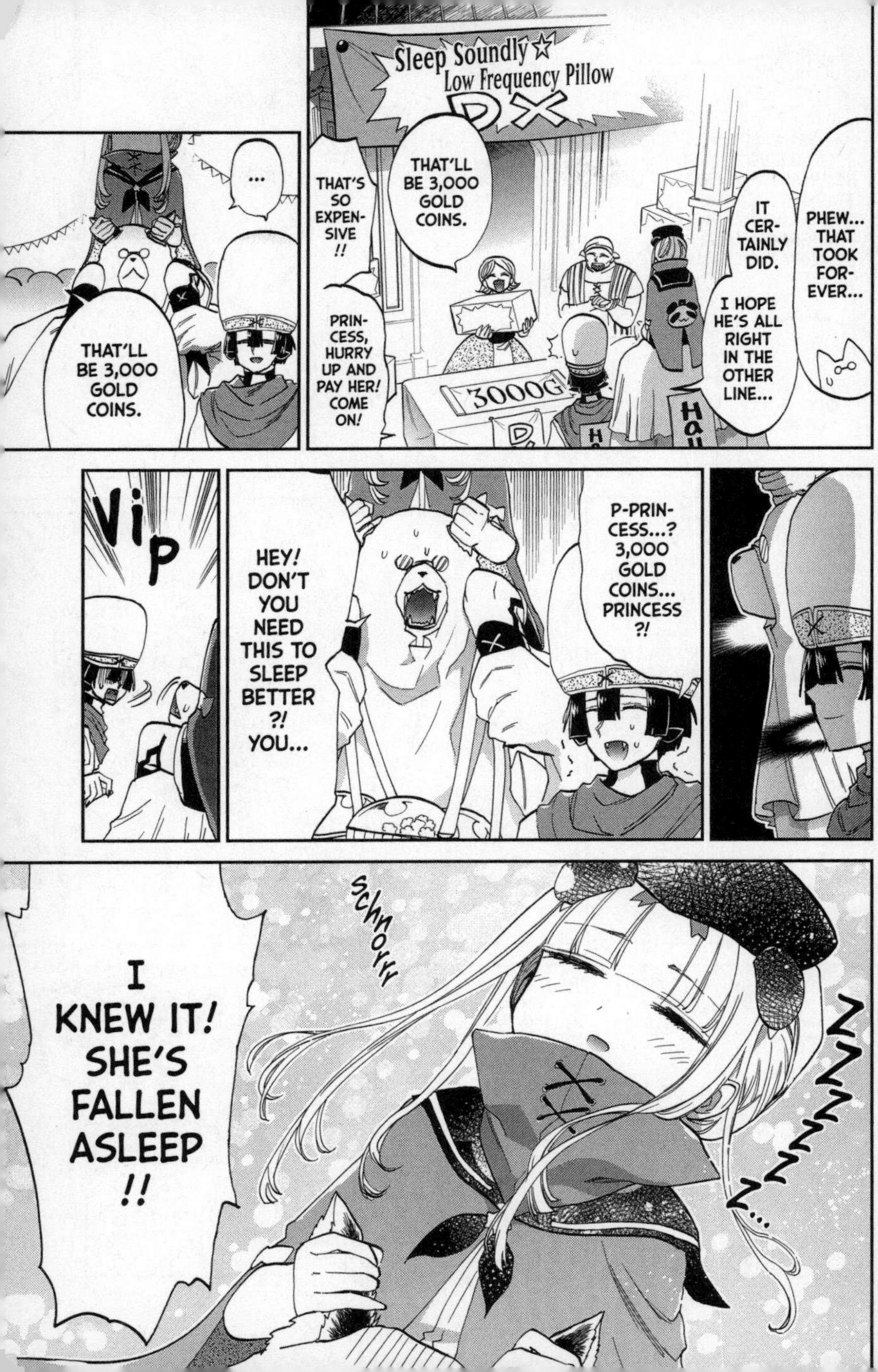
Sleep Soundly☆ Low Frequency Pillow DX
PHEW... THAT TOOK FOR-EVER...
IT CER-TAINLY DID.
I HOPE HE'S ALL RIGHT IN THE OTHER LINE...
THAT'LL BE 3,000 GOLD COINS.
THAT'S SO EXPEN-SIVE!!
PRIN-CESS, HURRY UP AND PAY HER! COME ON!
3000G
...
THAT'LL BE 3,000 GOLD COINS.
P-PRIN-CESS...? 3,000 GOLD COINS... PRINCESS?!
HEY! DON'T YOU NEED THIS TO SLEEP BETTER?! YOU...
ViP
ZZZZZZZ...
schnorrr
I KNEW IT! SHE'S FALLEN ASLEEP!!

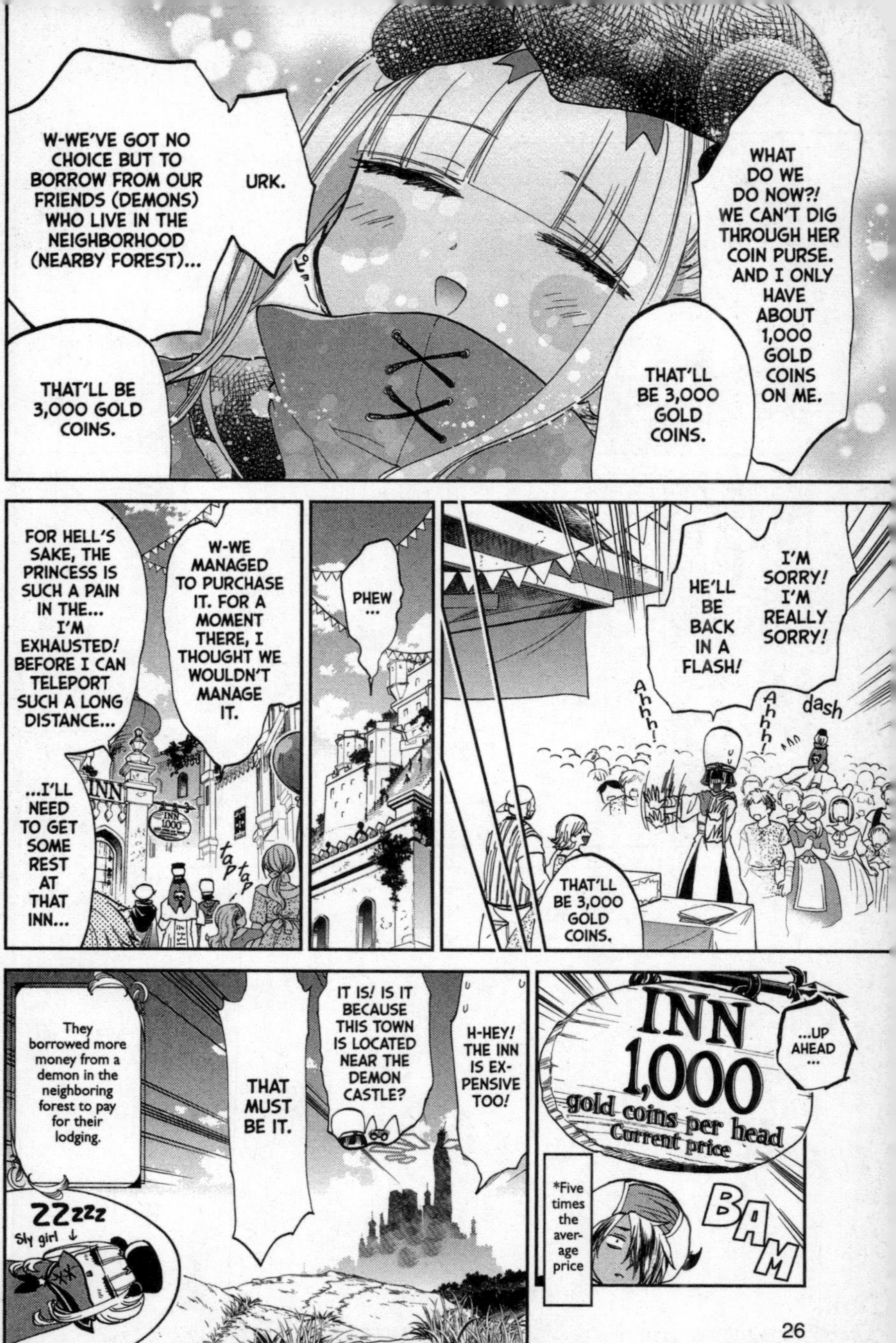

WHAT DO WE DO NOW?! WE CAN'T DIG THROUGH HER COIN PURSE. AND I ONLY HAVE ABOUT 1,000 GOLD COINS ON ME.
THAT'LL BE 3,000 GOLD COINS.
URK.
W-WE'VE GOT NO CHOICE BUT TO BORROW FROM OUR FRIENDS (DEMONS) WHO LIVE IN THE NEIGHBORHOOD (NEARBY FOREST)...
THAT'LL BE 3,000 GOLD COINS.
I'M SORRY! I'M REALLY SORRY!
dash
Ahhh!
HE'LL BE BACK IN A FLASH!
Ahhh!
THAT'LL BE 3,000 GOLD COINS.
PHEW...
W-WE MANAGED TO PURCHASE IT. FOR A MOMENT THERE, I THOUGHT WE WOULDN'T MANAGE IT.
FOR HELL'S SAKE, THE PRINCESS IS SUCH A PAIN IN THE... I'M EXHAUSTED! BEFORE I CAN TELEPORT SUCH A LONG DISTANCE...
tap tap
...I'LL NEED TO GET SOME REST AT THAT INN...
INN
...UP AHEAD...
INN 1,000 gold coins per head Current price
*Five times the average price
BAM
H-HEY! THE INN IS EXPENSIVE TOO!
IT IS! IS IT BECAUSE THIS TOWN IS LOCATED NEAR THE DEMON CASTLE?
THAT MUST BE IT.
They borrowed more money from a demon in the neighboring forest to pay for their lodging.
ZZzzz
Sly girl ↓

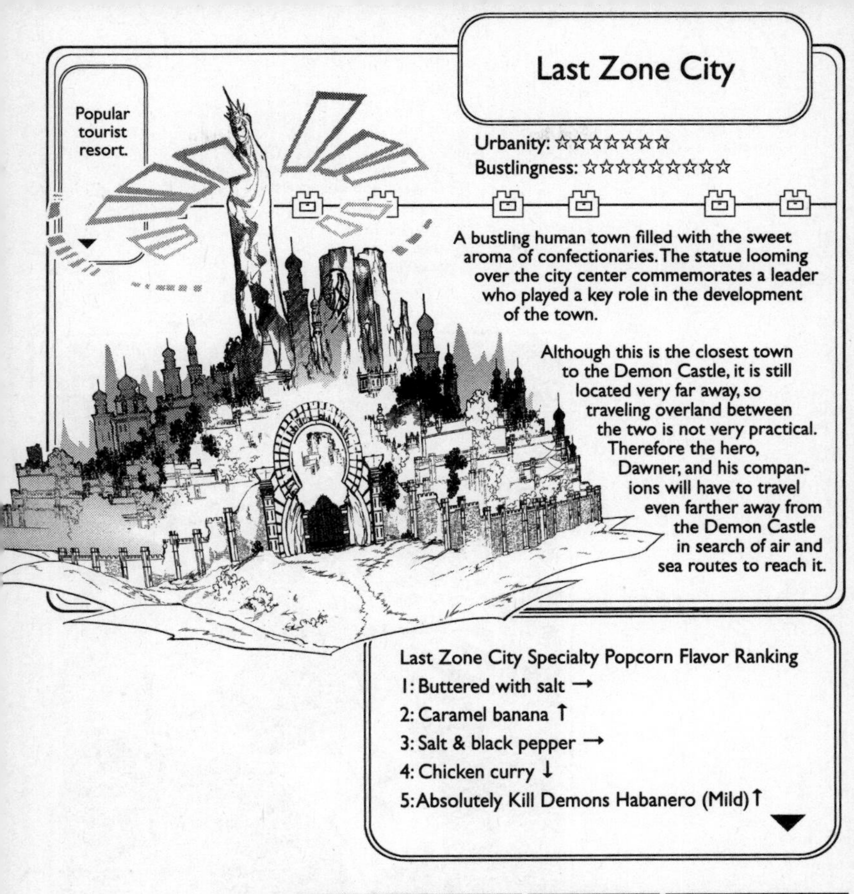
Popular tourist resort.

Last Zone City

Urbanity: ☆☆☆☆☆☆☆

Bustlingness: ☆☆☆☆☆☆☆☆☆

A bustling human town filled with the sweet aroma of confectionaries. The statue looming over the city center commemorates a leader who played a key role in the development of the town.

Although this is the closest town to the Demon Castle, it is still located very far away, so traveling overland between the two is not very practical. Therefore the hero, Dawner, and his companions will have to travel even farther away from the Demon Castle in search of air and sea routes to reach it.

Last Zone City Specialty Popcorn Flavor Ranking

1: Buttered with salt →

2: Caramel banana ↑

3: Salt & black pepper →

4: Chicken curry ↓

5: Absolutely Kill Demons Habanero (Mild) ↑

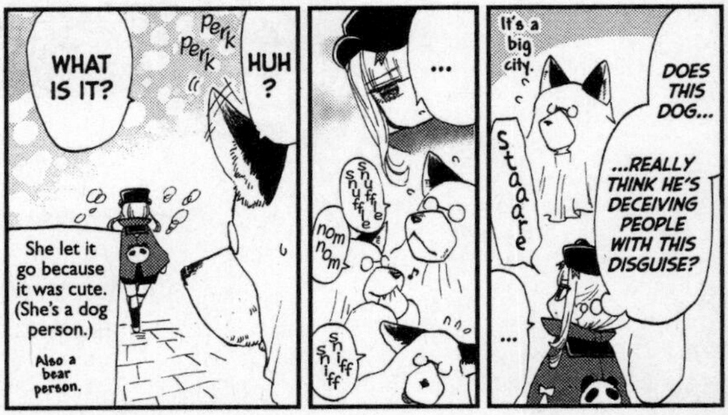
It's a big city.
DOES THIS DOG...
...REALLY THINK HE'S DECEIVING PEOPLE WITH THIS DISGUISE?
Staaare
...
...
snuffle snuffle
nom nom
sniff sniff
HUH?
Perk Perk
WHAT IS IT?
She let it go because it was cute. (She's a dog person.)
Also a bear person.

Would you like to change
your class?
10 changes
remaining

▶Yes

No ▼

Traveler

"Just buttered with salt
is best...♡"

▼

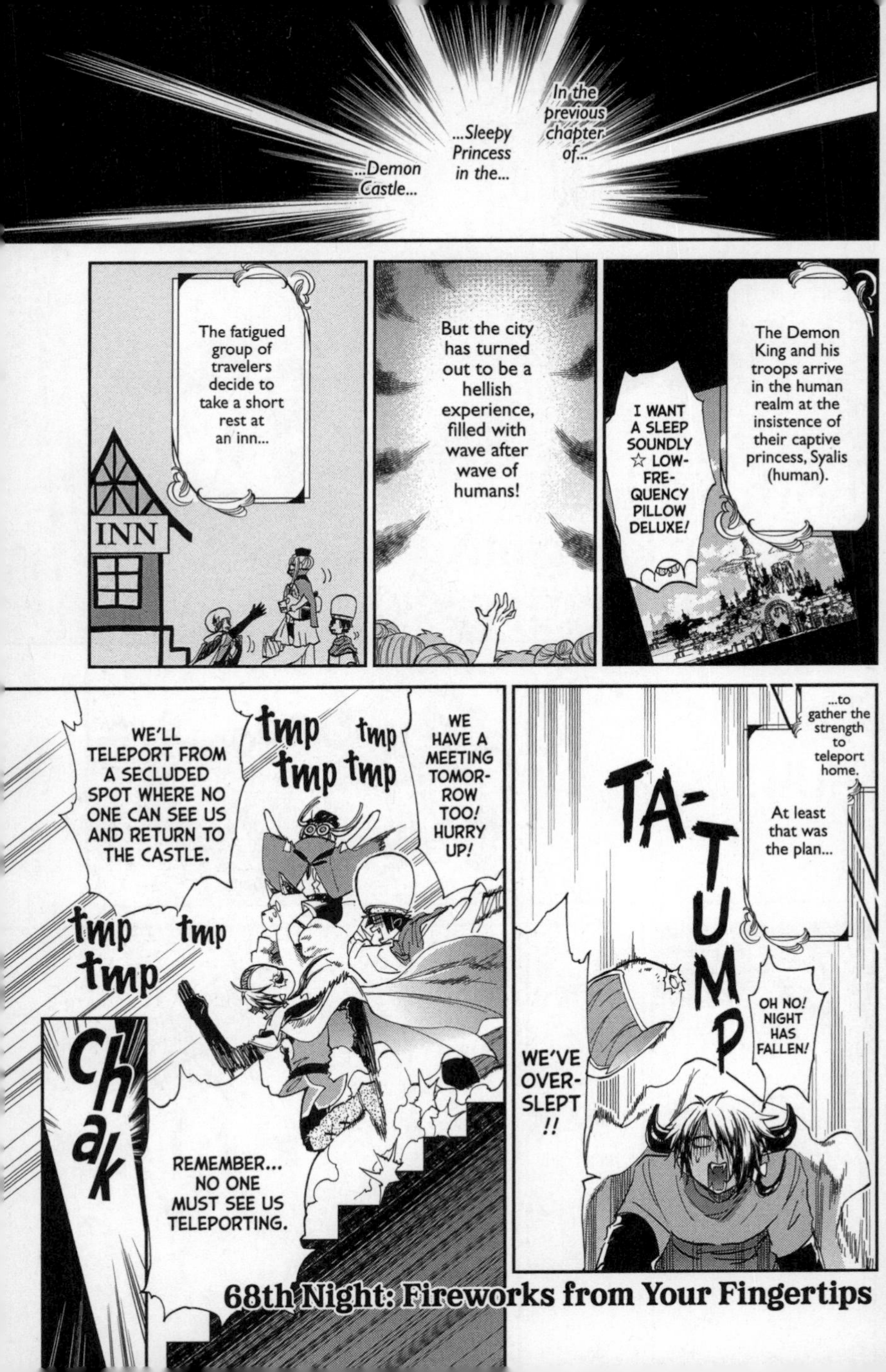
In the previous chapter of...
...Sleepy Princess in the...
...Demon Castle...
The Demon King and his troops arrive in the human realm at the insistence of their captive princess, Syalis (human).
I WANT A SLEEP SOUNDLY ☆ LOW-FREQUENCY PILLOW DELUXE!
But the city has turned out to be a hellish experience, filled with wave after wave of humans!
The fatigued group of travelers decide to take a short rest at an inn...
INN
...to gather the strength to teleport home.
At least that was the plan...
TA-TUMP
OH NO! NIGHT HAS FALLEN!
WE'VE OVER-SLEPT!!
WE HAVE A MEETING TOMORROW TOO! HURRY UP!
tmp tmp
tmp tmp
WE'LL TELEPORT FROM A SECLUDED SPOT WHERE NO ONE CAN SEE US AND RETURN TO THE CASTLE.
tmp tmp
tmp
Chak
REMEMBER... NO ONE MUST SEE US TELEPORTING.

68th Night: Fireworks from Your Fingertips

68th Night: Fireworks from Your Fingertips

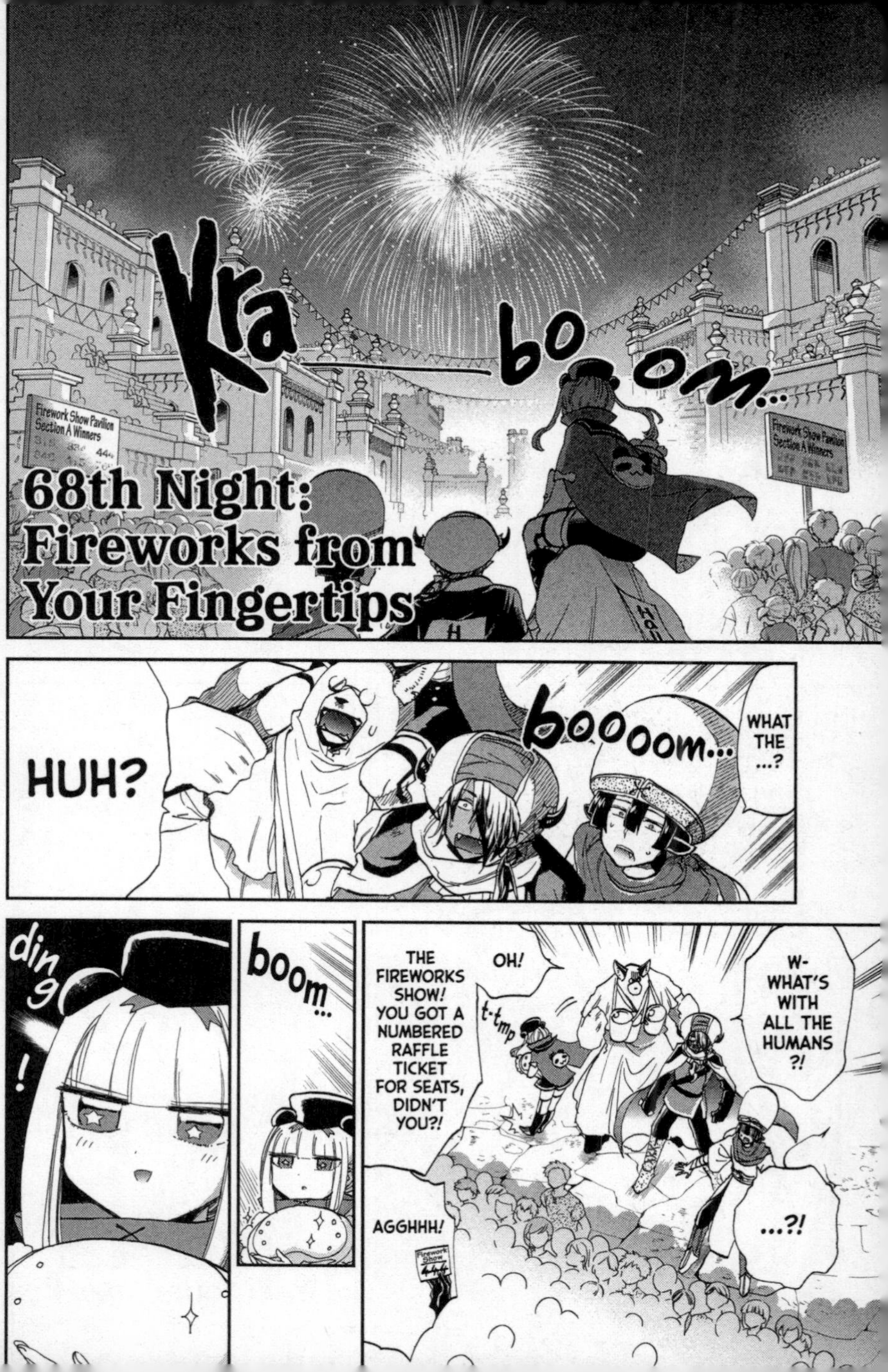
Kra—boom...
Firework Show Pavilion Section A Winners
Firework Show Pavilion Section A Winners
WHAT THE ...?
booooom...
HUH?
W- WHAT'S WITH ALL THE HUMANS ?!
OH!
THE FIREWORKS SHOW! YOU GOT A NUMBERED RAFFLE TICKET FOR SEATS, DIDN'T YOU?!
t-tmp
...?!
AGGHHH!
Firework Show
boom...
ding
!

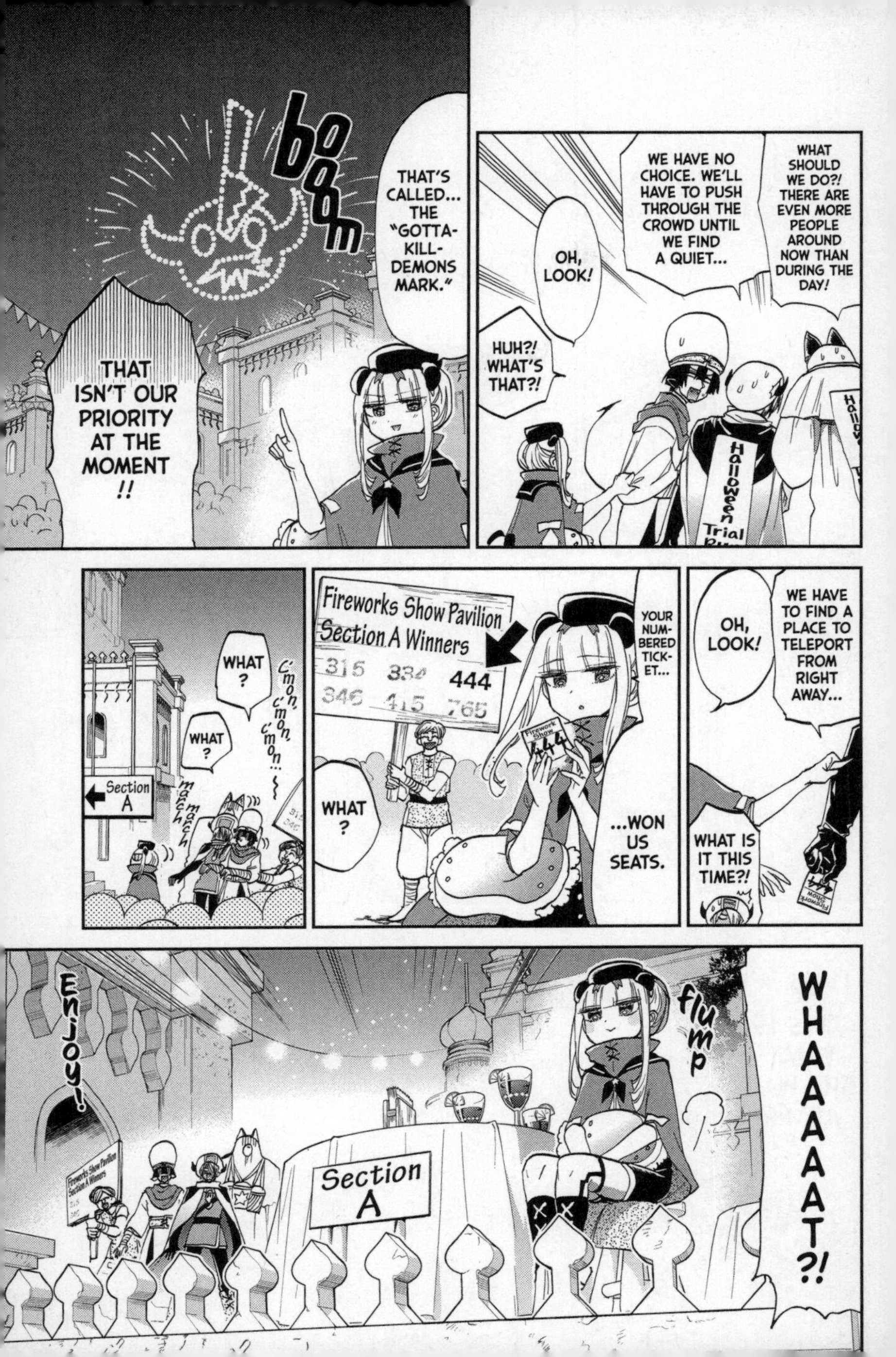
WHAT SHOULD WE DO?! THERE ARE EVEN MORE PEOPLE AROUND NOW THAN DURING THE DAY!
WE HAVE NO CHOICE. WE'LL HAVE TO PUSH THROUGH THE CROWD UNTIL WE FIND A QUIET...
OH, LOOK!
HUH?! WHAT'S THAT?!
Halloween Trial
boom
THAT'S CALLED... THE "GOTTA-KILL-DEMONS MARK."
THAT ISN'T OUR PRIORITY AT THE MOMENT!!
WE HAVE TO FIND A PLACE TO TELEPORT FROM RIGHT AWAY...
OH, LOOK!
WHAT IS IT THIS TIME?!
YOUR NUMBERED TICKET...
Fireworks Show Pavilion
Section A Winners
315 334 444
346 415 765
Firework Show 444
...WON US SEATS.
WHAT?
WHAT?
WHAT?
c'mon, c'mon, c'mon!!
Section A
march march
WHAAAAAAT?!
flump
Section A
Enjoy!

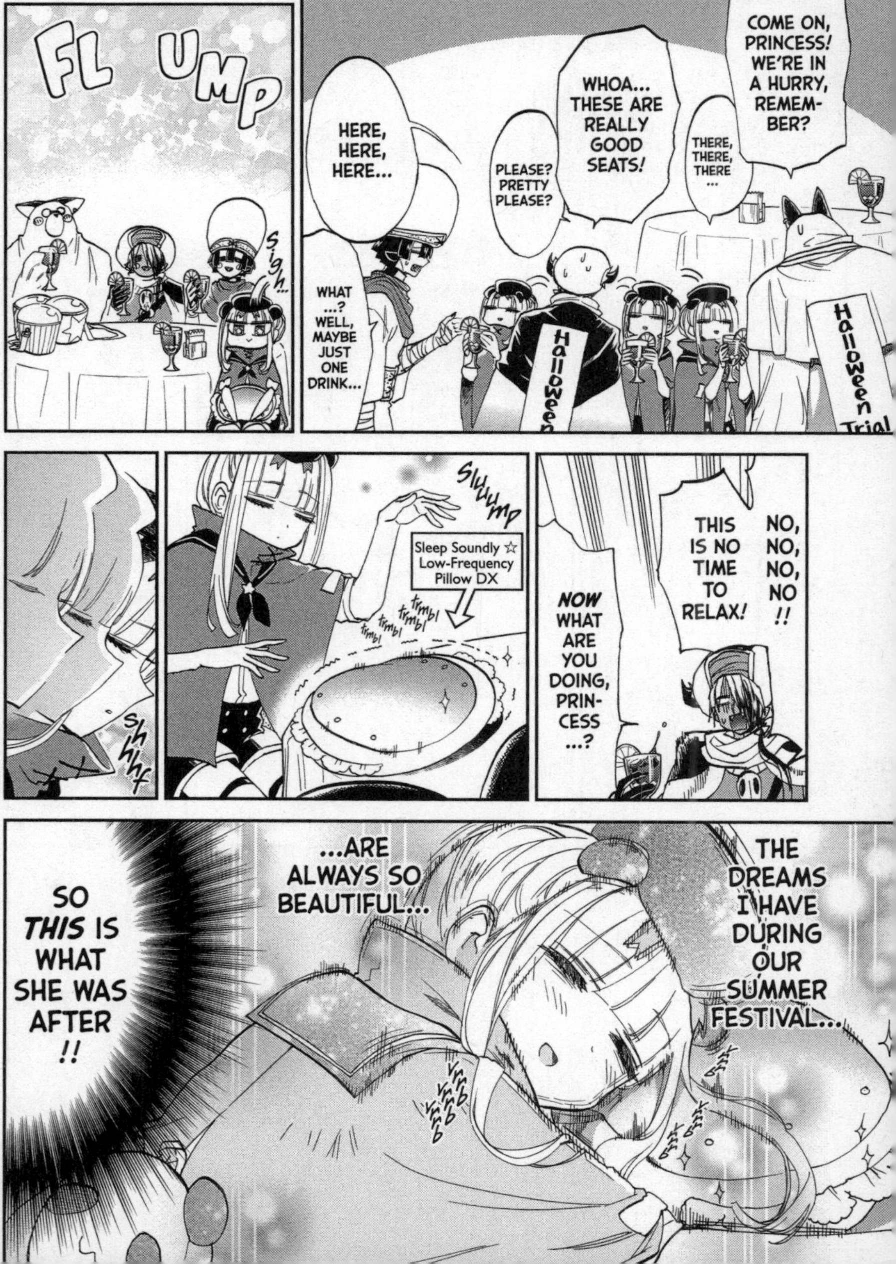
COME ON, PRINCESS! WE'RE IN A HURRY, REMEMBER?
THERE, THERE, THERE ...
WHOA... THESE ARE REALLY GOOD SEATS!
PLEASE? PRETTY PLEASE?
HERE, HERE, HERE...
WHAT ...? WELL, MAYBE JUST ONE DRINK...
Halloween Trial
Halloween
FL UMP
Sigh...
NO, NO, NO, NO!!
THIS IS NO TIME TO RELAX!
NOW WHAT ARE YOU DOING, PRINCESS ...?
Sluuump
Sleep Soundly ☆ Low-Frequency Pillow DX
trmbl trmbl trmbl trmbl
shhhf
THE DREAMS I HAVE DURING OUR SUMMER FESTIVAL...
...ARE ALWAYS SO BEAUTIFUL...
SO THIS IS WHAT SHE WAS AFTER!!
vrrrb vrrrb vrrrb
vrrrb vrrrb

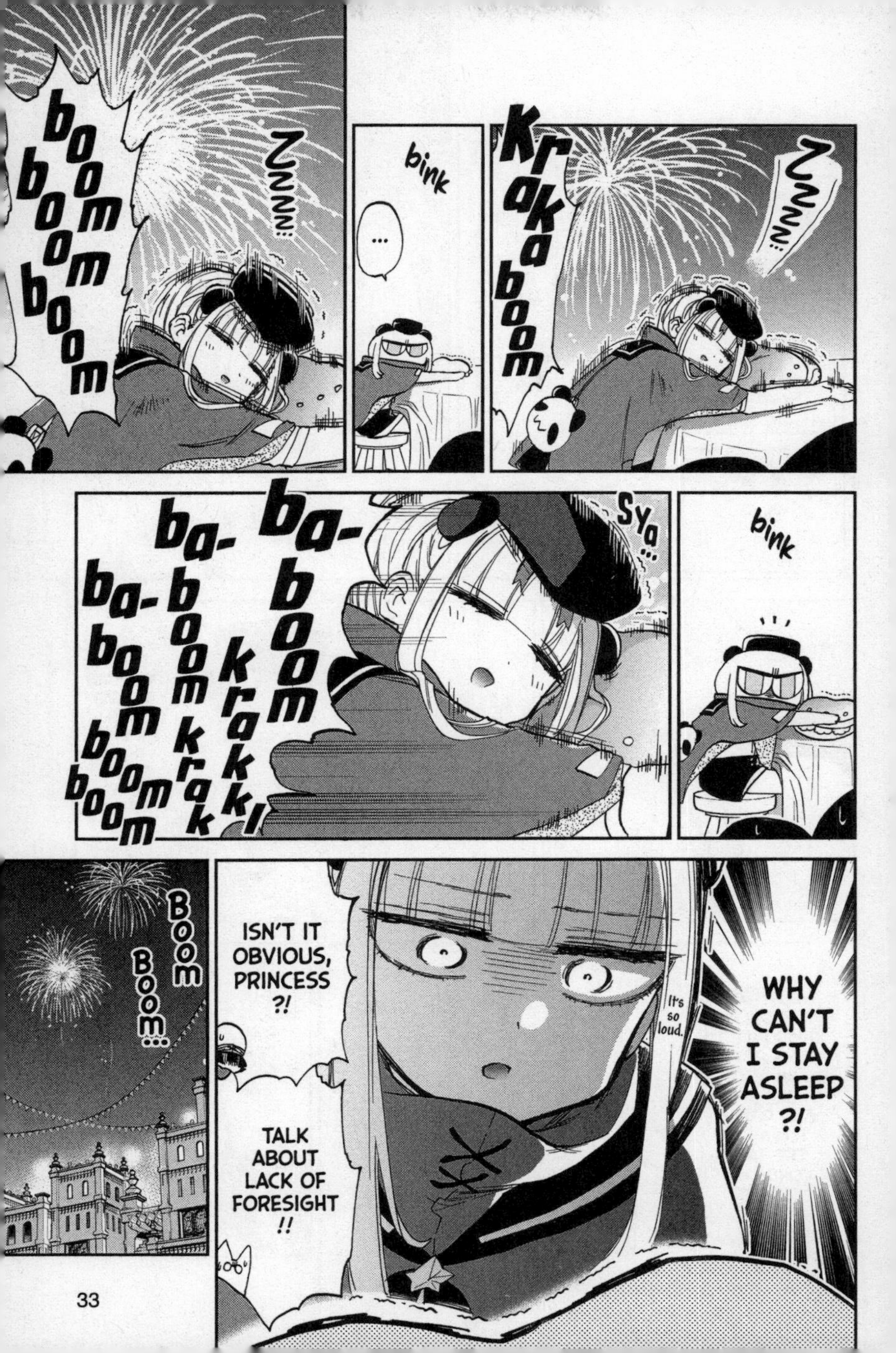

Kraka boom
Zzzz...
bink
...
boom boom boom boom
Zzzz...
bink
Sya...
ba-boom
krakkl
ba-boom krak
ba-boom boom boom
WHY CAN'T I STAY ASLEEP?!
It's so loud.
ISN'T IT OBVIOUS, PRINCESS?!
TALK ABOUT LACK OF FORESIGHT!!
Boom Boom...

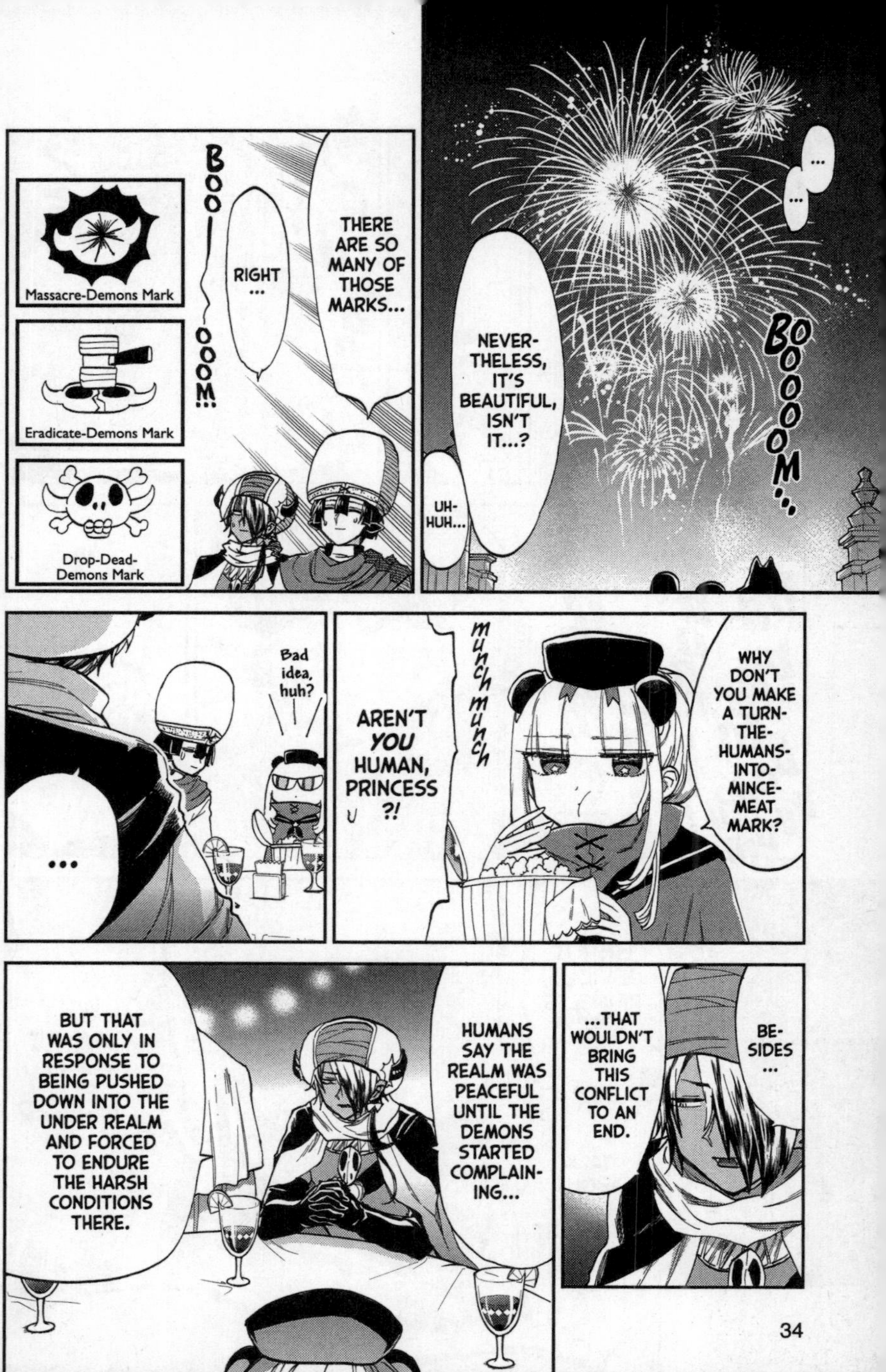
...
...
NEVER-THELESS, IT'S BEAUTIFUL, ISN'T IT...?
UH-HUH...
BOOOOOOM...
THERE ARE SO MANY OF THOSE MARKS...
RIGHT...
BOO—OOOM!!
Massacre-Demons Mark
Eradicate-Demons Mark
Drop-Dead-Demons Mark
WHY DON'T YOU MAKE A TURN-THE-HUMANS-INTO-MINCE-MEAT MARK?
munch munch
AREN'T *YOU* HUMAN, PRINCESS?!
Bad idea, huh?
...
BE-SIDES...
...THAT WOULDN'T BRING THIS CONFLICT TO AN END.
HUMANS SAY THE REALM WAS PEACEFUL UNTIL THE DEMONS STARTED COMPLAIN-ING...
BUT THAT WAS ONLY IN RESPONSE TO BEING PUSHED DOWN INTO THE UNDER REALM AND FORCED TO ENDURE THE HARSH CONDITIONS THERE.

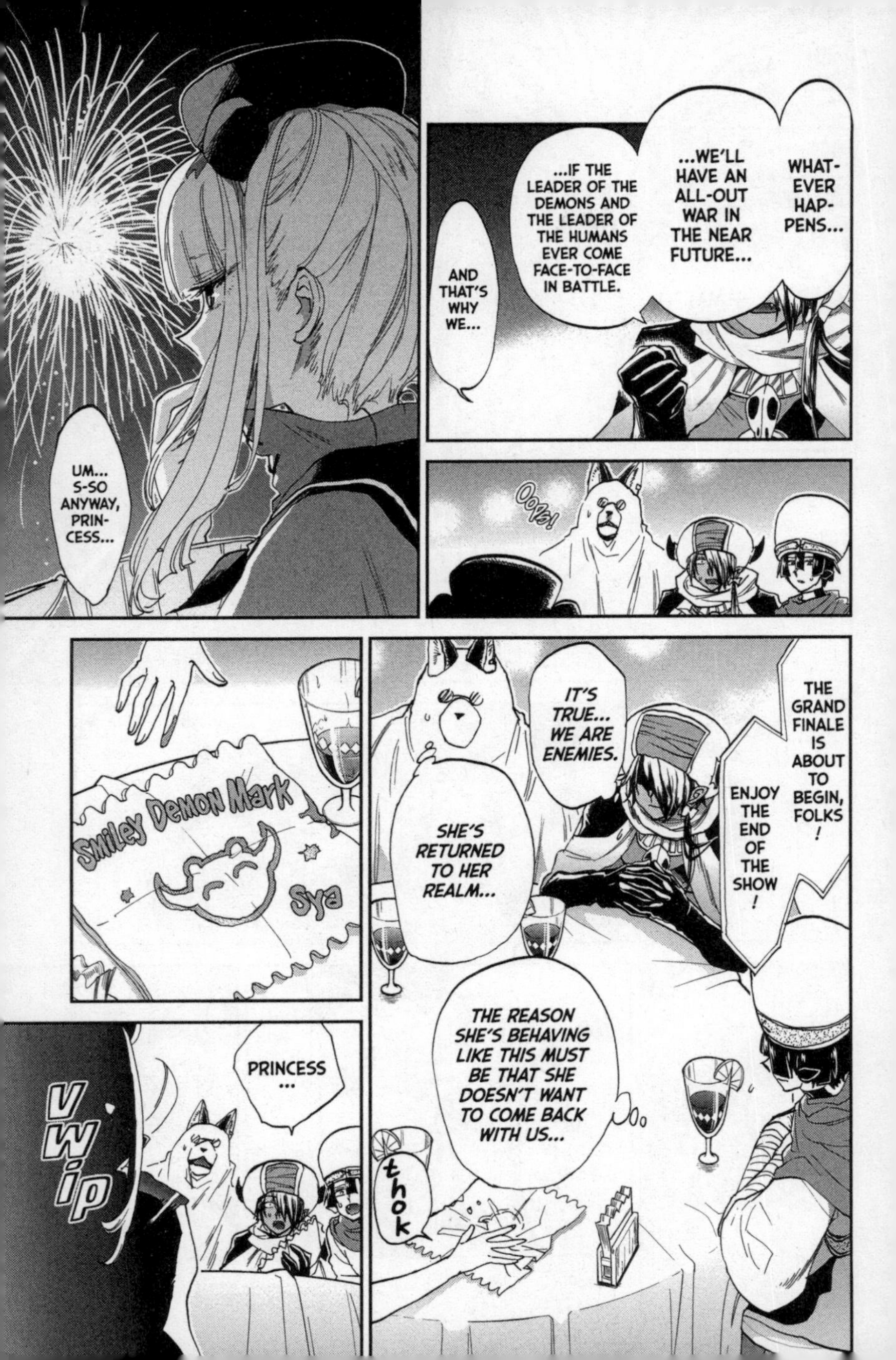
WHAT-EVER HAP-PENS...
...WE'LL HAVE AN ALL-OUT WAR IN THE NEAR FUTURE...
...IF THE LEADER OF THE DEMONS AND THE LEADER OF THE HUMANS EVER COME FACE-TO-FACE IN BATTLE.
AND THAT'S WHY WE...
Oops!
UM... S-SO ANYWAY, PRIN-CESS...
THE GRAND FINALE IS ABOUT TO BEGIN, FOLKS!
ENJOY THE END OF THE SHOW!
IT'S TRUE... WE ARE ENEMIES.
SHE'S RETURNED TO HER REALM...
THE REASON SHE'S BEHAVING LIKE THIS MUST BE THAT SHE DOESN'T WANT TO COME BACK WITH US...
thok
Smiley Demon Mark
Sya
PRINCESS...
Vwip

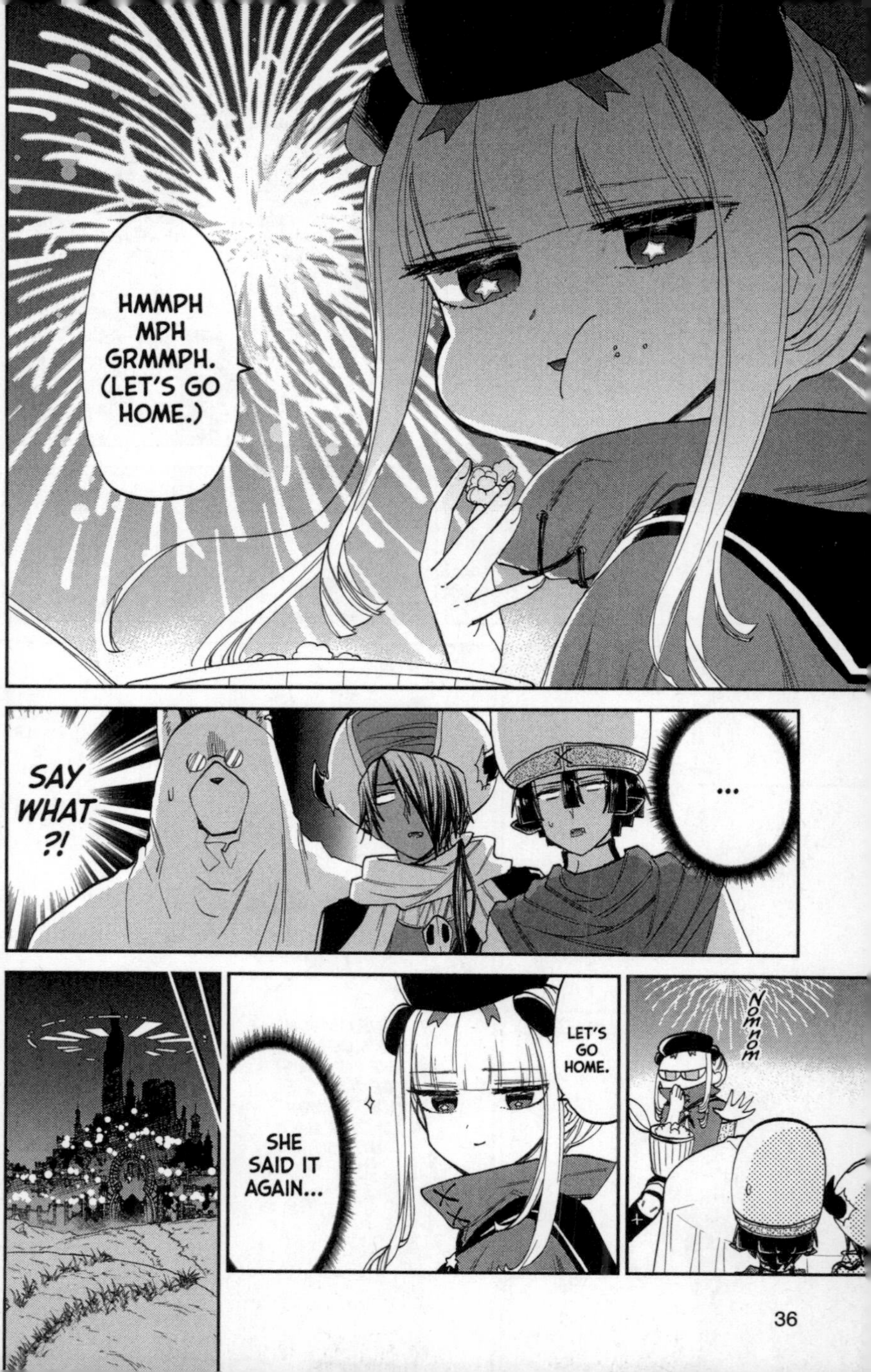
HMMPH MPH GRMMPH. (LET'S GO HOME.)
...
SAY WHAT ?!
Nomnom
LET'S GO HOME.
SHE SAID IT AGAIN...

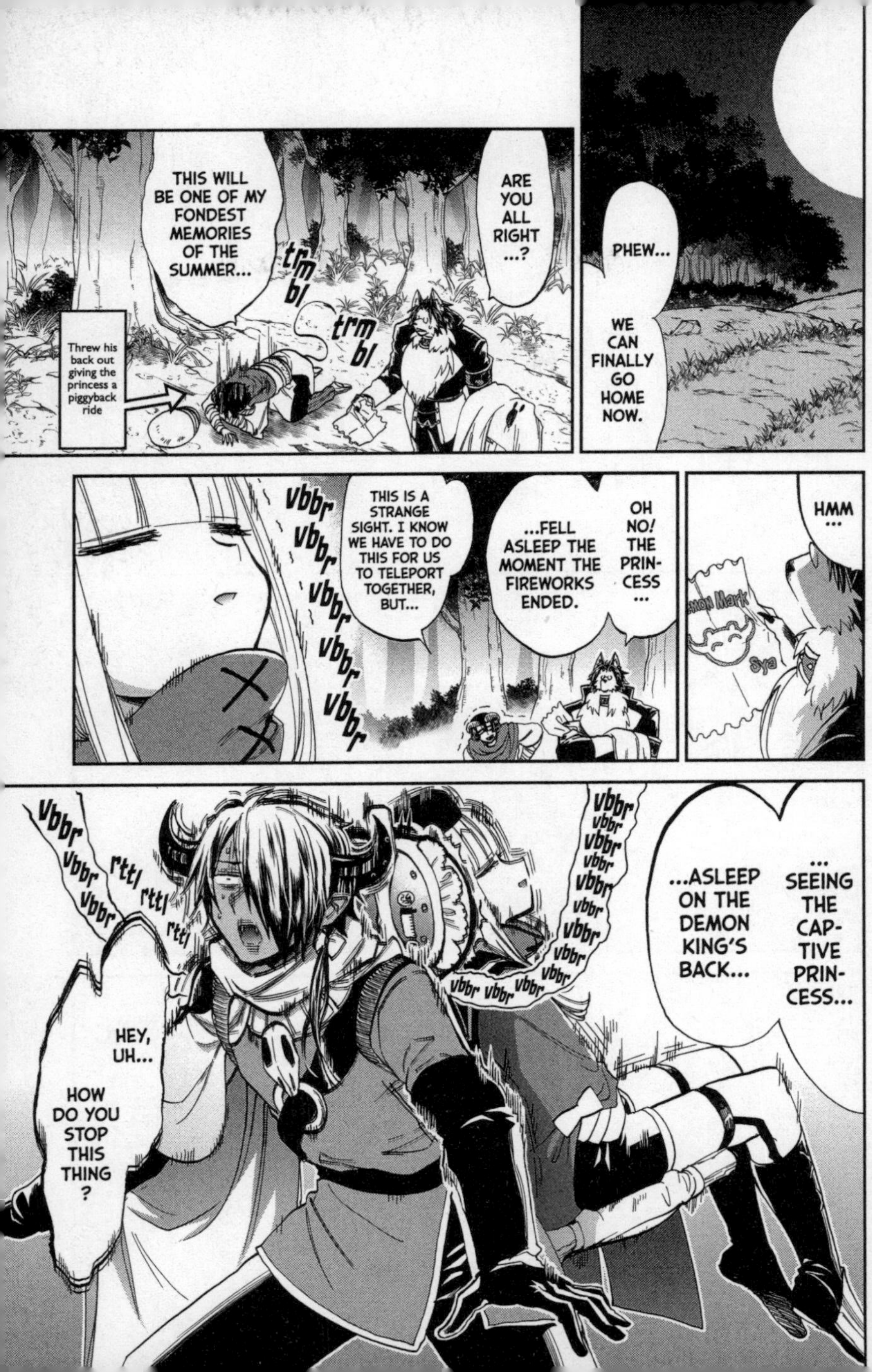
PHEW...
WE CAN FINALLY GO HOME NOW.
ARE YOU ALL RIGHT ...?
THIS WILL BE ONE OF MY FONDEST MEMORIES OF THE SUMMER...
trm bl
trm bl
Threw his back out giving the princess a piggyback ride
HMM ...
Sya
OH NO! THE PRIN-CESS ...
...FELL ASLEEP THE MOMENT THE FIREWORKS ENDED.
THIS IS A STRANGE SIGHT. I KNOW WE HAVE TO DO THIS FOR US TO TELEPORT TOGETHER, BUT...
vbbr vbbr vbbr vbbr vbbr
... SEEING THE CAP-TIVE PRIN-CESS...
...ASLEEP ON THE DEMON KING'S BACK...
vbbr vbbr vbbr vbbr vbbr vbbr vbbr vbbr vbbr vbbr vbbr vbbr vbbr
vbbr vbbr vbbr
rttl rttl rttl
HEY, UH...
HOW DO YOU STOP THIS THING ?

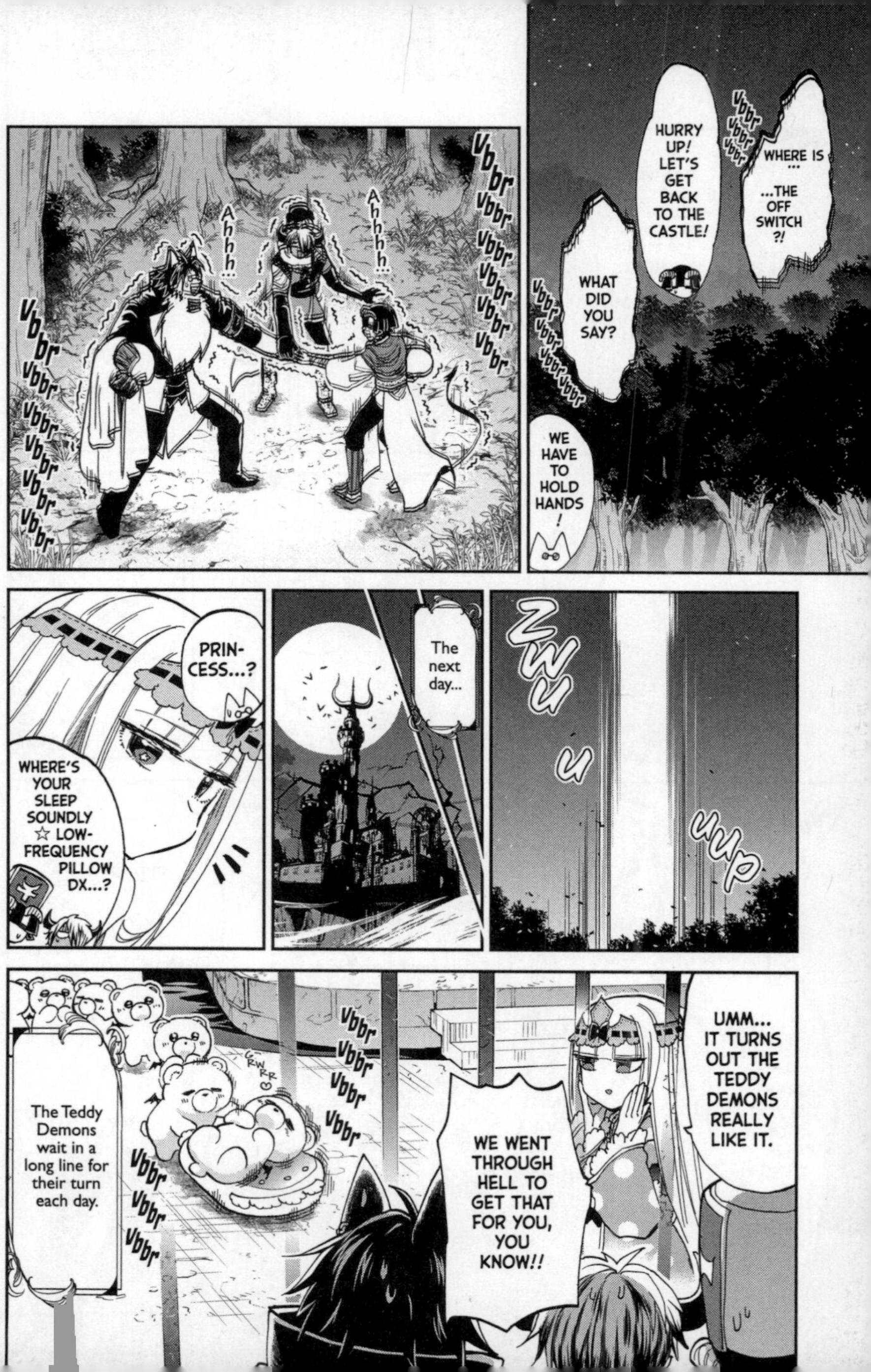
WHERE IS... ...THE OFF SWITCH?!
Vbbr vbbr vbbr
HURRY UP! LET'S GET BACK TO THE CASTLE!
WHAT DID YOU SAY?
Vbbr vbbr vbbr vbbr vbbr
WE HAVE TO HOLD HANDS!
Ahhhh...
Ahhh...
Vbbr vbbr vbbr vbbr vbbr vbbr vbbr
Vbbr vbbr vbbr vbbr vbbr vbbr vbbr
ZWUuuuup
The next day...
PRIN-CESS...?
WHERE'S YOUR SLEEP SOUNDLY ☆ LOW-FREQUENCY PILLOW DX...?
UMM... IT TURNS OUT THE TEDDY DEMONS REALLY LIKE IT.
WE WENT THROUGH HELL TO GET THAT FOR YOU, YOU KNOW!!
Vbbr vbbr vbbr vbbr
GRWRR
Vbbr vbbr vbbr
The Teddy Demons wait in a long line for their turn each day.

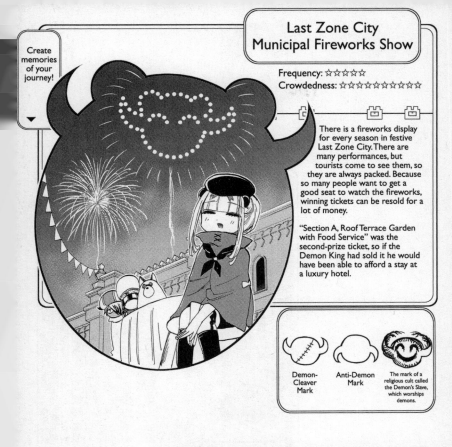

Create memories of your journey!

Last Zone City Municipal Fireworks Show

Frequency: ☆☆☆☆☆

Crowdedness: ☆☆☆☆☆☆☆☆☆☆☆☆

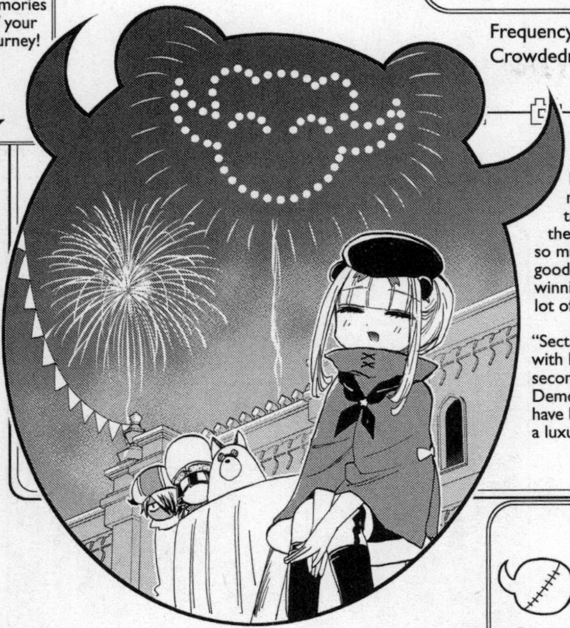

There is a fireworks display for every season in festive Last Zone City. There are many performances, but tourists come to see them, so they are always packed. Because so many people want to get a good seat to watch the fireworks, winning tickets can be resold for a lot of money.

"Section A, Roof Terrace Garden with Food Service" was the second-prize ticket, so if the Demon King had sold it he would have been able to afford a stay at a luxury hotel.

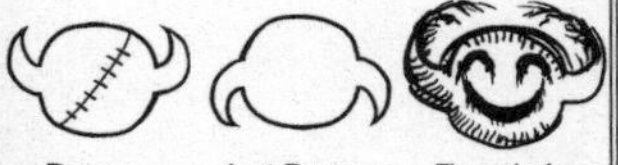

Demon-Cleaver Mark

Anti-Demon Mark

The mark of a religious cult called the Demon's Slave, which worships demons.

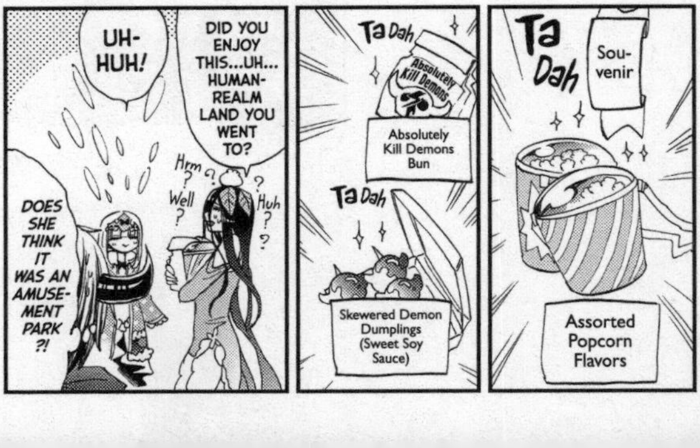
Ta Dah
Sou-venir
Assorted Popcorn Flavors
Ta Dah
Absolutely Kill Demons
Absolutely Kill Demons Bun
Ta Dah
Skewered Demon Dumplings (Sweet Soy Sauce)
DID YOU ENJOY THIS...UH... HUMAN-REALM LAND YOU WENT TO?
UH-HUH!
Hrm?
Well?
Huh??
DOES SHE THINK IT WAS AN AMUSEMENT PARK?!

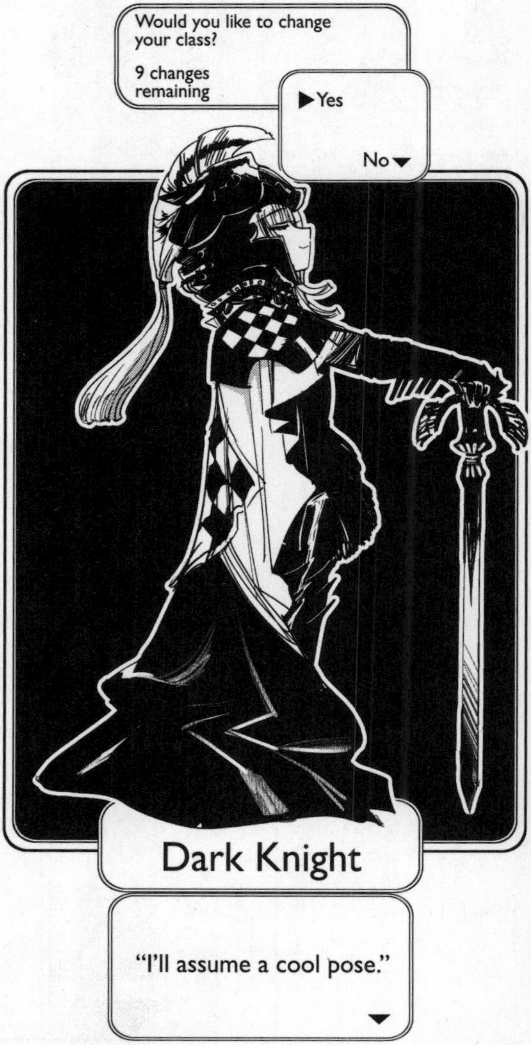
Would you like to change your class?
9 changes remaining
▶Yes
No
Dark Knight
"I'll assume a cool pose."

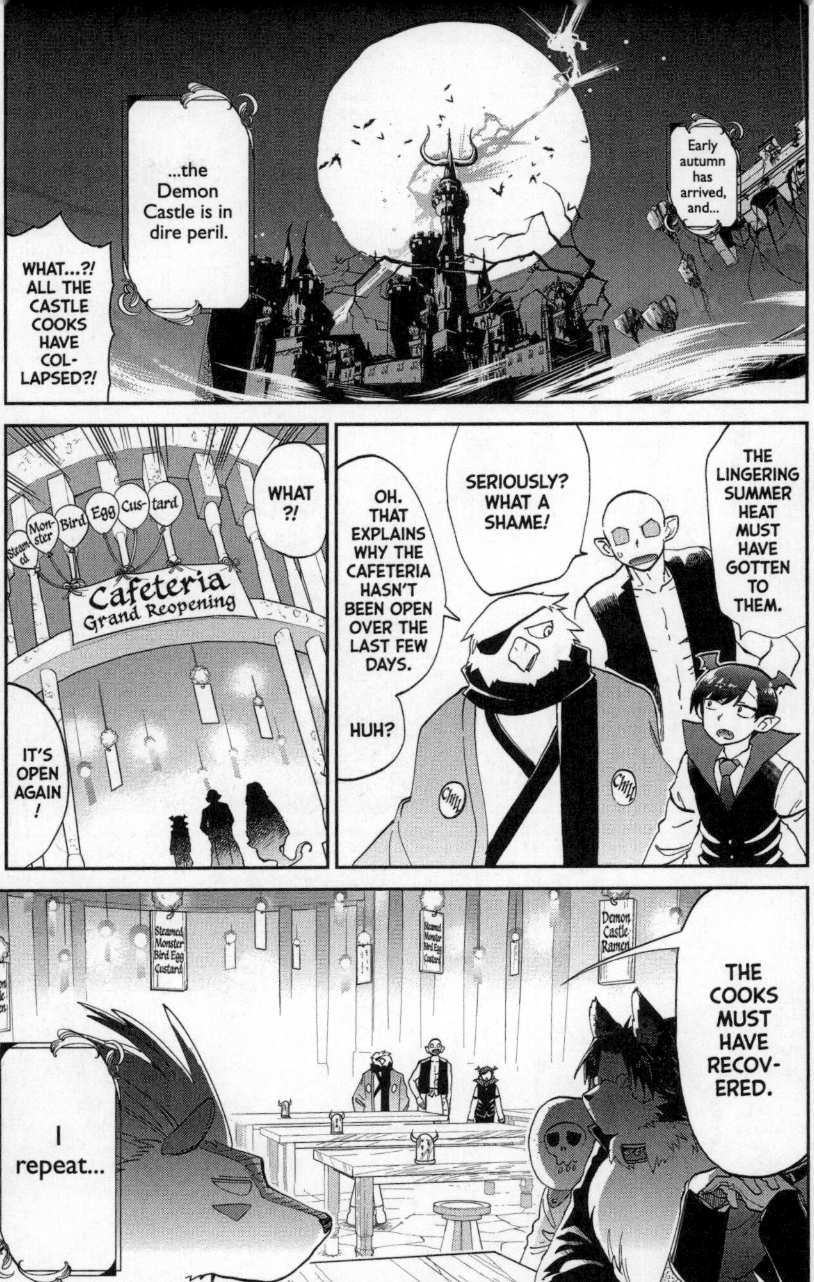
Early autumn has arrived, and...
...the Demon Castle is in dire peril.
WHAT...?! ALL THE CASTLE COOKS HAVE COL-LAPSED?!
THE LINGERING SUMMER HEAT MUST HAVE GOTTEN TO THEM.
SERIOUSLY? WHAT A SHAME!
OH. THAT EXPLAINS WHY THE CAFETERIA HASN'T BEEN OPEN OVER THE LAST FEW DAYS.
HUH?
WHAT ?!
Steam-ed Mon-ster Bird Egg Cus-tard
Cafeteria Grand Reopening
IT'S OPEN AGAIN!
THE COOKS MUST HAVE RECOV-ERED.
Demon Castle Ramen
Steamed Monster Bird Egg Custard
Steamed Monster Bird Egg Custard
Demon Castle Ramen
I repeat...

69th Night: Wobble Wobble, I Don't Taste Bad

...the Demon Castle...

...is in dire peril!

69th Night: Wobble Wobble, I Don't Taste Bad

Eek!

I WILL BEGIN BY MAKING THE STEAMED MONSTER EGG CUSTARD.

WELCOME, EVERYONE...

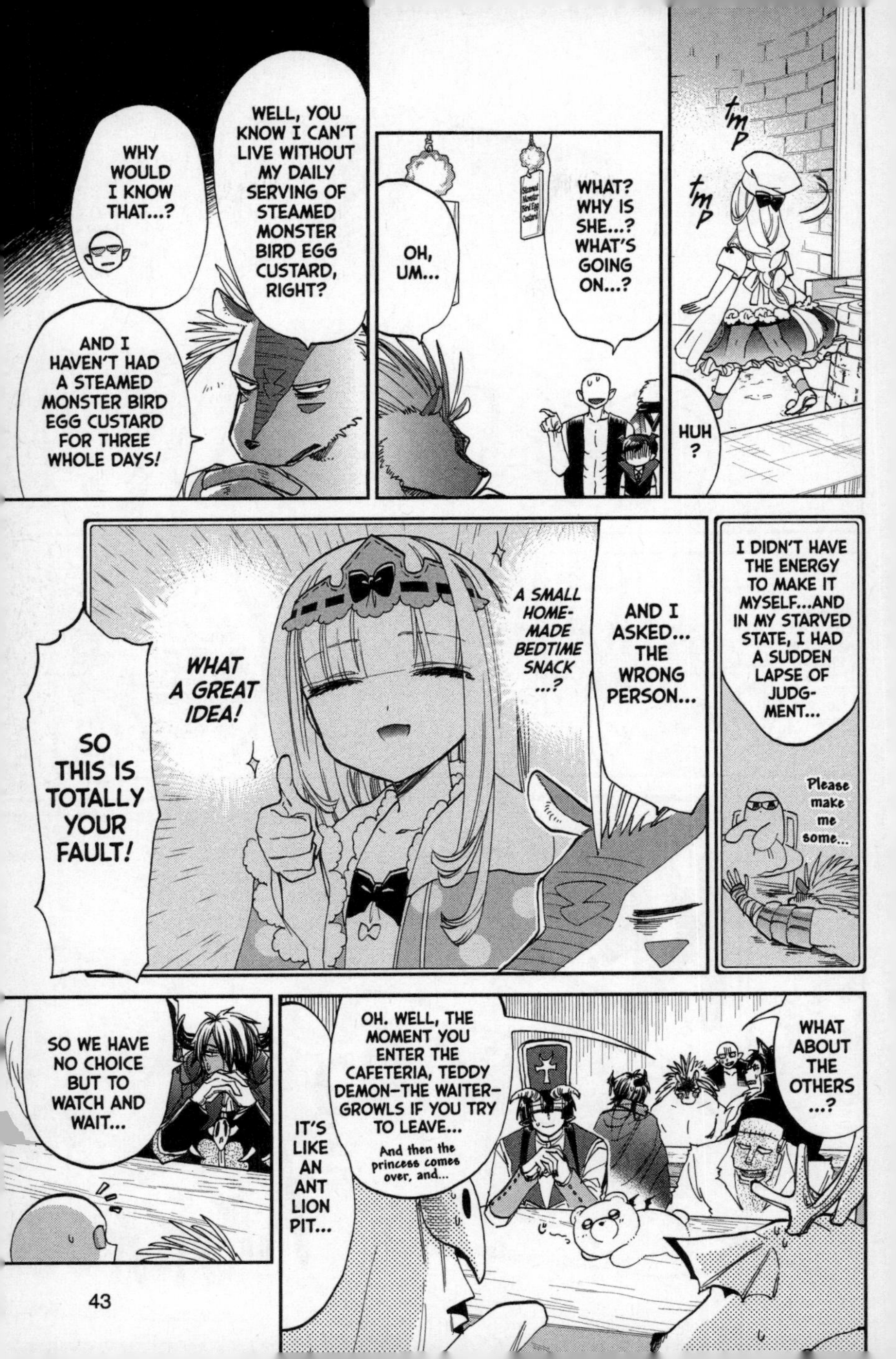
tmp
tmp
HUH?
WHAT? WHY IS SHE...? WHAT'S GOING ON...?
Steamed Monster Bird Egg Custard
OH, UM...
WELL, YOU KNOW I CAN'T LIVE WITHOUT MY DAILY SERVING OF STEAMED MONSTER BIRD EGG CUSTARD, RIGHT?
WHY WOULD I KNOW THAT...?
AND I HAVEN'T HAD A STEAMED MONSTER BIRD EGG CUSTARD FOR THREE WHOLE DAYS!
I DIDN'T HAVE THE ENERGY TO MAKE IT MYSELF...AND IN MY STARVED STATE, I HAD A SUDDEN LAPSE OF JUDG-MENT...
Please make me some...
AND I ASKED... THE WRONG PERSON...
A SMALL HOME-MADE BEDTIME SNACK...?
WHAT A GREAT IDEA!
SO THIS IS TOTALLY YOUR FAULT!
WHAT ABOUT THE OTHERS...?
OH. WELL, THE MOMENT YOU ENTER THE CAFETERIA, TEDDY DEMON—THE WAITER—GROWLS IF YOU TRY TO LEAVE...
And then the princess comes over, and...
IT'S LIKE AN ANT LION PIT...
SO WE HAVE NO CHOICE BUT TO WATCH AND WAIT...

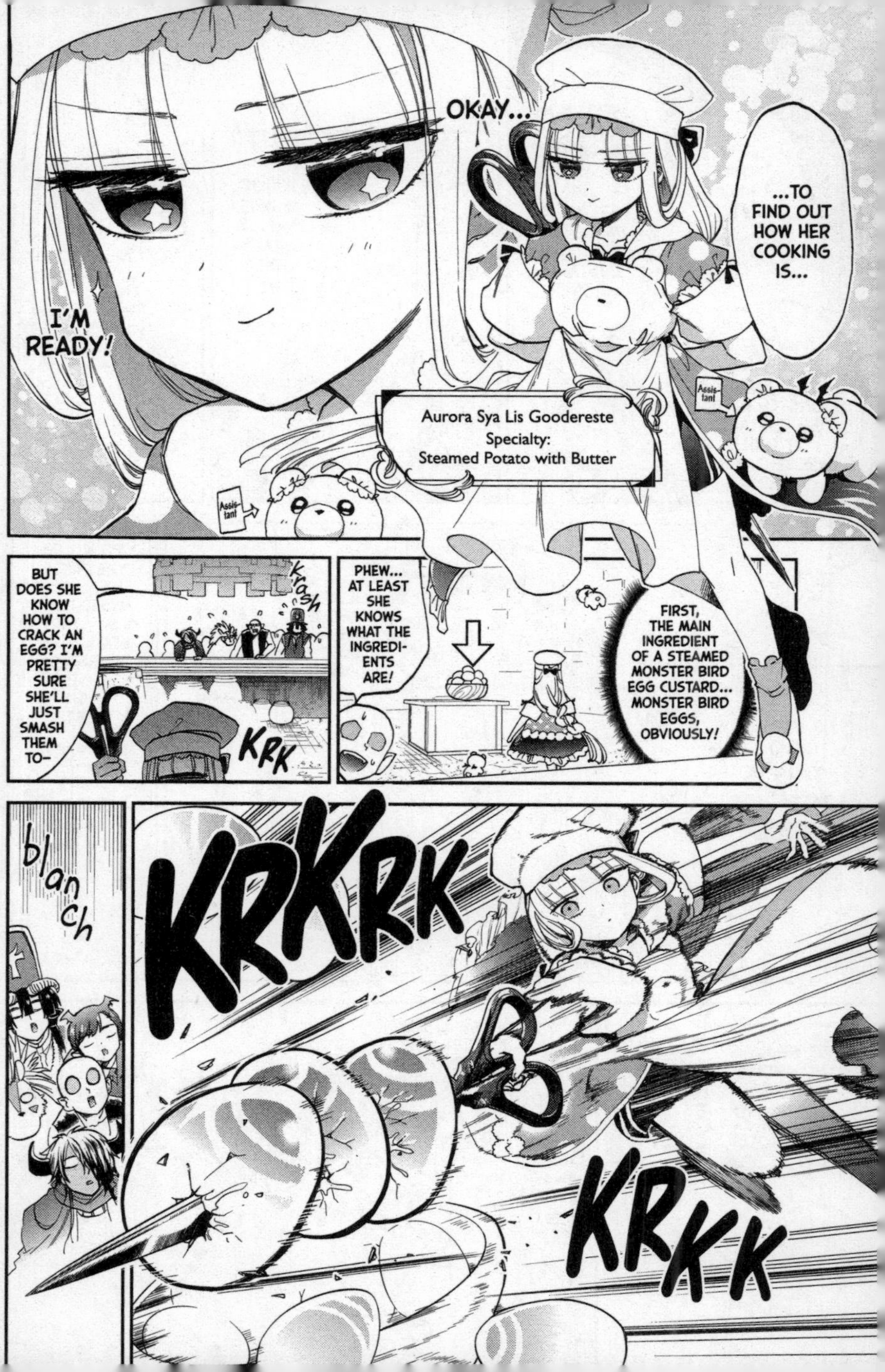
OKAY...
...TO FIND OUT HOW HER COOKING IS...
I'M READY!
Aurora Sya Lis Goodereste
Specialty:
Steamed Potato with Butter
Assis-tant
Assis-tant
FIRST, THE MAIN INGREDIENT OF A STEAMED MONSTER BIRD EGG CUSTARD... MONSTER BIRD EGGS, OBVIOUSLY!
PHEW... AT LEAST SHE KNOWS WHAT THE INGREDI-ENTS ARE!
krash
BUT DOES SHE KNOW HOW TO CRACK AN EGG? I'M PRETTY SURE SHE'LL JUST SMASH THEM TO—
KRK
KRKRK
KRKK
blanch

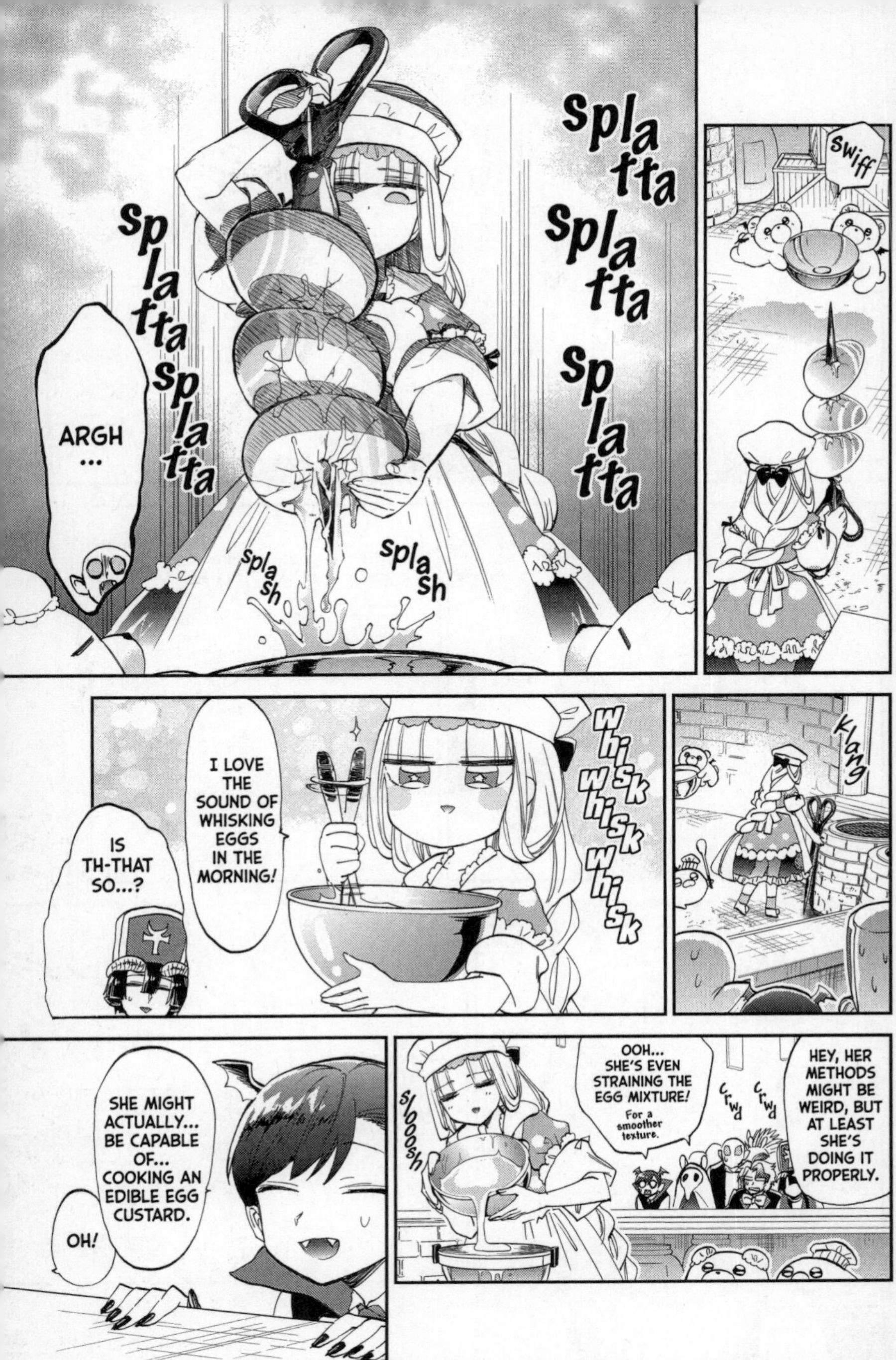
SWIFF
SPLATTA SPLATTA SPLATTA
SPLATTA SPLATTA
ARGH ...
SPLASH
SPLASH
KLANG
WHISK WHISK WHISK
I LOVE THE SOUND OF WHISKING EGGS IN THE MORNING!
IS TH-THAT SO...?
HEY, HER METHODS MIGHT BE WEIRD, BUT AT LEAST SHE'S DOING IT PROPERLY.
CRWD CRWD
OOH... SHE'S EVEN STRAINING THE EGG MIXTURE!
For a smoother texture.
SLOOOSH
SHE MIGHT ACTUALLY... BE CAPABLE OF... COOKING AN EDIBLE EGG CUSTARD.
OH!

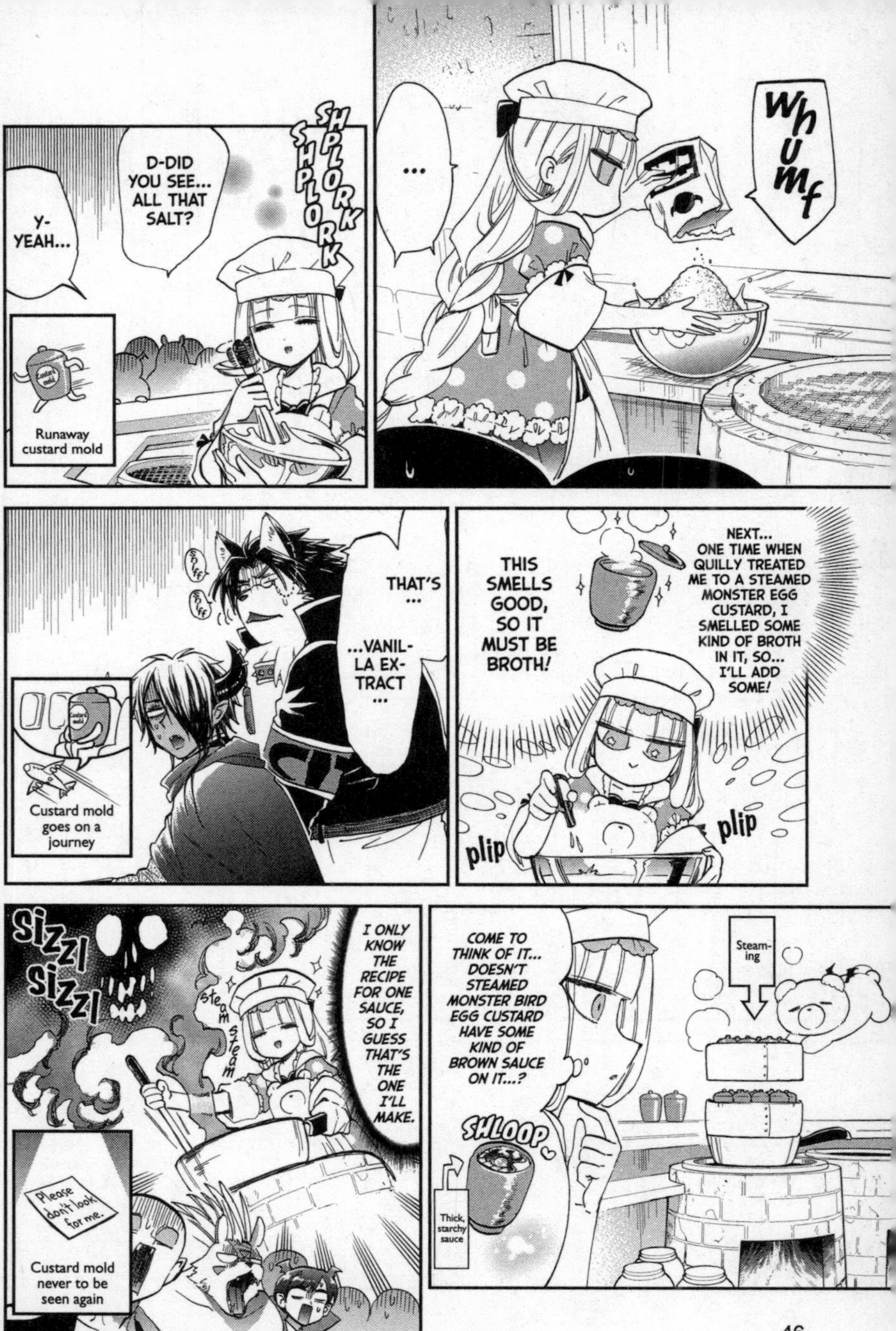
Whumf
...
SHPLORK
SHPLORK
D-DID YOU SEE... ALL THAT SALT?
Y-YEAH...
Custard mold
Runaway custard mold
NEXT... ONE TIME WHEN QUILLY TREATED ME TO A STEAMED MONSTER EGG CUSTARD, I SMELLED SOME KIND OF BROTH IN IT, SO... I'LL ADD SOME!
THIS SMELLS GOOD, SO IT MUST BE BROTH!
plip
plip
sniff
sniff
THAT'S...
...VANILLA EXTRACT...
Custard mold
Custard mold goes on a journey
COME TO THINK OF IT... DOESN'T STEAMED MONSTER BIRD EGG CUSTARD HAVE SOME KIND OF BROWN SAUCE ON IT...?
Steaming
SHLOOP
Thick, starchy sauce
I ONLY KNOW THE RECIPE FOR ONE SAUCE, SO I GUESS THAT'S THE ONE I'LL MAKE.
sizzl
sizzl
steam
steam
Please don't look for me.
Custard mold never to be seen again

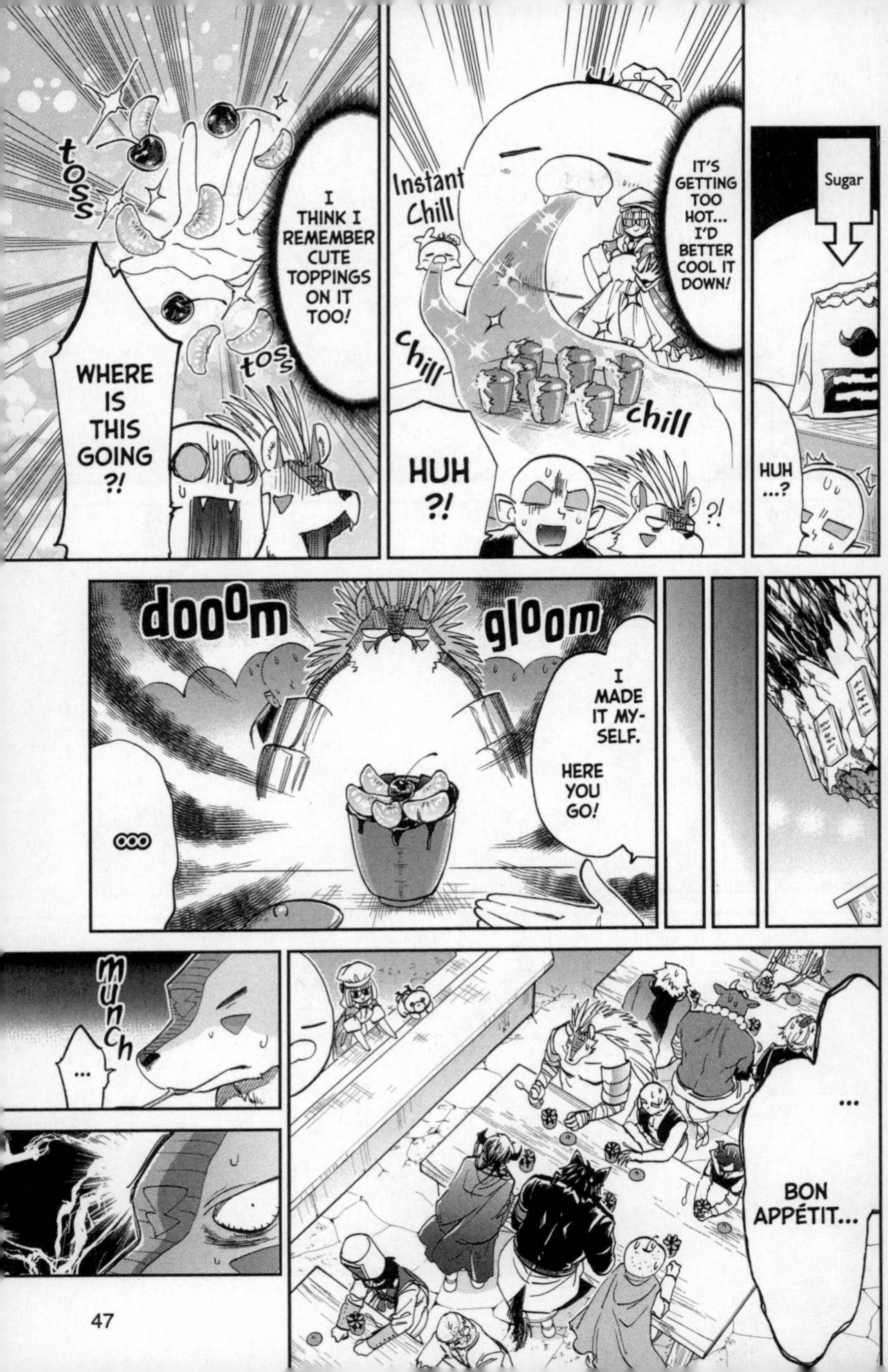
Sugar
HUH ...?
IT'S GETTING TOO HOT... I'D BETTER COOL IT DOWN!
Instant Chill
chill
chill
HUH ?!
?!
I THINK I REMEMBER CUTE TOPPINGS ON IT TOO!
toss
toss
WHERE IS THIS GOING ?!
dooom
gloom
I MADE IT MY-SELF.
HERE YOU GO!
...
...
BON APPÉTIT...
munch
...

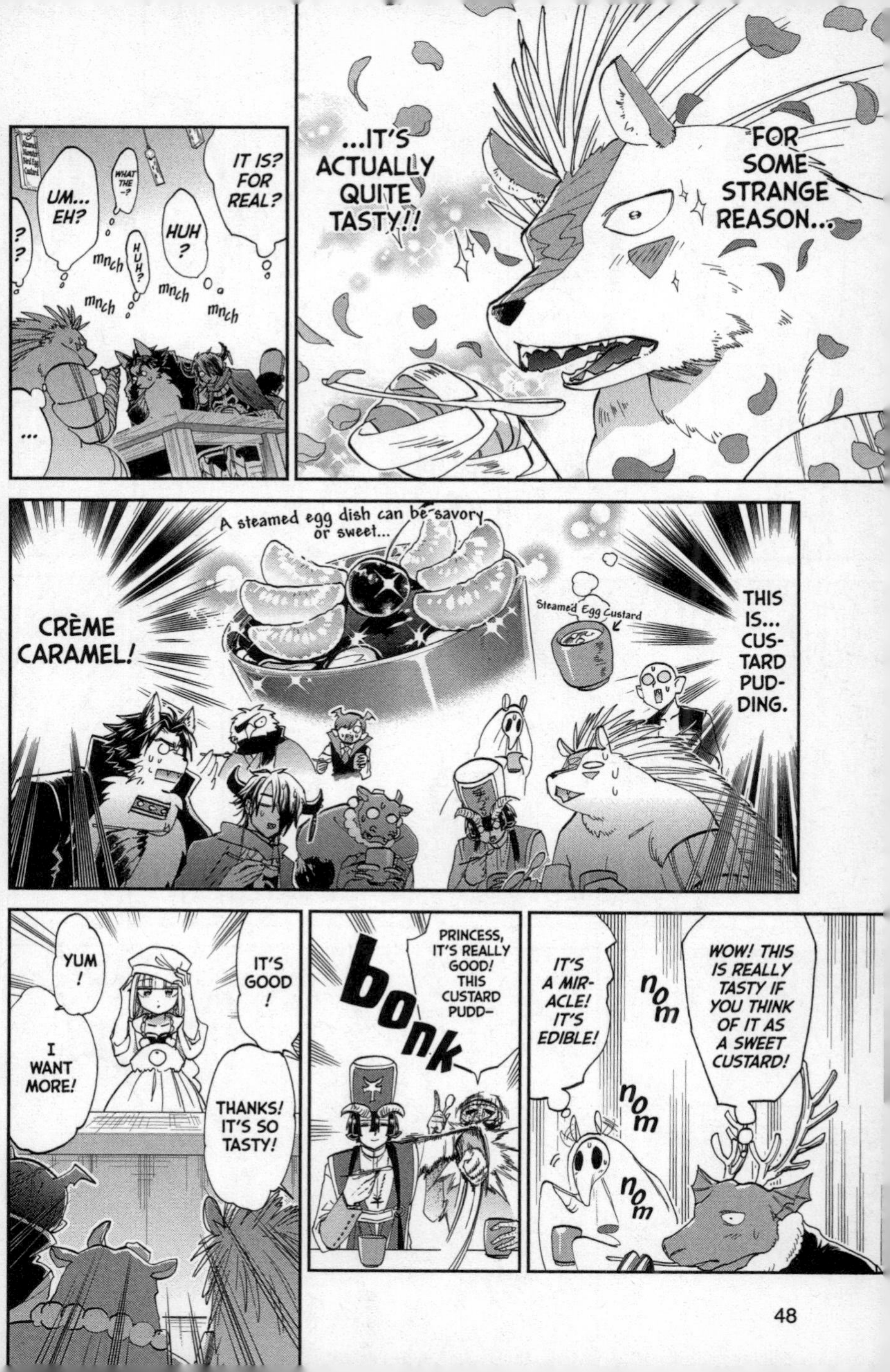

FOR SOME STRANGE REASON...
...IT'S ACTUALLY QUITE TASTY!!
IT IS? FOR REAL?
HUH?
WHAT THE--?
HUH?
mnch
mnch
mnch
mnch
UM... EH?
??
...
A steamed egg dish can be savory or sweet...
THIS IS... CUSTARD PUDDING.
Steamed Egg Custard
CRÈME CARAMEL!
WOW! THIS IS REALLY TASTY IF YOU THINK OF IT AS A SWEET CUSTARD!
nom
nom
nom
IT'S A MIRACLE! IT'S EDIBLE!
PRINCESS, IT'S REALLY GOOD! THIS CUSTARD PUDD—
bonk
IT'S GOOD!
YUM!
THANKS! IT'S SO TASTY!
I WANT MORE!

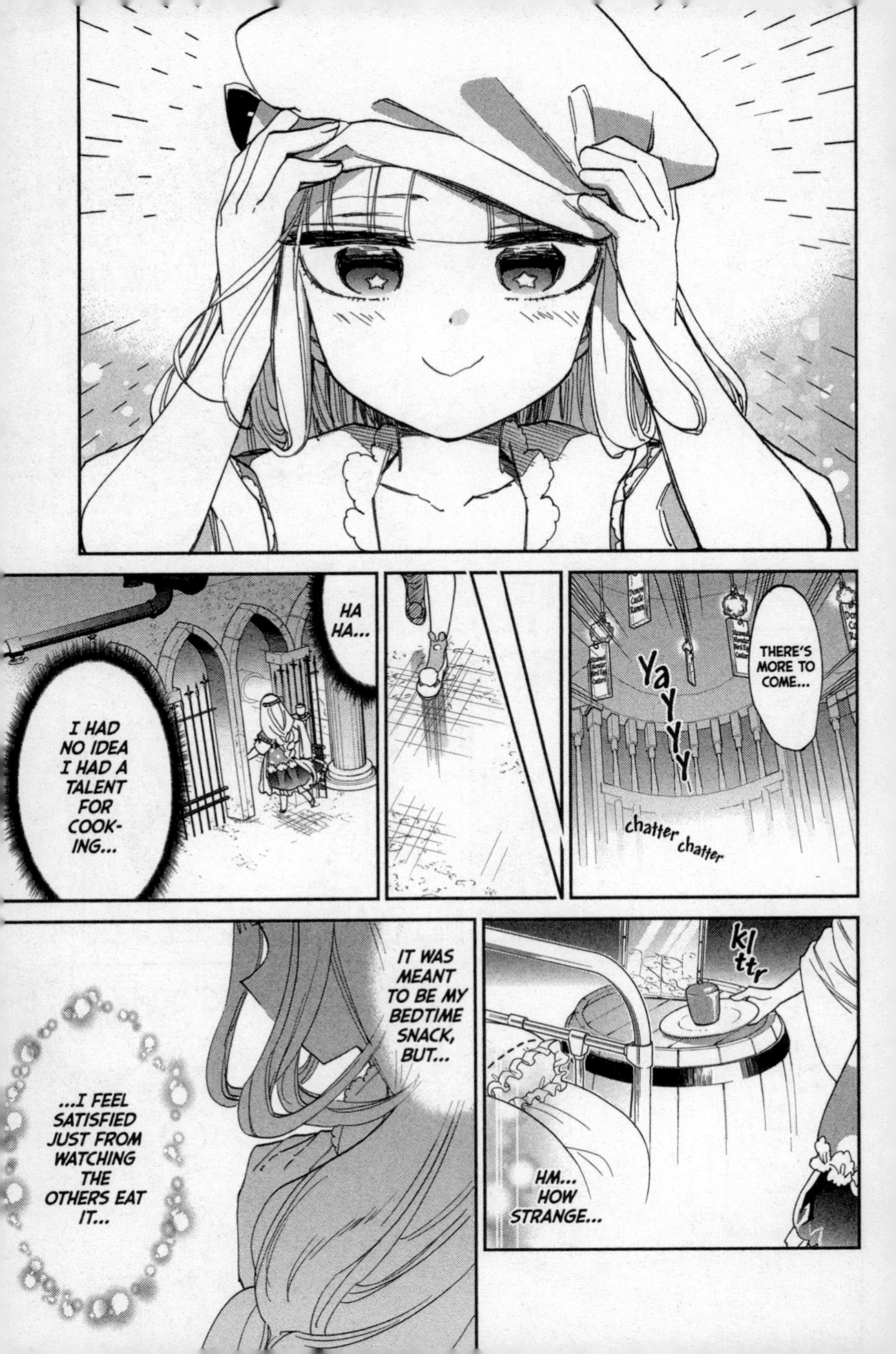
THERE'S MORE TO COME...
YaYYYY
chatter chatter
HA HA...
I HAD NO IDEA I HAD A TALENT FOR COOKING...
kl ttr
HM... HOW STRANGE...
IT WAS MEANT TO BE MY BEDTIME SNACK, BUT...
...I FEEL SATISFIED JUST FROM WATCHING THE OTHERS EAT IT...

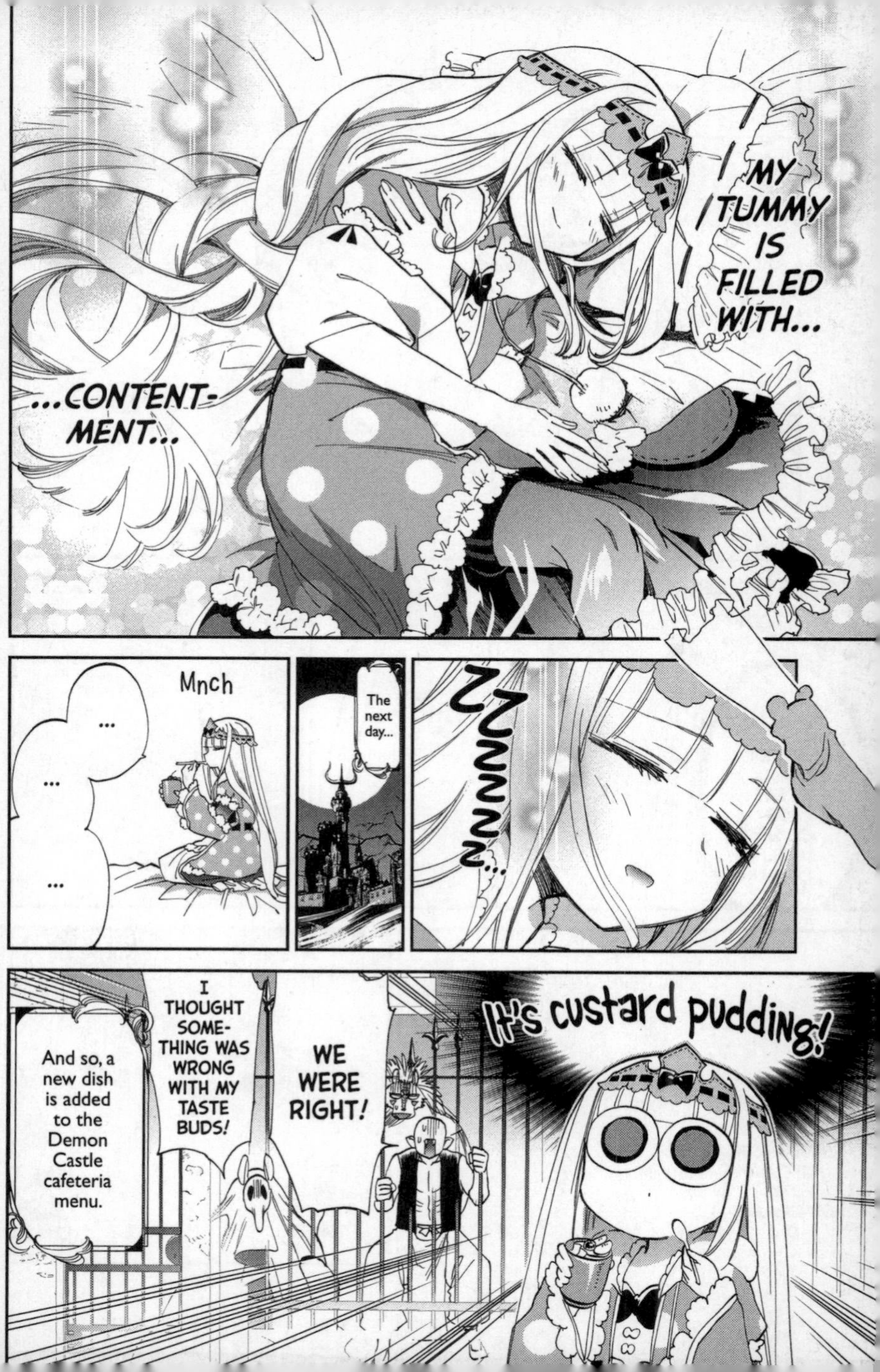
MY TUMMY IS FILLED WITH...
...CONTENT-MENT...
ZZZZZZZ...
The next day...
Mnch
...
...
...
It's custard pudding!
WE WERE RIGHT!
I THOUGHT SOME-THING WAS WRONG WITH MY TASTE BUDS!
And so, a new dish is added to the Demon Castle cafeteria menu.

Steamed Monster Bird Egg Custard

Monster Bird Pudding à la Mode

Popularity: ☆☆☆☆☆☆☆☆☆☆
Deliciousness: ☆☆☆☆☆☆☆☆☆☆

It's not at all poisonous.

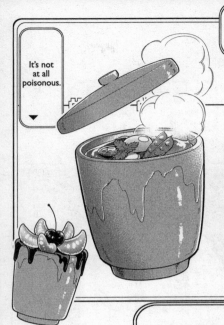

A classic Demon Castle cafeteria dish, beloved by everyone for hundreds of years since the original Demon Castle cafeteria opened. It is so popular with the Demon King, Quilladillo and the other demons that it even sells well during the summer. Consequently, members of the Monster Bird Union, who lay and supply the eggs, are far from poor...

The new dessert created by Princess Syalis, Monster Bird Pudding à la Mode, is very popular too.

Fan Reviews

"I can't think straight if I don't eat this at least once a day."
Mr. Q, Demon Castle employee

"It's my favorite snack. I'll use my authority to keep it on the menu."
Mr. T, Demon King

"Someone punched me and my head went blank the first time I had the custard pudding. It felt really good, so it's been a staple of my diet ever since."
Mr. F, Demon Castle employee

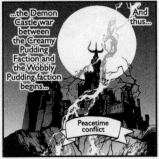

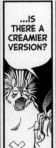

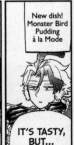

New dish! Monster Bird Pudding à la Mode
IT'S TASTY, BUT...
...IS THERE A CREAMIER VERSION?
And thus...
...the Demon Castle war between the Creamy Pudding Faction and the Wobbly Pudding faction begins...
Peacetime conflict

Would you like to change your class?
8 changes remaining
▶Yes
No
Puppet Master
"It dances better than me."

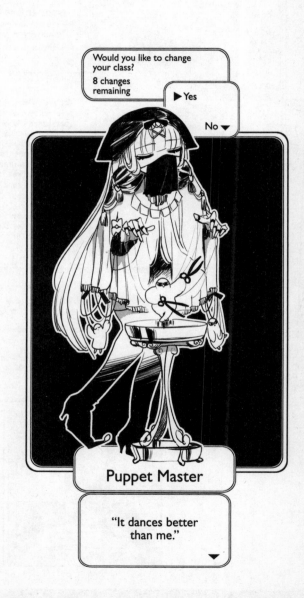

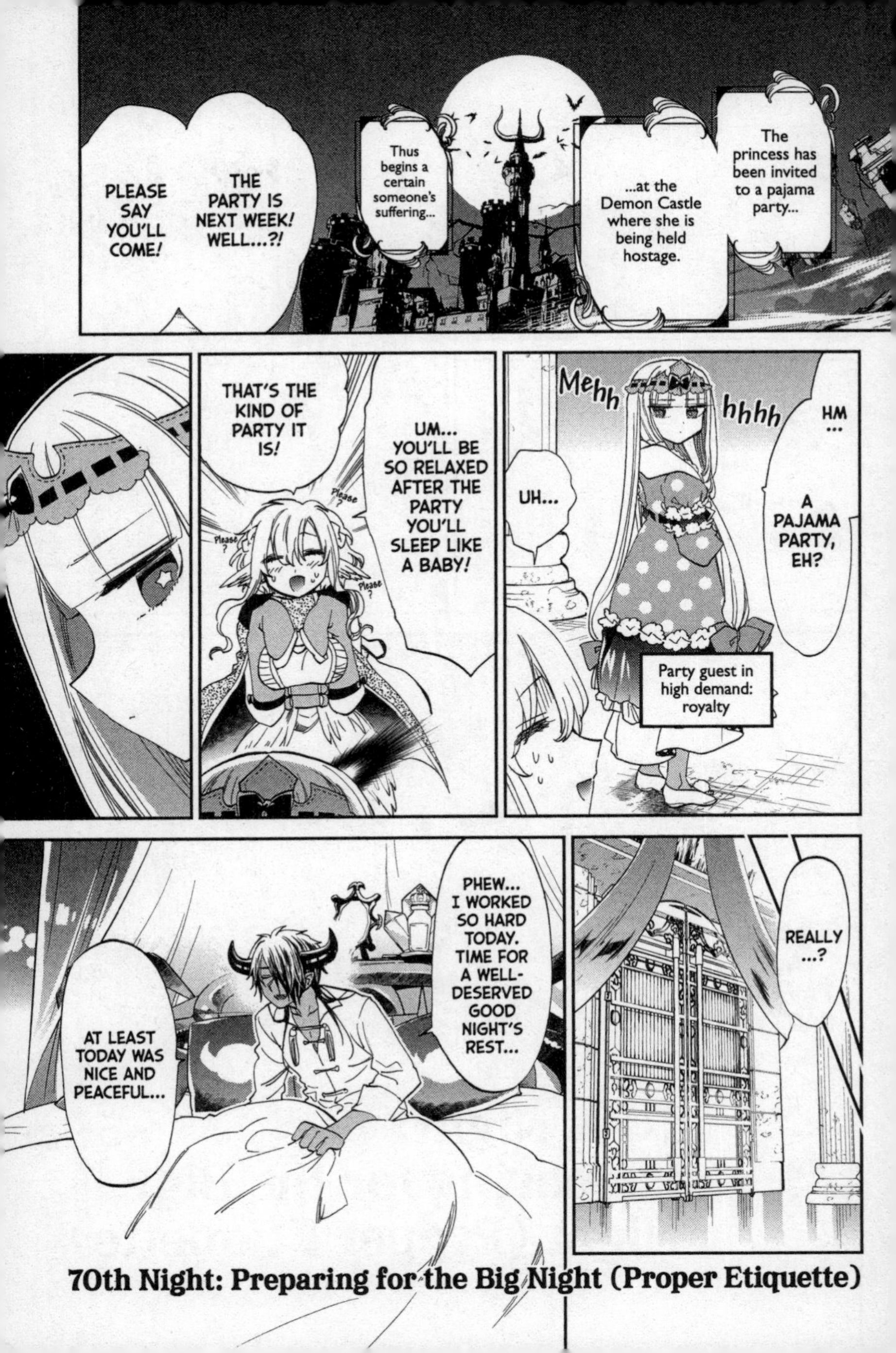
The princess has been invited to a pajama party...
...at the Demon Castle where she is being held hostage.
Thus begins a certain someone's suffering...
THE PARTY IS NEXT WEEK! WELL...?!
PLEASE SAY YOU'LL COME!
HM ...
A PAJAMA PARTY, EH?
Mehhhhhh
Party guest in high demand: royalty
UH...
UM... YOU'LL BE SO RELAXED AFTER THE PARTY YOU'LL SLEEP LIKE A BABY!
Please?
Please?
Please?
THAT'S THE KIND OF PARTY IT IS!
REALLY ...?
PHEW... I WORKED SO HARD TODAY. TIME FOR A WELL-DESERVED GOOD NIGHT'S REST...
AT LEAST TODAY WAS NICE AND PEACEFUL...

70th Night: Preparing for the Big Night (Proper Etiquette)

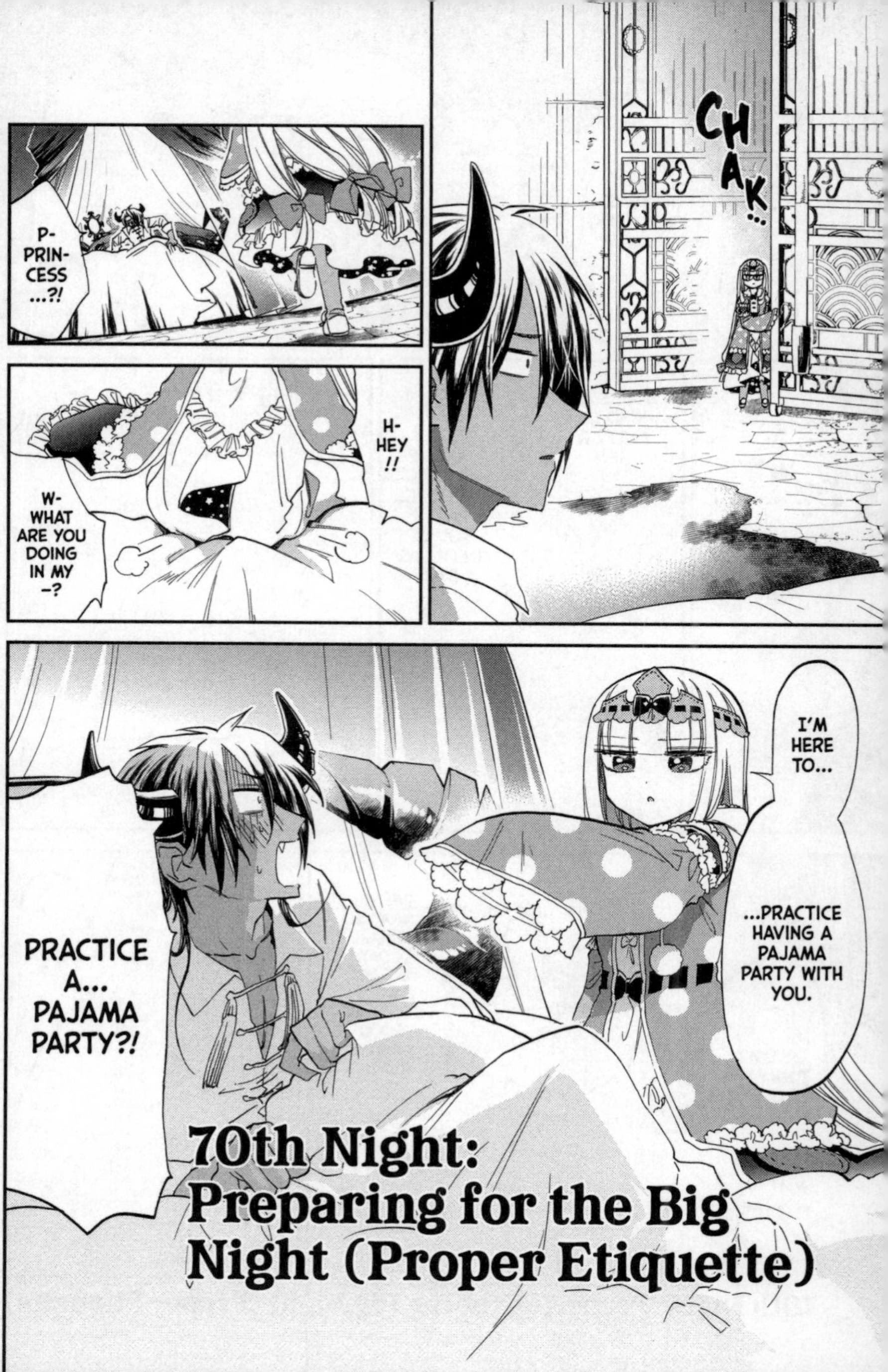
CHAK...
P-PRINCESS...?!
H-HEY!!
W-WHAT ARE YOU DOING IN MY–?
I'M HERE TO...
...PRACTICE HAVING A PAJAMA PARTY WITH YOU.
PRACTICE A... PAJAMA PARTY?!
70th Night: Preparing for the Big Night (Proper Etiquette)

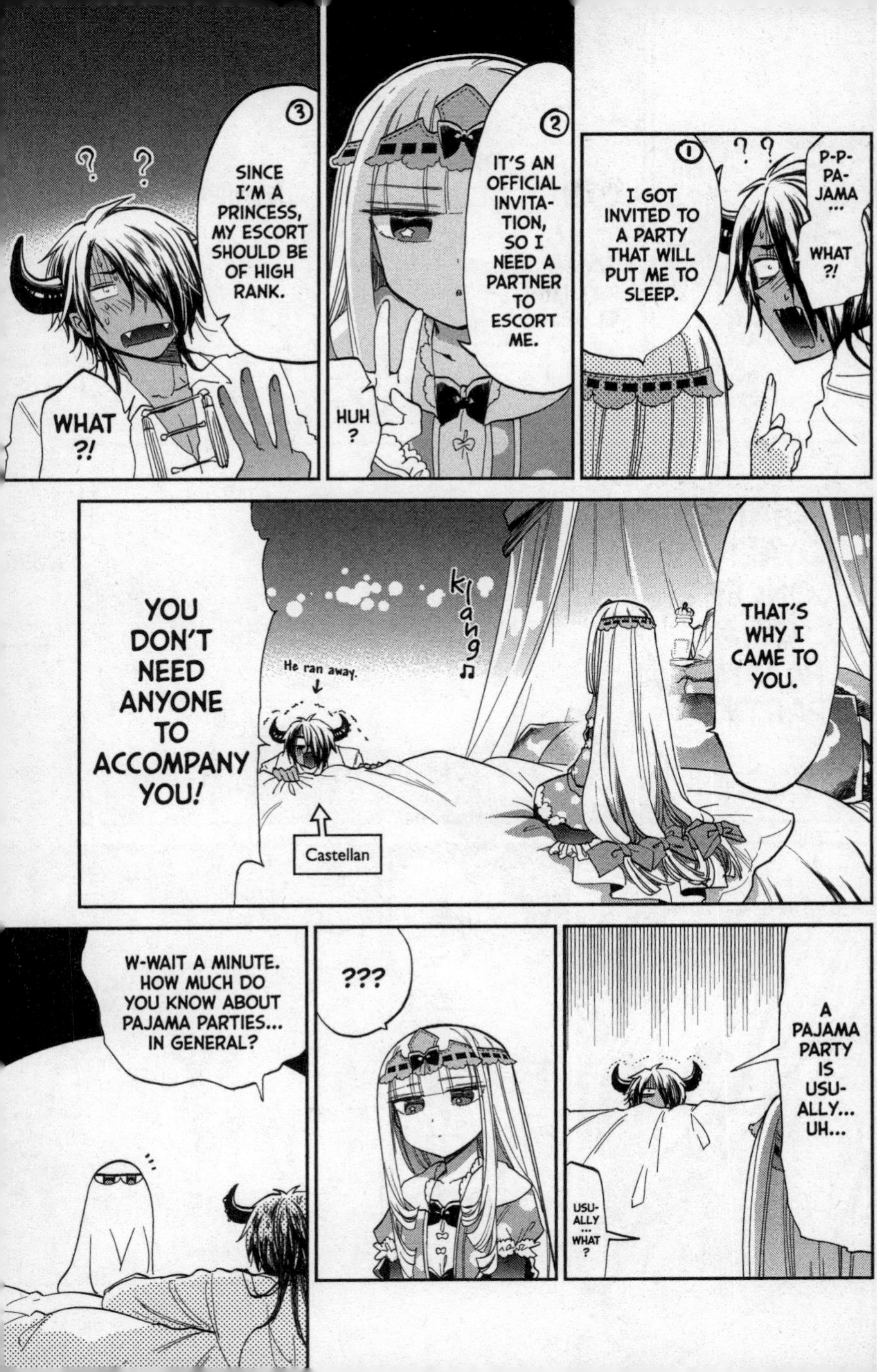
P-P-PAJAMA...
WHAT?!
① I GOT INVITED TO A PARTY THAT WILL PUT ME TO SLEEP.
② IT'S AN OFFICIAL INVITATION, SO I NEED A PARTNER TO ESCORT ME.
HUH?
③ SINCE I'M A PRINCESS, MY ESCORT SHOULD BE OF HIGH RANK.
WHAT?!
THAT'S WHY I CAME TO YOU.
klang♫
He ran away.
Castellan
YOU DON'T NEED ANYONE TO ACCOMPANY YOU!
A PAJAMA PARTY IS USUALLY... UH...
USUALLY... WHAT?
???
W-WAIT A MINUTE. HOW MUCH DO YOU KNOW ABOUT PAJAMA PARTIES... IN GENERAL?

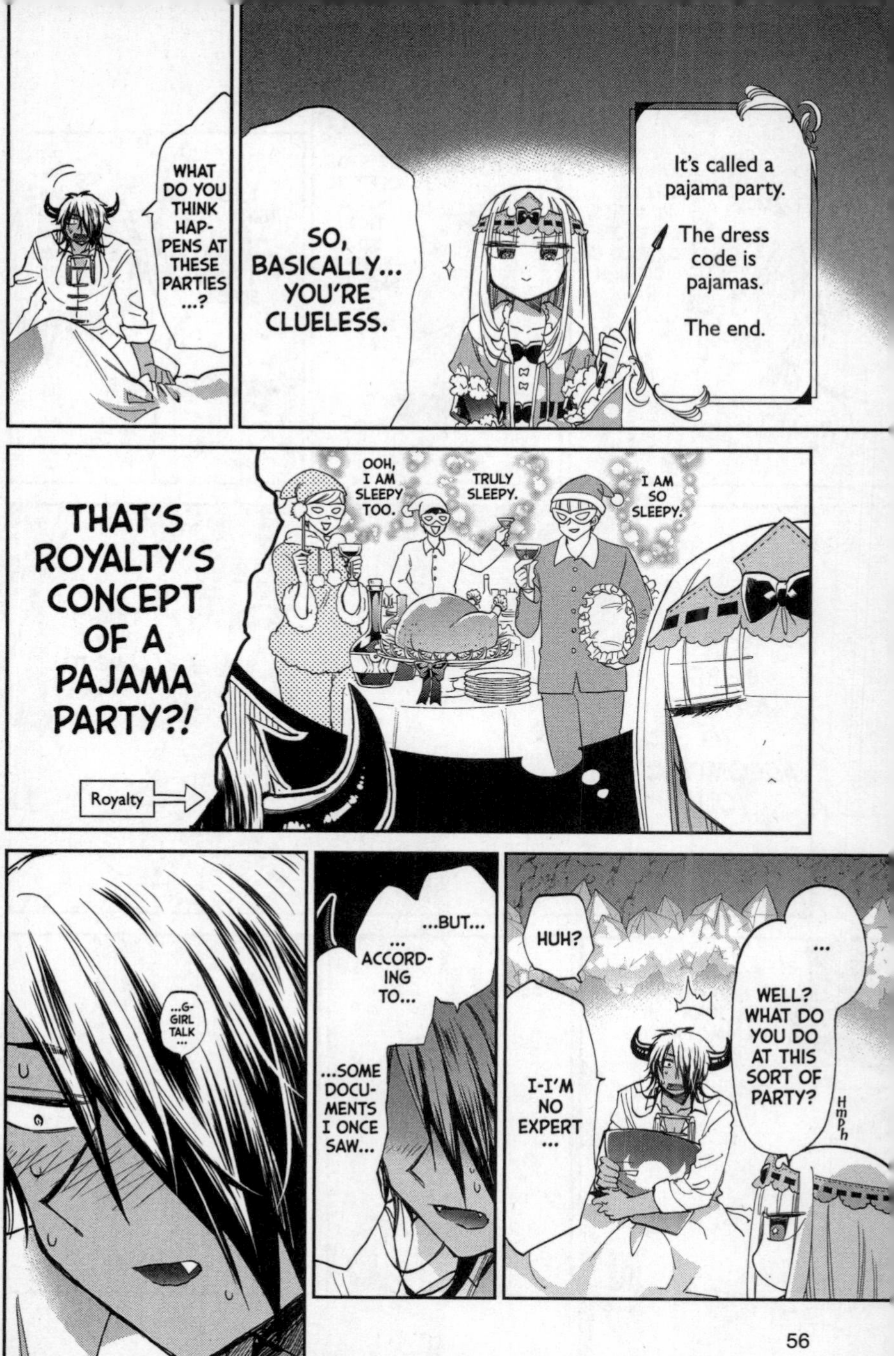
It's called a pajama party.
The dress code is pajamas.
The end.
SO, BASICALLY... YOU'RE CLUELESS.
WHAT DO YOU THINK HAPPENS AT THESE PARTIES ...?
I AM SO SLEEPY.
TRULY SLEEPY.
OOH, I AM SLEEPY TOO.
THAT'S ROYALTY'S CONCEPT OF A PAJAMA PARTY?!
Royalty
...
WELL? WHAT DO YOU DO AT THIS SORT OF PARTY?
Hmph
HUH?
I-I'M NO EXPERT ...
...BUT...
... ACCORDING TO...
...SOME DOCUMENTS I ONCE SAW...
...G-GIRL TALK ...

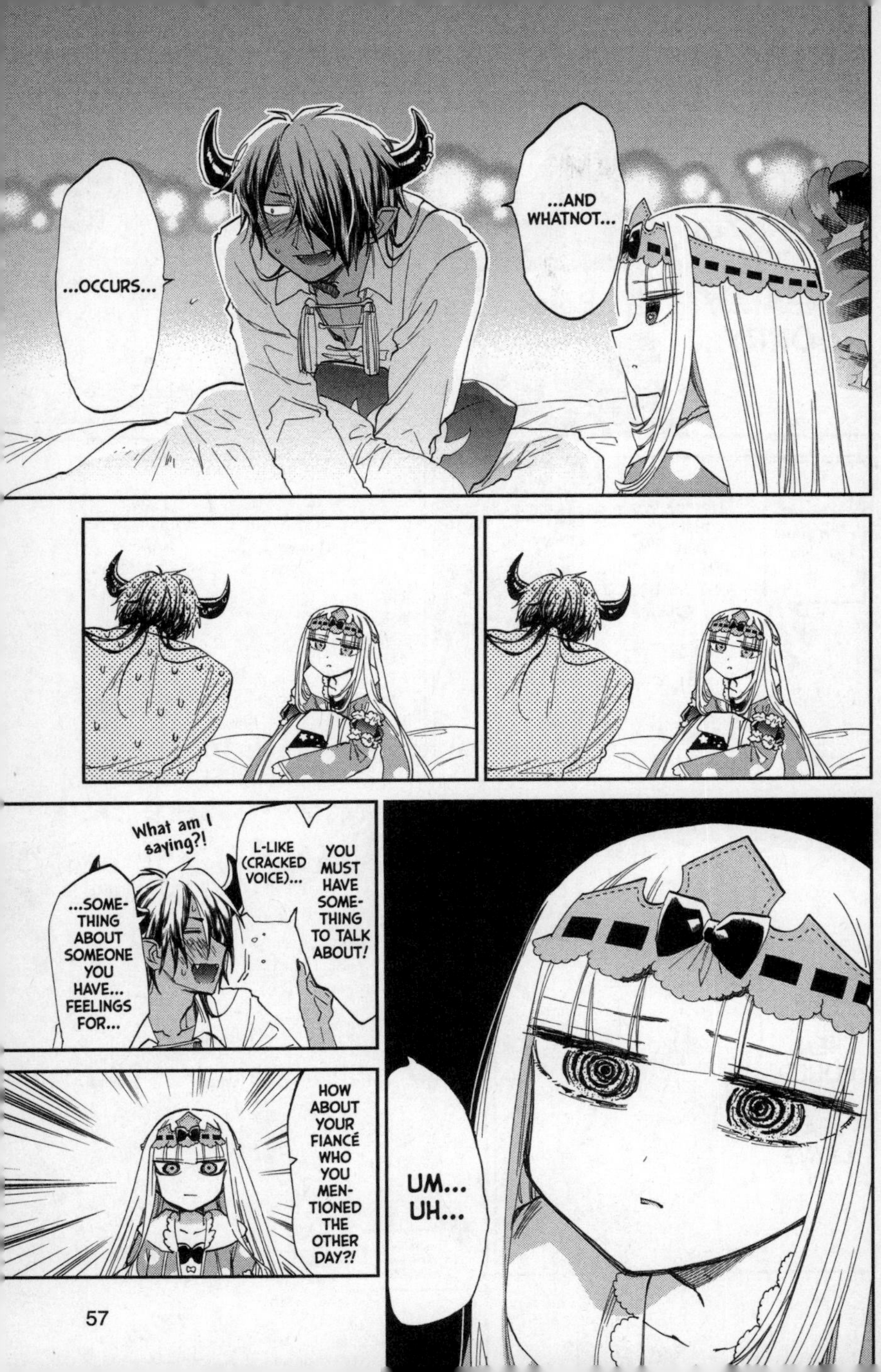
...AND WHATNOT...
...OCCURS...
UM... UH...
YOU MUST HAVE SOMETHING TO TALK ABOUT!
L-LIKE (CRACKED VOICE)...
What am I saying?!
...SOMETHING ABOUT SOMEONE YOU HAVE... FEELINGS FOR...
HOW ABOUT YOUR FIANCÉ WHO YOU MENTIONED THE OTHER DAY?!

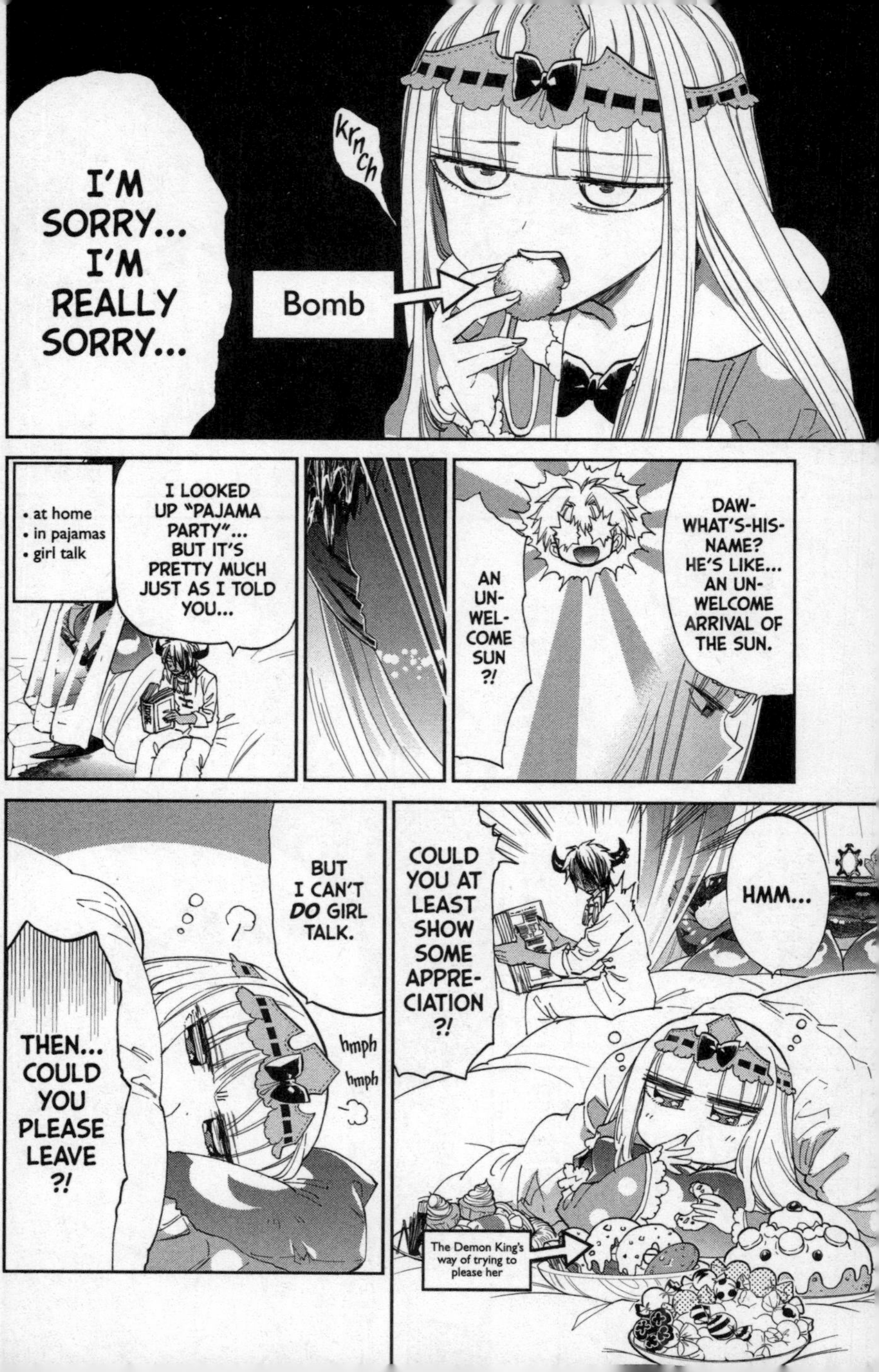

krnch
Bomb
I'M SORRY... I'M REALLY SORRY...
DAW-WHAT'S-HIS-NAME? HE'S LIKE... AN UN-WELCOME ARRIVAL OF THE SUN.
AN UN-WEL-COME SUN ?!
I LOOKED UP "PAJAMA PARTY"... BUT IT'S PRETTY MUCH JUST AS I TOLD YOU...
• at home
• in pajamas
• girl talk
HMM...
COULD YOU AT LEAST SHOW SOME APPRE-CIATION ?!
The Demon King's way of trying to please her
BUT I CAN'T *DO* GIRL TALK.
hmph
hmph
THEN... COULD YOU PLEASE LEAVE ?!

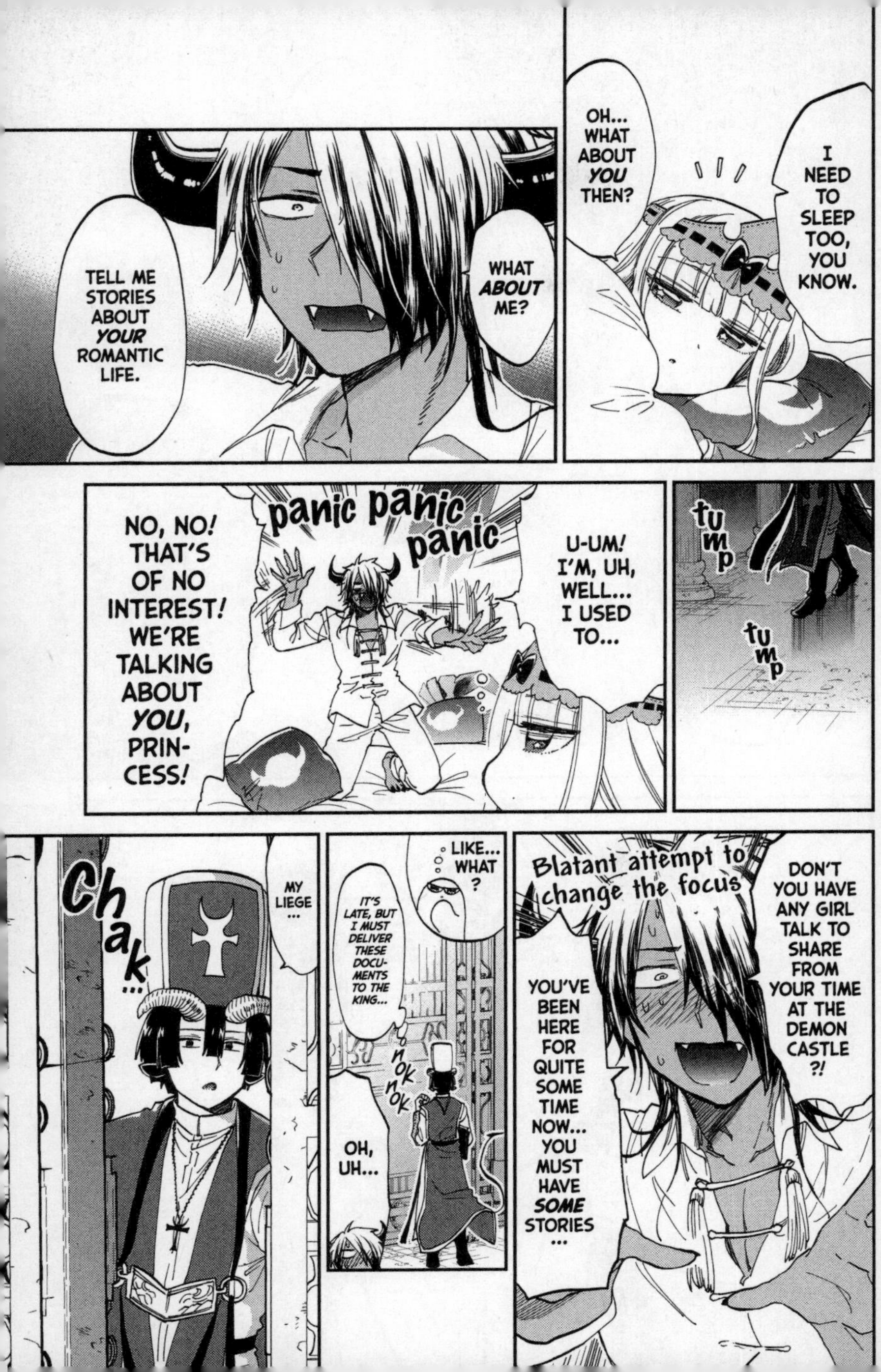
I NEED TO SLEEP TOO, YOU KNOW.
OH... WHAT ABOUT *YOU* THEN?
WHAT *ABOUT* ME?
TELL ME STORIES ABOUT *YOUR* ROMANTIC LIFE.
tump
tump
U-UM! I'M, UH, WELL... I USED TO...
panic panic panic
NO, NO! THAT'S OF NO INTEREST! WE'RE TALKING ABOUT *YOU*, PRIN-CESS!
DON'T YOU HAVE ANY GIRL TALK TO SHARE FROM YOUR TIME AT THE DEMON CASTLE?!
Blatant attempt to change the focus
YOU'VE BEEN HERE FOR QUITE SOME TIME NOW... YOU MUST HAVE *SOME* STORIES...
LIKE... WHAT?
IT'S LATE, BUT I MUST DELIVER THESE DOCU-MENTS TO THE KING...
nok nok
OH, UH...
MY LIEGE...
Chak...

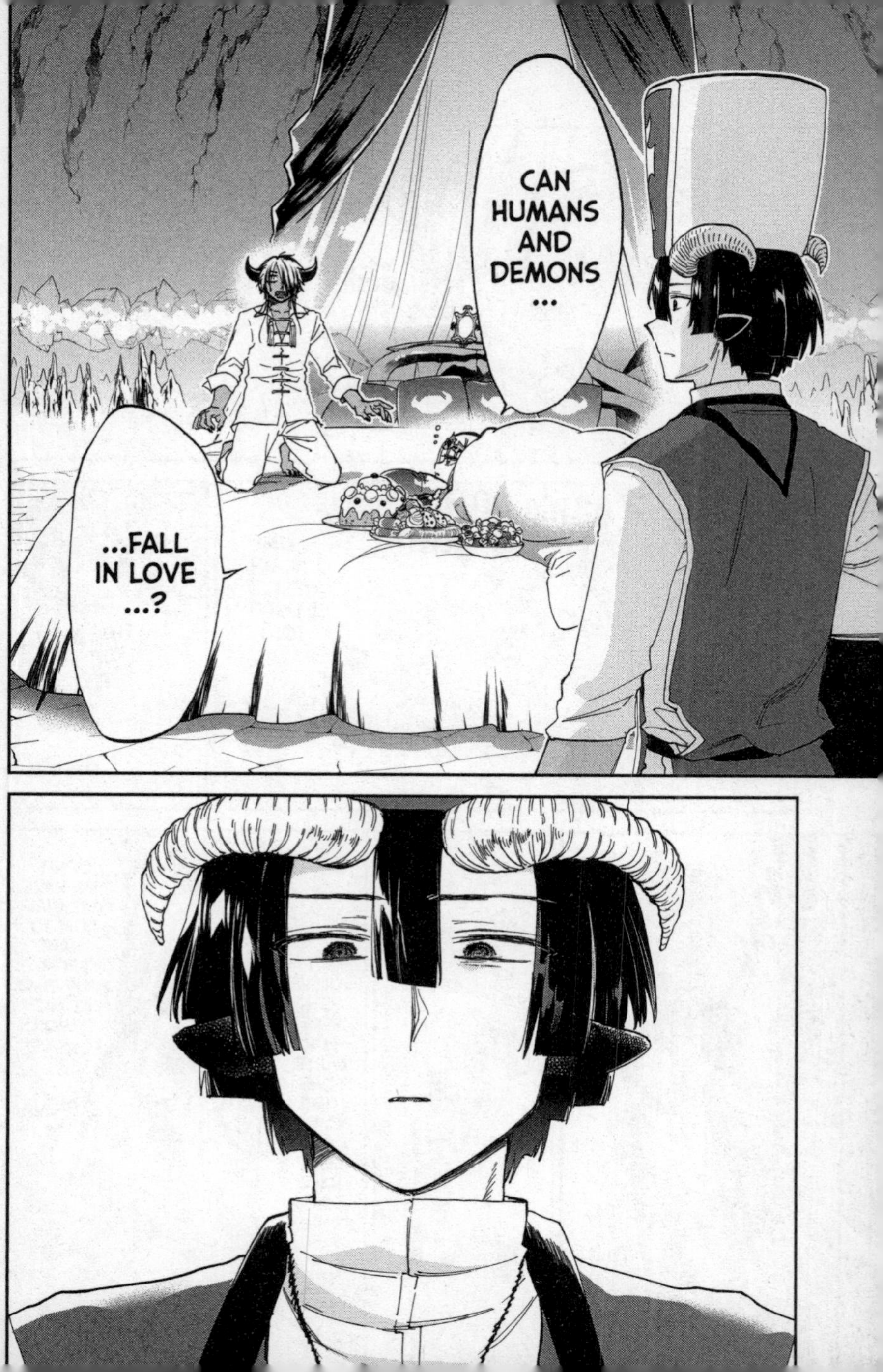
CAN HUMANS AND DEMONS ...
...FALL IN LOVE ...?

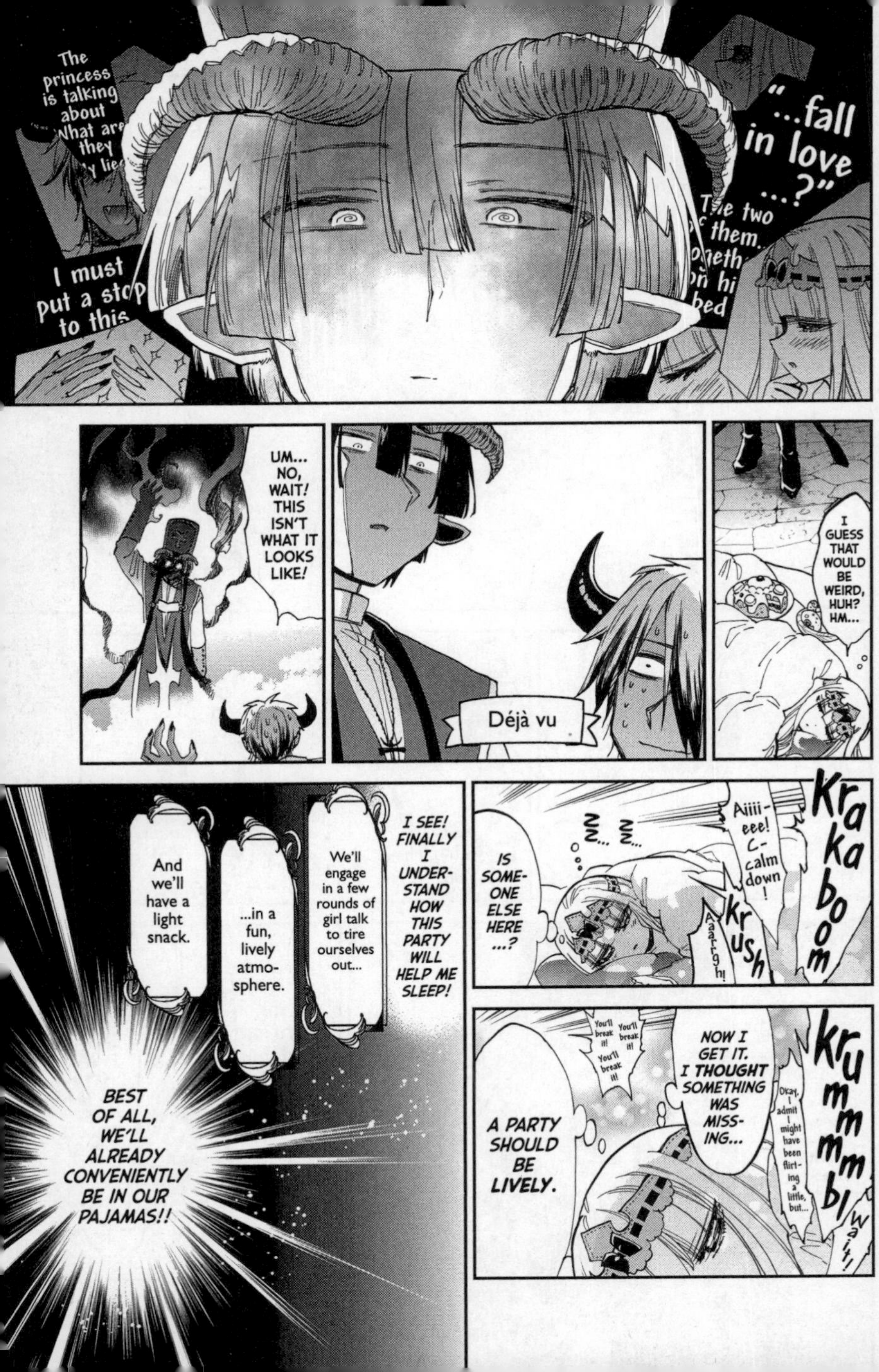
"...fall in love ...?"
The two
bed
The princess is talking about
What are they
I must put a stop to this
I GUESS THAT WOULD BE WEIRD, HUH? HM...
Déjà vu
UM... NO, WAIT! THIS ISN'T WHAT IT LOOKS LIKE!
Krakaboom
Aiiieee! C-calm down!
Krush
Aaargh!
ZZ... ZZ...
IS SOMEONE ELSE HERE ...?
Krummmbl
Wait!!
Okay, I admit I might have been flirting a little, but...
NOW I GET IT. I THOUGHT SOMETHING WAS MISSING...
You'll break it! You'll break it! You'll break it!
A PARTY SHOULD BE LIVELY.
I SEE! FINALLY I UNDERSTAND HOW THIS PARTY WILL HELP ME SLEEP!
We'll engage in a few rounds of girl talk to tire ourselves out...
...in a fun, lively atmosphere.
And we'll have a light snack.
BEST OF ALL, WE'LL ALREADY CONVENIENTLY BE IN OUR PAJAMAS!!

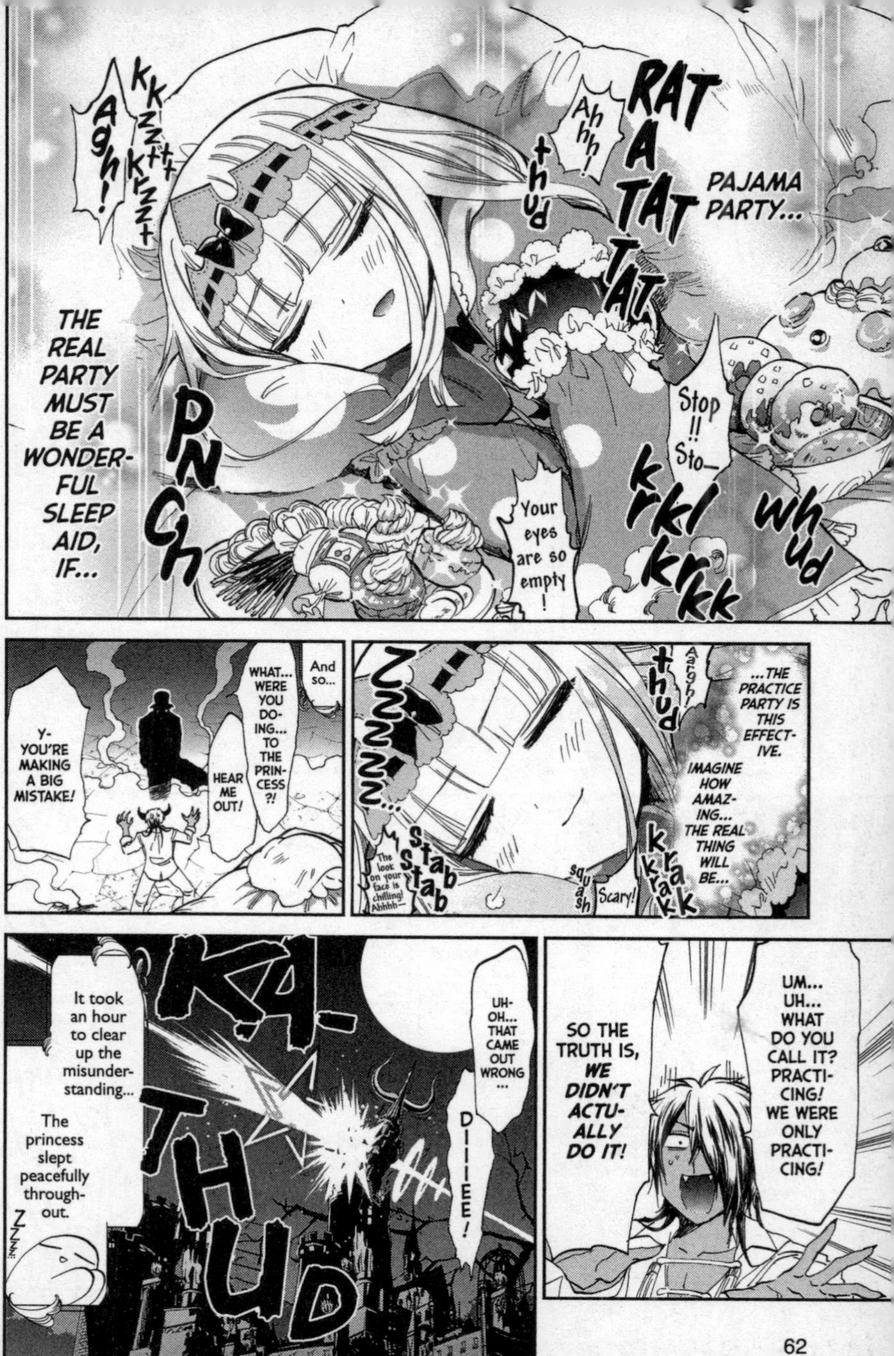
PAJAMA PARTY...
RAT A TAT TAT
Ahhh!
thud
kkzzttt krzzt
Agh!
THE REAL PARTY MUST BE A WONDER-FUL SLEEP AID, IF...
Stop!! Sto—
whud
krkl krrkk
Your eyes are so empty!
PNCh
...THE PRACTICE PARTY IS THIS EFFECT-IVE.
IMAGINE HOW AMAZ-ING... THE REAL THING WILL BE...
Aargh!
thud
krak krak
Scary!
squash
ZZZZZ...
stab stab
The look on your face is chilling! Ahhhh—
And so...
WHAT... WERE YOU DO-ING... TO THE PRIN-CESS?!
HEAR ME OUT!
Y-YOU'RE MAKING A BIG MISTAKE!
UM... UH... WHAT DO YOU CALL IT? PRACTI-CING! WE WERE ONLY PRACTI-CING!
SO THE TRUTH IS, WE DIDN'T ACTU-ALLY DO IT!
UH-OH... THAT CAME OUT WRONG...
DIIIEE!
KA-THUD
It took an hour to clear up the misunder-standing...
The princess slept peacefully through-out.
Zzz...

Hall of the Demon King

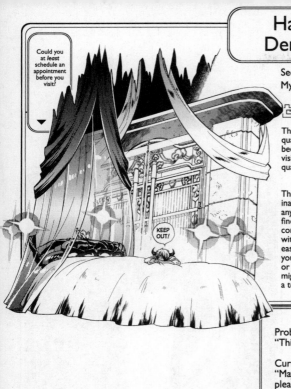

Could you at *least* schedule an appointment before you visit?
KEEP OUT!

Security: ☆

Mystery: ☆☆☆☆☆☆☆☆☆

The Demon King's personal quarters. In addition to the bedroom, which the princess often visits, there are quite large living quarters in back.

The security may seem terribly inadequate, but if you try to go any farther into the room, you will find yourself lost in a never-ending corridor. The effect is created with a magic spell, so you can easily escape by turning back. If you somehow manage to disable or bypass the spell, however, you might just come face-to-face with a terrifying being...

Problem until ten years ago:
"This bed is too big for me."

Current problem:
"May I have some privacy, please?!"

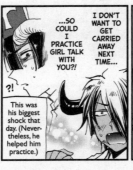

An hour later ...
MY APOLOGIES... I SEEM TO HAVE BEEN UNDER A MISAPPREHENSION.
huf huf
IT'S U-UNDERSTANDABLE... I'VE NEVER DONE GIRL TALK BEFORE, SO I MIGHT HAVE GOTTEN A LITTLE CARRIED AWAY...
huf huf
I'LL TIDY UP...
UM ...
I DON'T WANT TO GET CARRIED AWAY NEXT TIME...
...SO COULD I PRACTICE GIRL TALK WITH YOU?!
?!
This was his biggest shock that day. (Nevertheless, he helped him practice.)

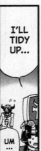

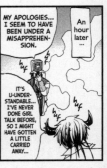

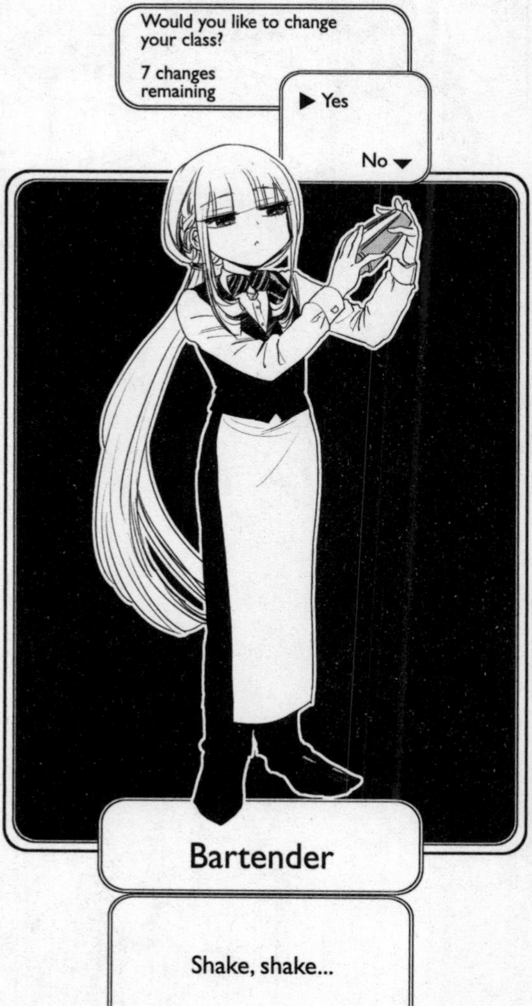
Would you like to change your class?
7 changes remaining
▶ Yes
No
Bartender
Shake, shake...

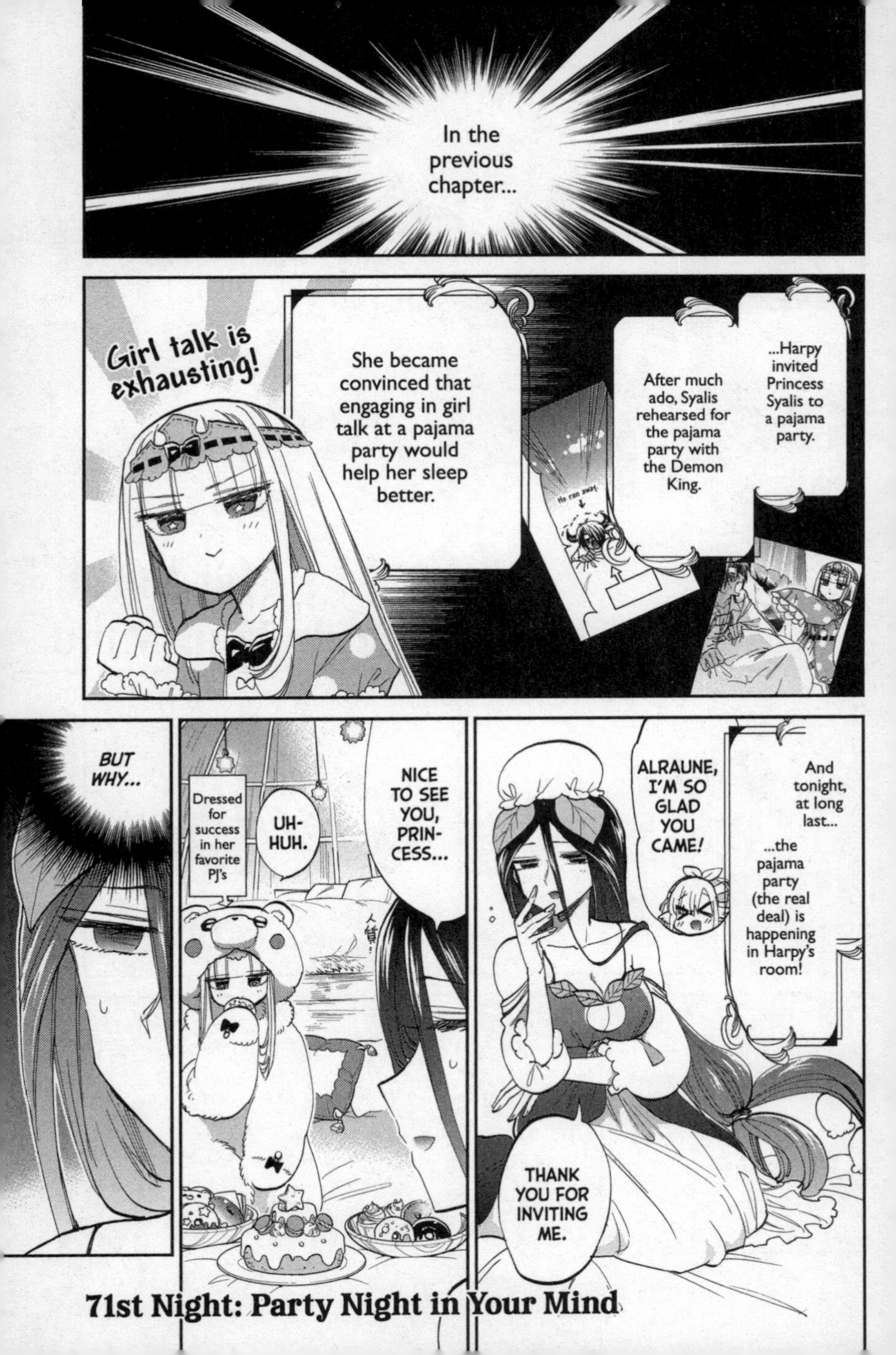
In the previous chapter...
...Harpy invited Princess Syalis to a pajama party.
After much ado, Syalis rehearsed for the pajama party with the Demon King.
He ran away.
She became convinced that engaging in girl talk at a pajama party would help her sleep better.
Girl talk is exhausting!
And tonight, at long last...
...the pajama party (the real deal) is happening in Harpy's room!
ALRAUNE, I'M SO GLAD YOU CAME!
THANK YOU FOR INVITING ME.
NICE TO SEE YOU, PRINCESS...
UH-HUH.
Dressed for success in her favorite PJ's
BUT WHY...

71st Night: Party Night in Your Mind

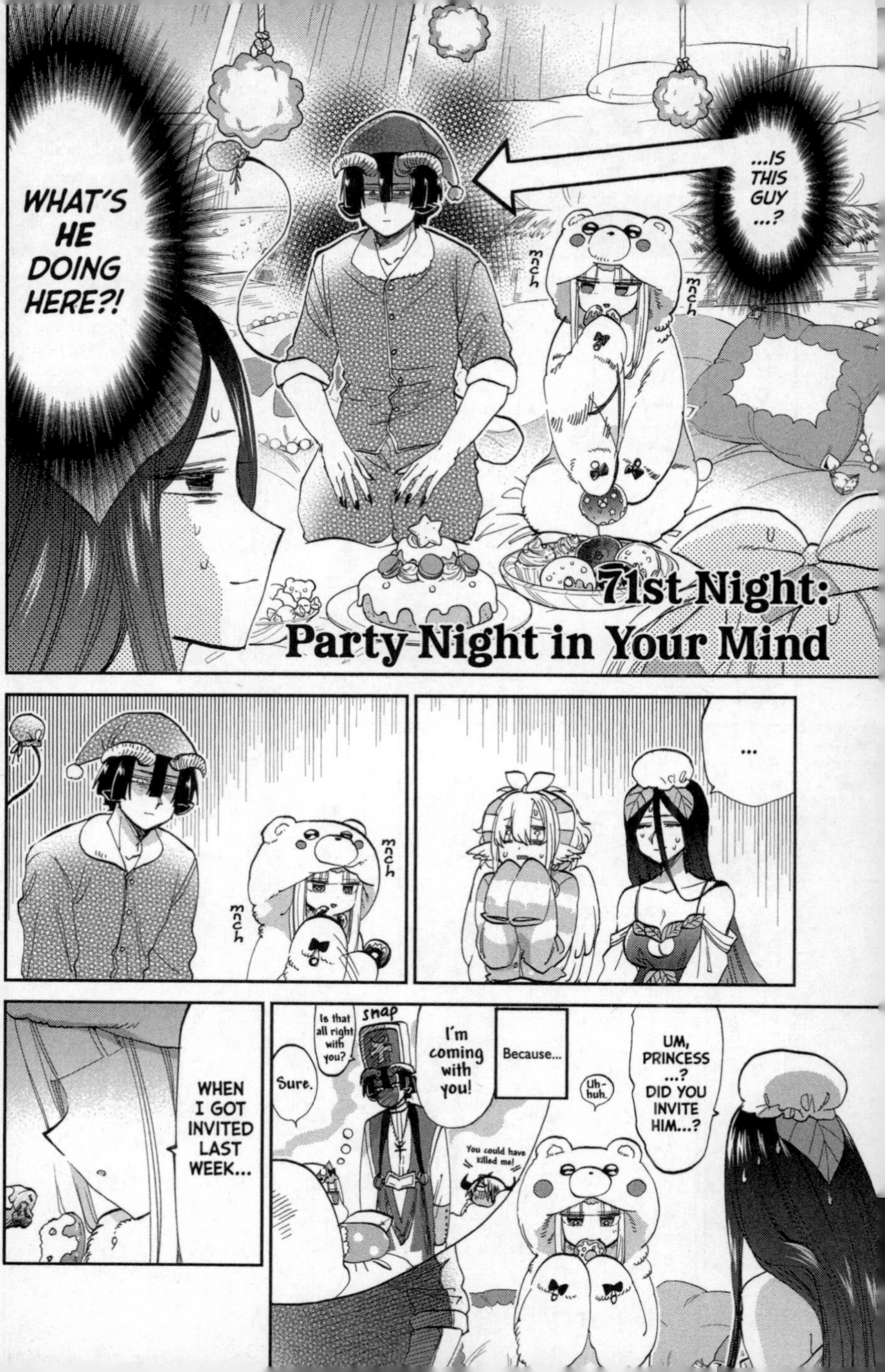
...IS THIS GUY ...?
mnch
mnch
WHAT'S HE DOING HERE?!
71st Night: Party Night in Your Mind
...
mnch
mnch
UM, PRINCESS ...? DID YOU INVITE HIM...?
Uh-huh.
Because...
I'm coming with you!
Is that all right with you?
snap
Sure.
You could have killed me!
WHEN I GOT INVITED LAST WEEK...

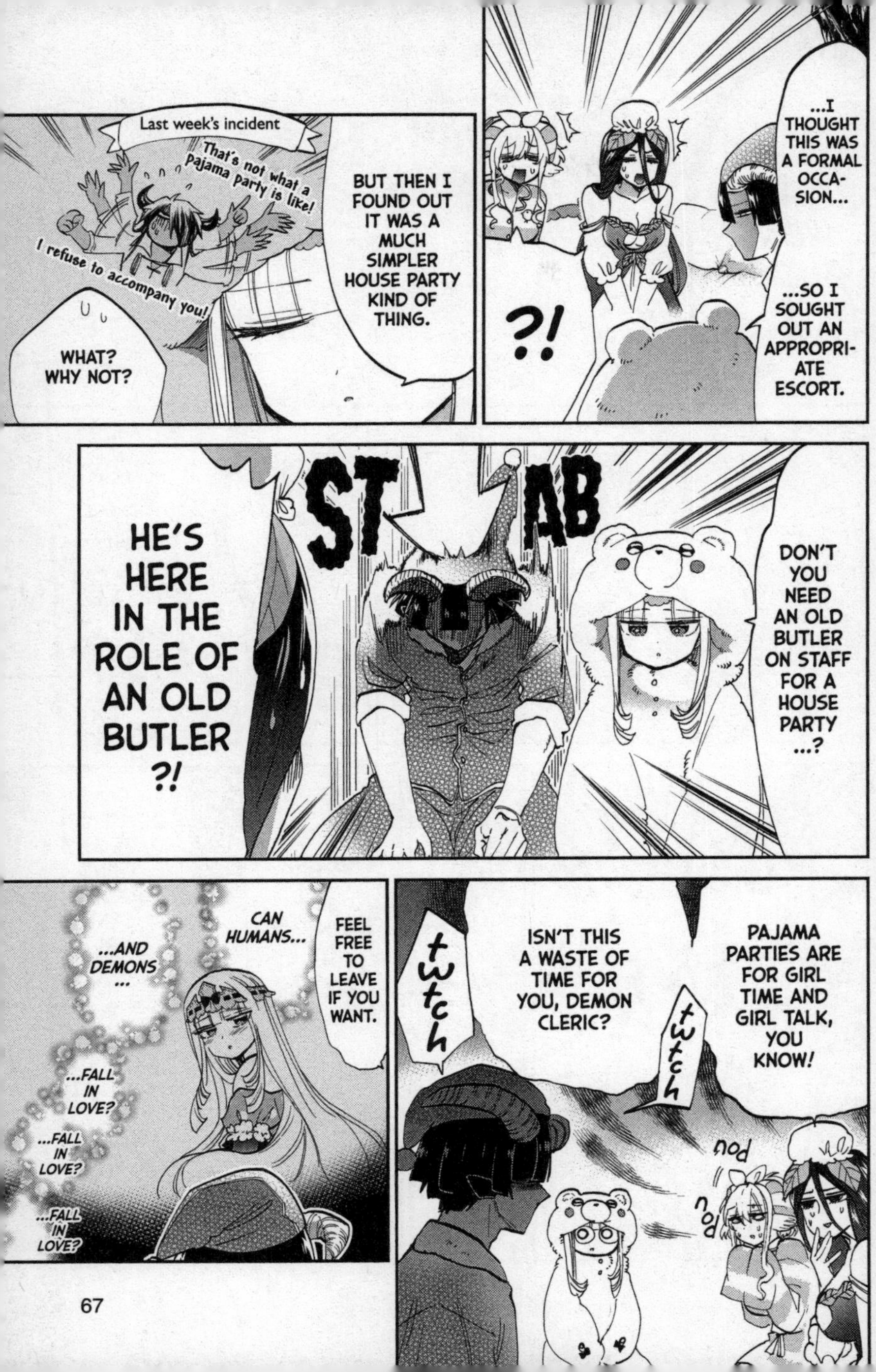
...I THOUGHT THIS WAS A FORMAL OCCASION...
...SO I SOUGHT OUT AN APPROPRIATE ESCORT.
?!
Last week's incident
BUT THEN I FOUND OUT IT WAS A MUCH SIMPLER HOUSE PARTY KIND OF THING.
That's not what a pajama party is like!
I refuse to accompany you!
WHAT? WHY NOT?
DON'T YOU NEED AN OLD BUTLER ON STAFF FOR A HOUSE PARTY ...?
STAB
HE'S HERE IN THE ROLE OF AN OLD BUTLER ?!
PAJAMA PARTIES ARE FOR GIRL TIME AND GIRL TALK, YOU KNOW!
ISN'T THIS A WASTE OF TIME FOR YOU, DEMON CLERIC?
twitch
twitch
pou
pou
FEEL FREE TO LEAVE IF YOU WANT.
CAN HUMANS...
...AND DEMONS ...
...FALL IN LOVE?
...FALL IN LOVE?
...FALL IN LOVE?

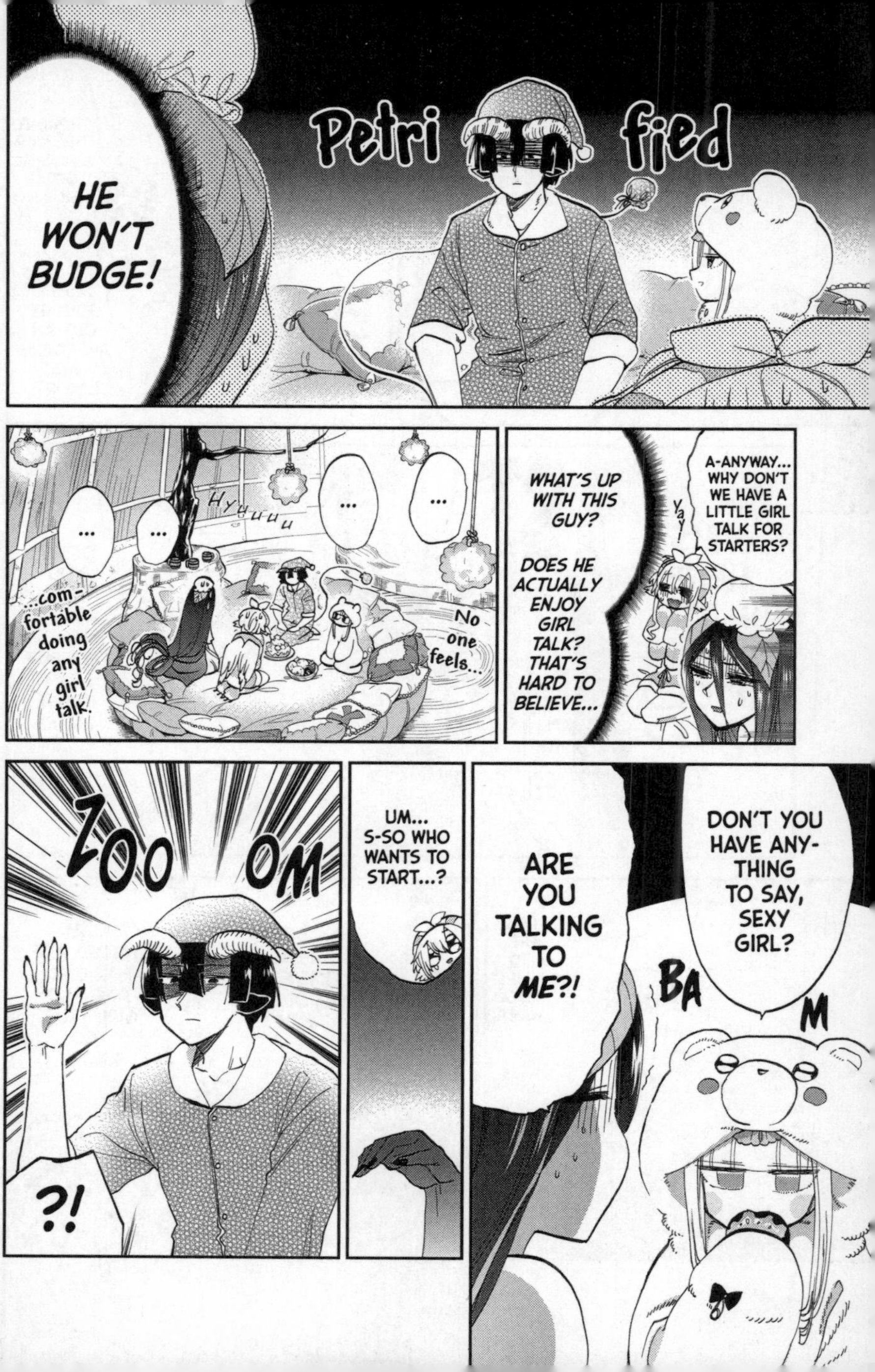
Petri fied
HE WON'T BUDGE!
A-ANYWAY... WHY DON'T WE HAVE A LITTLE GIRL TALK FOR STARTERS?
Yay!
WHAT'S UP WITH THIS GUY?
DOES HE ACTUALLY ENJOY GIRL TALK? THAT'S HARD TO BELIEVE...
...
...
...
...
Hyuuuuu
No one feels...
...comfortable doing any girl talk.
DON'T YOU HAVE ANYTHING TO SAY, SEXY GIRL?
BAM
ARE YOU TALKING TO ME?!
UM... S-SO WHO WANTS TO START...?
ZOOOM
?!

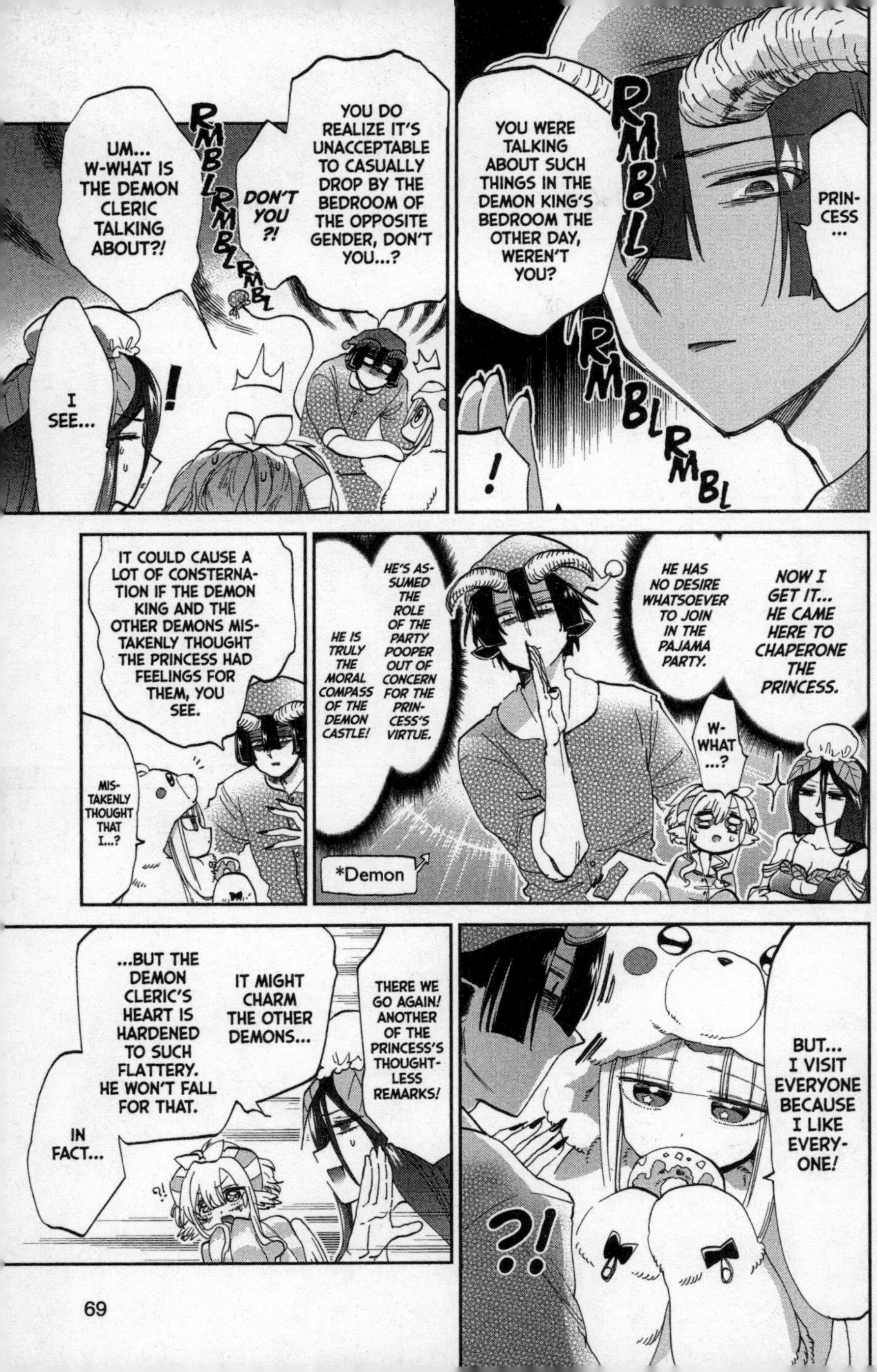
PRIN-CESS...
YOU WERE TALKING ABOUT SUCH THINGS IN THE DEMON KING'S BEDROOM THE OTHER DAY, WEREN'T YOU?
RMBL
RMBLRMBL
!
YOU DO REALIZE IT'S UNACCEPTABLE TO CASUALLY DROP BY THE BEDROOM OF THE OPPOSITE GENDER, DON'T YOU...?
DON'T YOU ?!
UM... W-WHAT IS THE DEMON CLERIC TALKING ABOUT?!
RMBLRMBLRMBL
!
I SEE...
NOW I GET IT... HE CAME HERE TO CHAPERONE THE PRINCESS.
HE HAS NO DESIRE WHATSOEVER TO JOIN IN THE PAJAMA PARTY.
HE'S AS-SUMED THE ROLE OF THE PARTY POOPER OUT OF CONCERN FOR THE PRIN-CESS'S VIRTUE.
HE IS TRULY THE MORAL COMPASS OF THE DEMON CASTLE!
W-WHAT ...?
*Demon
IT COULD CAUSE A LOT OF CONSTERNA-TION IF THE DEMON KING AND THE OTHER DEMONS MIS-TAKENLY THOUGHT THE PRINCESS HAD FEELINGS FOR THEM, YOU SEE.
MIS-TAKENLY THOUGHT THAT I...?
BUT... I VISIT EVERYONE BECAUSE I LIKE EVERY-ONE!
?!
THERE WE GO AGAIN! ANOTHER OF THE PRINCESS'S THOUGHT-LESS REMARKS!
IT MIGHT CHARM THE OTHER DEMONS...
...BUT THE DEMON CLERIC'S HEART IS HARDENED TO SUCH FLATTERY. HE WON'T FALL FOR THAT.
IN FACT...
?!

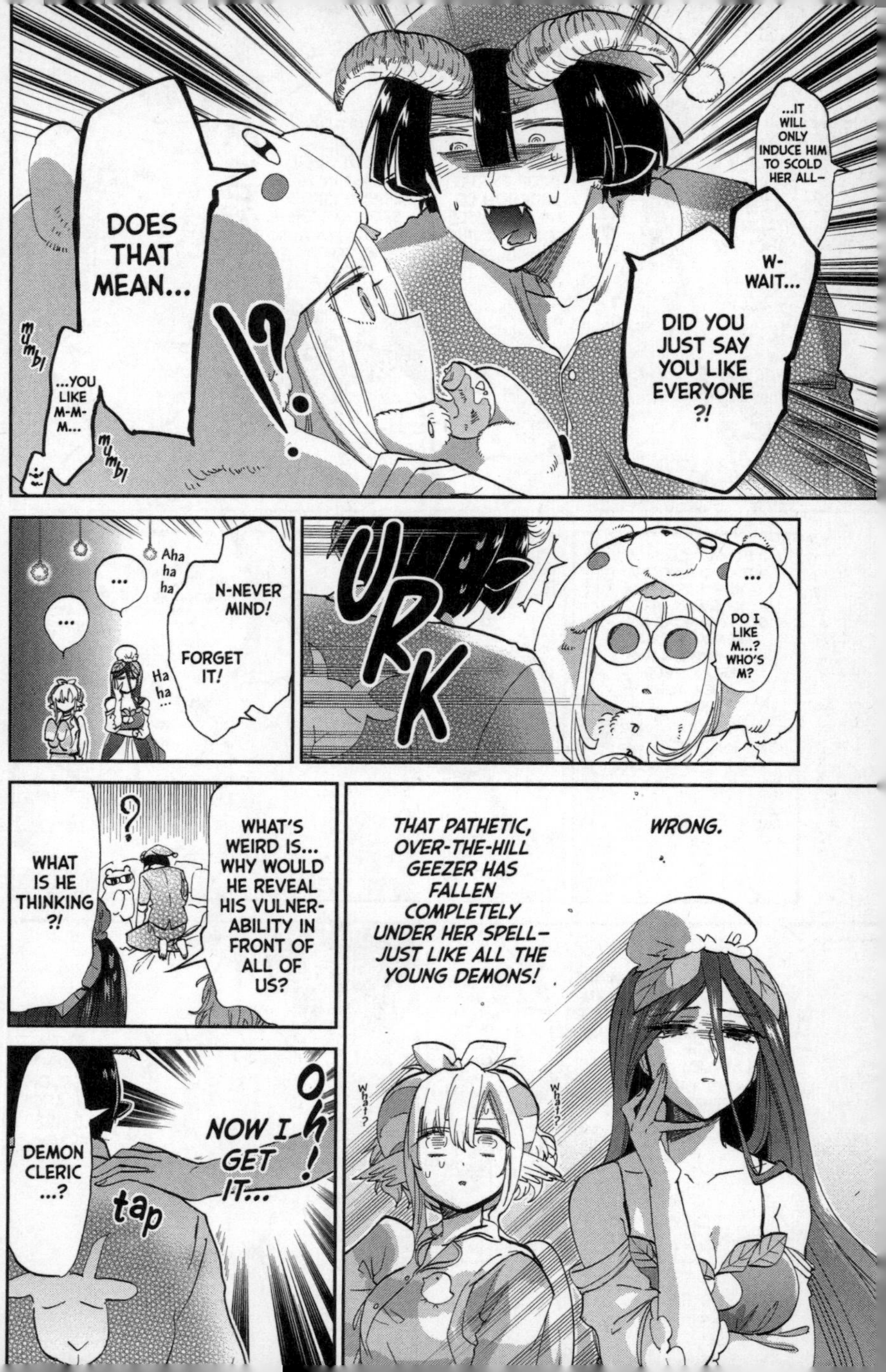
...IT WILL ONLY INDUCE HIM TO SCOLD HER ALL—
W- WAIT...
DID YOU JUST SAY YOU LIKE EVERYONE ?!
!?
DOES THAT MEAN...
mumbl
...YOU LIKE M-M-M...
mumbl
URK
...
DO I LIKE M...? WHO'S M?
N-NEVER MIND!
FORGET IT!
Aha ha ha
Ha ha ...
...
...
WRONG.
THAT PATHETIC, OVER-THE-HILL GEEZER HAS FALLEN COMPLETELY UNDER HER SPELL— JUST LIKE ALL THE YOUNG DEMONS!
What?
What?
WHAT'S WEIRD IS... WHY WOULD HE REVEAL HIS VULNER-ABILITY IN FRONT OF ALL OF US?
?
WHAT IS HE THINKING ?!
Oh!
NOW I GET IT...
DEMON CLERIC ...?
tap

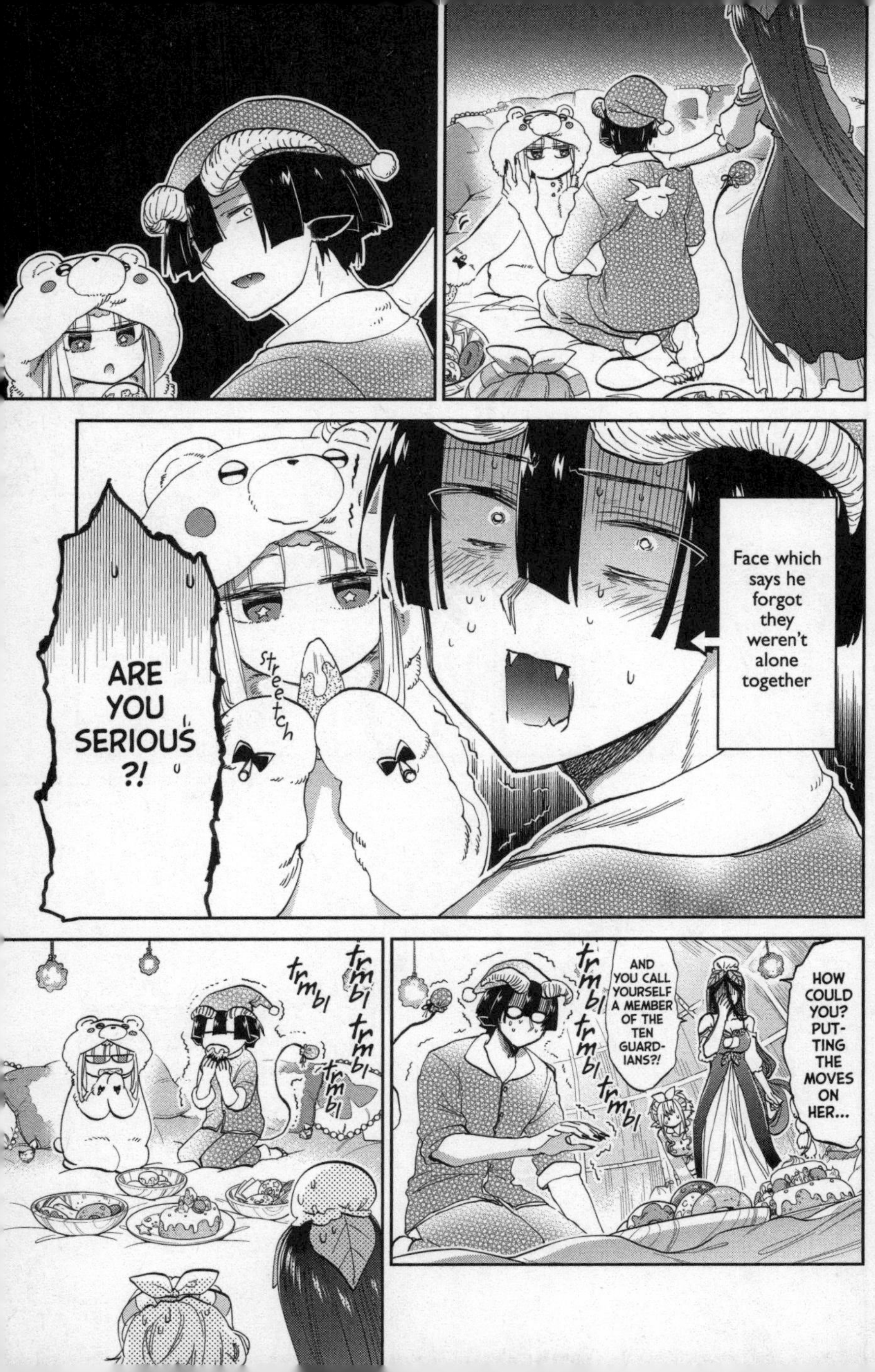
Face which says he forgot they weren't alone together
streeetch
ARE YOU SERIOUS?!
HOW COULD YOU? PUTTING THE MOVES ON HER...
AND YOU CALL YOURSELF A MEMBER OF THE TEN GUARDIANS?!
trmbl trmbl trmbl
trmbl trmbl trmbl trmbl

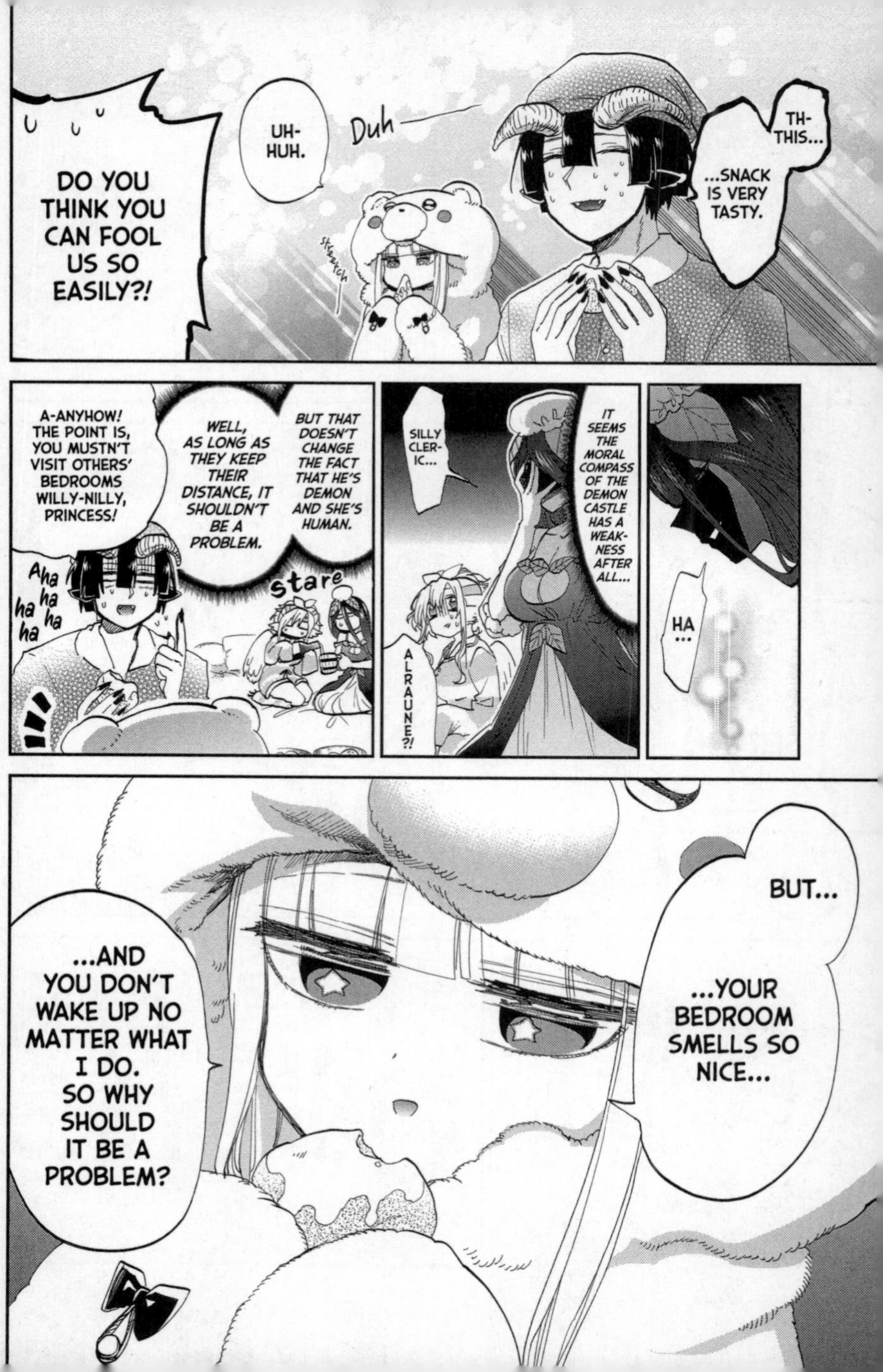
TH-THIS...
...SNACK IS VERY TASTY.
Duh
UH-HUH.
DO YOU THINK YOU CAN FOOL US SO EASILY?!
HA...
IT SEEMS THE MORAL COMPASS OF THE DEMON CASTLE HAS A WEAKNESS AFTER ALL...
SILLY CLERIC...
ALRAUNE?!
BUT THAT DOESN'T CHANGE THE FACT THAT HE'S DEMON AND SHE'S HUMAN.
WELL, AS LONG AS THEY KEEP THEIR DISTANCE, IT SHOULDN'T BE A PROBLEM.
A-ANYHOW! THE POINT IS, YOU MUSTN'T VISIT OTHERS' BEDROOMS WILLY-NILLY, PRINCESS!
stare
Aha ha ha ha ha
BUT...
...YOUR BEDROOM SMELLS SO NICE...
...AND YOU DON'T WAKE UP NO MATTER WHAT I DO. SO WHY SHOULD IT BE A PROBLEM?

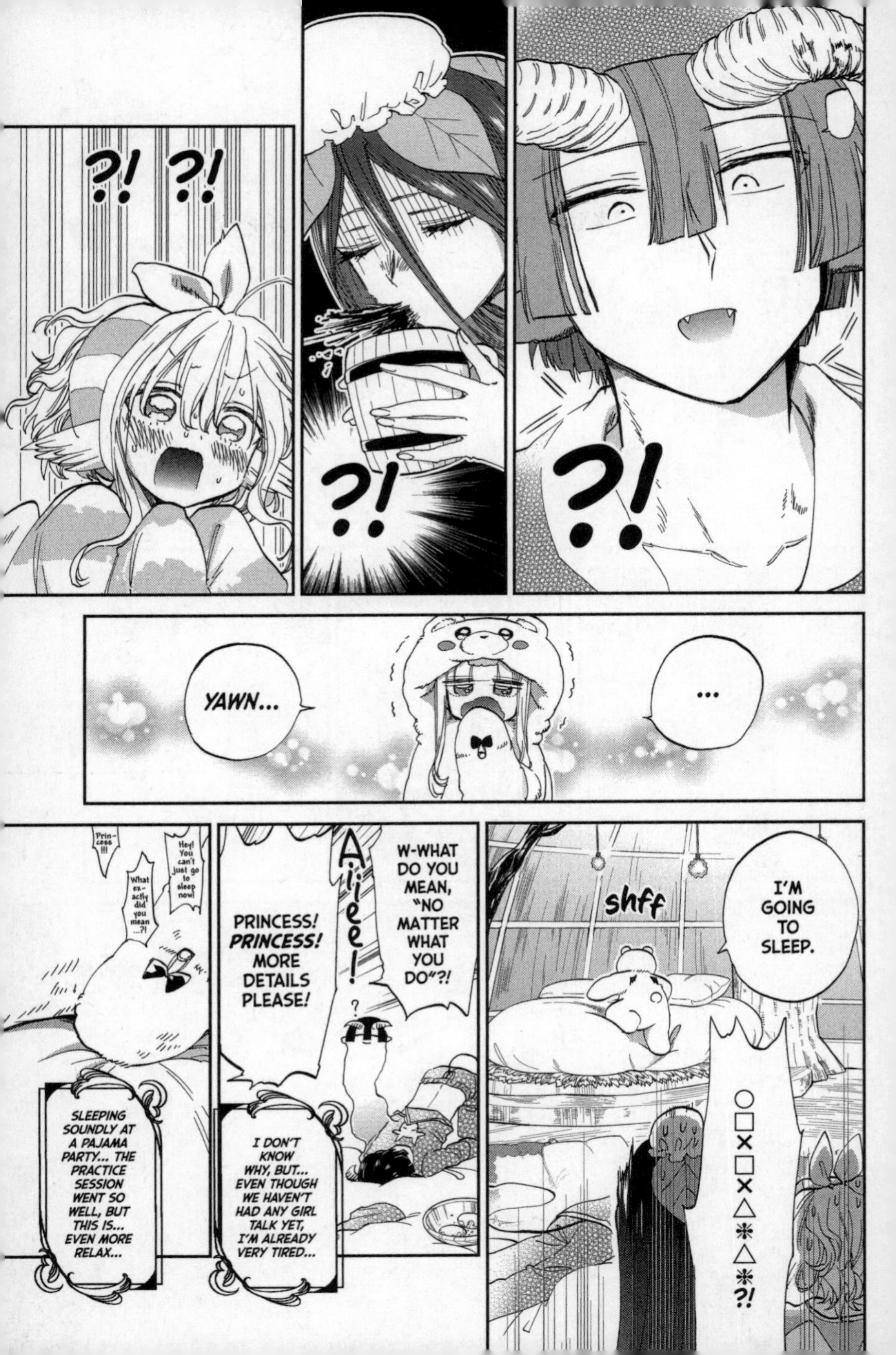
?!
?!
?! ?!
...
YAWN...
I'M GOING TO SLEEP.
shff
○□×□×△*△*?!
W-WHAT DO YOU MEAN, "NO MATTER WHAT YOU DO"?!
Aiiee!
PRINCESS! PRINCESS! MORE DETAILS PLEASE!
?
I DON'T KNOW WHY, BUT... EVEN THOUGH WE HAVEN'T HAD ANY GIRL TALK YET, I'M ALREADY VERY TIRED...
Hey! You can't just go to sleep now!
Princess!!!
What exactly did you mean...?!
SLEEPING SOUNDLY AT A PAJAMA PARTY... THE PRACTICE SESSION WENT SO WELL, BUT THIS IS... EVEN MORE RELAX...

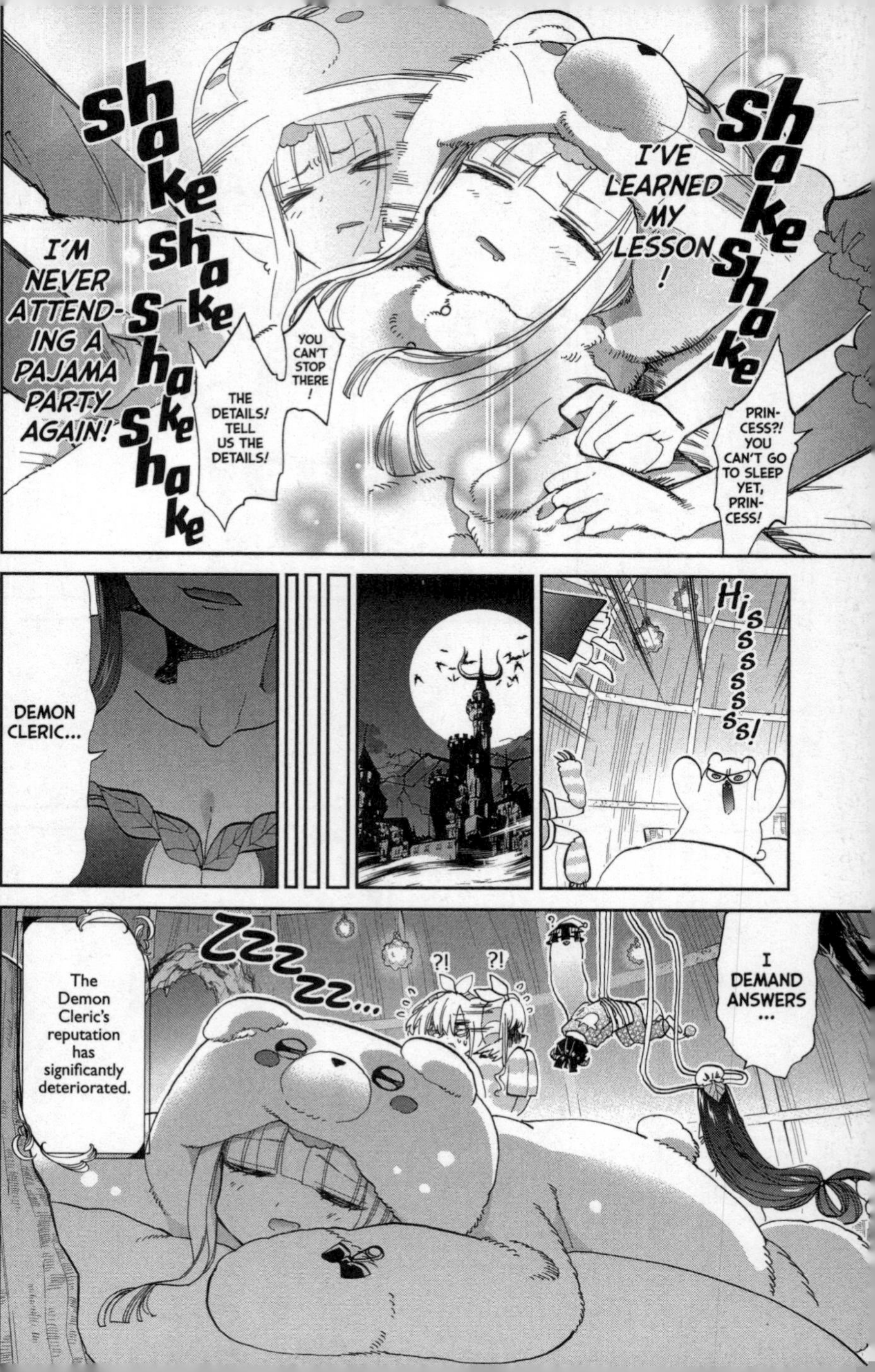
Shake Shake
I'VE LEARNED MY LESSON!
PRIN-CESS?! YOU CAN'T GO TO SLEEP YET, PRIN-CESS!
YOU CAN'T STOP THERE!
THE DETAILS! TELL US THE DETAILS!
I'M NEVER ATTEND-ING A PAJAMA PARTY AGAIN!
shake shake Shake Shake
Hissssssss!
DEMON CLERIC...
I DEMAND ANSWERS...
?!
?!
Zzzzzz...
The Demon Cleric's reputation has significantly deteriorated.

Harpy's Room

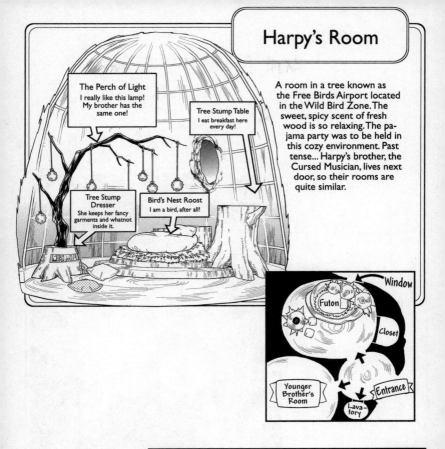

A room in a tree known as the Free Birds Airport located in the Wild Bird Zone. The sweet, spicy scent of fresh wood is so relaxing. The pajama party was to be held in this cozy environment. Past tense... Harpy's brother, the Cursed Musician, lives next door, so their rooms are quite similar.

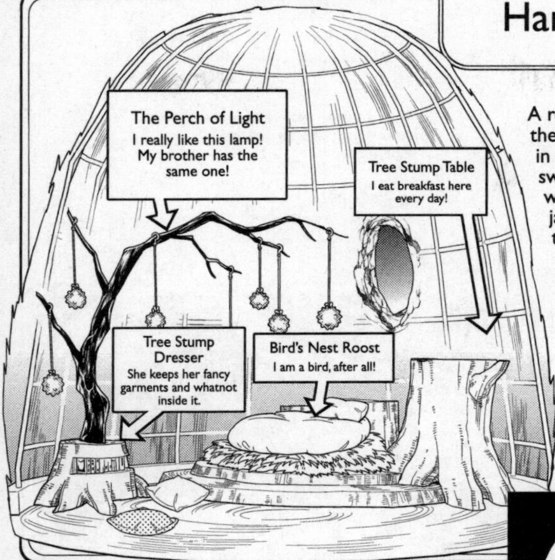
The Perch of Light
I really like this lamp! My brother has the same one!
Tree Stump Table
I eat breakfast here every day!
Tree Stump Dresser
She keeps her fancy garments and whatnot inside it.
Bird's Nest Roost
I am a bird, after all!

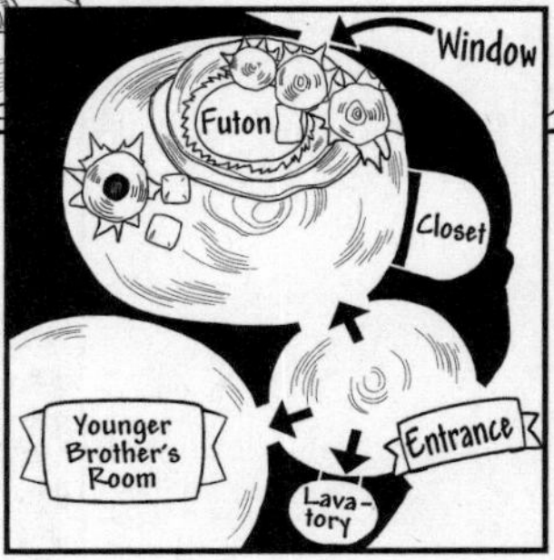
Window
Futon
Closet
Younger Brother's Room
Entrance
Lavatory

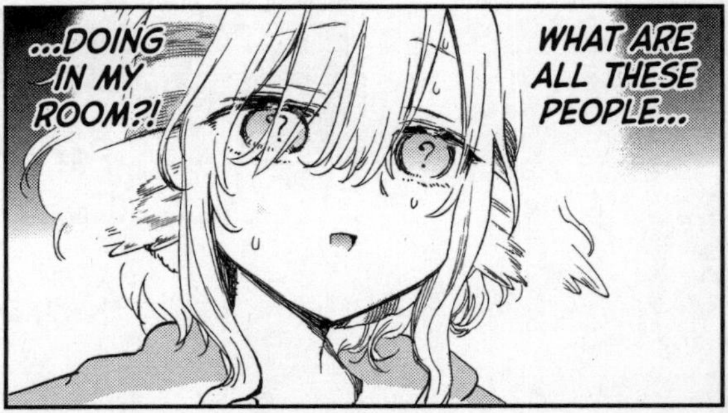
WHAT ARE ALL THESE PEOPLE...
...DOING IN MY ROOM?!

Would you like to change
your class?

6 changes
remaining

▶ Yes

No ▼

Partisan

"Deadly attack."

▼

72nd Night: Teddy Demon Grwrland, the Happiest Place in the Realm

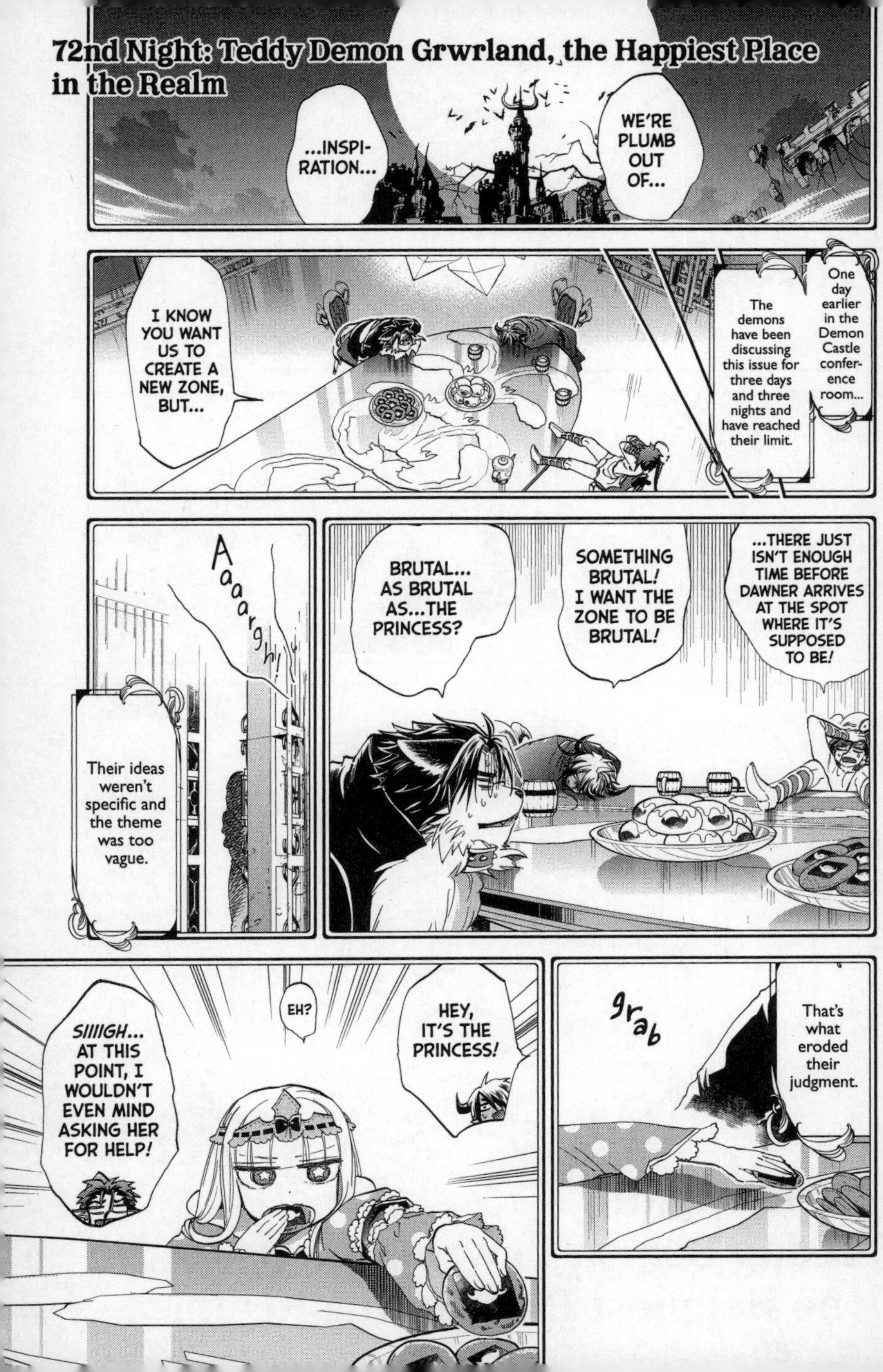
WE'RE PLUMB OUT OF...
...INSPIRATION...
One day earlier in the Demon Castle conference room...
The demons have been discussing this issue for three days and three nights and have reached their limit.
I KNOW YOU WANT US TO CREATE A NEW ZONE, BUT...
...THERE JUST ISN'T ENOUGH TIME BEFORE DAWNER ARRIVES AT THE SPOT WHERE IT'S SUPPOSED TO BE!
SOMETHING BRUTAL! I WANT THE ZONE TO BE BRUTAL!
BRUTAL... AS BRUTAL AS...THE PRINCESS?
Aaaargh!
Their ideas weren't specific and the theme was too vague.
That's what eroded their judgment.
grab
SIIIIGH... AT THIS POINT, I WOULDN'T EVEN MIND ASKING HER FOR HELP!
EH?
HEY, IT'S THE PRINCESS!

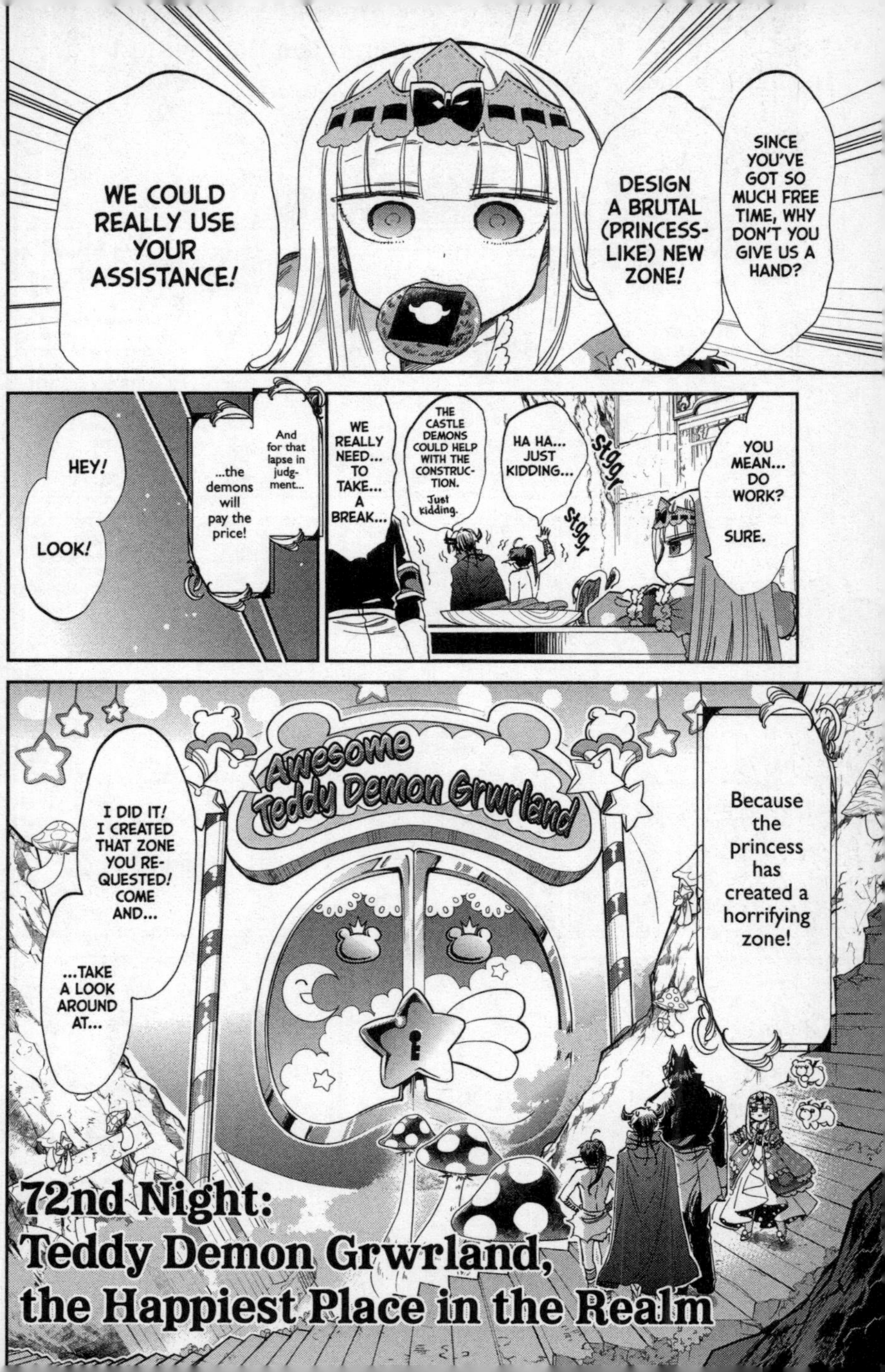
SINCE YOU'VE GOT SO MUCH FREE TIME, WHY DON'T YOU GIVE US A HAND?
DESIGN A BRUTAL (PRINCESS-LIKE) NEW ZONE!
WE COULD REALLY USE YOUR ASSISTANCE!
YOU MEAN... DO WORK?
SURE.
stggr
stggr
HA HA... JUST KIDDING...
THE CASTLE DEMONS COULD HELP WITH THE CONSTRUCTION.
Just kidding.
WE REALLY NEED... TO TAKE... A BREAK...
And for that lapse in judg-ment...
...the demons will pay the price!
HEY!
LOOK!
Because the princess has created a horrifying zone!
Awesome Teddy Demon Grwrland
I DID IT! I CREATED THAT ZONE YOU RE-QUESTED! COME AND...
...TAKE A LOOK AROUND AT...

72nd Night: Teddy Demon Grwrland, the Happiest Place in the Realm

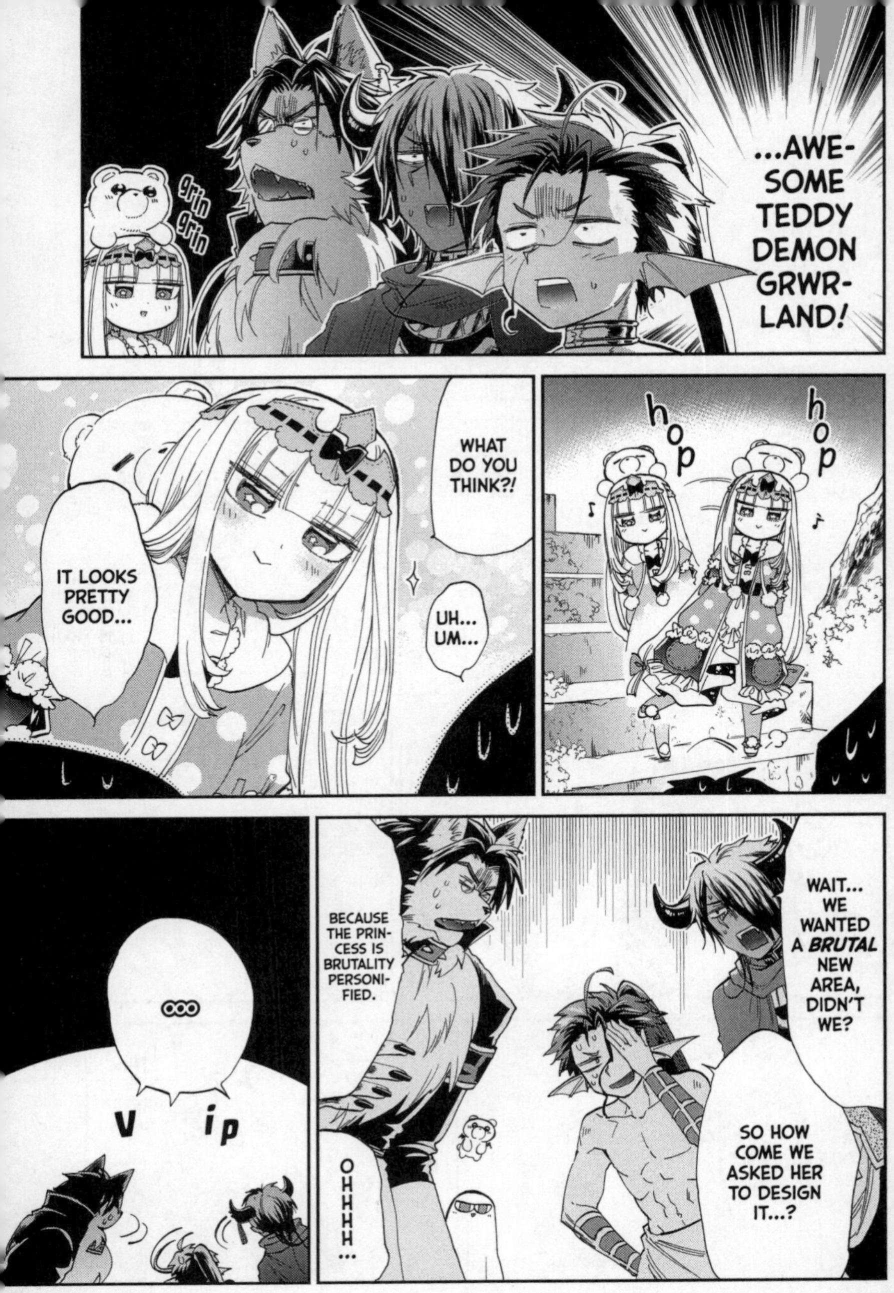
...AWE-SOME TEDDY DEMON GRWR-LAND!
grin grin
hop hop
WHAT DO YOU THINK?!
UH... UM...
IT LOOKS PRETTY GOOD...
WAIT... WE WANTED A *BRUTAL* NEW AREA, DIDN'T WE?
SO HOW COME WE ASKED HER TO DESIGN IT...?
BECAUSE THE PRIN-CESS IS BRUTALITY PERSONI-FIED.
OHHHH...
V ip

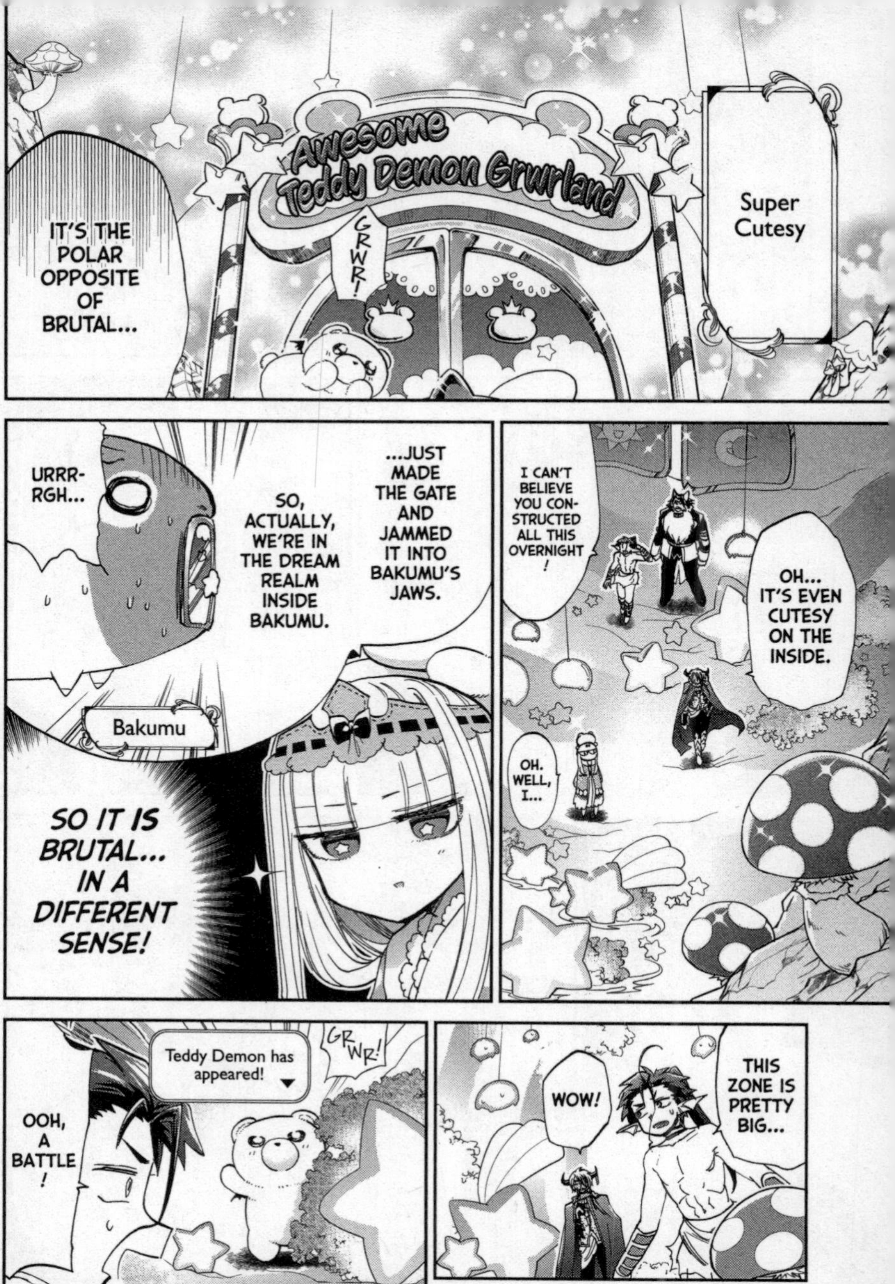
Super Cutesy
Awesome Teddy Demon Grurland
GRWR!
IT'S THE POLAR OPPOSITE OF BRUTAL...
OH... IT'S EVEN CUTESY ON THE INSIDE.
I CAN'T BELIEVE YOU CONSTRUCTED ALL THIS OVERNIGHT!
OH. WELL, I...
...JUST MADE THE GATE AND JAMMED IT INTO BAKUMU'S JAWS.
SO, ACTUALLY, WE'RE IN THE DREAM REALM INSIDE BAKUMU.
URRR-RGH...
Bakumu
SO IT IS BRUTAL... IN A DIFFERENT SENSE!
THIS ZONE IS PRETTY BIG...
WOW!
GRWR!
Teddy Demon has appeared!
OOH, A BATTLE!

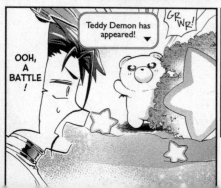

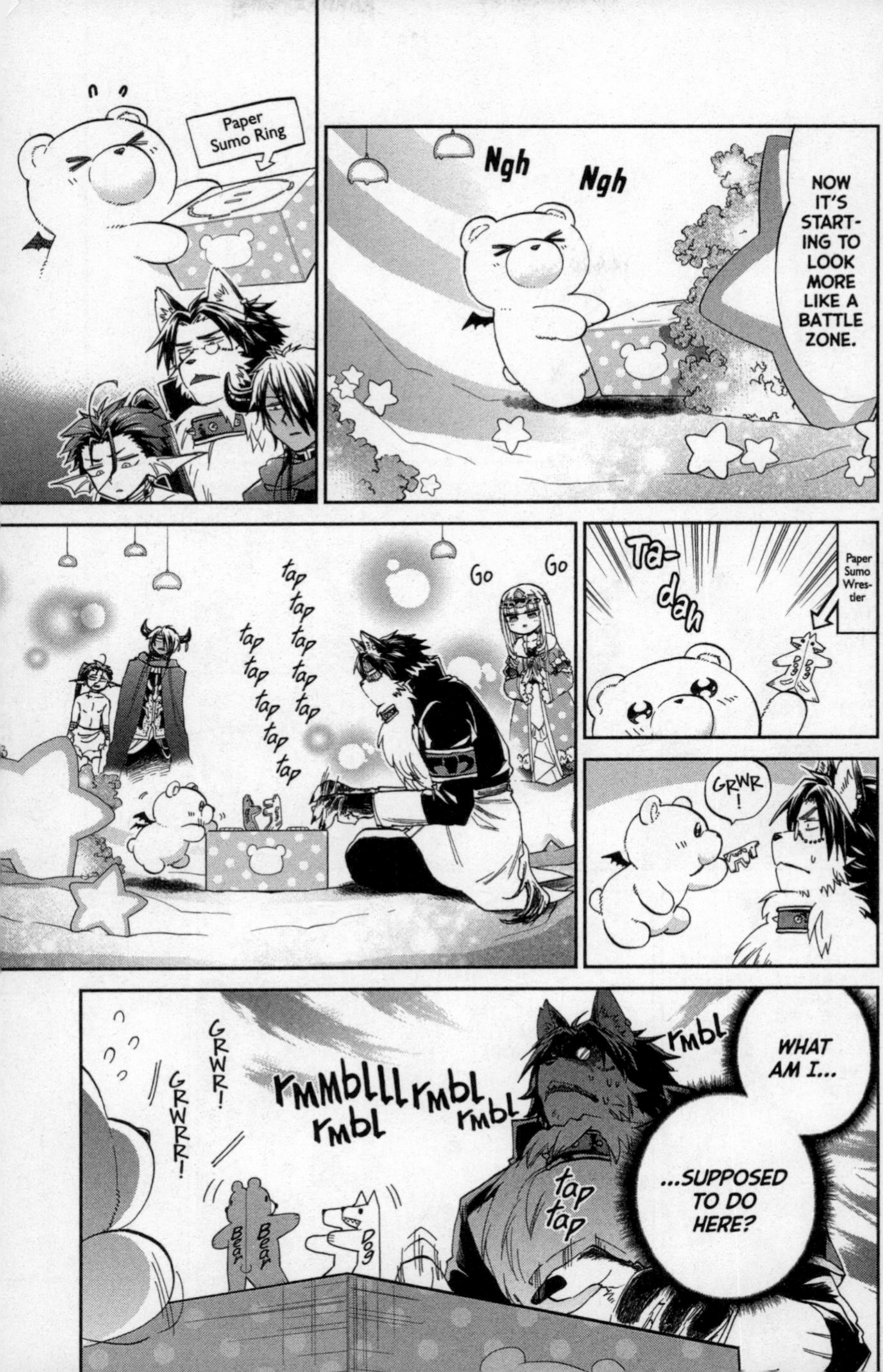
Ngh
Ngh
NOW IT'S STARTING TO LOOK MORE LIKE A BATTLE ZONE.
Paper Sumo Ring
Ta-dah
Paper Sumo Wrestler
GRWR!
Go
Go
tap tap tap tap tap
tap tap tap tap tap tap
WHAT AM I...
...SUPPOSED TO DO HERE?
rmbl
rmbl
rmMblll rmbl
rmbl
tap tap
GRWR!
GRWRR!
Bear
Bear
Dog

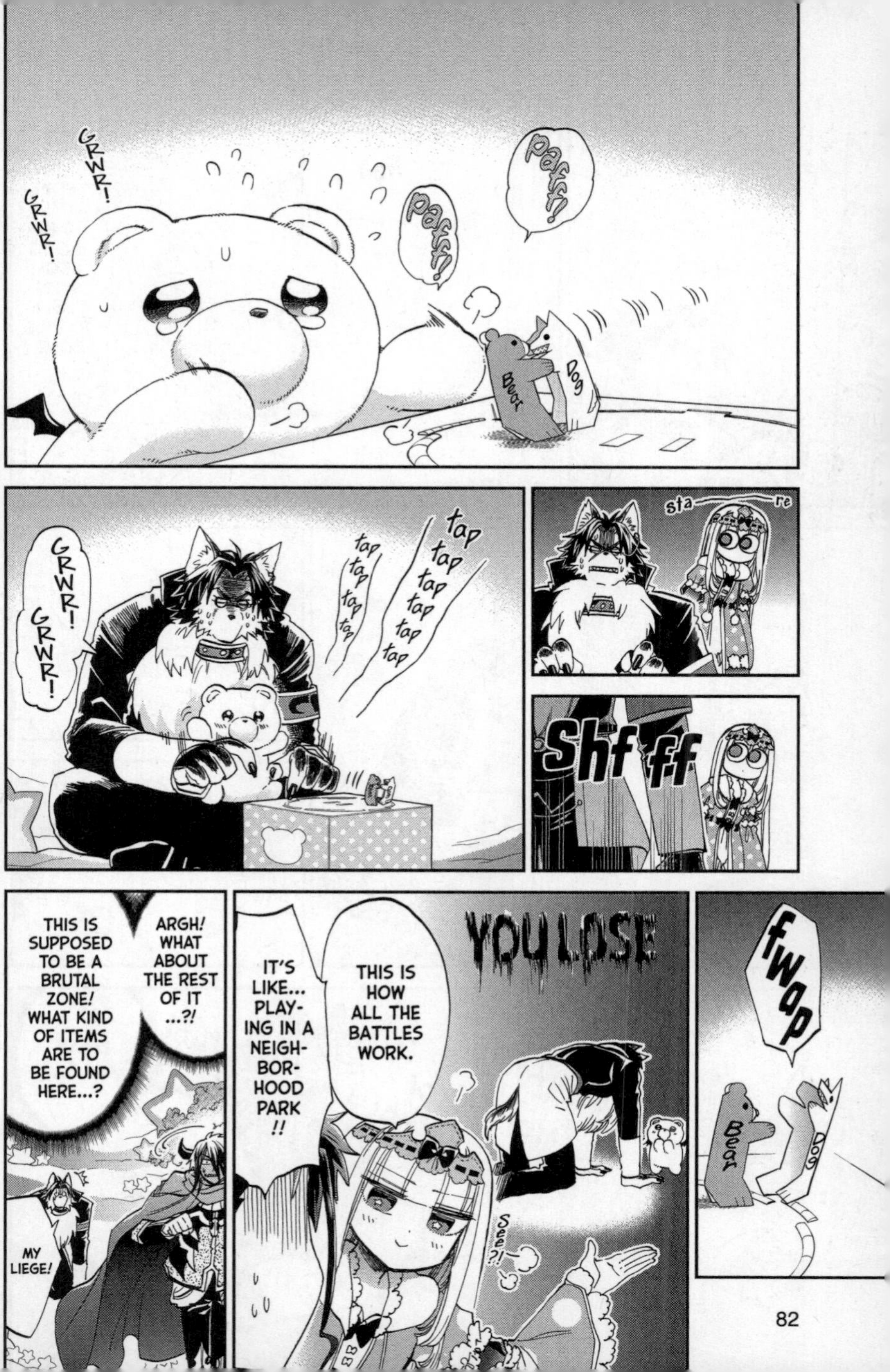
paff!
paff!
GRWR!
GRWR!
Dog
Bear
sta——re
Shf ff
tap tap tap tap tap tap
tap tap tap tap tap
GRWR! GRWR!
fwap
Bear
Dog
YOU LOSE
THIS IS HOW ALL THE BATTLES WORK.
IT'S LIKE... PLAY-ING IN A NEIGH-BOR-HOOD PARK!!
See?!
ARGH! WHAT ABOUT THE REST OF IT ...?!
THIS IS SUPPOSED TO BE A BRUTAL ZONE! WHAT KIND OF ITEMS ARE TO BE FOUND HERE...?
MY LIEGE!

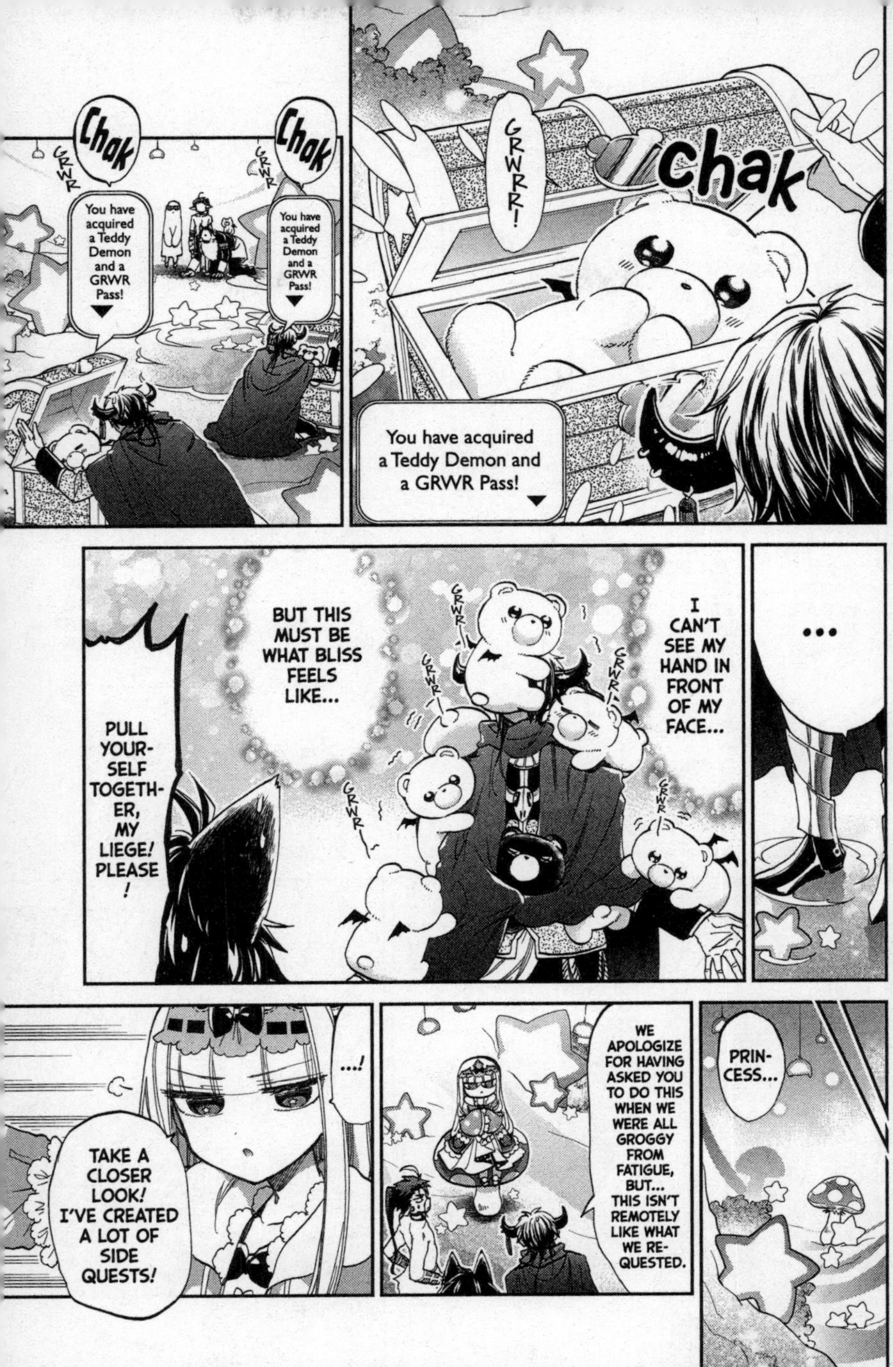
GRWRR!
Chak
You have acquired a Teddy Demon and a GRWR Pass!
Chak
GRWR
You have acquired a Teddy Demon and a GRWR Pass!
Chak
GRWR
You have acquired a Teddy Demon and a GRWR Pass!
...
I CAN'T SEE MY HAND IN FRONT OF MY FACE...
GRWR
GRWR
BUT THIS MUST BE WHAT BLISS FEELS LIKE...
GRWR
GRWR
GRWR
PULL YOURSELF TOGETHER, MY LIEGE! PLEASE!
PRINCESS...
WE APOLOGIZE FOR HAVING ASKED YOU TO DO THIS WHEN WE WERE ALL GROGGY FROM FATIGUE, BUT... THIS ISN'T REMOTELY LIKE WHAT WE REQUESTED.
...!
TAKE A CLOSER LOOK! I'VE CREATED A LOT OF SIDE QUESTS!

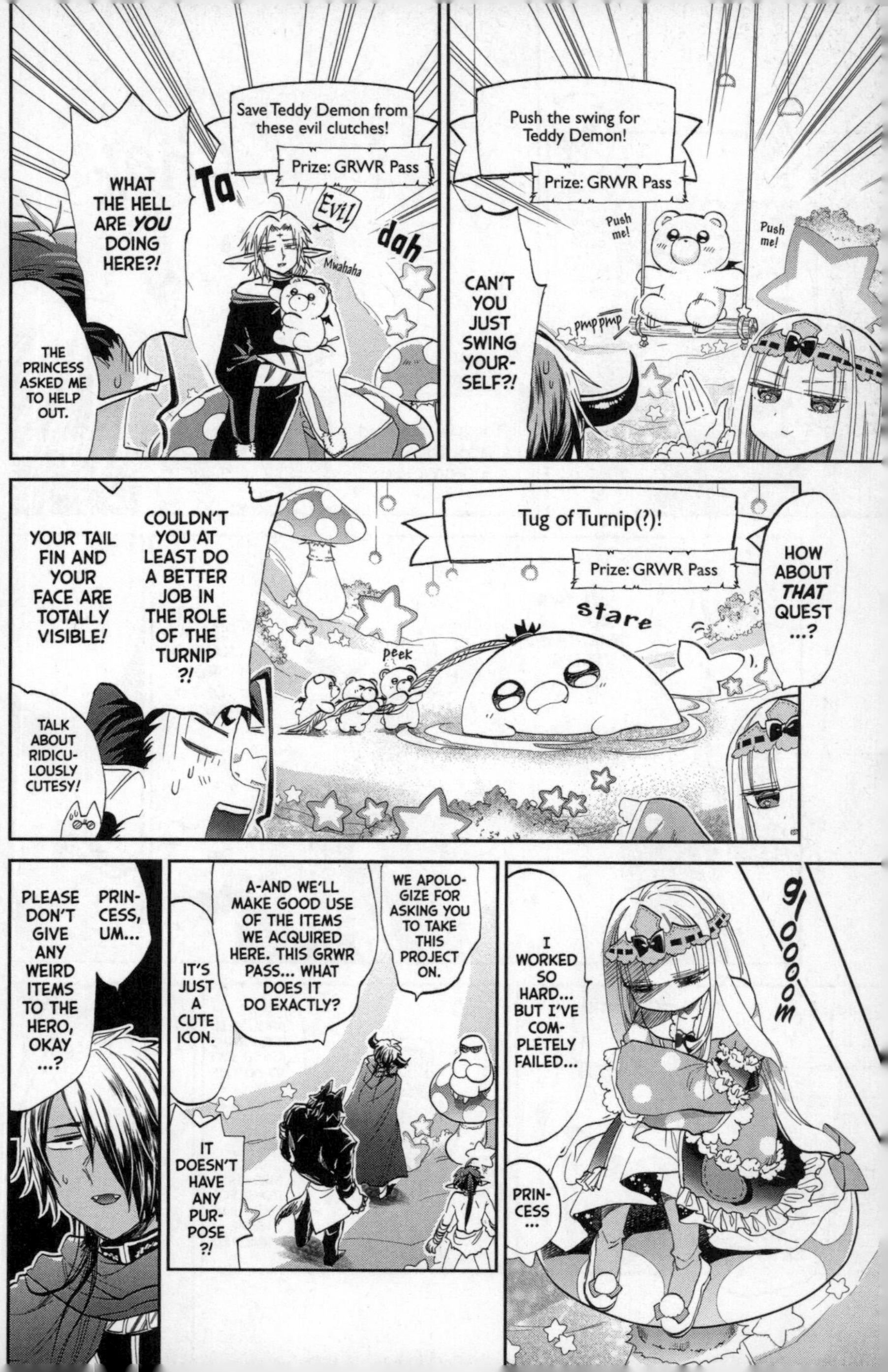
Push the swing for Teddy Demon!
Prize: GRWR Pass
Push me!
Push me!
CAN'T YOU JUST SWING YOURSELF?!
pmp pmp
Save Teddy Demon from these evil clutches!
Prize: GRWR Pass
Ta
Evil
dah
Mwahaha
WHAT THE HELL ARE *YOU* DOING HERE?!
THE PRINCESS ASKED ME TO HELP OUT.
HOW ABOUT *THAT* QUEST ...?
Tug of Turnip(?)!
Prize: GRWR Pass
stare
peek
COULDN'T YOU AT LEAST DO A BETTER JOB IN THE ROLE OF THE TURNIP?!
YOUR TAIL FIN AND YOUR FACE ARE TOTALLY VISIBLE!
TALK ABOUT RIDICULOUSLY CUTESY!
glooooom
I WORKED SO HARD... BUT I'VE COMPLETELY FAILED...
PRINCESS...
WE APOLOGIZE FOR ASKING YOU TO TAKE THIS PROJECT ON.
A-AND WE'LL MAKE GOOD USE OF THE ITEMS WE ACQUIRED HERE. THIS GRWR PASS... WHAT DOES IT DO EXACTLY?
IT'S JUST A CUTE ICON.
IT DOESN'T HAVE ANY PURPOSE?!
PRINCESS, UM...
PLEASE DON'T GIVE ANY WEIRD ITEMS TO THE HERO, OKAY...?

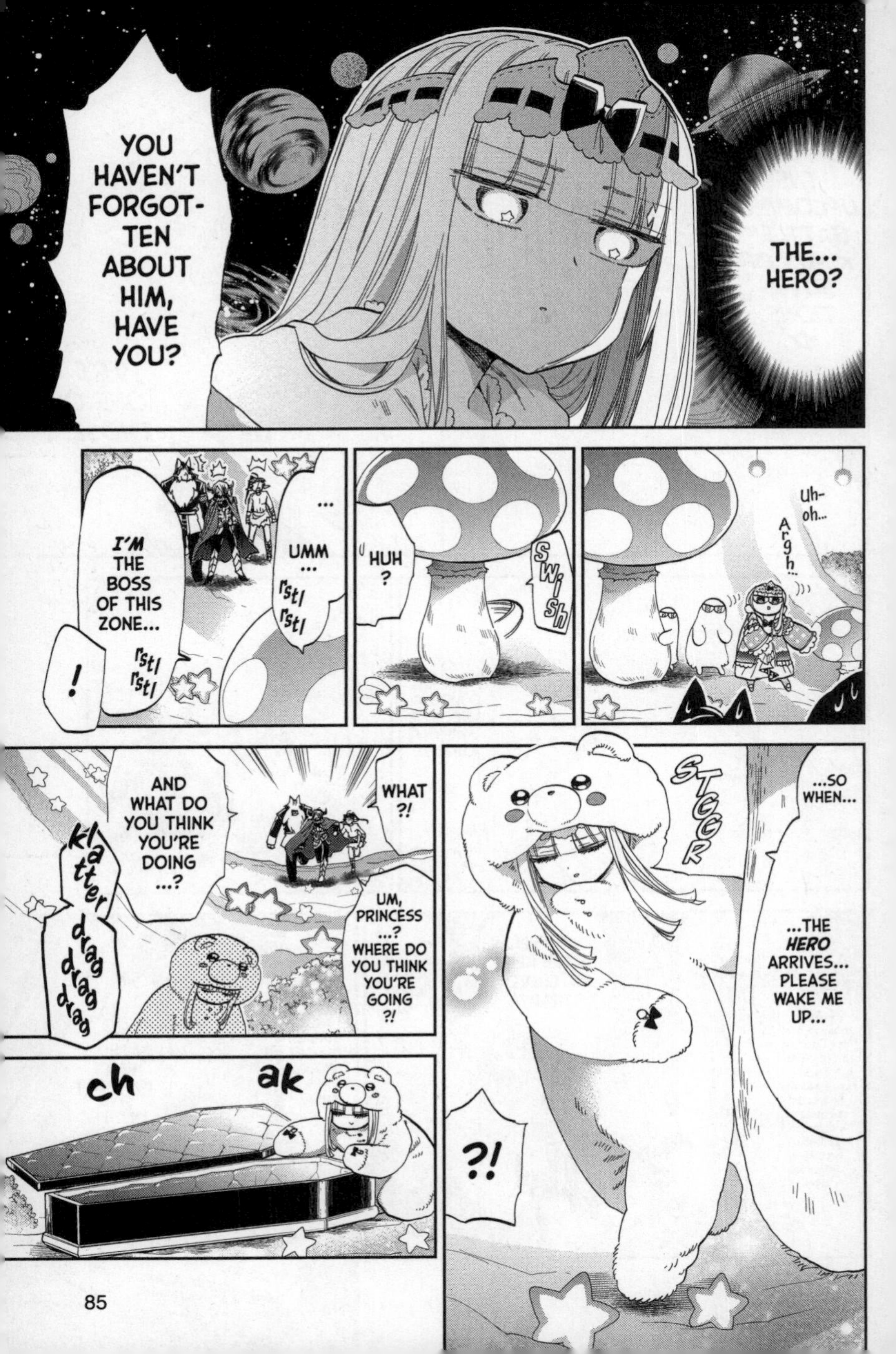
THE... HERO?
YOU HAVEN'T FORGOT-TEN ABOUT HIM, HAVE YOU?
Uh-oh...
Argh...
SWISH
HUH?
...
UMM... rstl rstl
I'M THE BOSS OF THIS ZONE...
rstl rstl
!
STGGR
...SO WHEN...
...THE HERO ARRIVES... PLEASE WAKE ME UP...
?!
WHAT?!
AND WHAT DO YOU THINK YOU'RE DOING...?
UM, PRINCESS...? WHERE DO YOU THINK YOU'RE GOING?!
klatter drag drag drag
ch ak

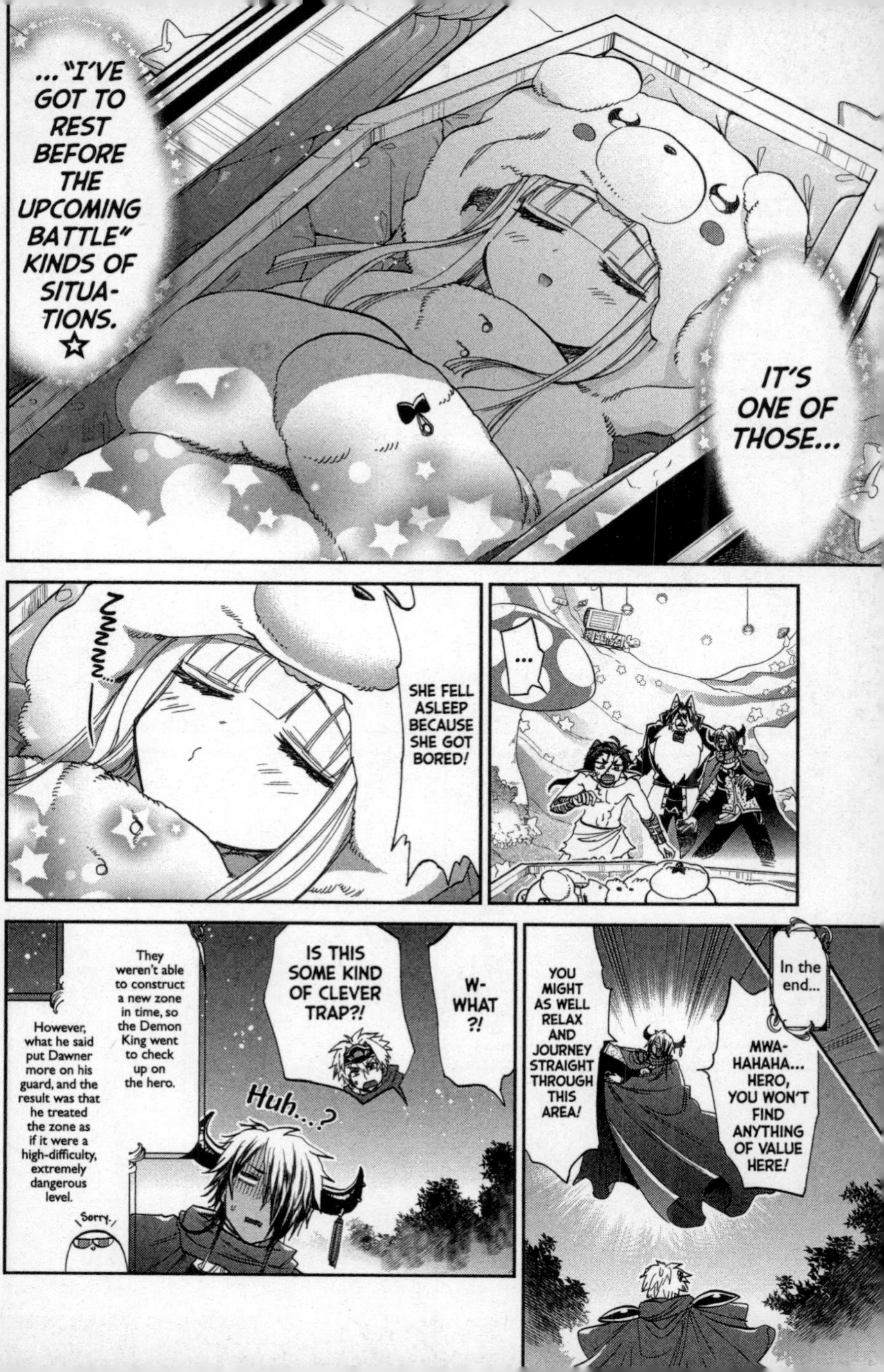
IT'S ONE OF THOSE...
..."I'VE GOT TO REST BEFORE THE UPCOMING BATTLE" KINDS OF SITUATIONS. ☆
...
SHE FELL ASLEEP BECAUSE SHE GOT BORED!
NNNNN...
In the end...
MWA-HAHAHA... HERO, YOU WON'T FIND ANYTHING OF VALUE HERE!
YOU MIGHT AS WELL RELAX AND JOURNEY STRAIGHT THROUGH THIS AREA!
W-WHAT?!
IS THIS SOME KIND OF CLEVER TRAP?!
They weren't able to construct a new zone in time, so the Demon King went to check up on the hero.
However, what he said put Dawner more on his guard, and the result was that he treated the zone as if it were a high-difficulty, extremely dangerous level.
Huh...?
Sorry.

Awesome Teddy Demon Grwrland

His favorite dish is green tea over rice.

▼

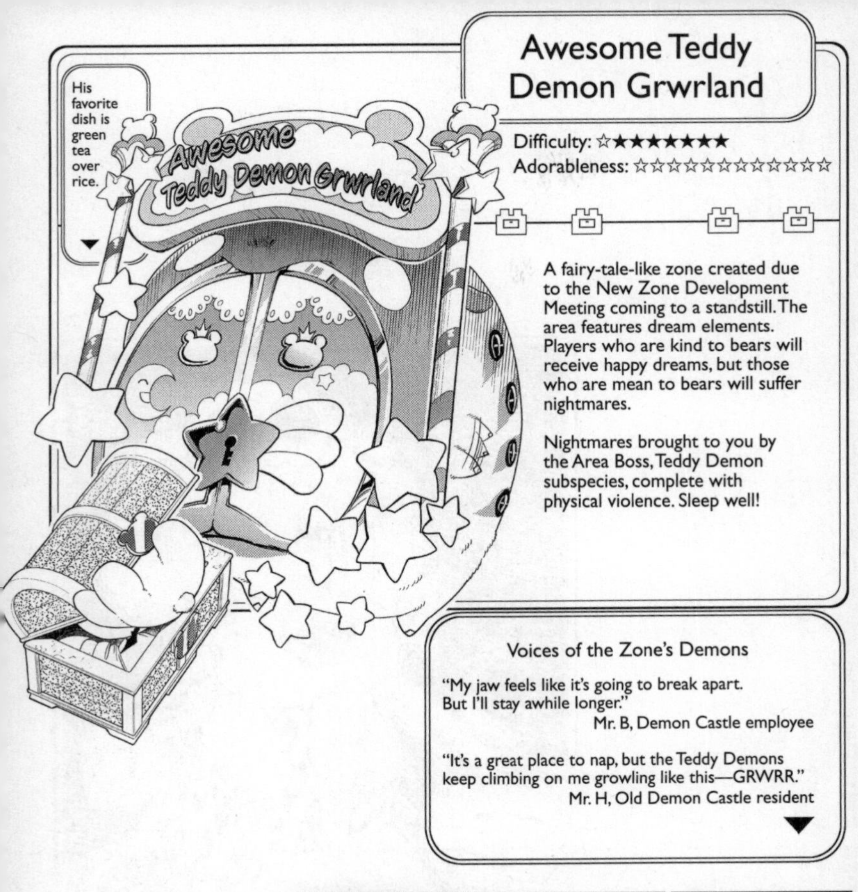
Awesome Teddy Demon Grwrland!

Difficulty: ☆★★★★★★★
Adorableness: ☆☆☆☆☆☆☆☆☆☆☆☆☆☆

A fairy-tale-like zone created due to the New Zone Development Meeting coming to a standstill. The area features dream elements. Players who are kind to bears will receive happy dreams, but those who are mean to bears will suffer nightmares.

Nightmares brought to you by the Area Boss, Teddy Demon subspecies, complete with physical violence. Sleep well!

Voices of the Zone's Demons

"My jaw feels like it's going to break apart. But I'll stay awhile longer."

Mr. B, Demon Castle employee

"It's a great place to nap, but the Teddy Demons keep climbing on me growling like this—GRWRR."

Mr. H, Old Demon Castle resident

▼

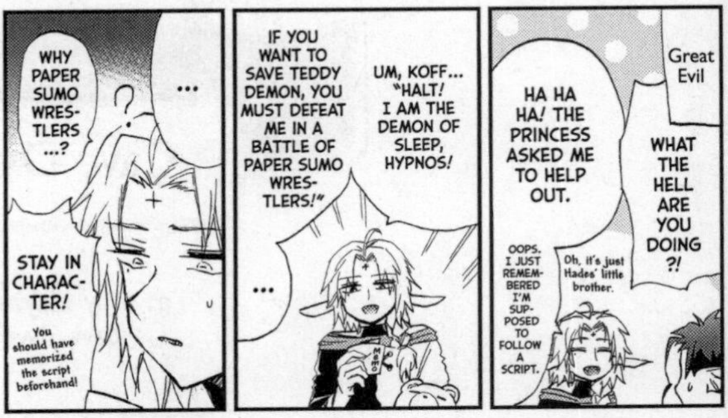
Great Evil
WHAT THE HELL ARE YOU DOING?!
HA HA HA! THE PRINCESS ASKED ME TO HELP OUT.
Oh, it's just Hades' little brother.
OOPS. I JUST REMEMBERED I'M SUPPOSED TO FOLLOW A SCRIPT.
UM, KOFF... "HALT! I AM THE DEMON OF SLEEP, HYPNOS!
IF YOU WANT TO SAVE TEDDY DEMON, YOU MUST DEFEAT ME IN A BATTLE OF PAPER SUMO WRESTLERS!"
...
MEMO
...
WHY PAPER SUMO WRESTLERS...?
STAY IN CHARACTER!
You should have memorized the script beforehand!

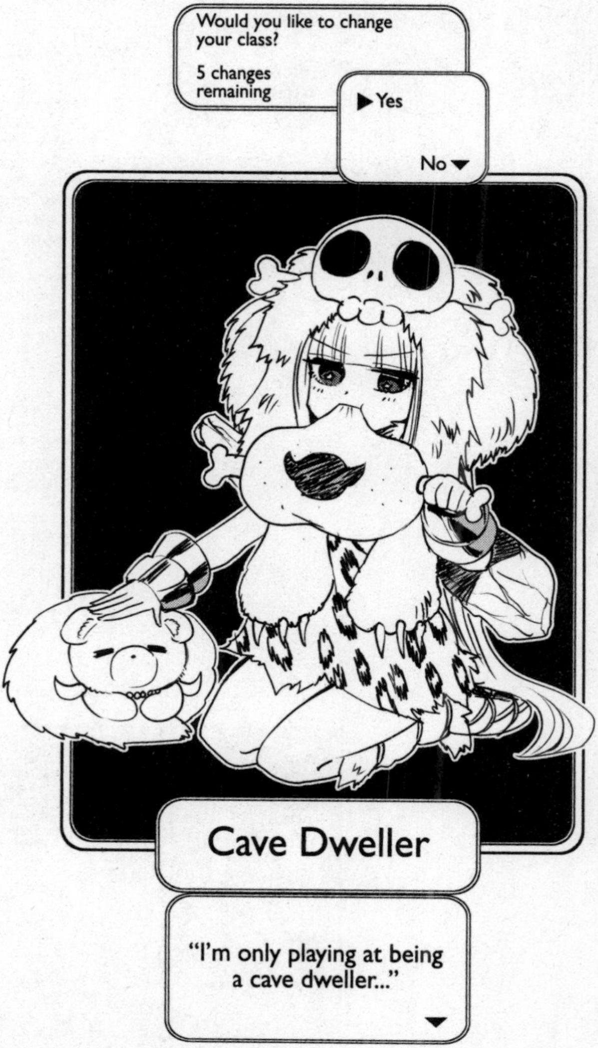
Would you like to change your class?
5 changes remaining
▶Yes
No
Cave Dweller
"I'm only playing at being a cave dweller..."

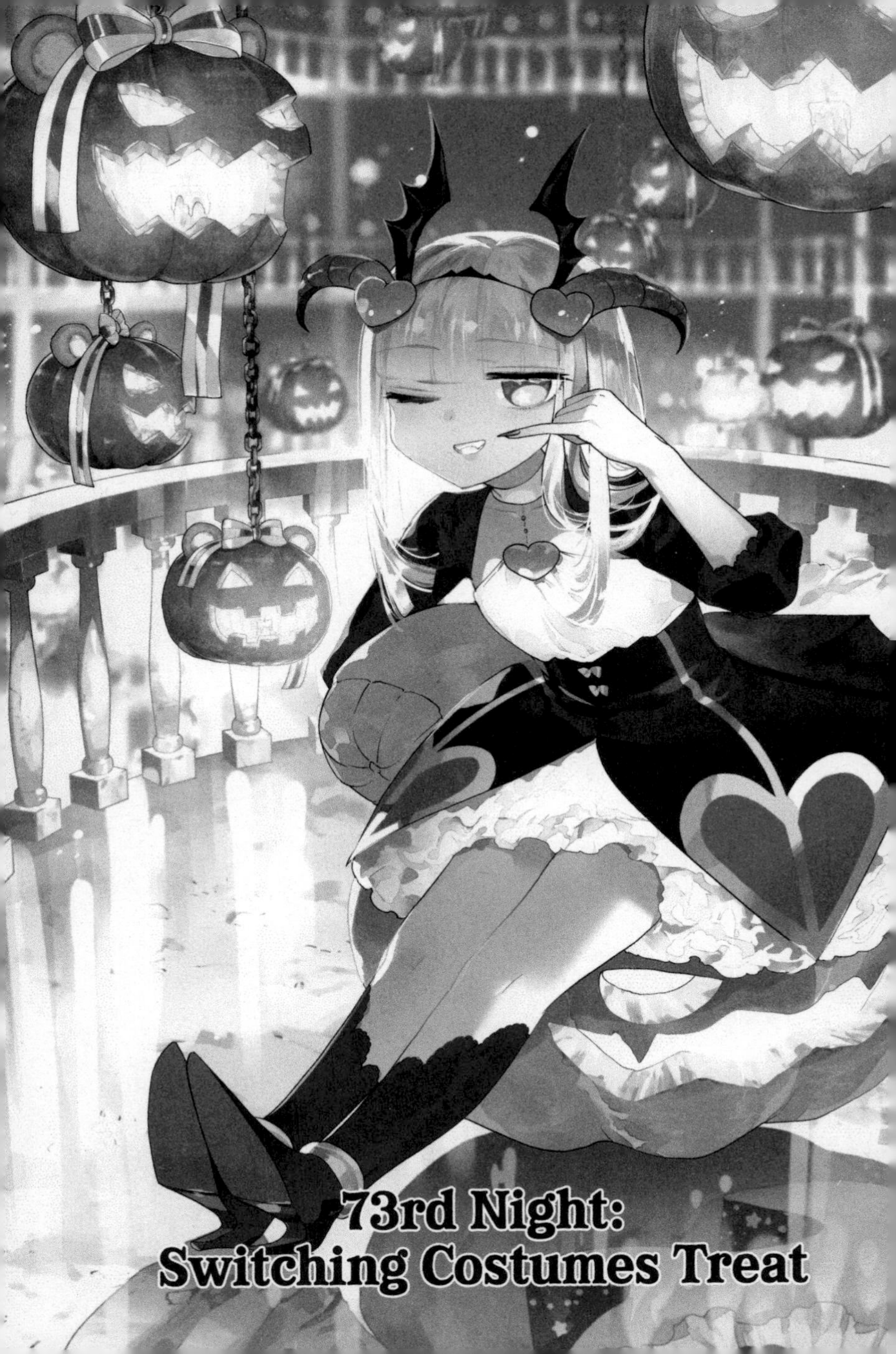
73rd Night:
Switching Costumes Treat

SLEEPY PRINCESS
IN THE
DEMON CASTLE

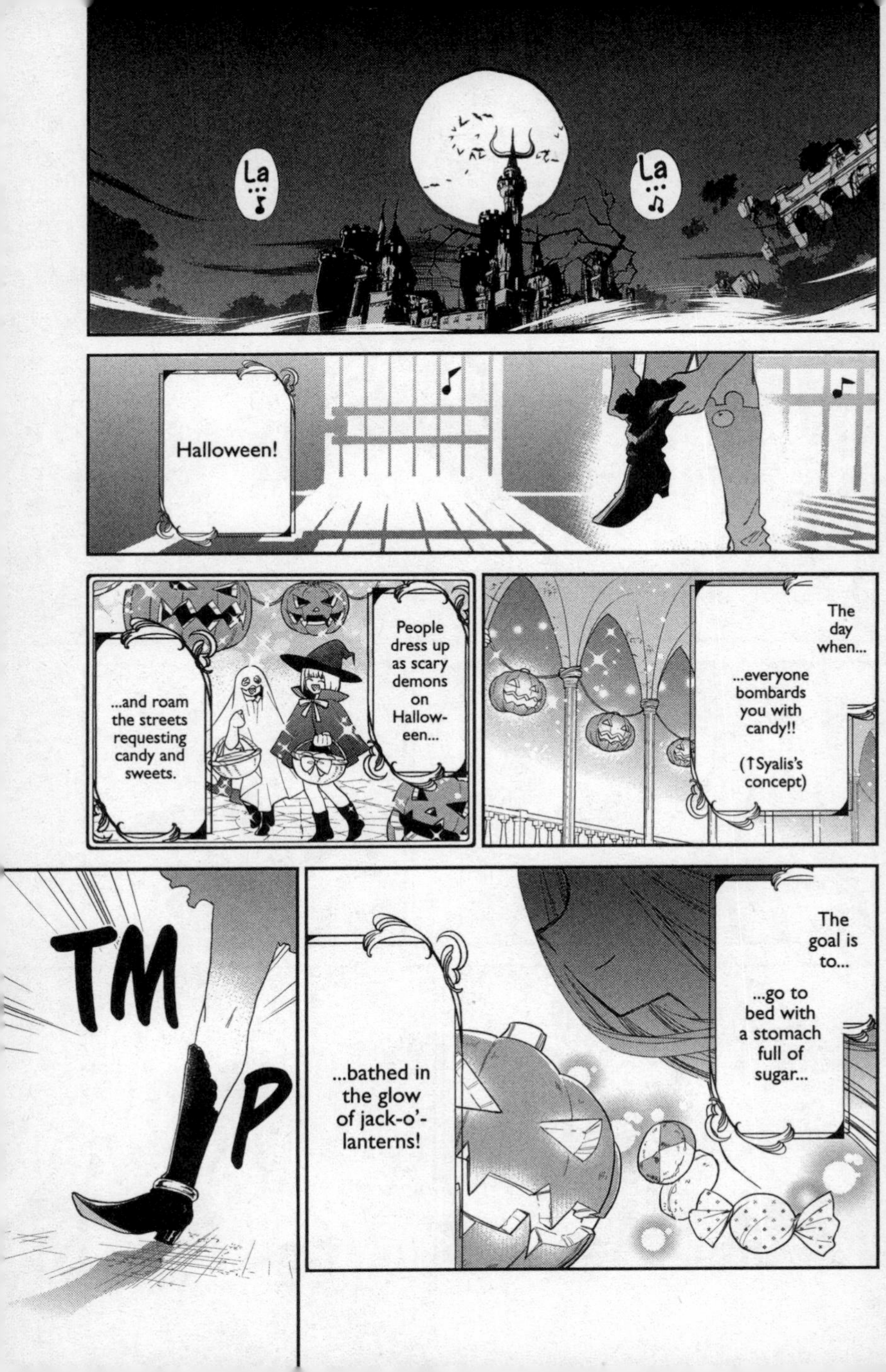
La...
La...
Halloween!
The day when...
...everyone bombards you with candy!!
(↑Syalis's concept)
People dress up as scary demons on Halloween...
...and roam the streets requesting candy and sweets.
The goal is to...
...go to bed with a stomach full of sugar...
...bathed in the glow of jack-o'-lanterns!
TMP

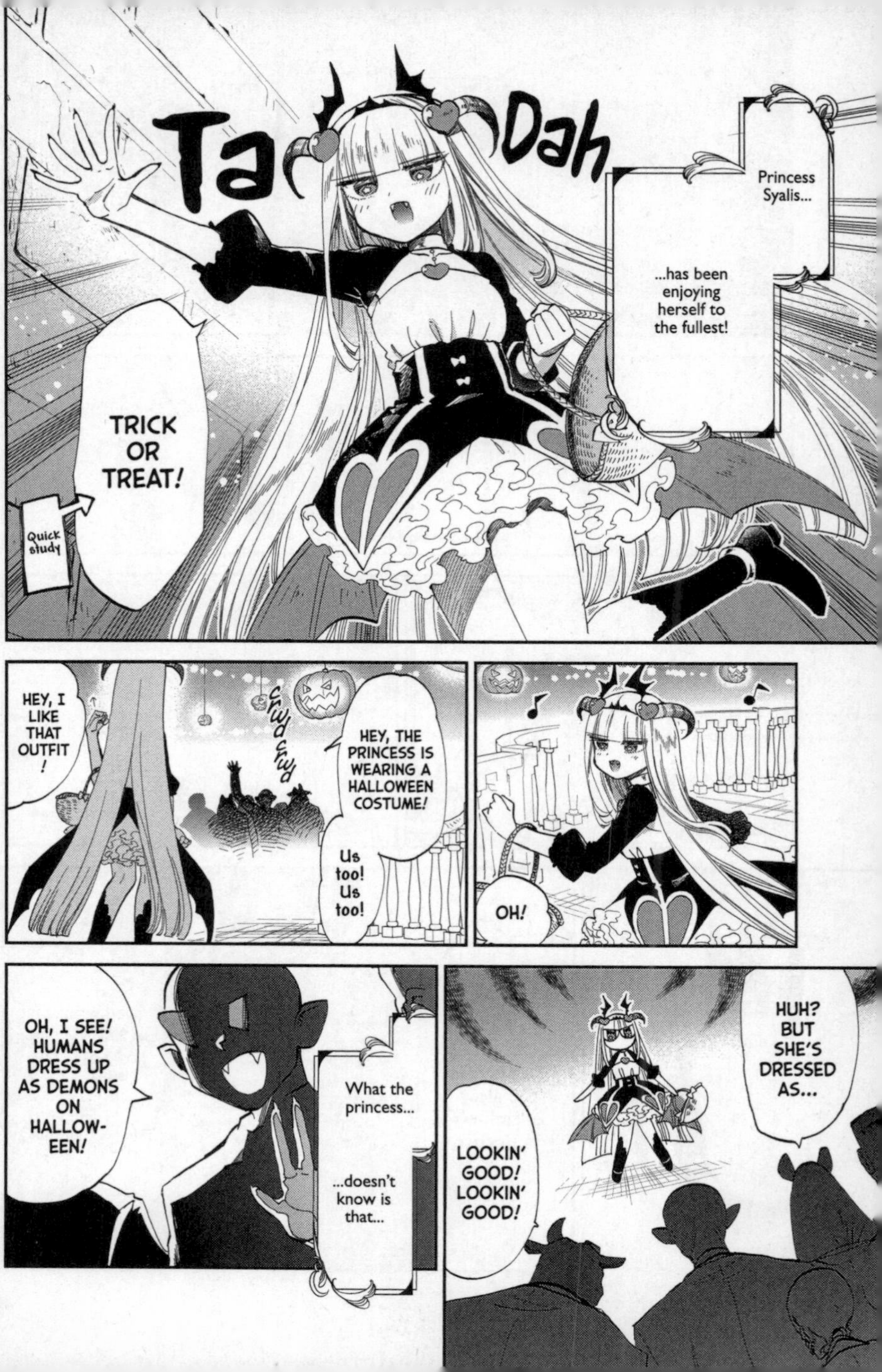

Princess Syalis...
...has been enjoying herself to the fullest!
Ta Dah
TRICK OR TREAT!
Quick study
OH!
HEY, THE PRINCESS IS WEARING A HALLOWEEN COSTUME!
crwd crwd
HEY, I LIKE THAT OUTFIT!
Us too! Us too!
HUH? BUT SHE'S DRESSED AS...
LOOKIN' GOOD! LOOKIN' GOOD!
OH, I SEE! HUMANS DRESS UP AS DEMONS ON HALLOW-EEN!
What the princess...
...doesn't know is that...

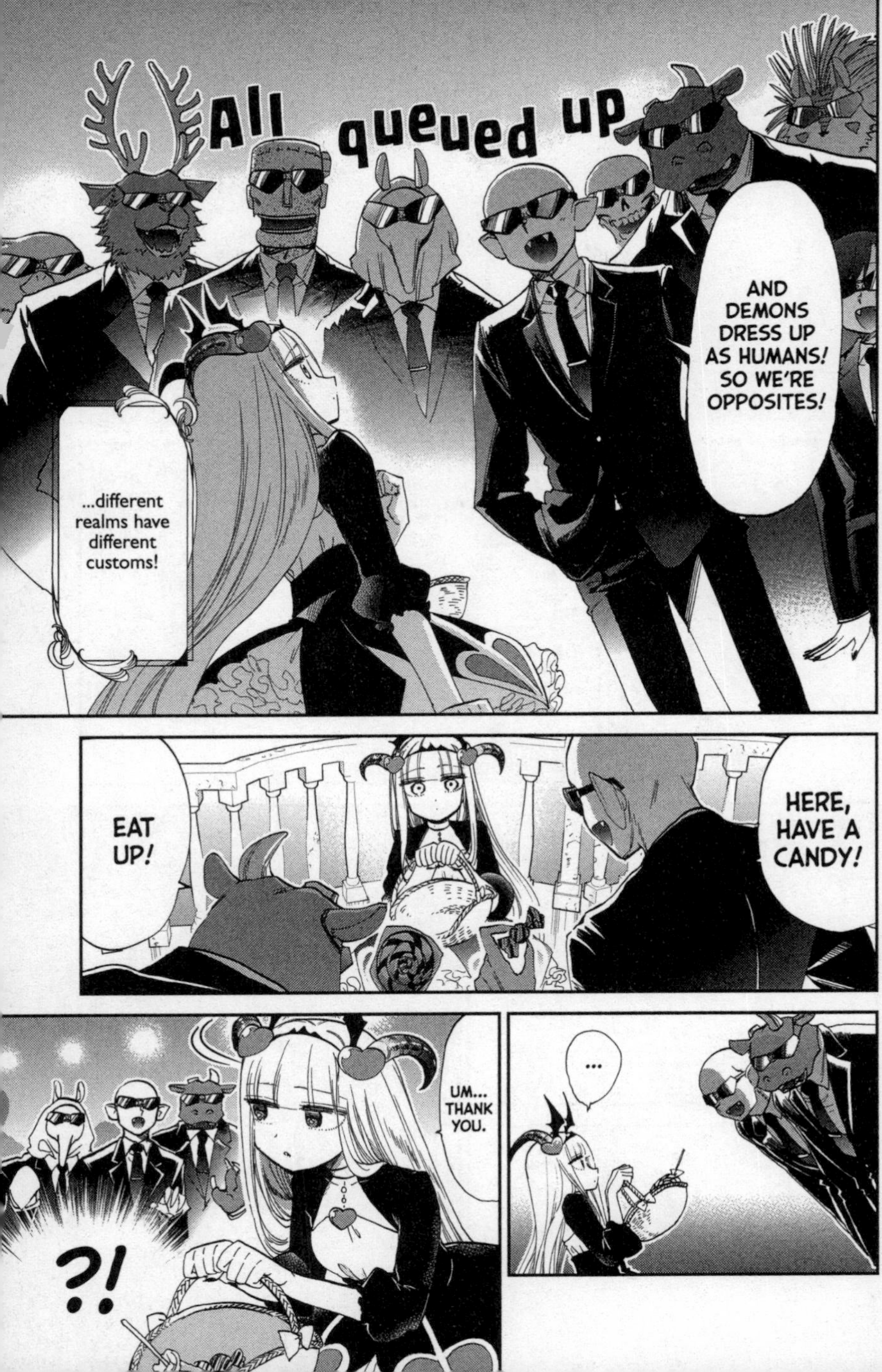
All queued up
AND DEMONS DRESS UP AS HUMANS! SO WE'RE OPPOSITES!
...different realms have different customs!
HERE, HAVE A CANDY!
EAT UP!
...
UM... THANK YOU.
?!

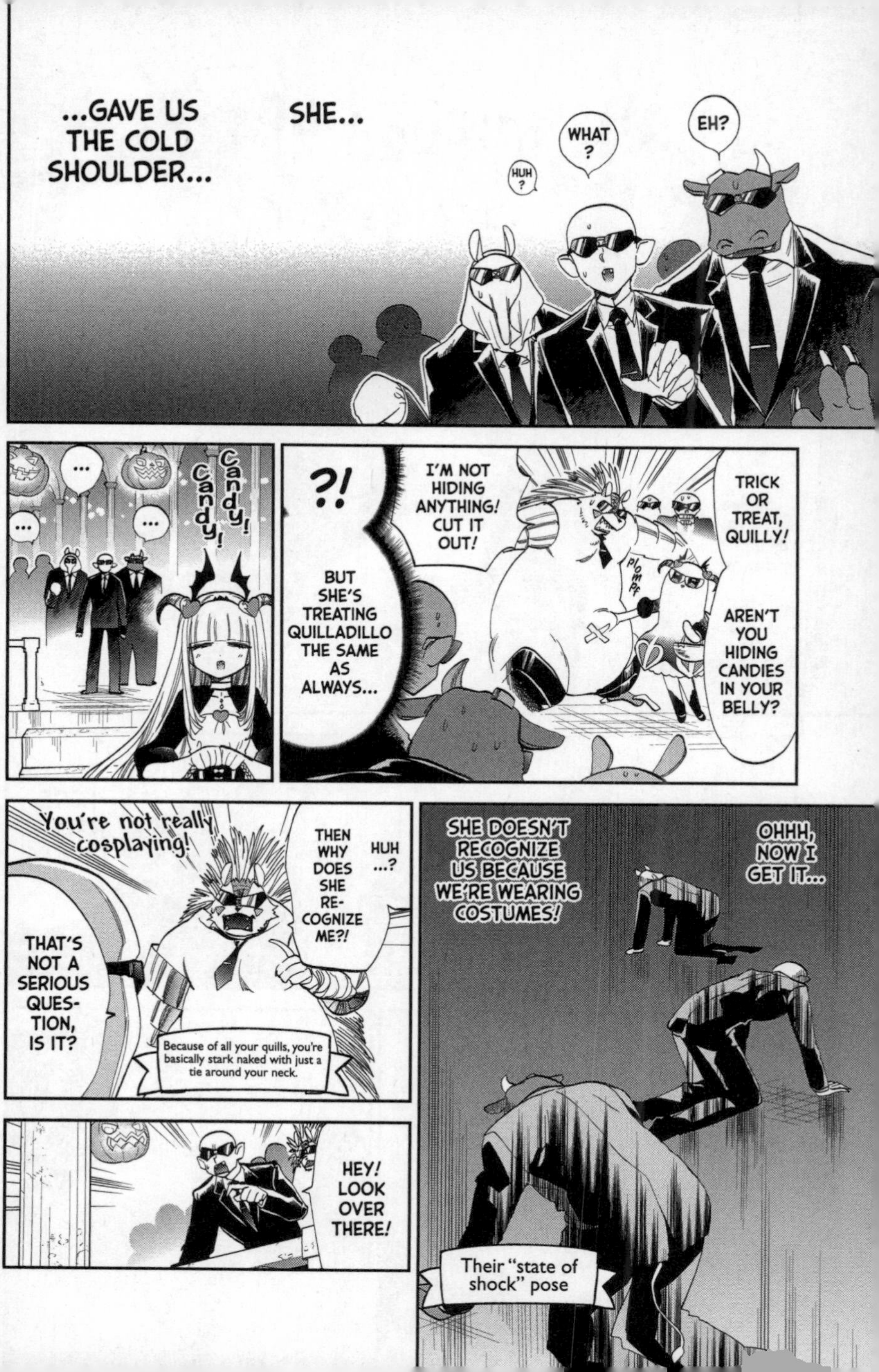
EH?
WHAT ?
HUH ?
SHE...
...GAVE US THE COLD SHOULDER...
TRICK OR TREAT, QUILLY!
AREN'T YOU HIDING CANDIES IN YOUR BELLY?
PLOMPF
I'M NOT HIDING ANYTHING! CUT IT OUT!
?!
BUT SHE'S TREATING QUILLADILLO THE SAME AS ALWAYS...
Candy! Candy!
...
...
...
OHHH, NOW I GET IT...
SHE DOESN'T RECOGNIZE US BECAUSE WE'RE WEARING COSTUMES!
Their "state of shock" pose
HUH ...?
THEN WHY DOES SHE RE-COGNIZE ME?!
You're not really cosplaying!
THAT'S NOT A SERIOUS QUES-TION, IS IT?
Because of all your quills, you're basically stark naked with just a tie around your neck.
HEY! LOOK OVER THERE!

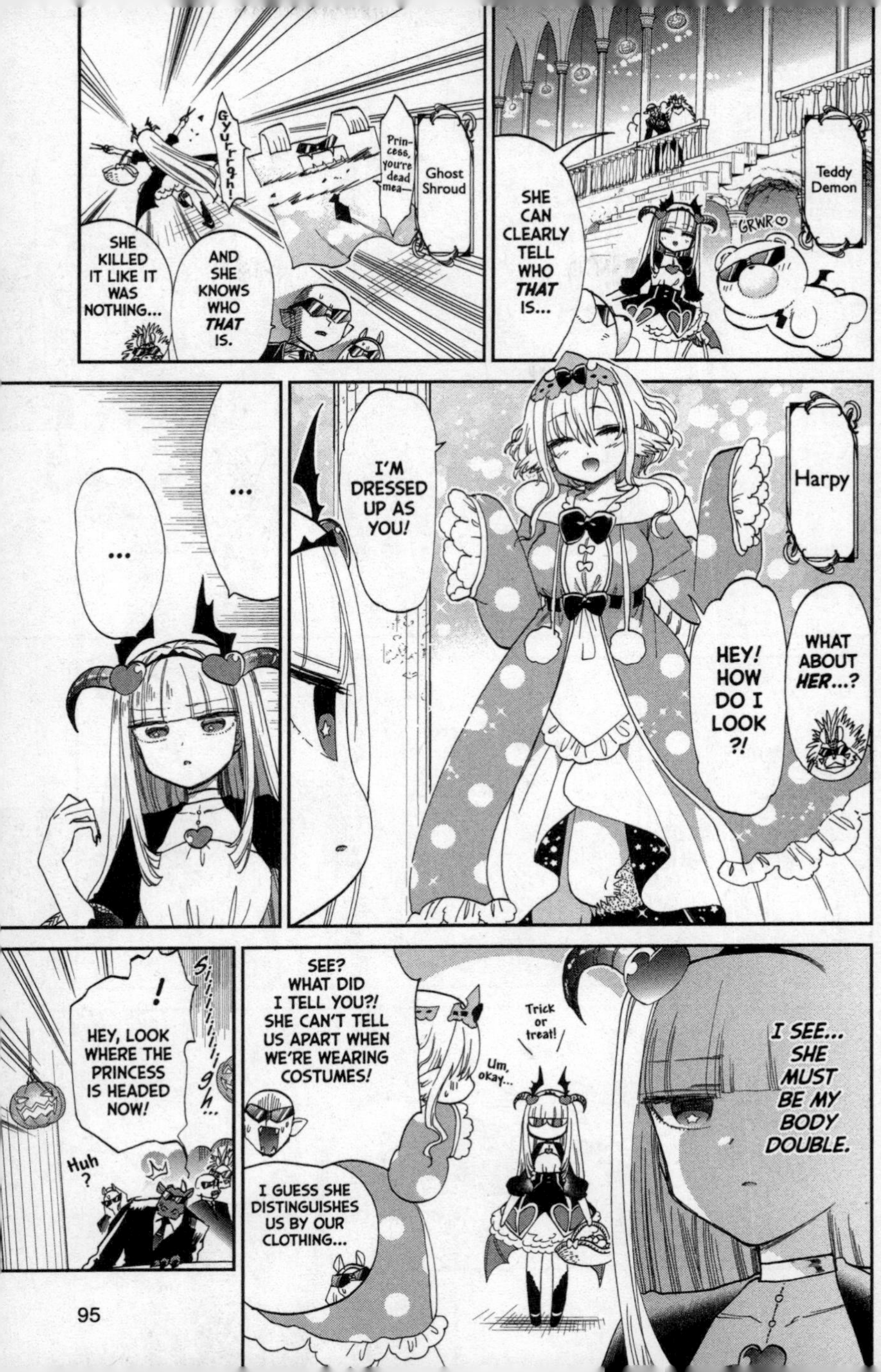
Teddy Demon
GRWR ♡
SHE CAN CLEARLY TELL WHO *THAT* IS...
Ghost Shroud
Princess, you're dead mea—
Gyurrrgh!
AND SHE KNOWS WHO *THAT* IS.
SHE KILLED IT LIKE IT WAS NOTHING...
Harpy
WHAT ABOUT *HER*...?
HEY! HOW DO I LOOK?!
I'M DRESSED UP AS YOU!
...
...
I SEE... SHE MUST BE MY BODY DOUBLE.
Trick or treat!
Um, okay...
SEE? WHAT DID I TELL YOU?! SHE CAN'T TELL US APART WHEN WE'RE WEARING COSTUMES!
I GUESS SHE DISTINGUISHES US BY OUR CLOTHING...
!
HEY, LOOK WHERE THE PRINCESS IS HEADED NOW!
Siiiiiiiigh...
Huh?

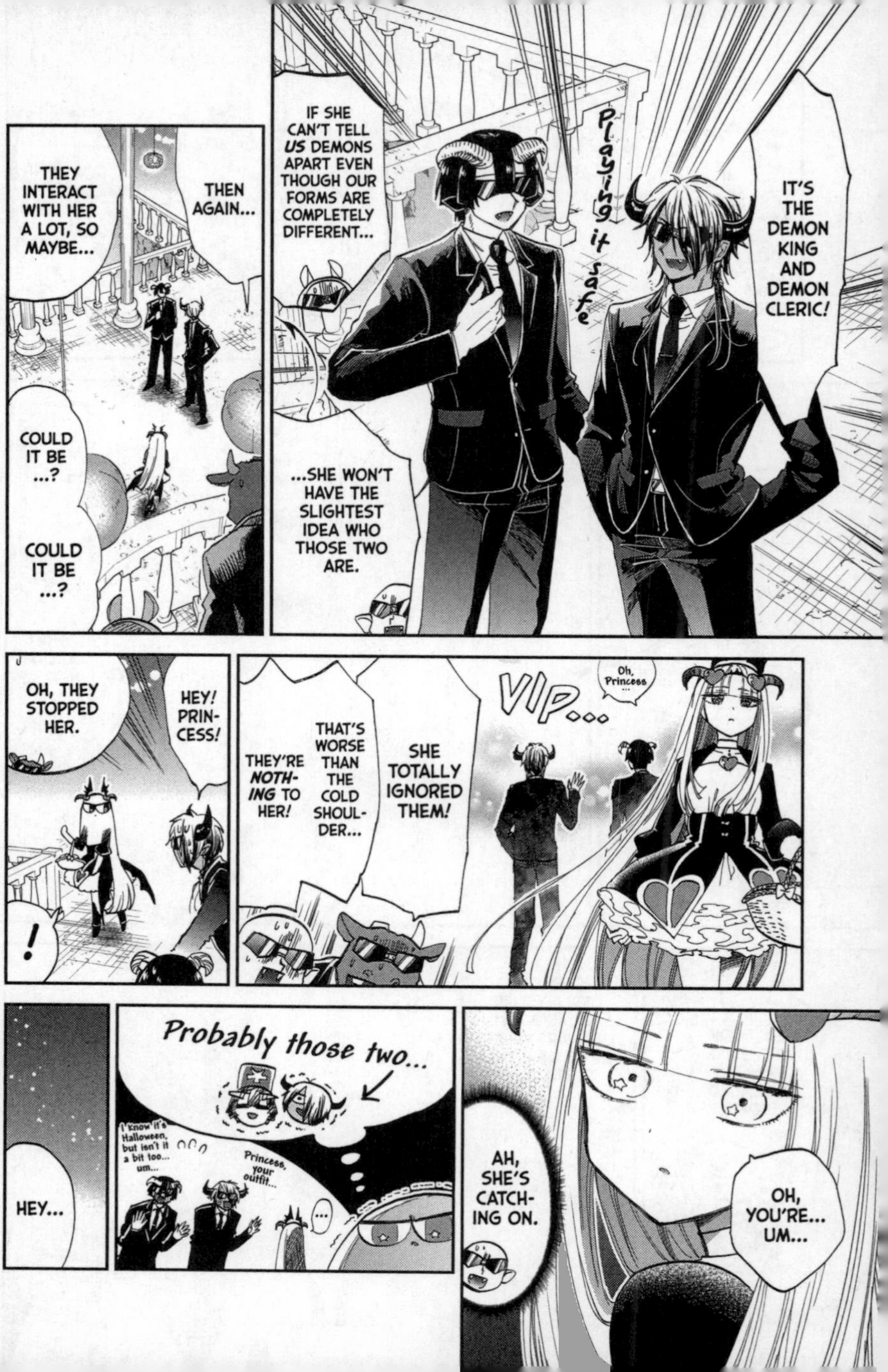
IT'S THE DEMON KING AND DEMON CLERIC!
Playing it safe
IF SHE CAN'T TELL *US* DEMONS APART EVEN THOUGH OUR FORMS ARE COMPLETELY DIFFERENT...
...SHE WON'T HAVE THE SLIGHTEST IDEA WHO THOSE TWO ARE.
THEN AGAIN...
THEY INTERACT WITH HER A LOT, SO MAYBE...
COULD IT BE ...?
COULD IT BE ...?
Oh, Princess ...
VIP...
SHE TOTALLY IGNORED THEM!
THAT'S WORSE THAN THE COLD SHOULDER...
THEY'RE *NOTHING* TO HER!
HEY! PRINCESS!
OH, THEY STOPPED HER.
!
OH, YOU'RE... UM...
AH, SHE'S CATCHING ON.
Probably those two...
Princess, your outfit...
I know it's Halloween, but isn't it a bit too... um...
...
HEY...

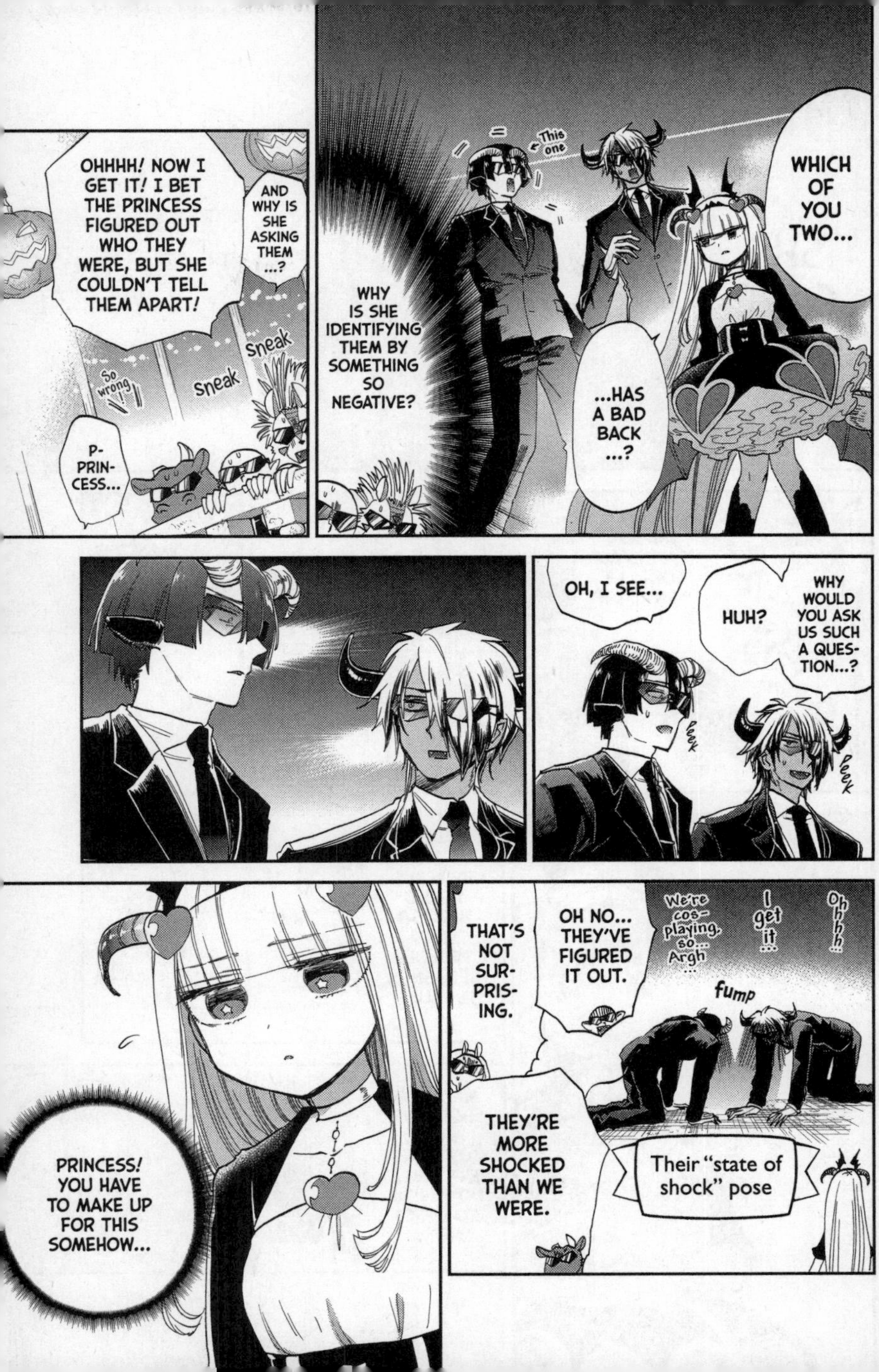
WHICH OF YOU TWO...
This one
...HAS A BAD BACK...?
WHY IS SHE IDENTIFYING THEM BY SOMETHING SO NEGATIVE?
AND WHY IS SHE ASKING THEM...?
OHHHH! NOW I GET IT! I BET THE PRINCESS FIGURED OUT WHO THEY WERE, BUT SHE COULDN'T TELL THEM APART!
Sneak
Sneak
So wrong
P-PRINCESS...
WHY WOULD YOU ASK US SUCH A QUESTION...?
HUH?
OH, I SEE...
Peek
Peek
Ohhhh...
I get it...
We're cos-playing, so... Argh...
OH NO... THEY'VE FIGURED IT OUT.
THAT'S NOT SURPRISING.
fump
Their "state of shock" pose
THEY'RE MORE SHOCKED THAN WE WERE.
PRINCESS! YOU HAVE TO MAKE UP FOR THIS SOMEHOW...

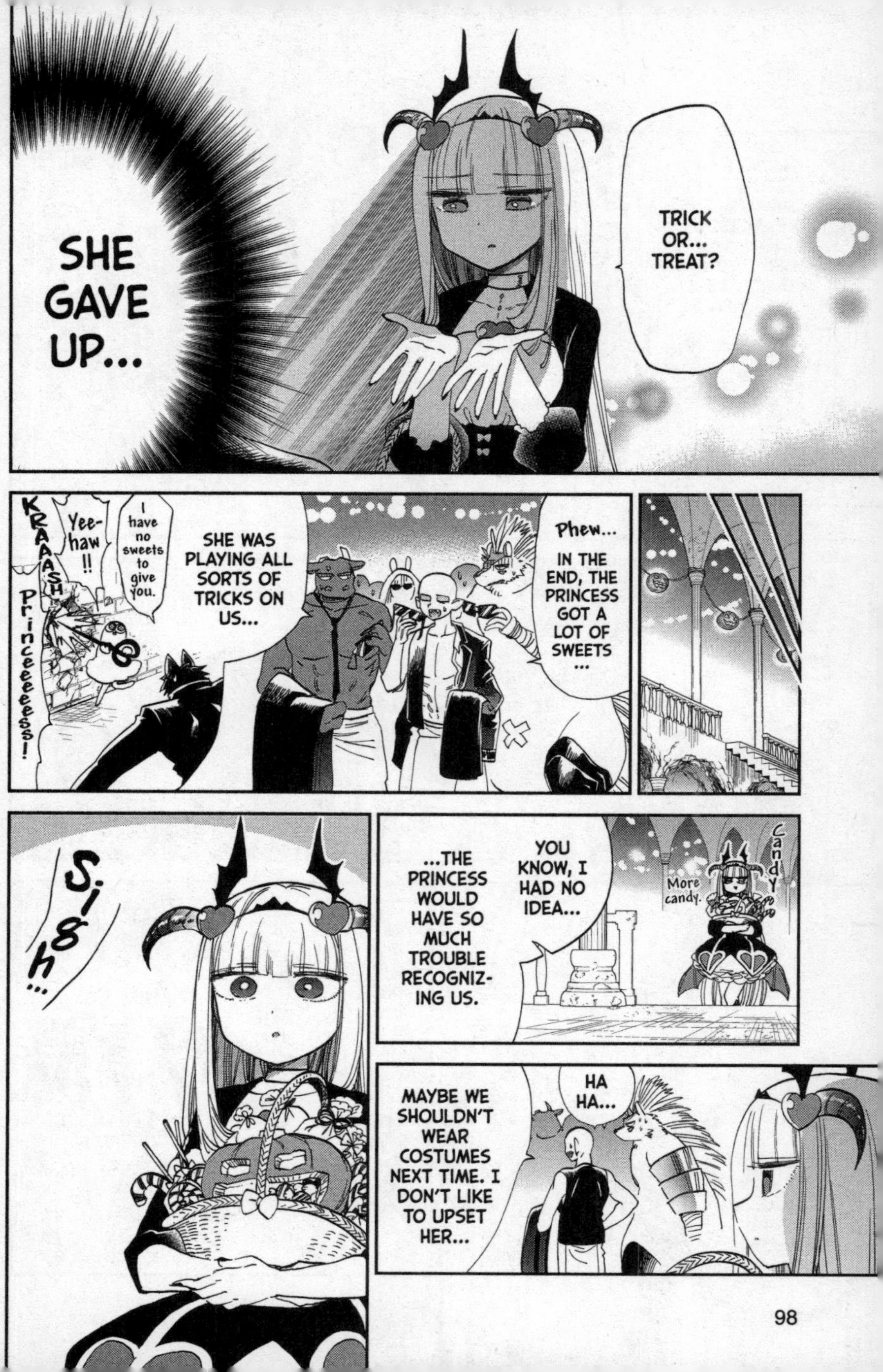
TRICK OR... TREAT?
SHE GAVE UP...
Phew...
IN THE END, THE PRINCESS GOT A LOT OF SWEETS ...
SHE WAS PLAYING ALL SORTS OF TRICKS ON US...
I have no sweets to give you.
Yee-haw !!
KRAAAASH
Princeeeeeess!
Candy
More candy.
YOU KNOW, I HAD NO IDEA...
...THE PRINCESS WOULD HAVE SO MUCH TROUBLE RECOGNIZ-ING US.
HA HA...
MAYBE WE SHOULDN'T WEAR COSTUMES NEXT TIME. I DON'T LIKE TO UPSET HER...
Sigh...

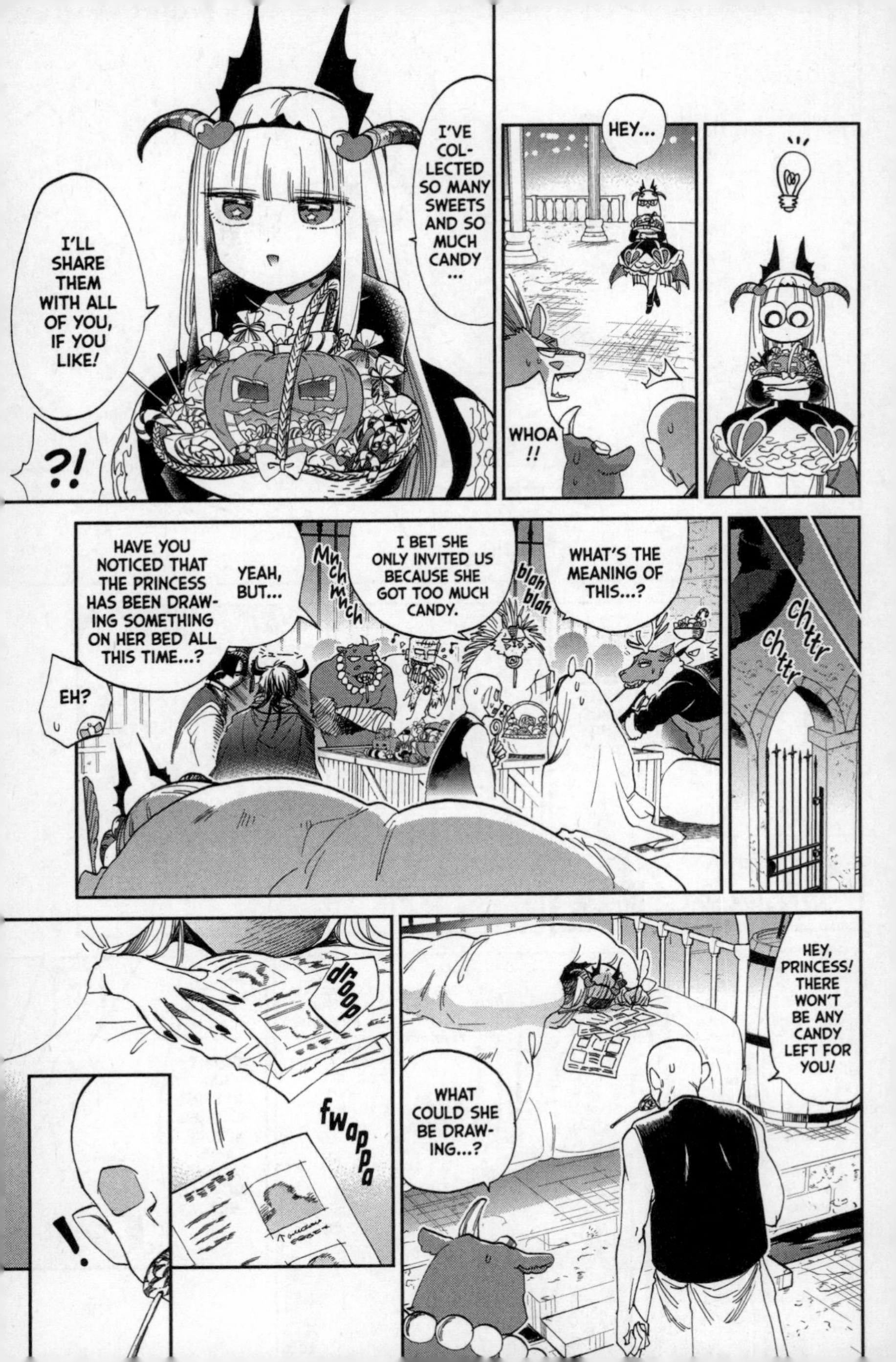
HEY...
WHOA!!
I'VE COLLECTED SO MANY SWEETS AND SO MUCH CANDY...
I'LL SHARE THEM WITH ALL OF YOU, IF YOU LIKE!
?!
chttr chttr
WHAT'S THE MEANING OF THIS...?
blah blah
I BET SHE ONLY INVITED US BECAUSE SHE GOT TOO MUCH CANDY.
Mnch mnch
YEAH, BUT...
HAVE YOU NOTICED THAT THE PRINCESS HAS BEEN DRAWING SOMETHING ON HER BED ALL THIS TIME...?
EH?
HEY, PRINCESS! THERE WON'T BE ANY CANDY LEFT FOR YOU!
WHAT COULD SHE BE DRAWING...?
droop
fwappa
!

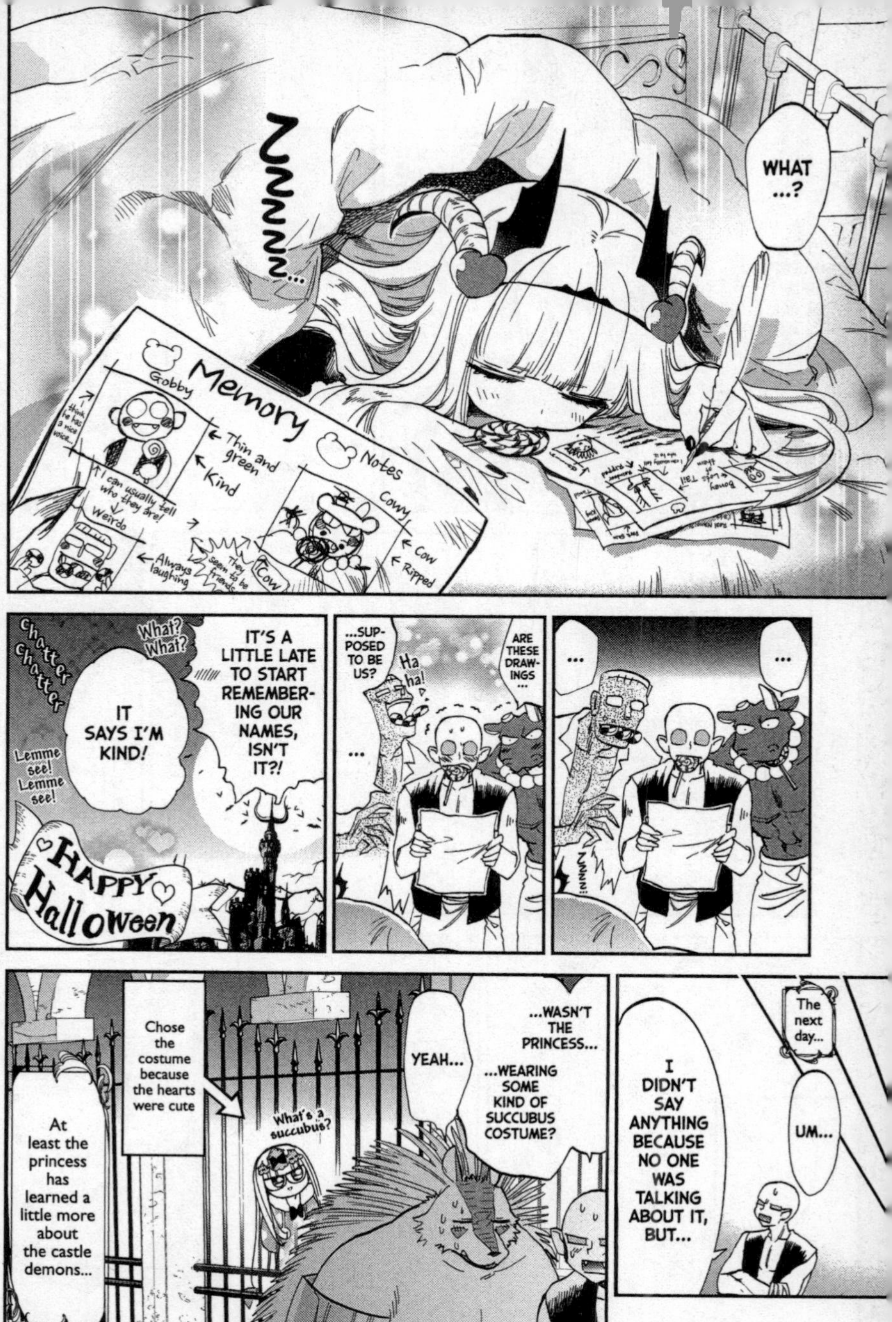

WHAT ...?
ZZZZZ...
Memory
Gobby
I think he has a nice voice...
Thin and green
Kind
I can usually tell who they are!
Weirdo
Always laughing
Notes
Cowy
Cow
Ripped
They seem to be friends
Cow
...
...
ARE THESE DRAWINGS ...
...SUPPOSED TO BE US?
Ha ha!
...
IT'S A LITTLE LATE TO START REMEMBERING OUR NAMES, ISN'T IT?!
What? What?
IT SAYS I'M KIND!
Chatter chatter
Lemme see! Lemme see!
HAPPY Halloween
The next day...
UM...
I DIDN'T SAY ANYTHING BECAUSE NO ONE WAS TALKING ABOUT IT, BUT...
...WASN'T THE PRINCESS...
...WEARING SOME KIND OF SUCCUBUS COSTUME?
YEAH...
What's a succubus?
Chose the costume because the hearts were cute
At least the princess has learned a little more about the castle demons...

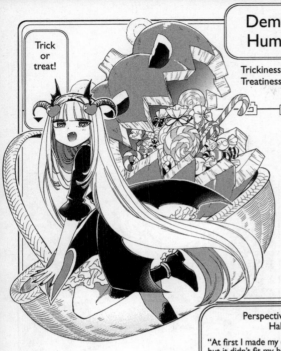

Demon Halloween
Human Halloween

Trick or treat!

Trickiness: ☆☆
Treatiness: ☆☆☆☆☆☆☆☆☆

This is the Halloween tradition practiced by demons: whereas humans dress as demons, demons dress up as humans and hand out candy.

Since the Demon Castle is populated by demons, Halloween is nothing more than a candy exchange party. It's based on a human tradition that got distorted when it reached the demon realm. It has become traditional for demons to wear black suits as costumes on Halloween in their best attempt to look human.

Perspectives from Demon Castle Halloween Revelers

"At first I made my costume exactly the same size, but it didn't fit my bust."

Ms. H, Demon Castle employee

"The costume I wore when I went to the human realm was the best I could do, so I'm not participating."

Mr. GRS, Demon Castle employee

I GOT SO MANY SWEETS! ♫
Milk Cookie
Yummy Sticks
Lollipop
...?! THIS IS... AMAZING!
SOMEONE GAVE ME A DELICIOUS-LOOKING CAKE!
WAIT... THIS IS PLASTIC!
Someone played a trick on the princess too.
Culprit
Ha ha ha ha ha!

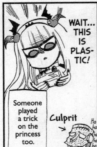

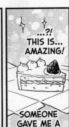

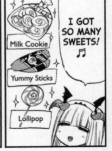

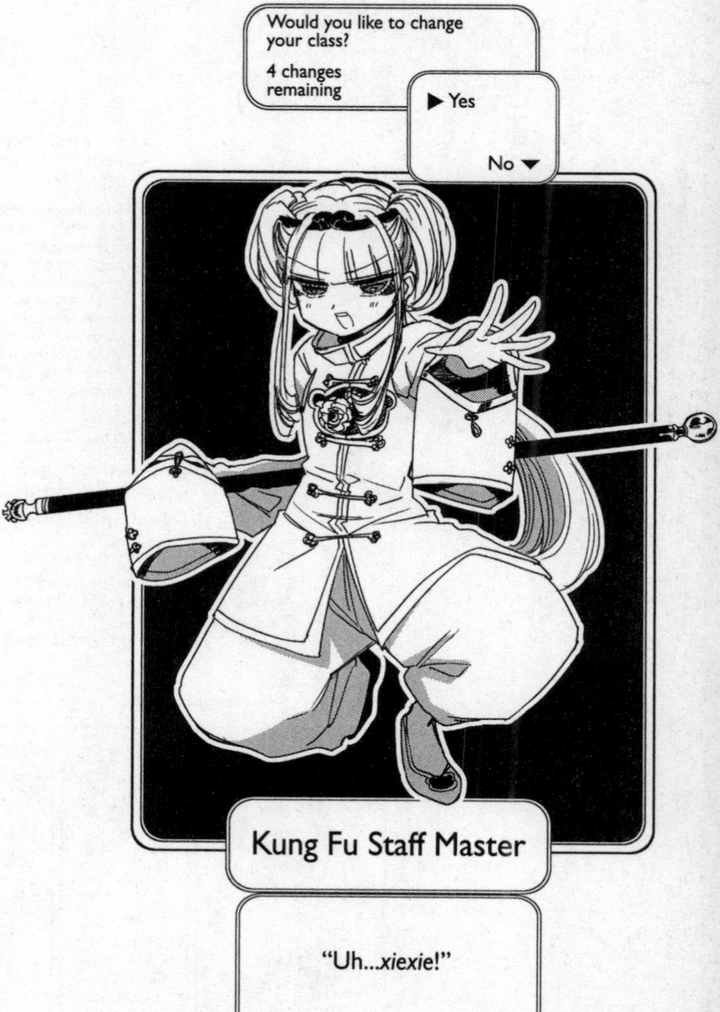
Would you like to change your class?
4 changes remaining
▶ Yes
No ▼
Kung Fu Staff Master
"Uh...*xiexie*!"

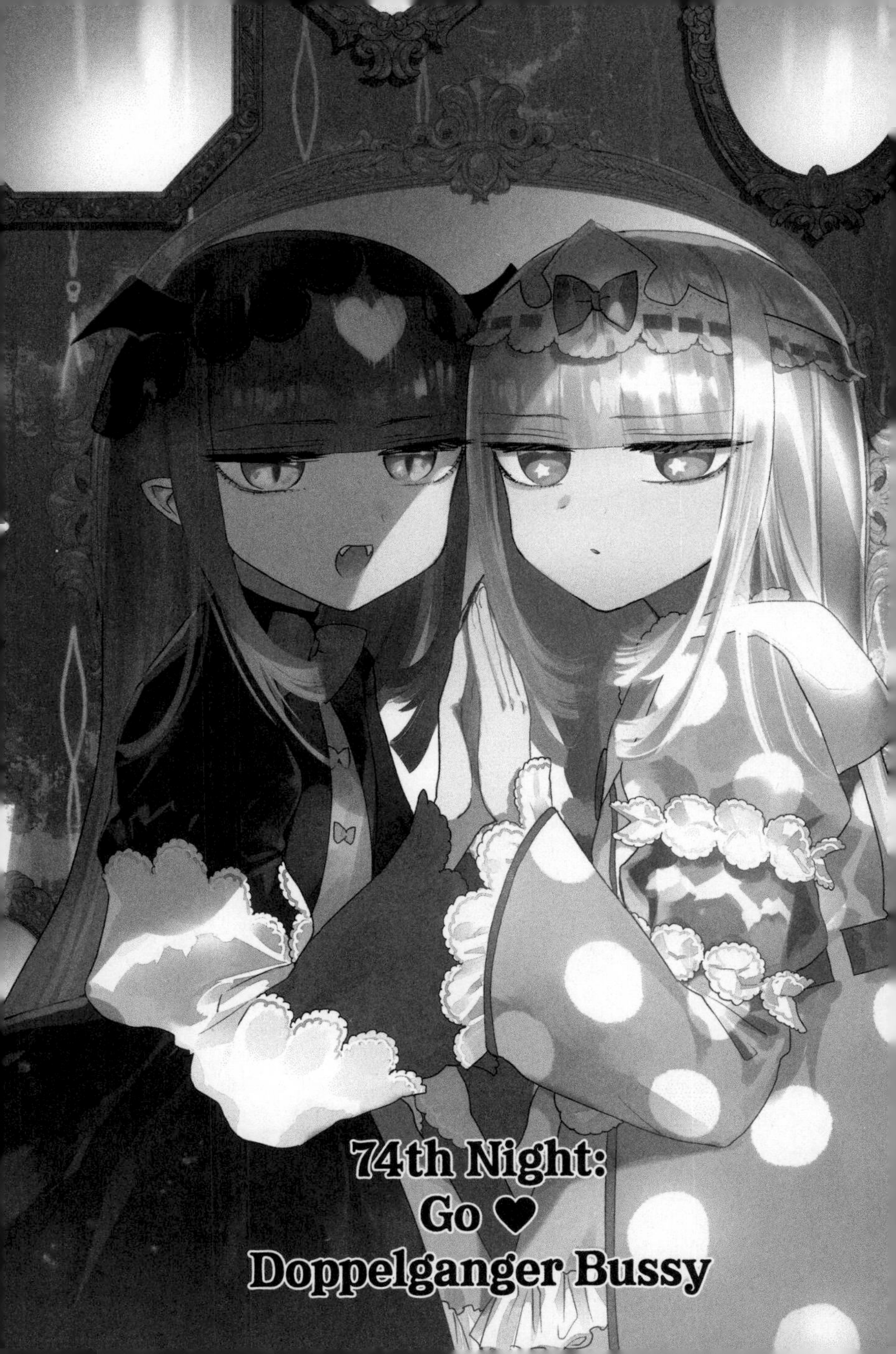
74th Night:
Go ♥
Doppelganger Bussy

SLEEPY PRINCESS
IN THE
DEMON CASTLE

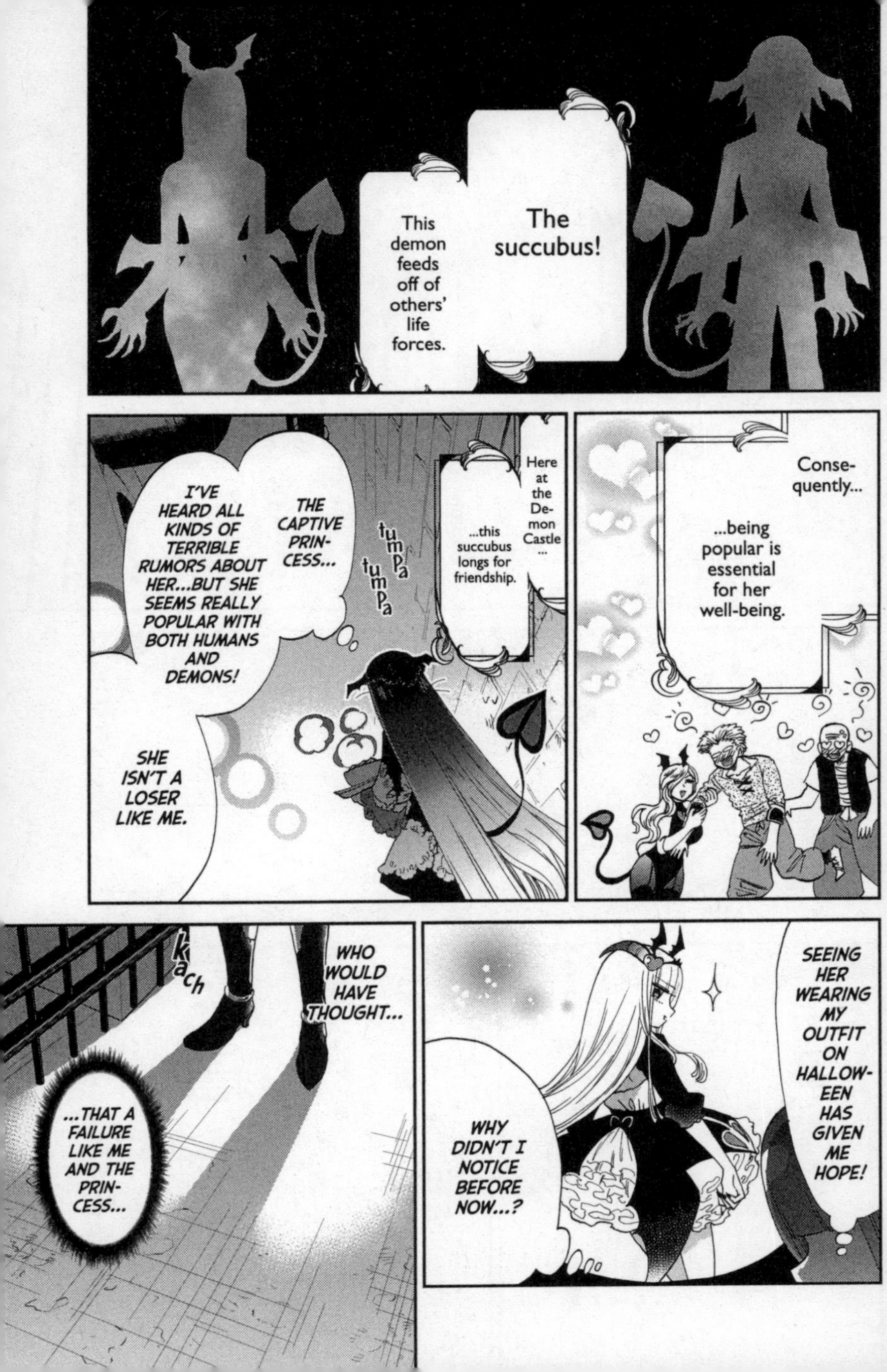
The succubus!
This demon feeds off of others' life forces.
Conse-quently...
...being popular is essential for her well-being.
Here at the De-mon Castle...
...this succubus longs for friendship.
tumpa tumpa
THE CAPTIVE PRIN-CESS...
I'VE HEARD ALL KINDS OF TERRIBLE RUMORS ABOUT HER...BUT SHE SEEMS REALLY POPULAR WITH BOTH HUMANS AND DEMONS!
SHE ISN'T A LOSER LIKE ME.
SEEING HER WEARING MY OUTFIT ON HALLOW-EEN HAS GIVEN ME HOPE!
WHY DIDN'T I NOTICE BEFORE NOW...?
kach
WHO WOULD HAVE THOUGHT...
...THAT A FAILURE LIKE ME AND THE PRIN-CESS...

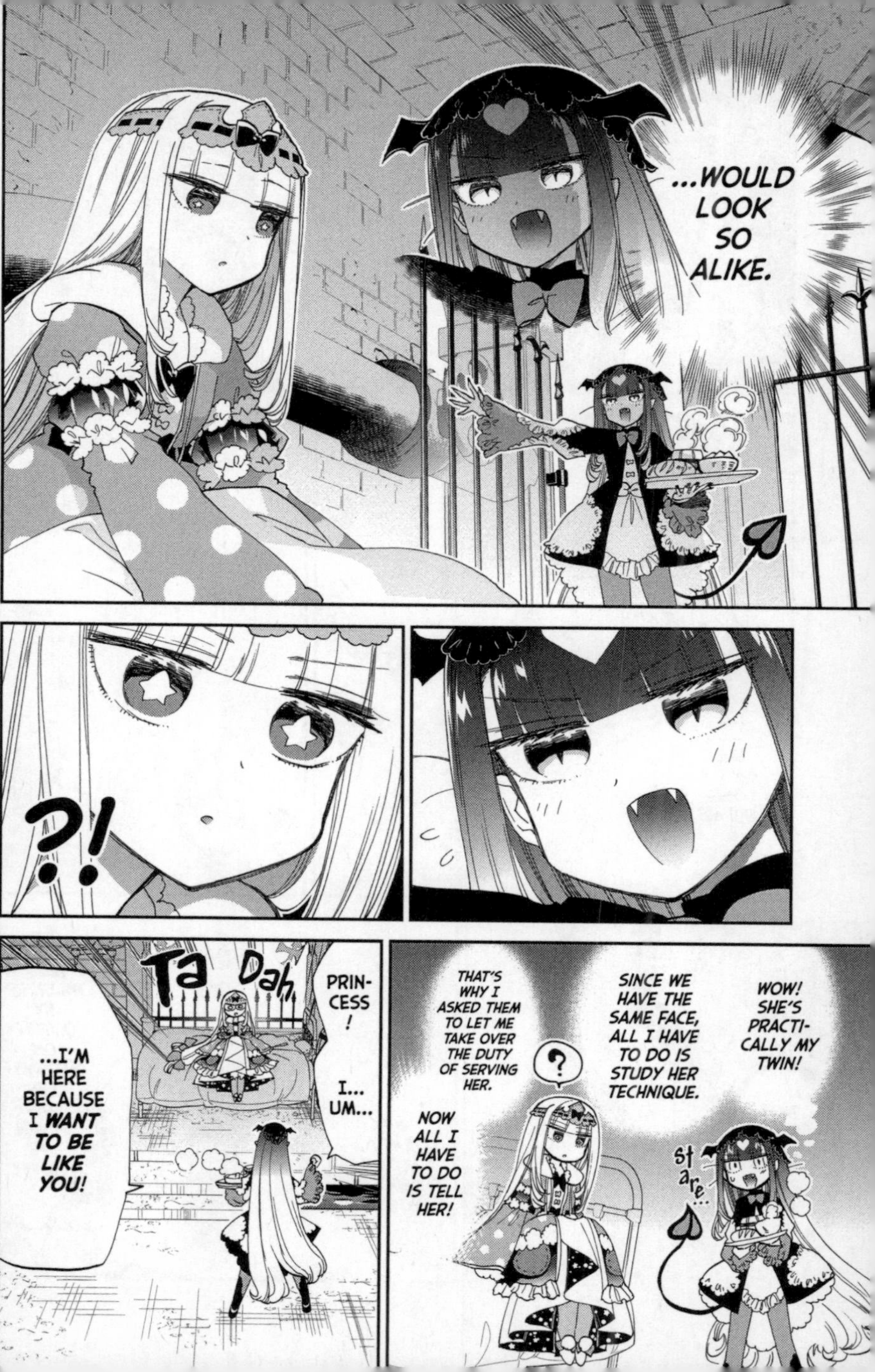
...WOULD LOOK SO ALIKE.
?!
WOW! SHE'S PRACTI-CALLY MY TWIN!
SINCE WE HAVE THE SAME FACE, ALL I HAVE TO DO IS STUDY HER TECHNIQUE.
THAT'S WHY I ASKED THEM TO LET ME TAKE OVER THE DUTY OF SERVING HER.
?
stare...
NOW ALL I HAVE TO DO IS TELL HER!
Ta Dah
PRIN-CESS!
I... UM...
...I'M HERE BECAUSE I *WANT* TO BE LIKE YOU!

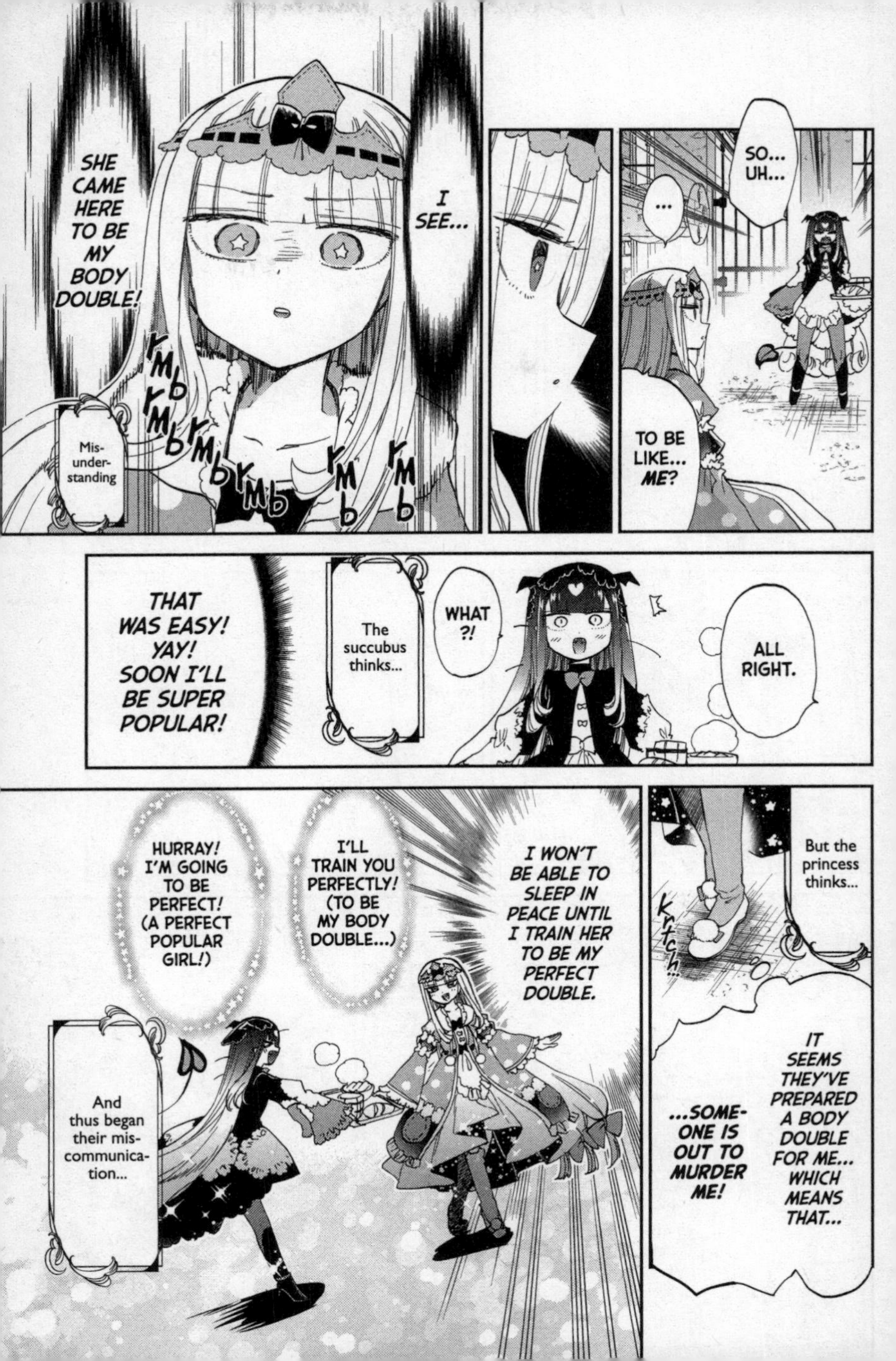
SO... UH...
...
TO BE LIKE... ME?
I SEE...
SHE CAME HERE TO BE MY BODY DOUBLE!
rmb rmb rmb rmb rmb rmb
Misunderstanding
ALL RIGHT.
WHAT?!
The succubus thinks...
THAT WAS EASY! YAY! SOON I'LL BE SUPER POPULAR!
But the princess thinks...
Krtch...
IT SEEMS THEY'VE PREPARED A BODY DOUBLE FOR ME... WHICH MEANS THAT...
...SOMEONE IS OUT TO MURDER ME!
I WON'T BE ABLE TO SLEEP IN PEACE UNTIL I TRAIN HER TO BE MY PERFECT DOUBLE.
I'LL TRAIN YOU PERFECTLY! (TO BE MY BODY DOUBLE...)
HURRAY! I'M GOING TO BE PERFECT! (A PERFECT POPULAR GIRL!)
And thus began their miscommunication...

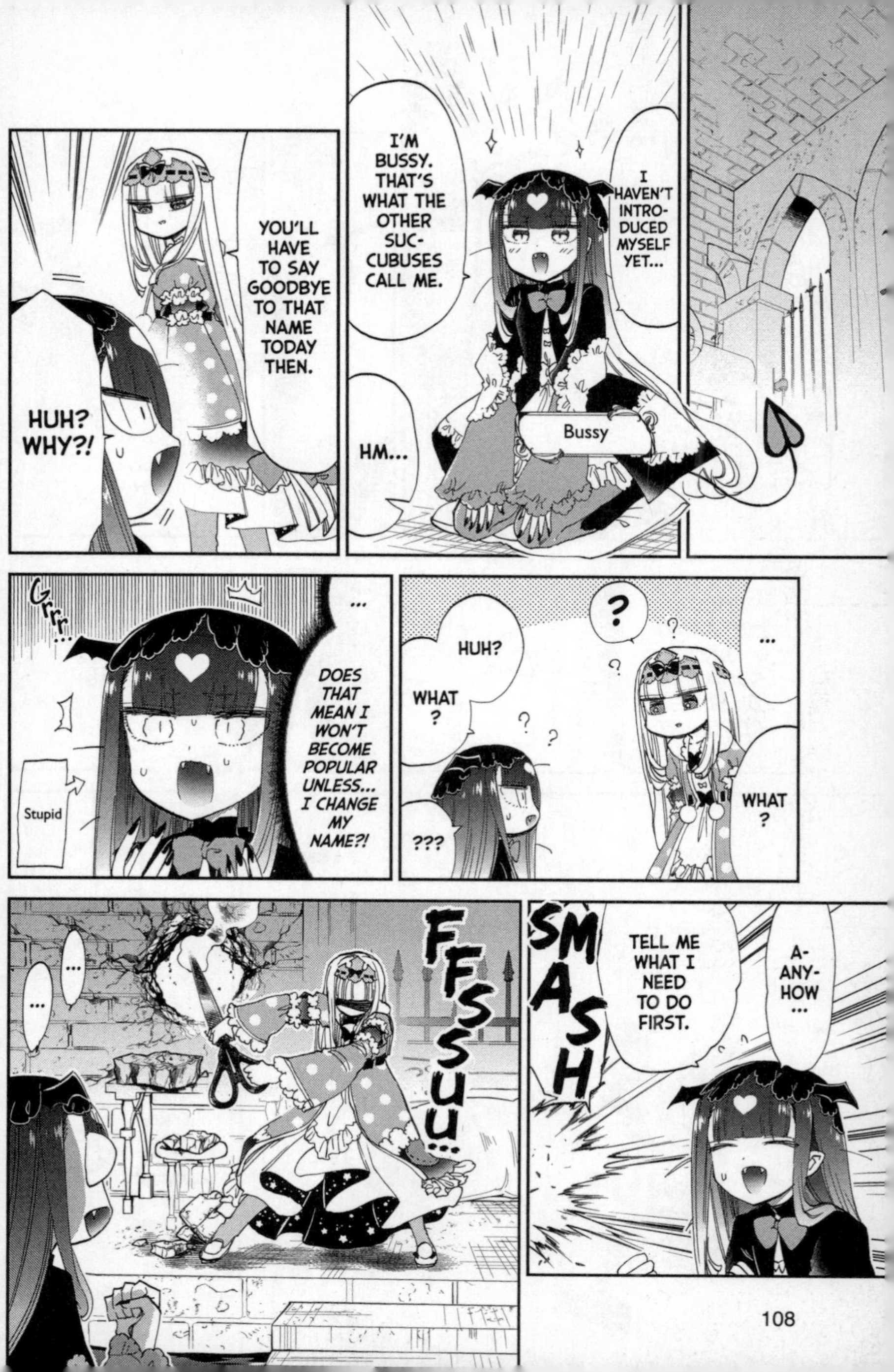
I HAVEN'T INTRODUCED MYSELF YET...
I'M BUSSY. THAT'S WHAT THE OTHER SUCCUBUSES CALL ME.
Bussy
HM...
YOU'LL HAVE TO SAY GOODBYE TO THAT NAME TODAY THEN.
HUH? WHY?!
...
?
HUH?
WHAT?
WHAT?
???
...
DOES THAT MEAN I WON'T BECOME POPULAR UNLESS... I CHANGE MY NAME?!
Grrr...
Stupid
A-ANYHOW...
TELL ME WHAT I NEED TO DO FIRST.
SMASH
FFSSUU...
...
...

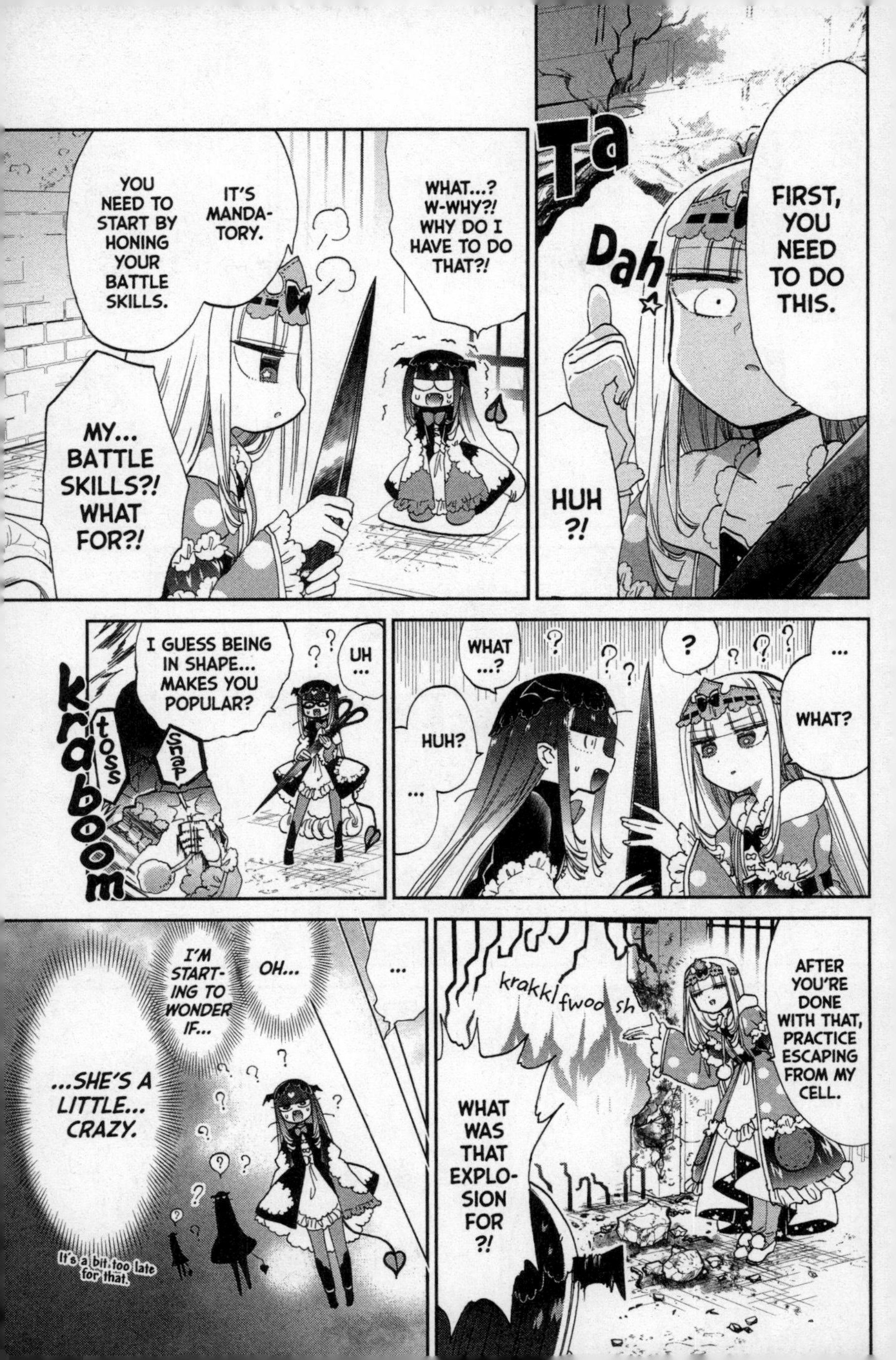
FIRST, YOU NEED TO DO THIS.
Ta Dah
HUH ?!
WHAT...? W-WHY?! WHY DO I HAVE TO DO THAT?!
IT'S MANDATORY.
YOU NEED TO START BY HONING YOUR BATTLE SKILLS.
MY... BATTLE SKILLS?! WHAT FOR?!
...
WHAT?
?
WHAT ...?
HUH?
...
UH ...
I GUESS BEING IN SHAPE... MAKES YOU POPULAR?
Snap
toss
kraboom
AFTER YOU'RE DONE WITH THAT, PRACTICE ESCAPING FROM MY CELL.
krakkl fwoosh
WHAT WAS THAT EXPLOSION FOR ?!
...
OH...
I'M STARTING TO WONDER IF...
...SHE'S A LITTLE... CRAZY.
It's a bit too late for that.

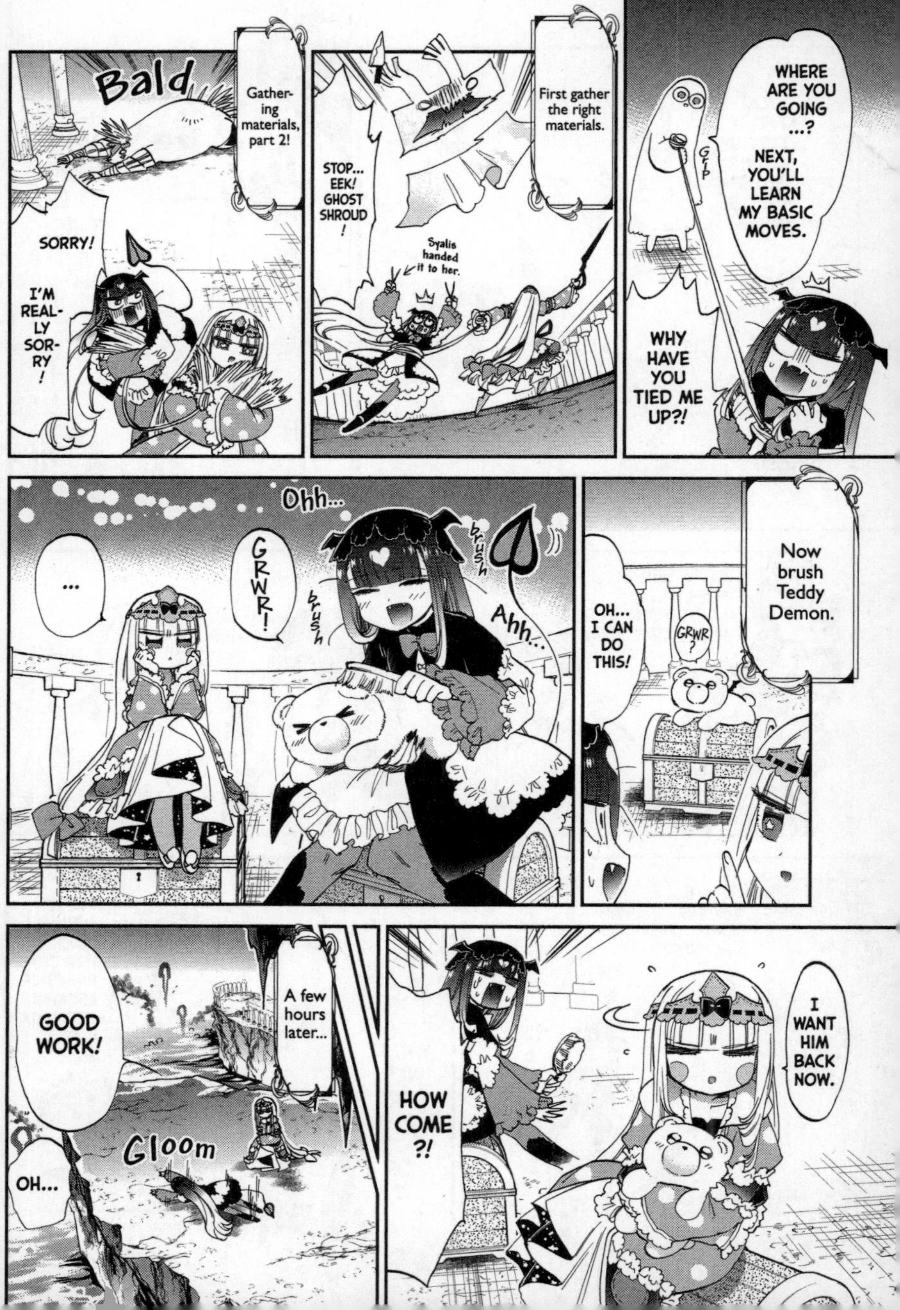
WHERE ARE YOU GOING ...?
NEXT, YOU'LL LEARN MY BASIC MOVES.
GRIP
WHY HAVE YOU TIED ME UP?!
First gather the right materials.
STOP... EEK! GHOST SHROUD!
Syalis handed it to her.
Gathering materials, part 2!
Bald
SORRY!
I'M REALLY SORRY!
Now brush Teddy Demon.
GRWR?
OH... I CAN DO THIS!
Ohh...
brush
GRWR!
brush
Ahh...
...
I WANT HIM BACK NOW.
HOW COME?!
A few hours later...
GOOD WORK!
Gloom
OH...

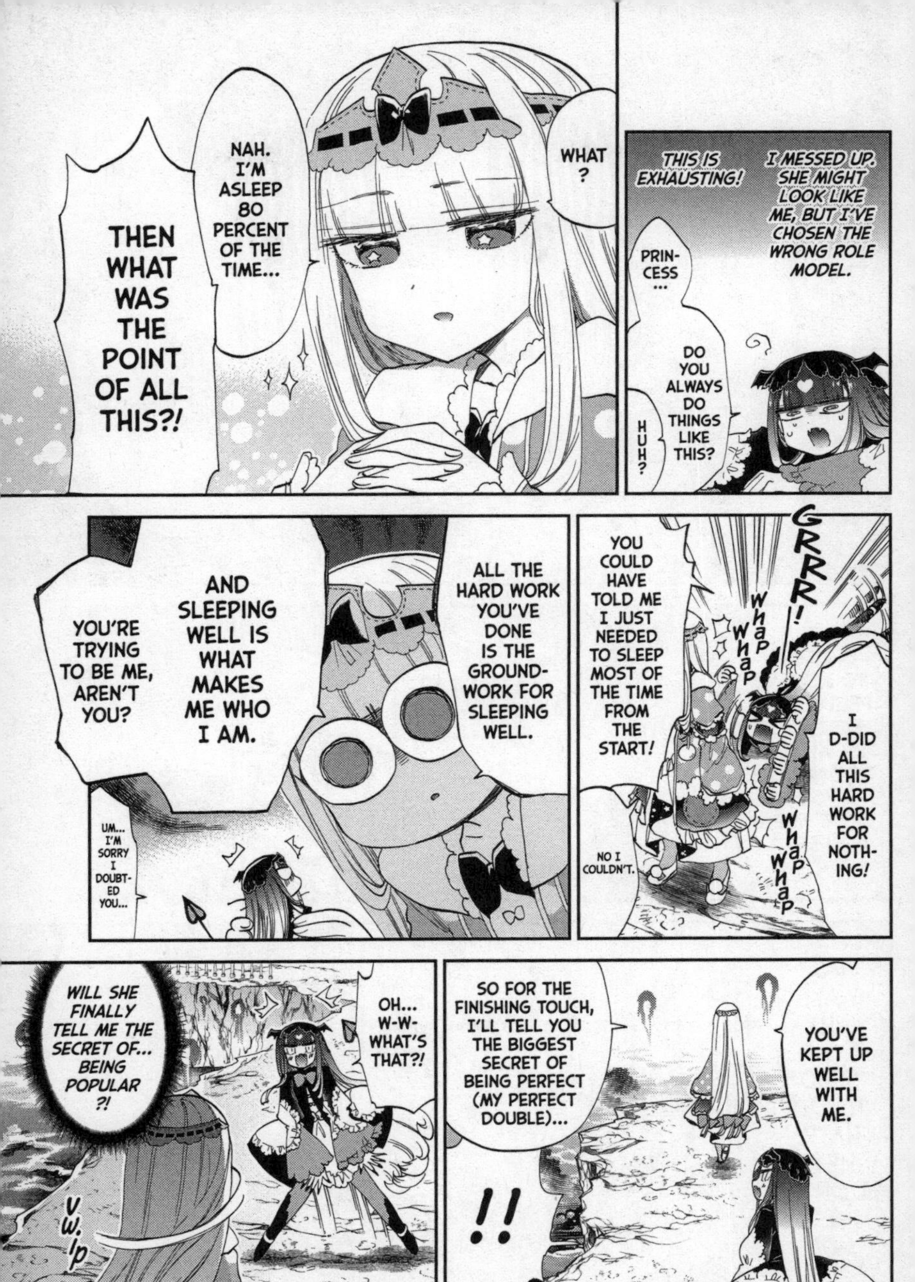
I MESSED UP. SHE MIGHT LOOK LIKE ME, BUT I'VE CHOSEN THE WRONG ROLE MODEL.
THIS IS EXHAUSTING!
PRINCESS...
DO YOU ALWAYS DO THINGS LIKE THIS?
HUH?
WHAT?
NAH. I'M ASLEEP 80 PERCENT OF THE TIME...
THEN WHAT WAS THE POINT OF ALL THIS?!
GRRR!
YOU COULD HAVE TOLD ME I JUST NEEDED TO SLEEP MOST OF THE TIME FROM THE START!
whap whap whap
I D-DID ALL THIS HARD WORK FOR NOTHING!
whap whap whap
NO I COULDN'T.
ALL THE HARD WORK YOU'VE DONE IS THE GROUND-WORK FOR SLEEPING WELL.
AND SLEEPING WELL IS WHAT MAKES ME WHO I AM.
YOU'RE TRYING TO BE ME, AREN'T YOU?
UM... I'M SORRY I DOUBTED YOU...
YOU'VE KEPT UP WELL WITH ME.
SO FOR THE FINISHING TOUCH, I'LL TELL YOU THE BIGGEST SECRET OF BEING PERFECT (MY PERFECT DOUBLE)...
!!
OH... W-W-WHAT'S THAT?!
WILL SHE FINALLY TELL ME THE SECRET OF... BEING POPULAR?!
vwip

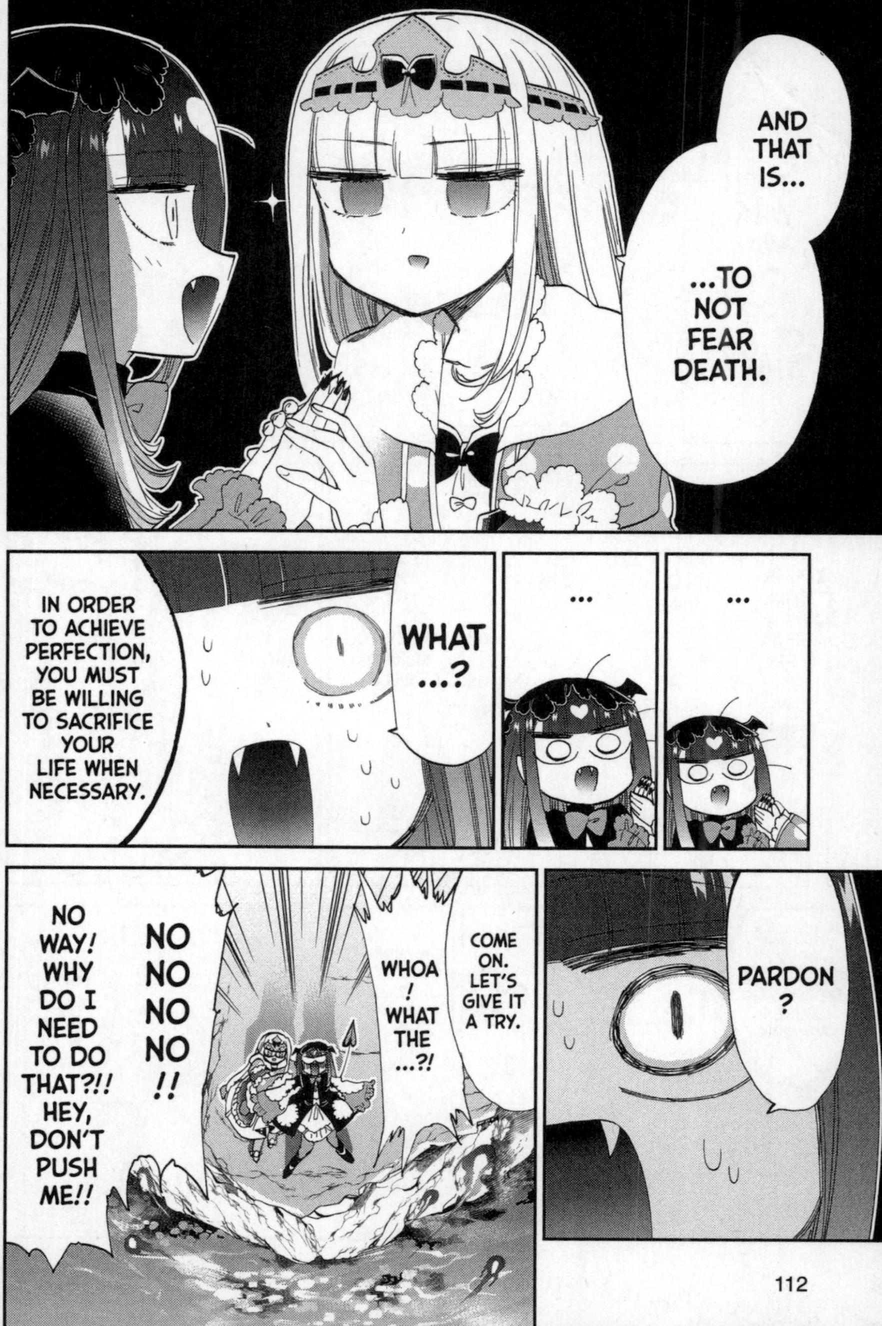
AND THAT IS...
...TO NOT FEAR DEATH.
...
...
WHAT ...?
IN ORDER TO ACHIEVE PERFECTION, YOU MUST BE WILLING TO SACRIFICE YOUR LIFE WHEN NECESSARY.
PARDON?
COME ON. LET'S GIVE IT A TRY.
WHOA! WHAT THE ...?!
NO NO NO NO!!
NO WAY! WHY DO I NEED TO DO THAT?!! HEY, DON'T PUSH ME!!

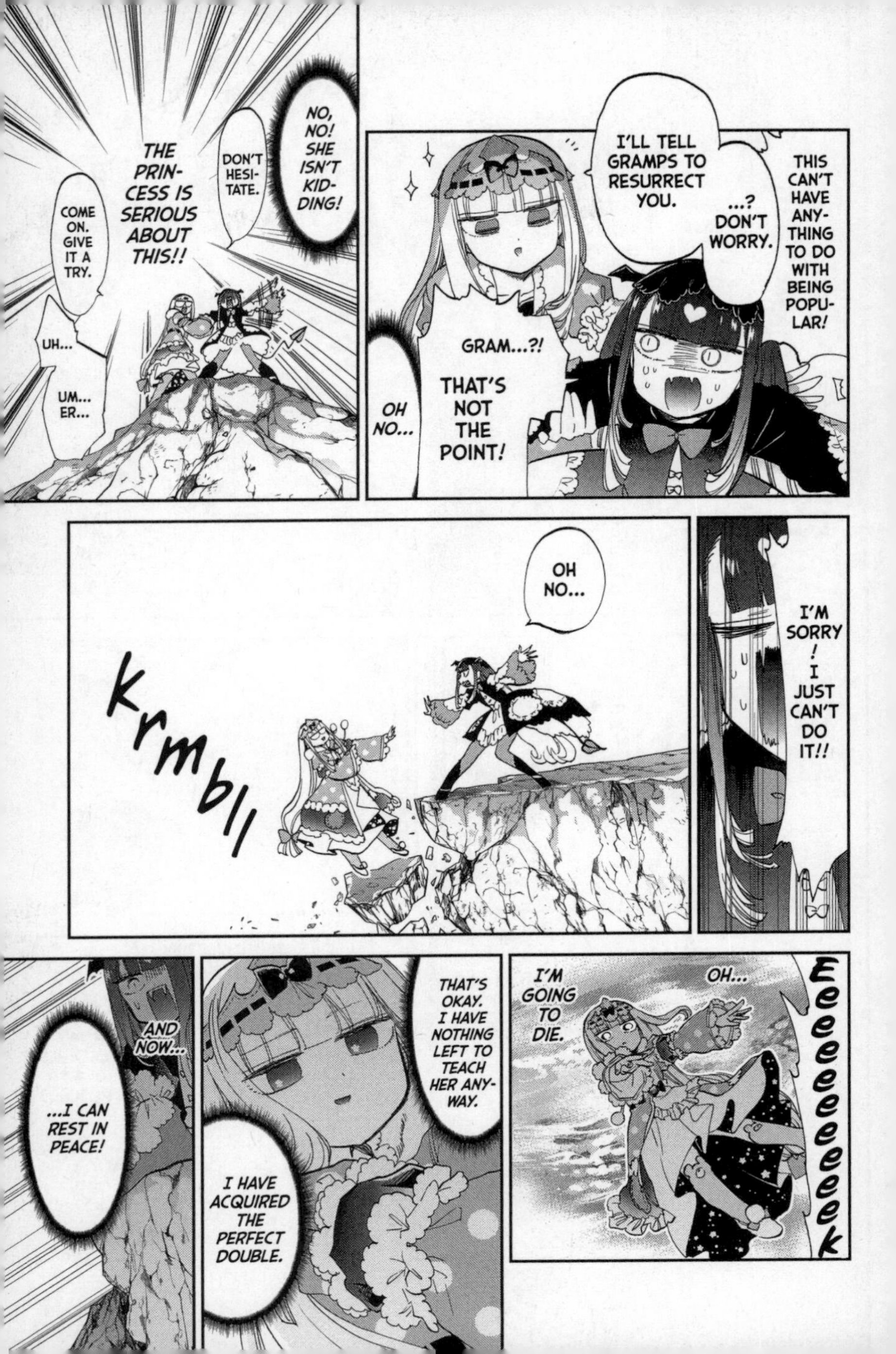
I'LL TELL GRAMPS TO RESURRECT YOU.
...? DON'T WORRY.
THIS CAN'T HAVE ANYTHING TO DO WITH BEING POPULAR!
GRAM...?!
THAT'S NOT THE POINT!
OH NO...
NO, NO! SHE ISN'T KIDDING!
DON'T HESITATE.
THE PRINCESS IS SERIOUS ABOUT THIS!!
COME ON. GIVE IT A TRY.
UH...
UM... ER...
I'M SORRY! I JUST CAN'T DO IT!!
OH NO...
krmbll
Eeeeeeeeeeek
OH...
I'M GOING TO DIE.
THAT'S OKAY. I HAVE NOTHING LEFT TO TEACH HER ANYWAY.
I HAVE ACQUIRED THE PERFECT DOUBLE.
AND NOW...
...I CAN REST IN PEACE!

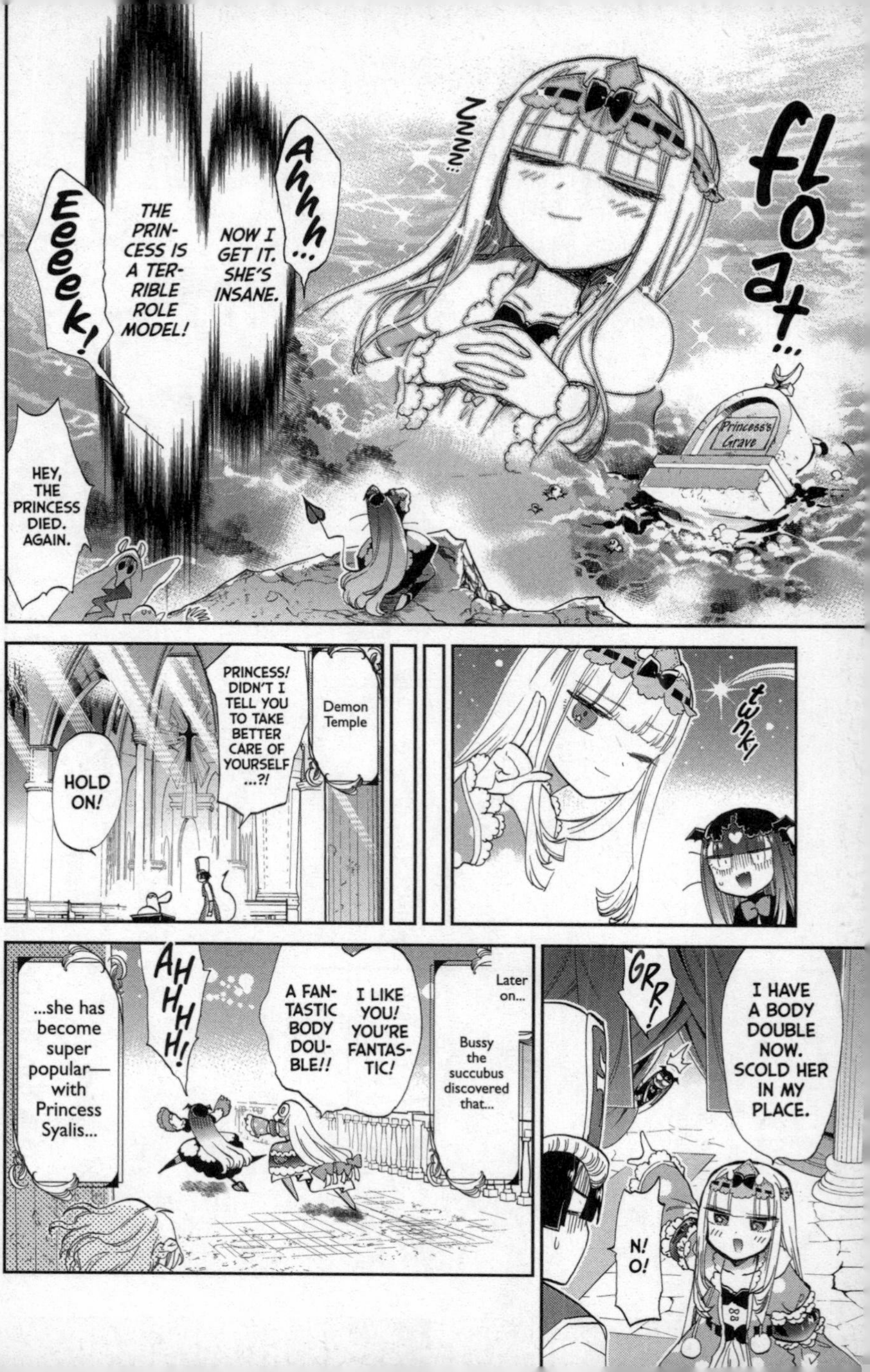
float...
Princess's Grave
Ahhh...
NOW I GET IT. SHE'S INSANE.
THE PRINCESS IS A TERRIBLE ROLE MODEL!
Eeeek!
HEY, THE PRINCESS DIED. AGAIN.
twnk!
Demon Temple
PRINCESS! DIDN'T I TELL YOU TO TAKE BETTER CARE OF YOURSELF...?!
HOLD ON!
GRR!
I HAVE A BODY DOUBLE NOW. SCOLD HER IN MY PLACE.
N! O!
Later on...
Bussy the succubus discovered that...
I LIKE YOU! YOU'RE FANTASTIC!
A FANTASTIC BODY DOUBLE!!
AHHHH!
...she has become super popular—with Princess Syalis...

Grrr!

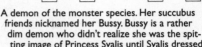

Bussy

Charisma: ☆
Seductiveness: ☆

A demon of the monster species. Her succubus friends nicknamed her Bussy. Bussy is a rather dim demon who didn't realize she was the spitting image of Princess Syalis until Syalis dressed in a succubus costume. Then again, the other demons also said, "Does she look like the princess? Nah... It must just be my imagination." This is due to the vast difference in their presence. In terms of the type of demon Bussy is, one could say she is loosely related to Hypnos. But the only thing they have in common is that the princess likes them both.

Bussy's favorite snack is the crispy edge of *fugashi* wheat-gluten crackers.

Former problem:
"I'm not popular!"

Current problem:
"Shoot! I've been forced to be a body double, and I'm still not popular!"

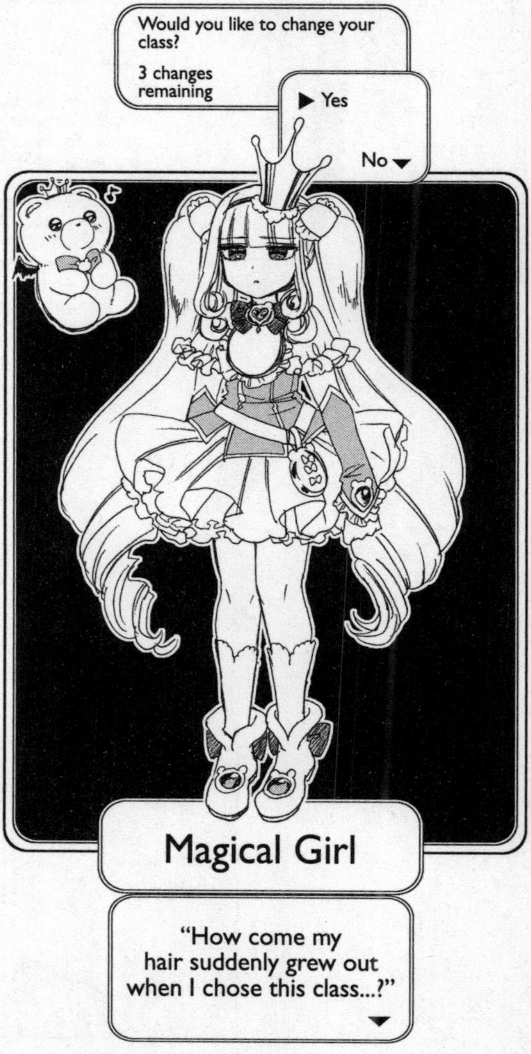
Would you like to change your class?
3 changes remaining
▶ Yes
No
Magical Girl
"How come my hair suddenly grew out when I chose this class...?"

75th Night: For That Worthless Victory

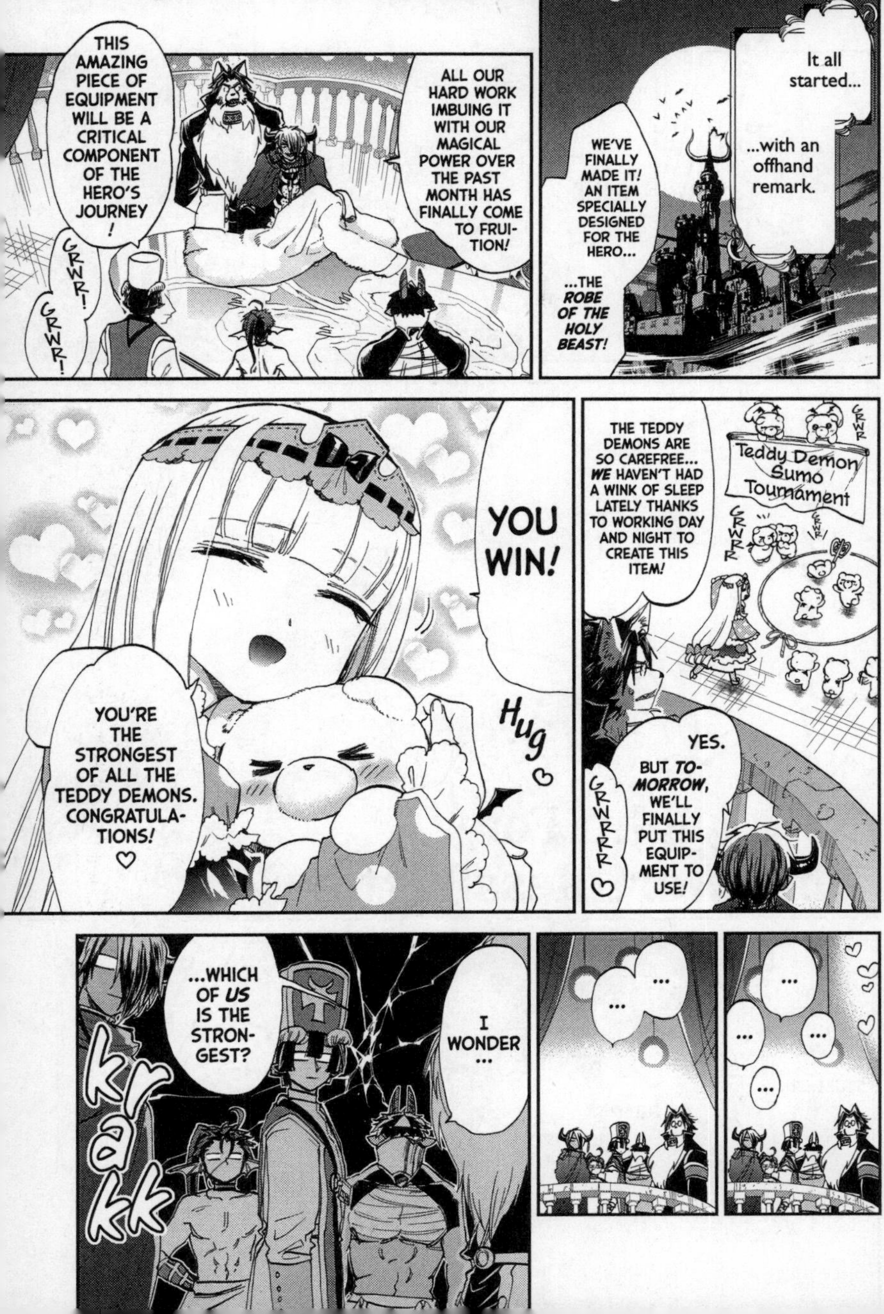
It all started...
...with an offhand remark.
WE'VE FINALLY MADE IT! AN ITEM SPECIALLY DESIGNED FOR THE HERO...
...THE *ROBE OF THE HOLY BEAST!*
ALL OUR HARD WORK IMBUING IT WITH OUR MAGICAL POWER OVER THE PAST MONTH HAS FINALLY COME TO FRUITION!
THIS AMAZING PIECE OF EQUIPMENT WILL BE A CRITICAL COMPONENT OF THE HERO'S JOURNEY!
GRWR! GRWR!
THE TEDDY DEMONS ARE SO CAREFREE... *WE* HAVEN'T HAD A WINK OF SLEEP LATELY THANKS TO WORKING DAY AND NIGHT TO CREATE THIS ITEM!
GRWR
Teddy Demon Sumo Tournament
GRWRR
YES. BUT *TOMORROW*, WE'LL FINALLY PUT THIS EQUIPMENT TO USE!
GRWRRR ♡
YOU WIN!
Hug ♡
YOU'RE THE STRONGEST OF ALL THE TEDDY DEMONS. CONGRATULATIONS! ♡
...
...
...
...
...
...
...
I WONDER...
...WHICH OF *US* IS THE STRONGEST?
krakk

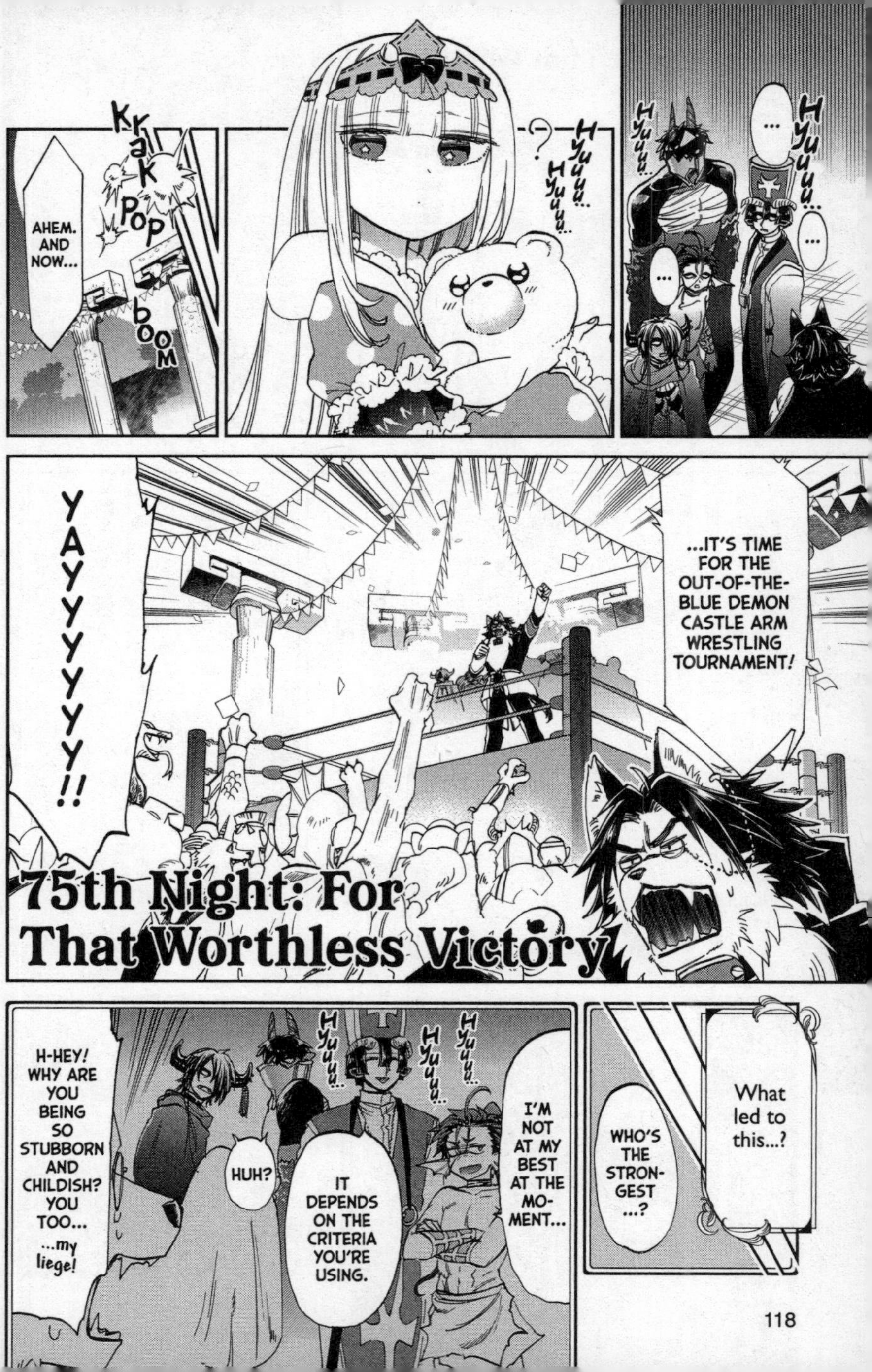
Hyuuu...
...
...
...
Hyuuu...
?
Hyuuu...
Hyuuu...
Krak
Pop
boom
AHEM. AND NOW...
...IT'S TIME FOR THE OUT-OF-THE-BLUE DEMON CASTLE ARM WRESTLING TOURNAMENT!
YAYYYYYYYY!!
75th Night: For That Worthless Victory
What led to this...?
WHO'S THE STRONGEST...?
I'M NOT AT MY BEST AT THE MOMENT...
Hyuuu...
Hyuuu...
Hyuuu...
IT DEPENDS ON THE CRITERIA YOU'RE USING.
HUH?
H-HEY! WHY ARE YOU BEING SO STUBBORN AND CHILDISH? YOU TOO...
...my liege!

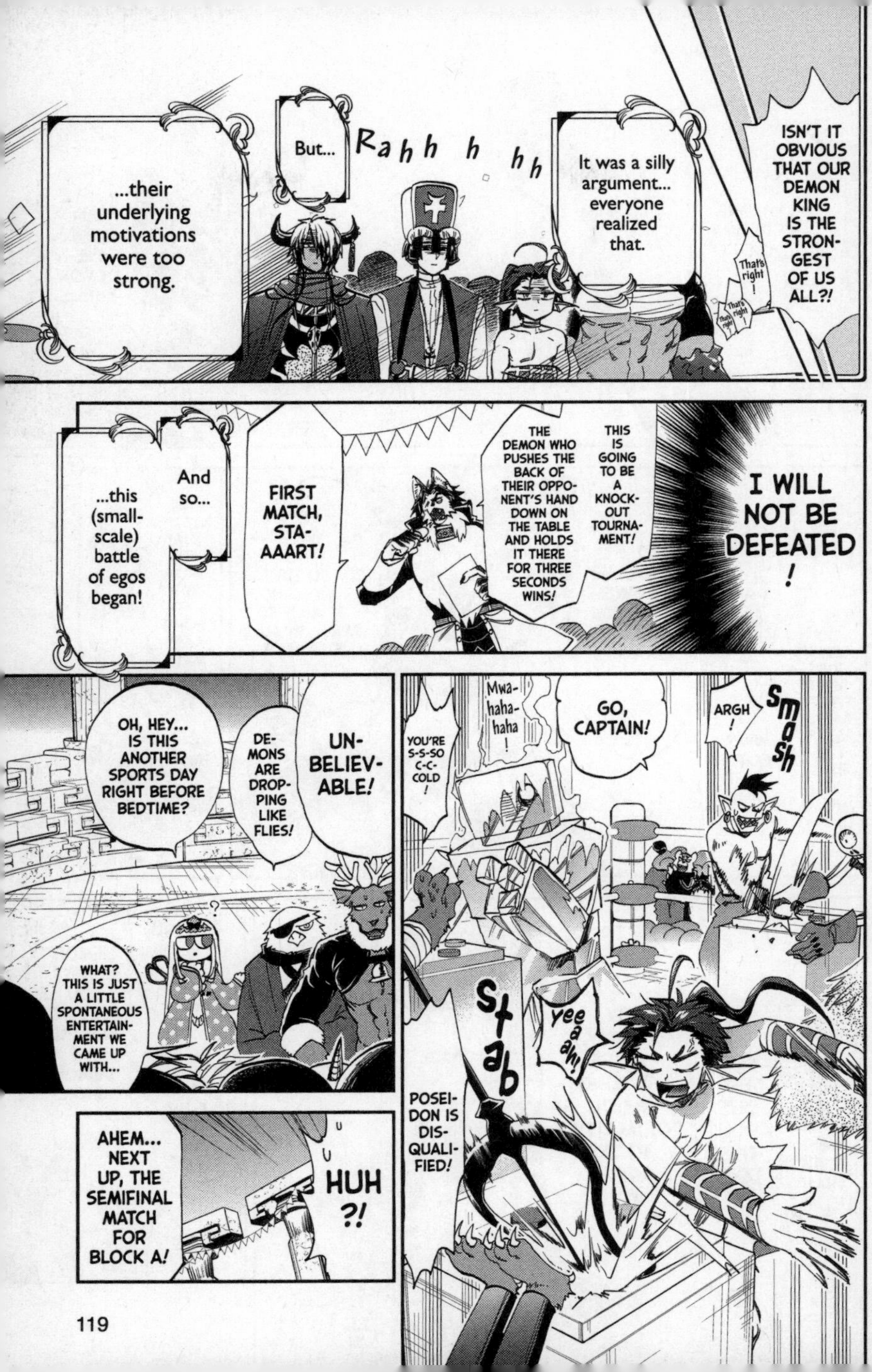
ISN'T IT OBVIOUS THAT OUR DEMON KING IS THE STRONGEST OF US ALL?!
That's right!
That's right!
That's right!
It was a silly argument... everyone realized that.
Rahhhhh
But...
...their underlying motivations were too strong.
I WILL NOT BE DEFEATED!
THIS IS GOING TO BE A KNOCKOUT TOURNAMENT!
THE DEMON WHO PUSHES THE BACK OF THEIR OPPONENT'S HAND DOWN ON THE TABLE AND HOLDS IT THERE FOR THREE SECONDS WINS!
FIRST MATCH, STA-AAART!
And so...
...this (small-scale) battle of egos began!
Smash
ARGH!
GO, CAPTAIN!
Mwahahahaha!
YOU'RE S-S-SO C-C-COLD!
yeeaah!
Stab
POSEIDON IS DISQUALIFIED!
UNBELIEVABLE!
DEMONS ARE DROPPING LIKE FLIES!
OH, HEY... IS THIS ANOTHER SPORTS DAY RIGHT BEFORE BEDTIME?
WHAT? THIS IS JUST A LITTLE SPONTANEOUS ENTERTAINMENT WE CAME UP WITH...
HUH?!
AHEM... NEXT UP, THE SEMIFINAL MATCH FOR BLOCK A!

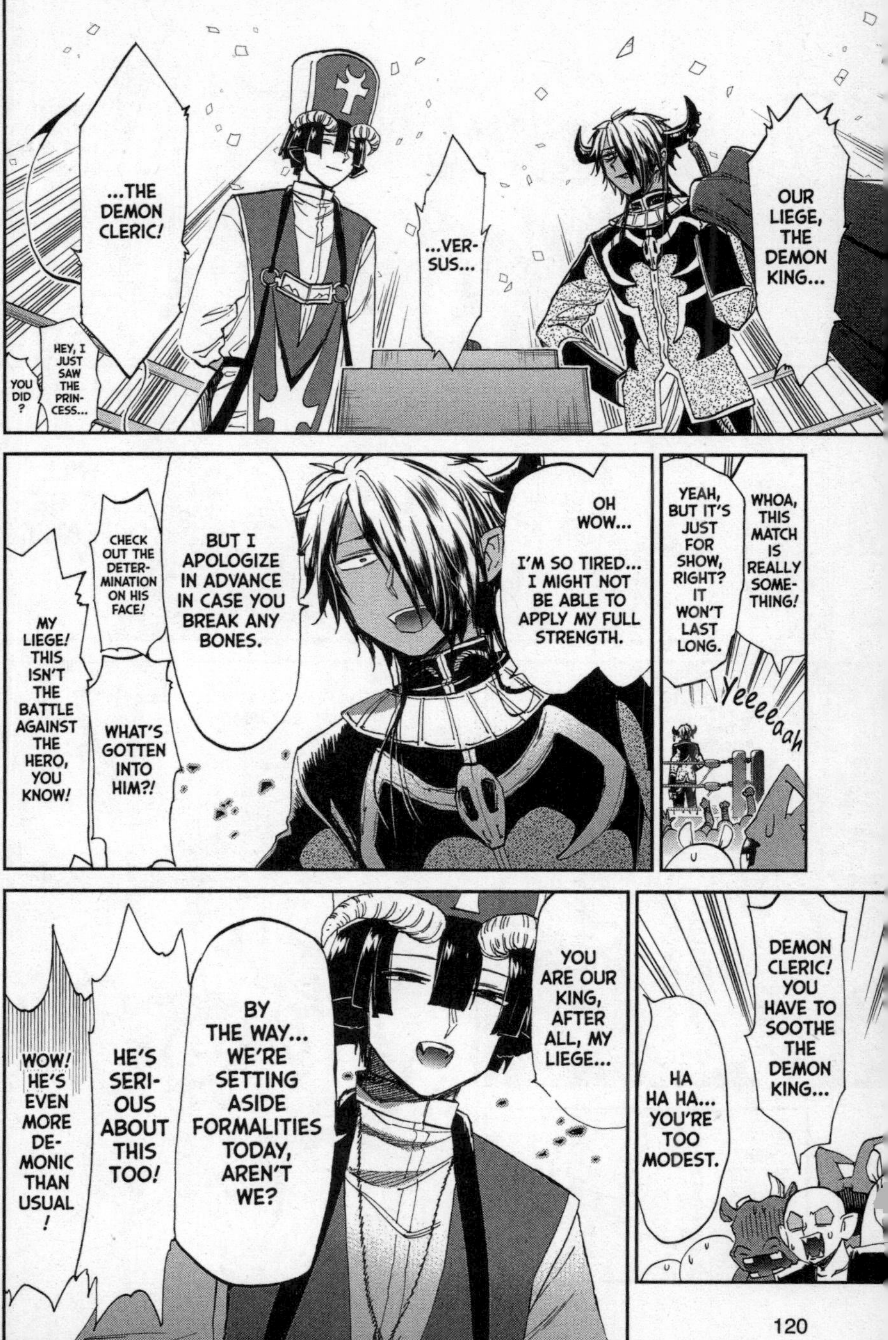
OUR LIEGE, THE DEMON KING...
...VERSUS...
...THE DEMON CLERIC!
HEY, I JUST SAW THE PRINCESS...
YOU DID?
WHOA, THIS MATCH IS REALLY SOMETHING!
YEAH, BUT IT'S JUST FOR SHOW, RIGHT? IT WON'T LAST LONG.
Yeeeeaah
OH WOW... I'M SO TIRED... I MIGHT NOT BE ABLE TO APPLY MY FULL STRENGTH.
BUT I APOLOGIZE IN ADVANCE IN CASE YOU BREAK ANY BONES.
CHECK OUT THE DETERMINATION ON HIS FACE!
WHAT'S GOTTEN INTO HIM?!
MY LIEGE! THIS ISN'T THE BATTLE AGAINST THE HERO, YOU KNOW!
DEMON CLERIC! YOU HAVE TO SOOTHE THE DEMON KING...
HA HA HA... YOU'RE TOO MODEST.
YOU ARE OUR KING, AFTER ALL, MY LIEGE...
BY THE WAY... WE'RE SETTING ASIDE FORMALITIES TODAY, AREN'T WE?
HE'S SERIOUS ABOUT THIS TOO!
WOW! HE'S EVEN MORE DEMONIC THAN USUAL!

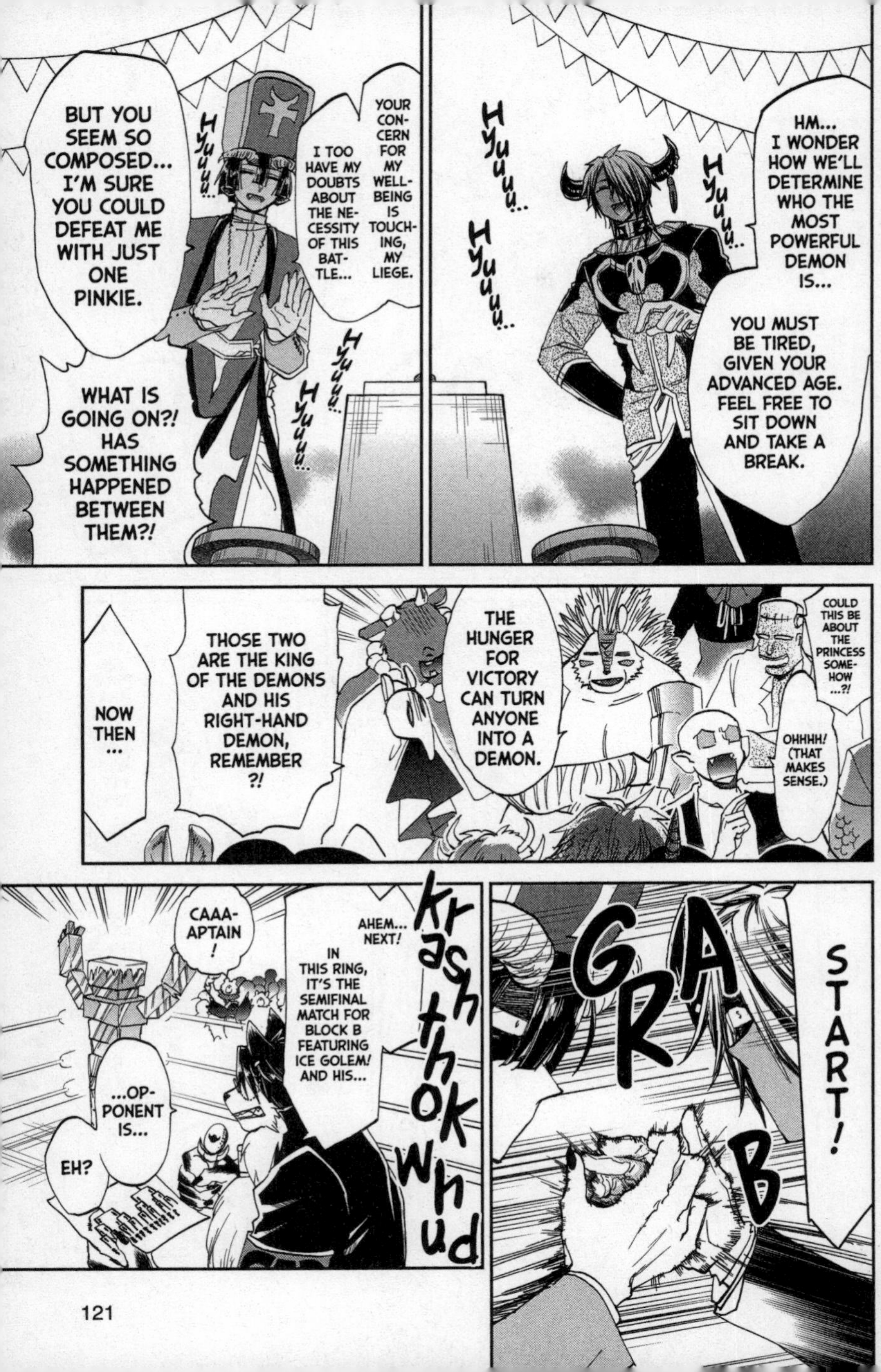
HM... I WONDER HOW WE'LL DETERMINE WHO THE MOST POWERFUL DEMON IS...
Hyuuuu...
Hyuuuu...
Hyuuuu...
YOU MUST BE TIRED, GIVEN YOUR ADVANCED AGE. FEEL FREE TO SIT DOWN AND TAKE A BREAK.
YOUR CONCERN FOR MY WELL-BEING IS TOUCHING, MY LIEGE.
I TOO HAVE MY DOUBTS ABOUT THE NECESSITY OF THIS BATTLE...
Hyuuuu...
BUT YOU SEEM SO COMPOSED... I'M SURE YOU COULD DEFEAT ME WITH JUST ONE PINKIE.
Hyuuuu...
Hyuuuu...
WHAT IS GOING ON?! HAS SOMETHING HAPPENED BETWEEN THEM?!
COULD THIS BE ABOUT THE PRINCESS SOMEHOW...?!
OHHHH! (THAT MAKES SENSE.)
THE HUNGER FOR VICTORY CAN TURN ANYONE INTO A DEMON.
THOSE TWO ARE THE KING OF THE DEMONS AND HIS RIGHT-HAND DEMON, REMEMBER?!
NOW THEN...
START!
GRAB
krash thok whud
AHEM... NEXT!
IN THIS RING, IT'S THE SEMIFINAL MATCH FOR BLOCK B FEATURING ICE GOLEM! AND HIS...
CAAA-APTAIN!
...OPPONENT IS...
EH?

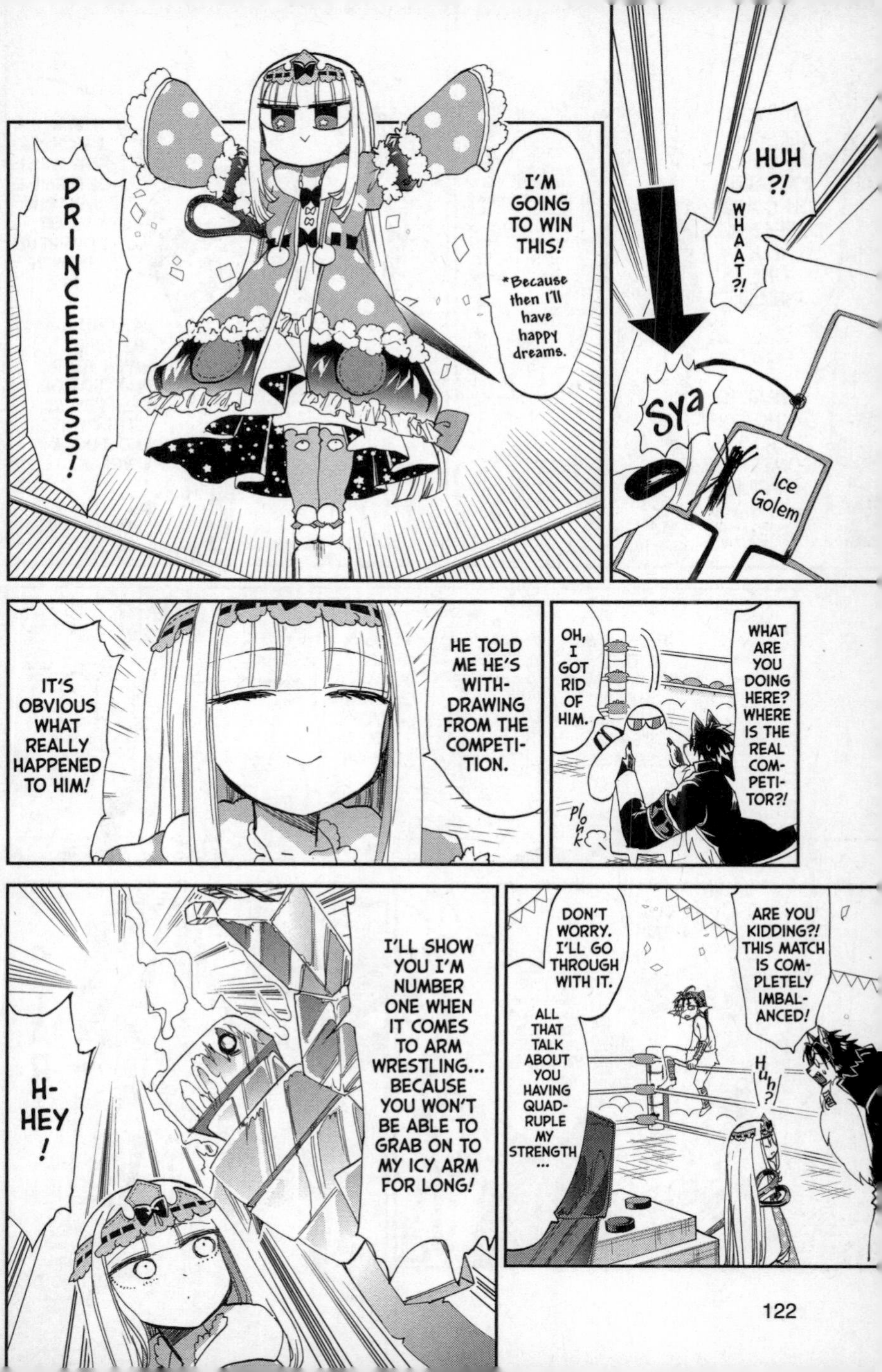
HUH?!
WHAAT?!
Sya
Ice Golem
I'M GOING TO WIN THIS!
*Because then I'll have happy dreams.
PRINCEEEEESS!
WHAT ARE YOU DOING HERE? WHERE IS THE REAL COMPETITOR?!
OH, I GOT RID OF HIM.
Plonk
HE TOLD ME HE'S WITHDRAWING FROM THE COMPETITION.
IT'S OBVIOUS WHAT REALLY HAPPENED TO HIM!
ARE YOU KIDDING?! THIS MATCH IS COMPLETELY IMBALANCED!
Huh?
DON'T WORRY. I'LL GO THROUGH WITH IT.
ALL THAT TALK ABOUT YOU HAVING QUADRUPLE MY STRENGTH...
I'LL SHOW YOU I'M NUMBER ONE WHEN IT COMES TO ARM WRESTLING... BECAUSE YOU WON'T BE ABLE TO GRAB ON TO MY ICY ARM FOR LONG!
H-HEY!

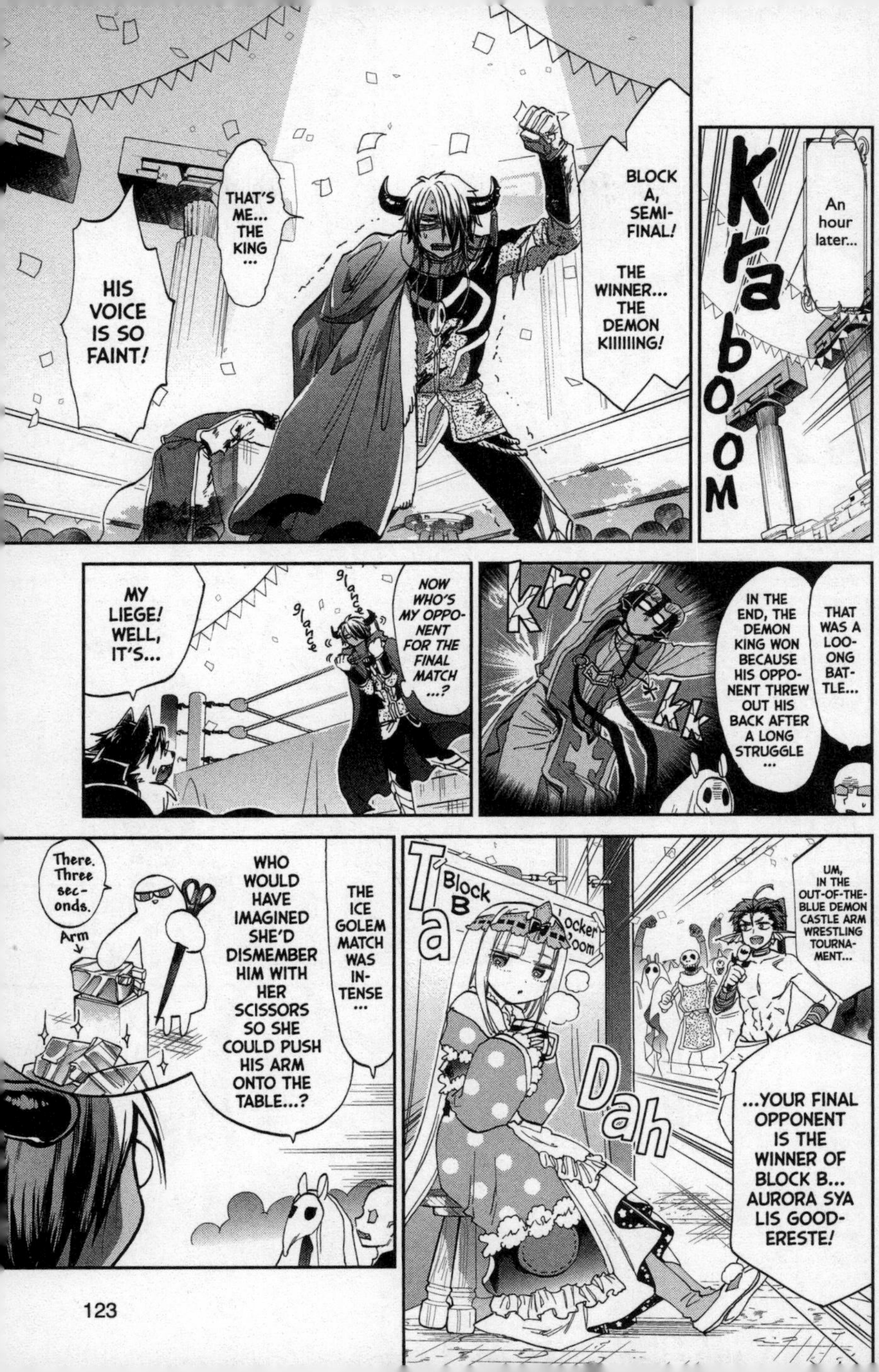
An hour later...
Kraboom
BLOCK A, SEMI-FINAL!
THE WINNER... THE DEMON KIIIIIING!
THAT'S ME... THE KING...
HIS VOICE IS SO FAINT!
THAT WAS A LOO-ONG BATTLE...
IN THE END, THE DEMON KING WON BECAUSE HIS OPPONENT THREW OUT HIS BACK AFTER A LONG STRUGGLE...
kri
kk
glance glance
NOW WHO'S MY OPPONENT FOR THE FINAL MATCH...?
MY LIEGE! WELL, IT'S...
UM, IN THE OUT-OF-THE-BLUE DEMON CASTLE ARM WRESTLING TOURNAMENT...
...YOUR FINAL OPPONENT IS THE WINNER OF BLOCK B... AURORA SYA LIS GOODERESTE!
Block B Locker Room
Ta
Dah
THE ICE GOLEM MATCH WAS INTENSE...
WHO WOULD HAVE IMAGINED SHE'D DISMEMBER HIM WITH HER SCISSORS SO SHE COULD PUSH HIS ARM ONTO THE TABLE...?
There. Three seconds.
Arm

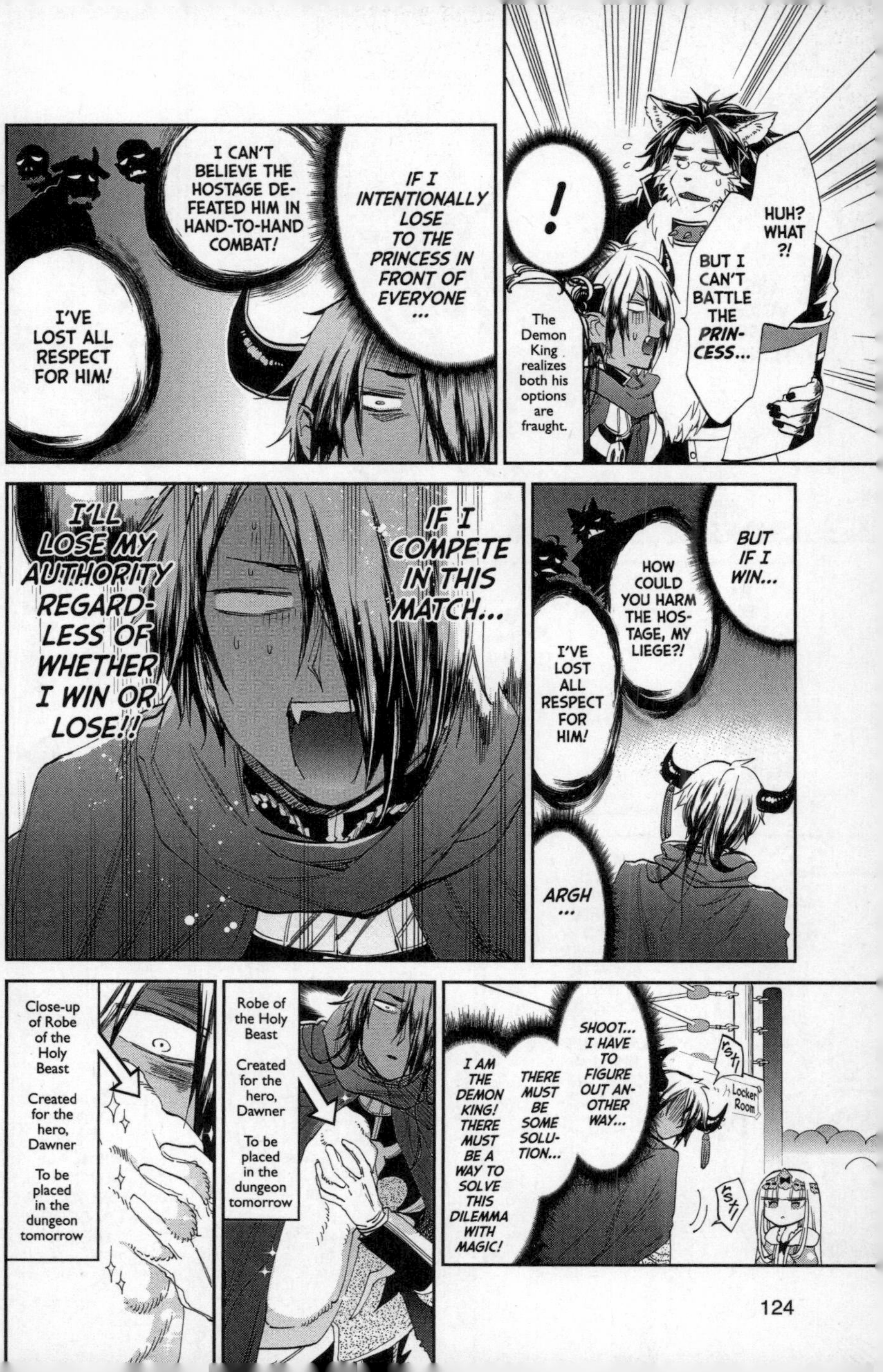
HUH? WHAT?!
BUT I CAN'T BATTLE THE PRINCESS...
!
The Demon King realizes both his options are fraught.
IF I INTENTIONALLY LOSE TO THE PRINCESS IN FRONT OF EVERYONE...
I CAN'T BELIEVE THE HOSTAGE DEFEATED HIM IN HAND-TO-HAND COMBAT!
I'VE LOST ALL RESPECT FOR HIM!
BUT IF I WIN...
HOW COULD YOU HARM THE HOSTAGE, MY LIEGE?!
I'VE LOST ALL RESPECT FOR HIM!
ARGH...
IF I COMPETE IN THIS MATCH...
I'LL LOSE MY AUTHORITY REGARDLESS OF WHETHER I WIN OR LOSE!!
Locker Room
SHOOT... I HAVE TO FIGURE OUT ANOTHER WAY...
THERE MUST BE SOME SOLUTION...
I AM THE DEMON KING! THERE MUST BE A WAY TO SOLVE THIS DILEMMA WITH MAGIC!
Robe of the Holy Beast
Created for the hero, Dawner
To be placed in the dungeon tomorrow
Close-up of Robe of the Holy Beast
Created for the hero, Dawner
To be placed in the dungeon tomorrow

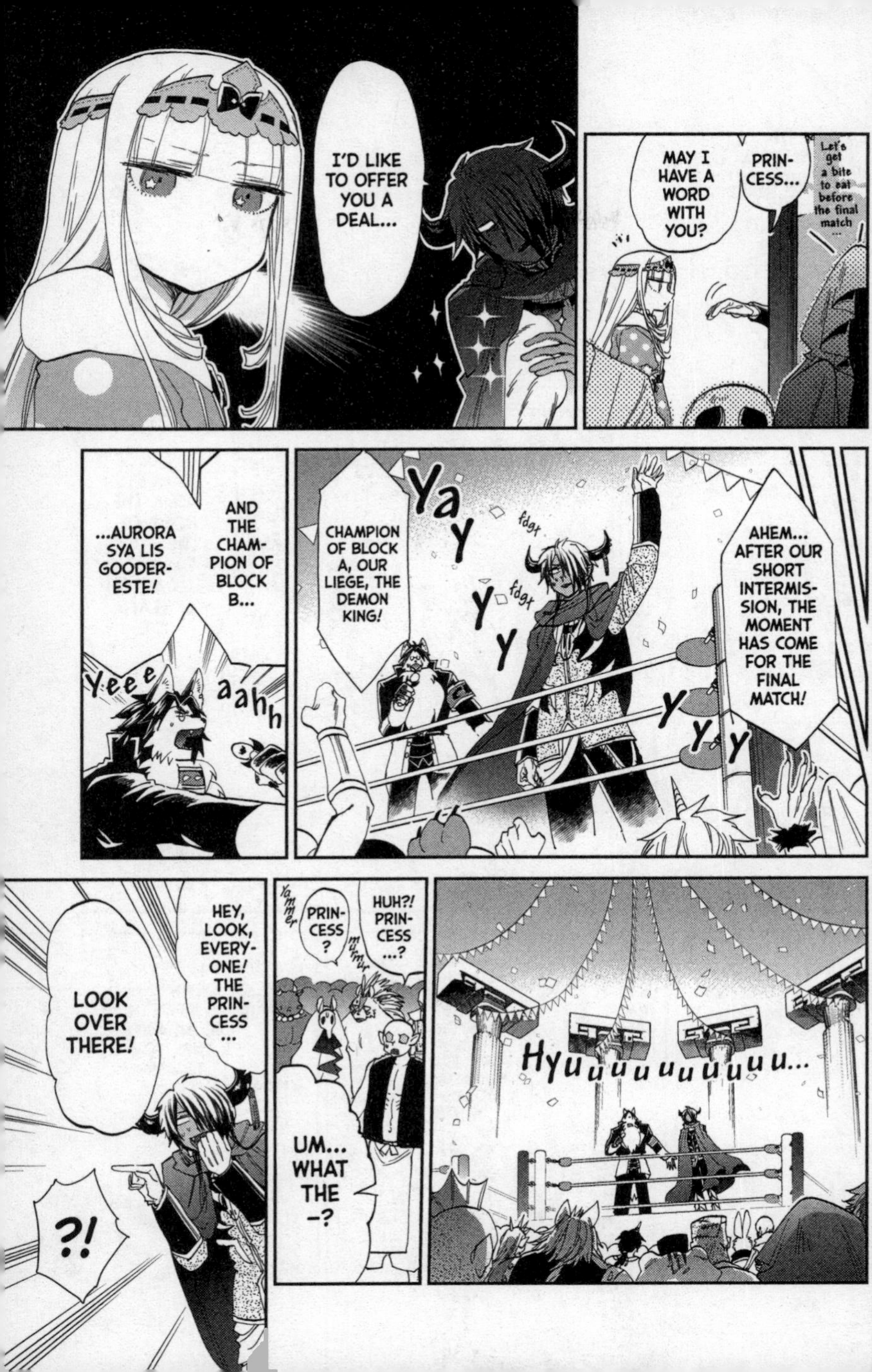
Let's get a bite to eat before the final match...
PRINCESS...
MAY I HAVE A WORD WITH YOU?
I'D LIKE TO OFFER YOU A DEAL...
AHEM... AFTER OUR SHORT INTERMISSION, THE MOMENT HAS COME FOR THE FINAL MATCH!
Yay
fdgt
fdgt
CHAMPION OF BLOCK A, OUR LIEGE, THE DEMON KING!
YYYYYY
AND THE CHAMPION OF BLOCK B...
...AURORA SYA LIS GOODERESTE!
Yeeeaahh
Hyuuuuuuuuuuuu...
HUH?! PRINCESS...?
murmur
PRINCESS?
Yammer
UM... WHAT THE—?
HEY, LOOK, EVERYONE! THE PRINCESS...
LOOK OVER THERE!
?!

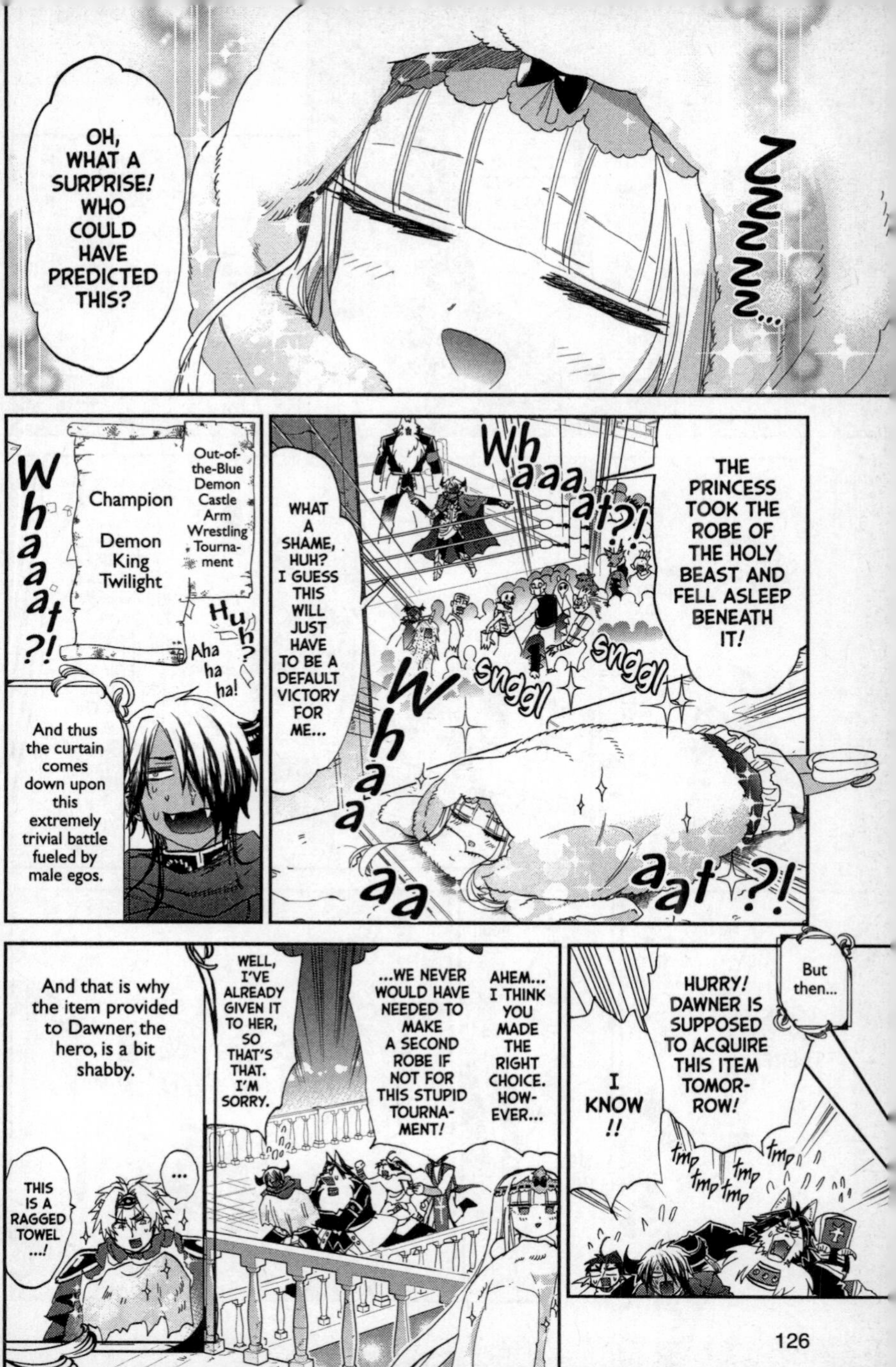

ZZZZZ...
OH, WHAT A SURPRISE! WHO COULD HAVE PREDICTED THIS?
THE PRINCESS TOOK THE ROBE OF THE HOLY BEAST AND FELL ASLEEP BENEATH IT!
Whaaaat?!
WHAT A SHAME, HUH? I GUESS THIS WILL JUST HAVE TO BE A DEFAULT VICTORY FOR ME...
snggl
snggl
Whaaaaaat?!
Out-of-the-Blue Demon Castle Arm Wrestling Tournament
Champion
Demon King Twilight
Whaaaat?!
Huh?
Aha ha ha!
And thus the curtain comes down upon this extremely trivial battle fueled by male egos.
But then...
HURRY! DAWNER IS SUPPOSED TO ACQUIRE THIS ITEM TOMORROW!
I KNOW!!
tmp tmp tmp tmp tmp tmp
AHEM... I THINK YOU MADE THE RIGHT CHOICE. HOWEVER...
...WE NEVER WOULD HAVE NEEDED TO MAKE A SECOND ROBE IF NOT FOR THIS STUPID TOURNAMENT!
WELL, I'VE ALREADY GIVEN IT TO HER, SO THAT'S THAT. I'M SORRY.
And that is why the item provided to Dawner, the hero, is a bit shabby.
...
THIS IS A RAGGED TOWEL...!

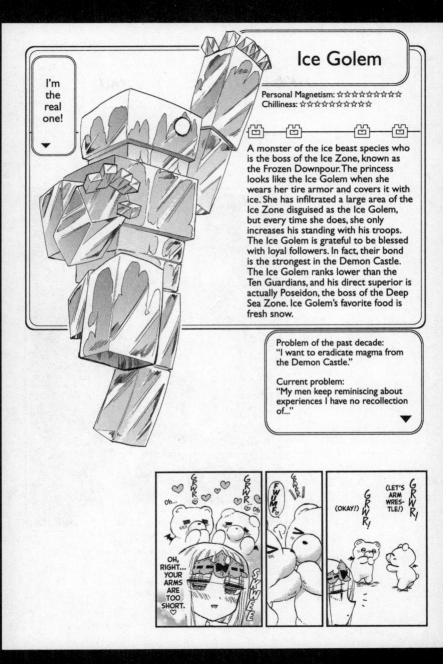

Ice Golem

Personal Magnetism: ☆☆☆☆☆☆☆☆☆☆
Chilliness: ☆☆☆☆☆☆☆☆☆☆

I'm the real one!

A monster of the ice beast species who is the boss of the Ice Zone, known as the Frozen Downpour. The princess looks like the Ice Golem when she wears her tire armor and covers it with ice. She has infiltrated a large area of the Ice Zone disguised as the Ice Golem, but every time she does, she only increases his standing with his troops. The Ice Golem is grateful to be blessed with loyal followers. In fact, their bond is the strongest in the Demon Castle. The Ice Golem ranks lower than the Ten Guardians, and his direct superior is actually Poseidon, the boss of the Deep Sea Zone. Ice Golem's favorite food is fresh snow.

Problem of the past decade:
"I want to eradicate magma from the Demon Castle."

Current problem:
"My men keep reminiscing about experiences I have no recollection of..."

(LET'S ARM WRES-TLE!)
GRWR!
(OKAY!)
GRWR!
GRWRR
FWUMF
GRWR...
Oh...
GRWR...
Oh
OH, RIGHT... YOUR ARMS ARE TOO SHORT.
SKWEE

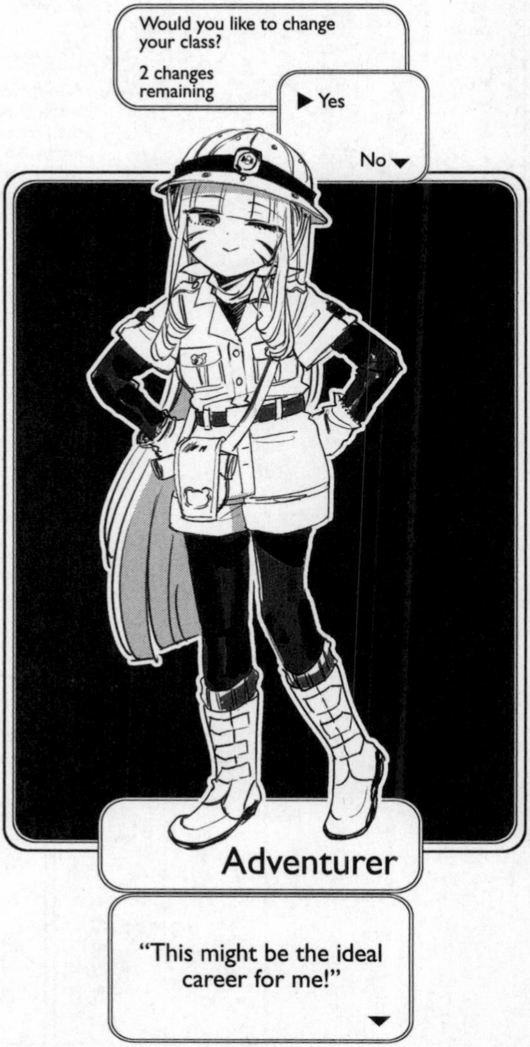
Would you like to change your class?
2 changes remaining
▶ Yes
No
Adventurer
"This might be the ideal career for me!"

76th Night: None Shall Sleep for a Few More Minutes

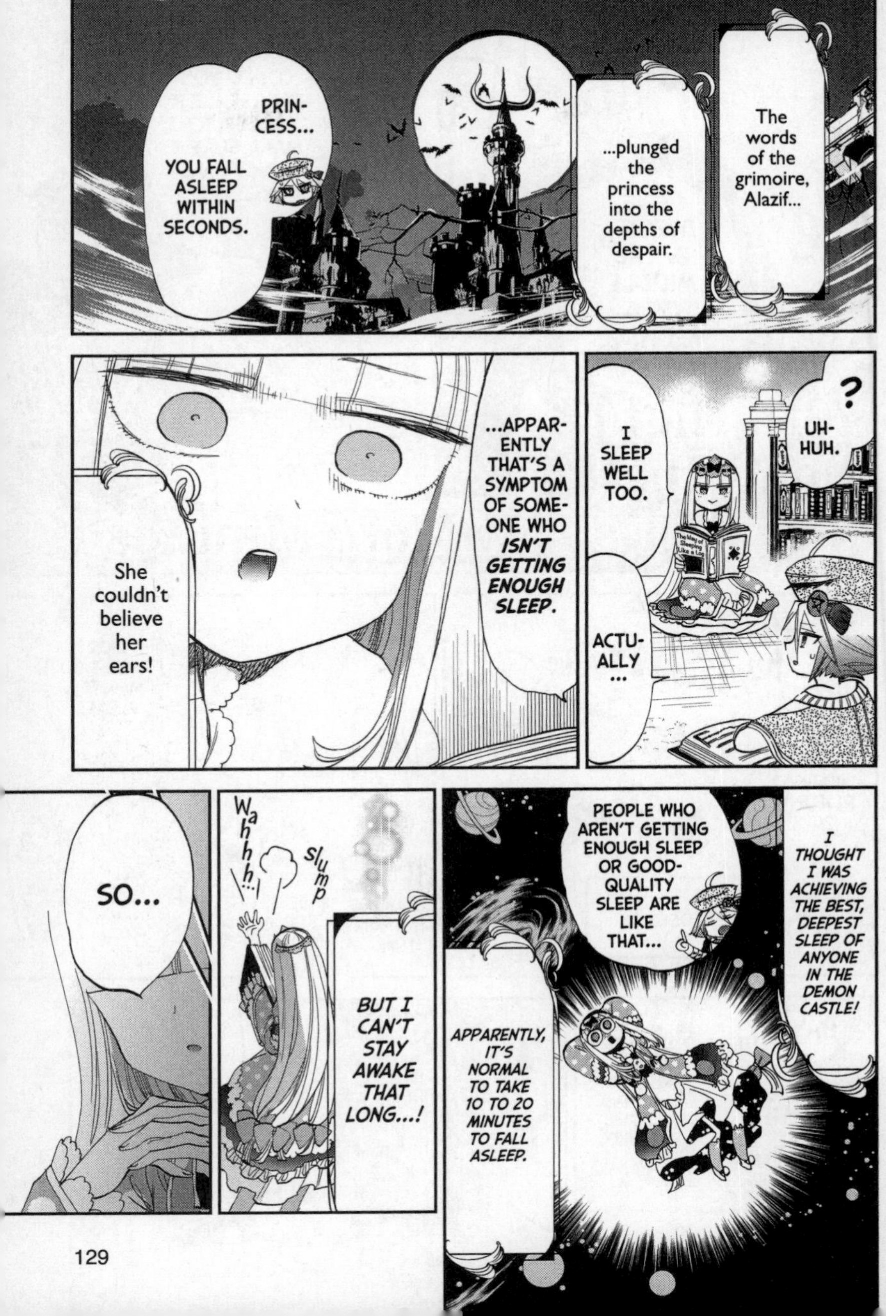

The words of the grimoire, Alazif...
...plunged the princess into the depths of despair.
PRINCESS... YOU FALL ASLEEP WITHIN SECONDS.
?
UH-HUH.
I SLEEP WELL TOO.
The Way of Sleeping Like a Log
ACTUALLY...
...APPARENTLY THAT'S A SYMPTOM OF SOMEONE WHO *ISN'T GETTING ENOUGH SLEEP.*
She couldn't believe her ears!
I THOUGHT I WAS ACHIEVING THE BEST, DEEPEST SLEEP OF ANYONE IN THE DEMON CASTLE!
PEOPLE WHO AREN'T GETTING ENOUGH SLEEP OR GOOD-QUALITY SLEEP ARE LIKE THAT...
APPARENTLY, IT'S NORMAL TO TAKE 10 TO 20 MINUTES TO FALL ASLEEP.
Wahhhh...!
slump
BUT I CAN'T STAY AWAKE THAT LONG...!
SO...

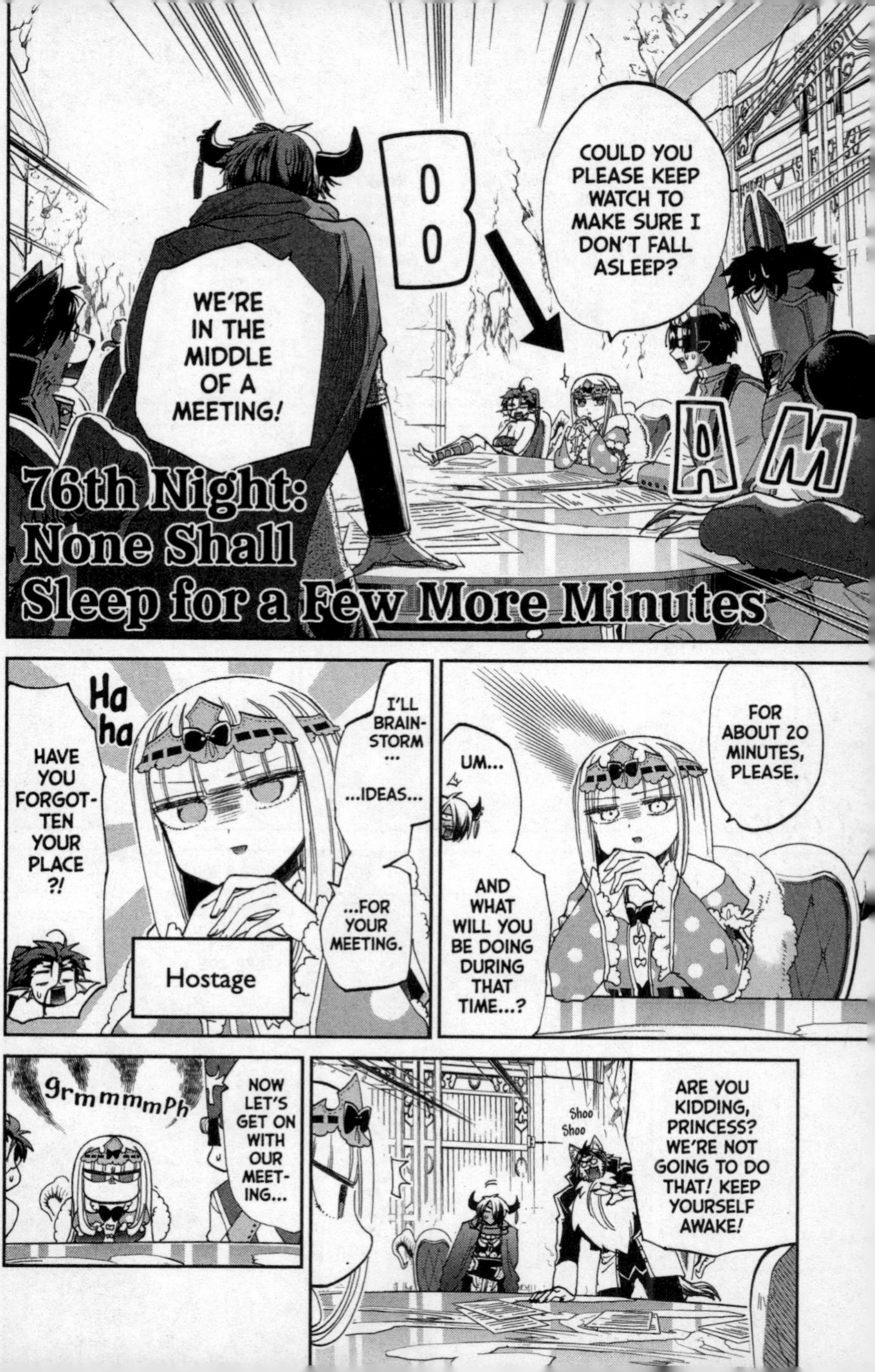
COULD YOU PLEASE KEEP WATCH TO MAKE SURE I DON'T FALL ASLEEP?
BAM
WE'RE IN THE MIDDLE OF A MEETING!
76th Night: None Shall Sleep for a Few More Minutes
FOR ABOUT 20 MINUTES, PLEASE.
UM...
AND WHAT WILL YOU BE DOING DURING THAT TIME...?
I'LL BRAIN-STORM ...
...IDEAS...
...FOR YOUR MEETING.
Ha ha
HAVE YOU FORGOT-TEN YOUR PLACE?!
Hostage
ARE YOU KIDDING, PRINCESS? WE'RE NOT GOING TO DO THAT! KEEP YOURSELF AWAKE!
Shoo Shoo
NOW LET'S GET ON WITH OUR MEET-ING...
grmmmmph

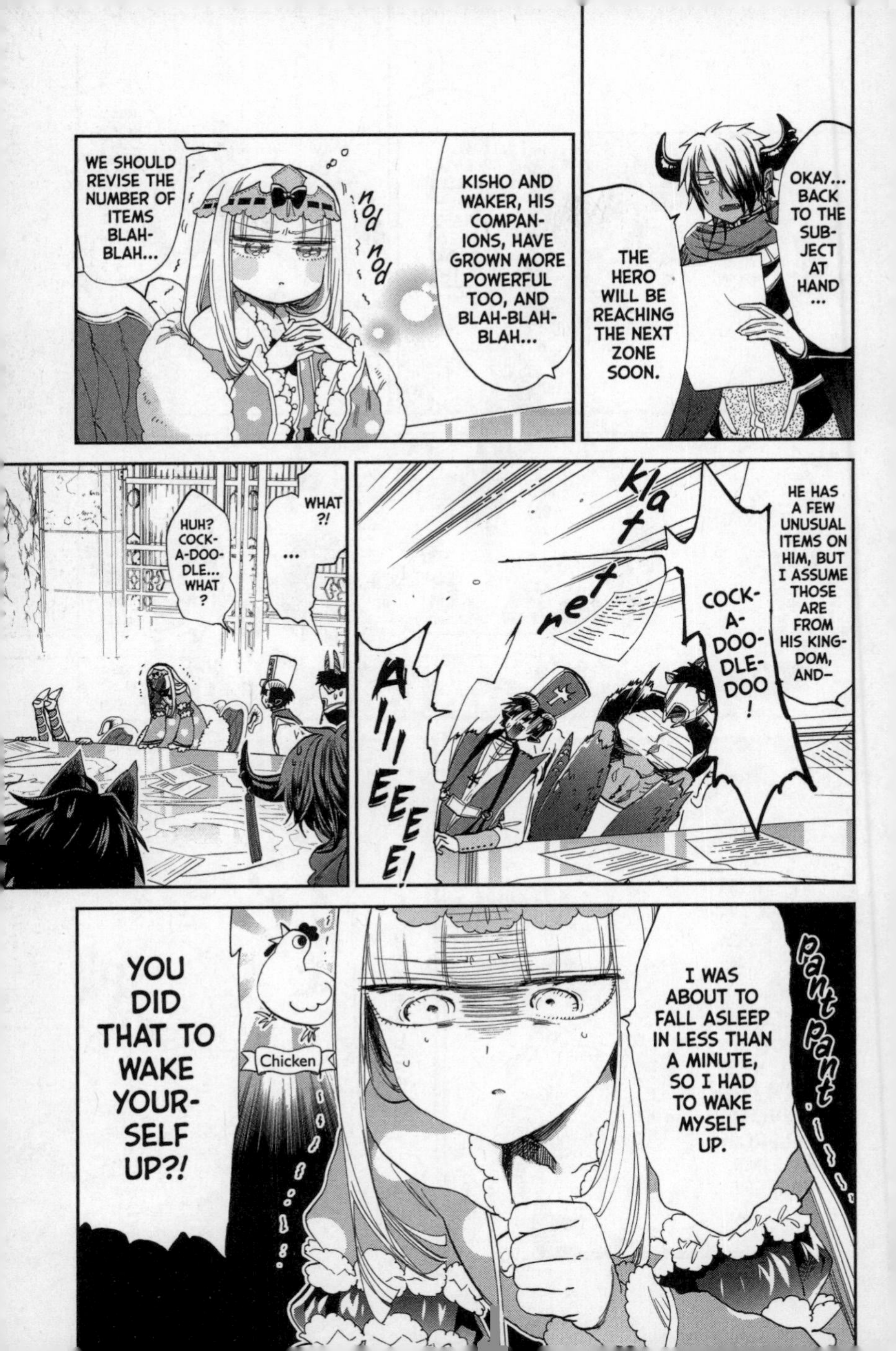
OKAY... BACK TO THE SUBJECT AT HAND...
THE HERO WILL BE REACHING THE NEXT ZONE SOON.
KISHO AND WAKER, HIS COMPANIONS, HAVE GROWN MORE POWERFUL TOO, AND BLAH-BLAH-BLAH...
nod nod
WE SHOULD REVISE THE NUMBER OF ITEMS BLAH-BLAH...
HE HAS A FEW UNUSUAL ITEMS ON HIM, BUT I ASSUME THOSE ARE FROM HIS KINGDOM, AND—
COCK-A-DOODLE-DOO!
klat
ret
AIIIIEEEEE!
WHAT?!
...
HUH? COCK-A-DOODLE... WHAT?
pant pant
I WAS ABOUT TO FALL ASLEEP IN LESS THAN A MINUTE, SO I HAD TO WAKE MYSELF UP.
Chicken
YOU DID THAT TO WAKE YOURSELF UP?!

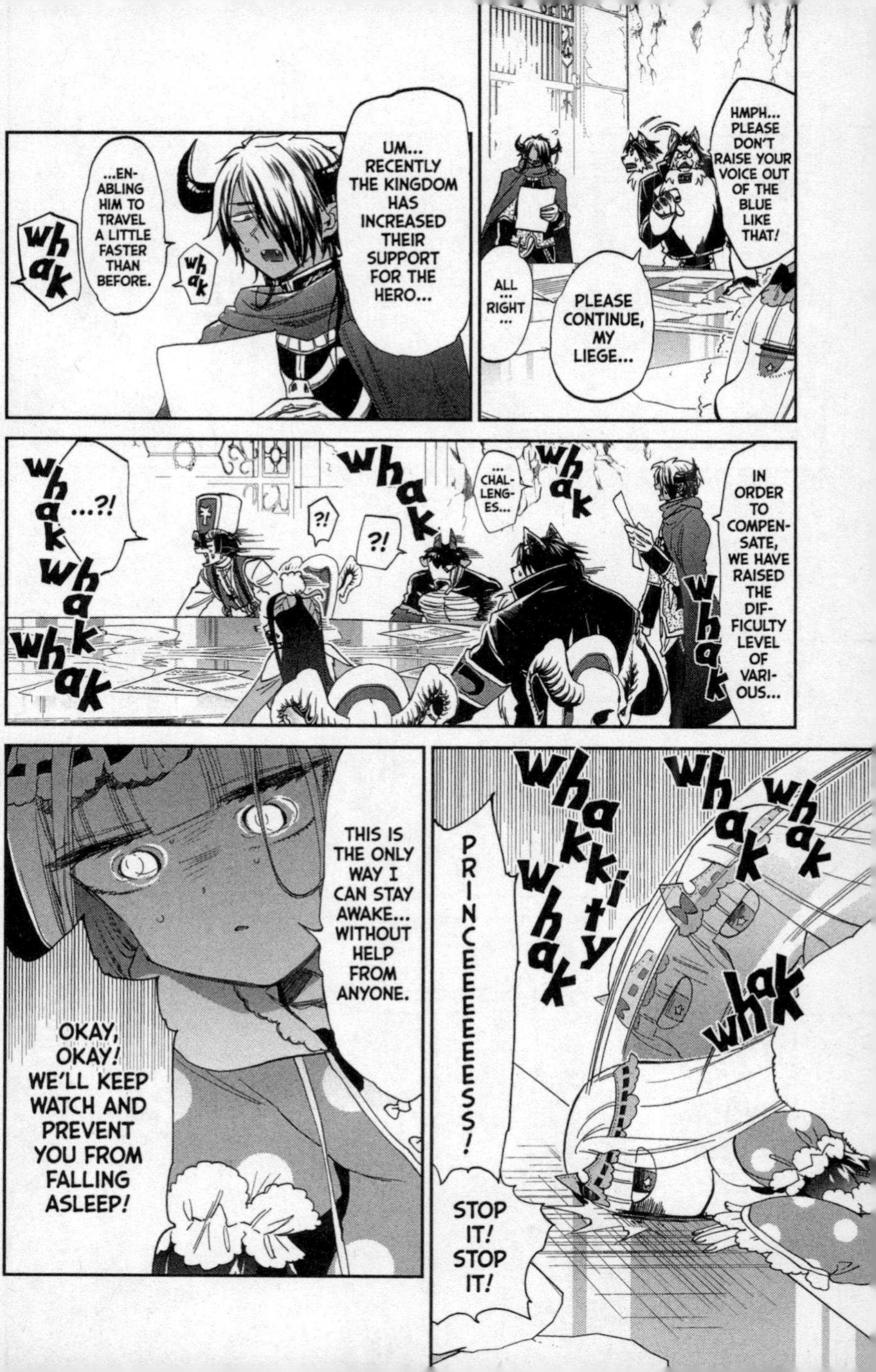
HMPH... PLEASE DON'T RAISE YOUR VOICE OUT OF THE BLUE LIKE THAT!
PLEASE CONTINUE, MY LIEGE...
ALL ... RIGHT ...
UM... RECENTLY THE KINGDOM HAS INCREASED THEIR SUPPORT FOR THE HERO...
whak
...EN-ABLING HIM TO TRAVEL A LITTLE FASTER THAN BEFORE.
whak
IN ORDER TO COMPEN-SATE, WE HAVE RAISED THE DIF-FICULTY LEVEL OF VARI-OUS...
whak
whak
...CHAL-LENG-ES...
whak
?!
?!
...?!
whak whak whak
whak whakkity whak
whak whak
whak
PRINCEEEEEEESS!
STOP IT! STOP IT!
THIS IS THE ONLY WAY I CAN STAY AWAKE... WITHOUT HELP FROM ANYONE.
OKAY, OKAY! WE'LL KEEP WATCH AND PREVENT YOU FROM FALLING ASLEEP!

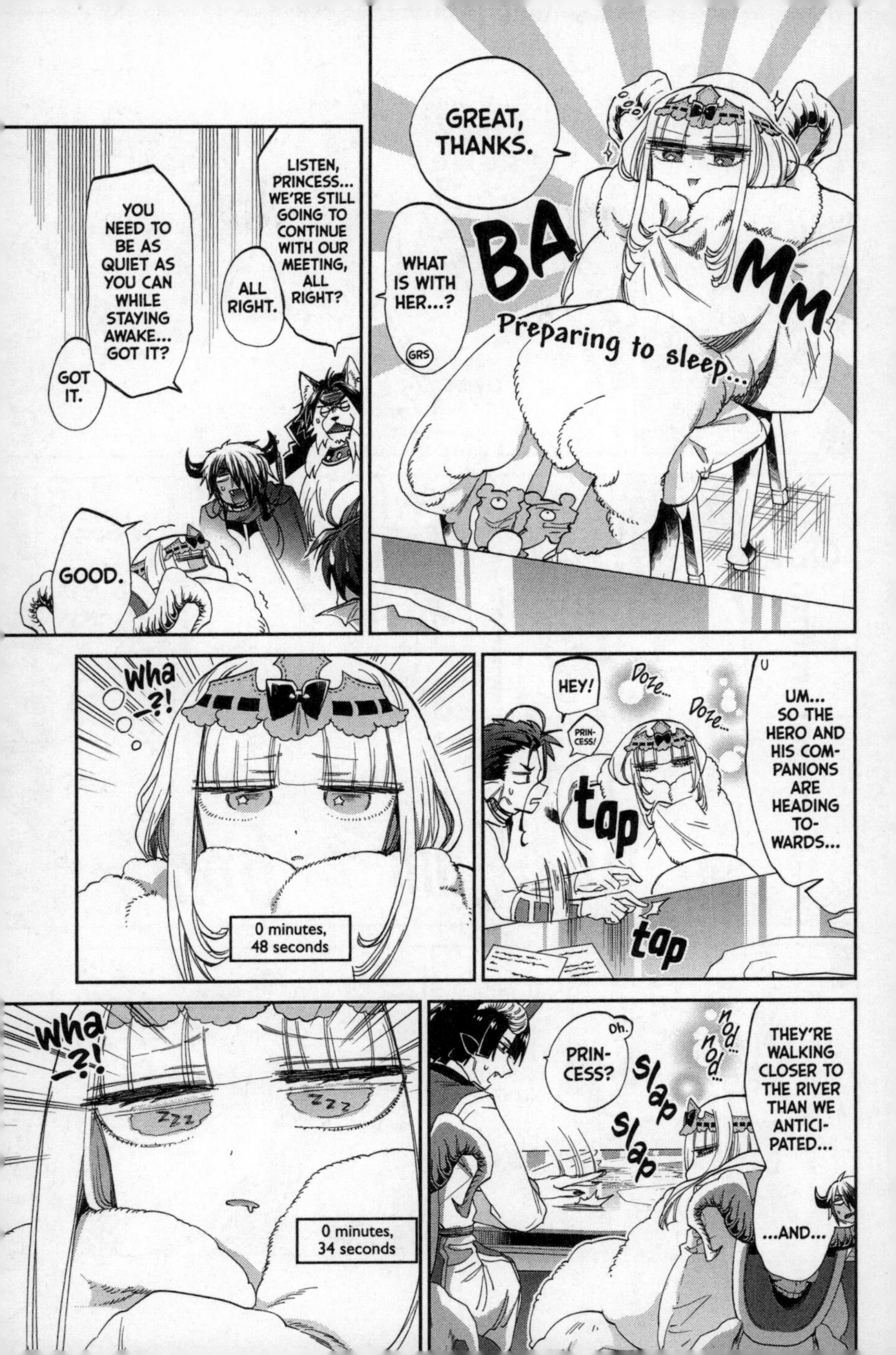
GREAT, THANKS.
WHAT IS WITH HER...?
GRS
BAMM
Preparing to sleep...
LISTEN, PRINCESS... WE'RE STILL GOING TO CONTINUE WITH OUR MEETING, ALL RIGHT?
ALL RIGHT.
YOU NEED TO BE AS QUIET AS YOU CAN WHILE STAYING AWAKE... GOT IT?
GOT IT.
GOOD.
UM... SO THE HERO AND HIS COMPANIONS ARE HEADING TOWARDS...
Doze... Doze...
HEY!
PRINCESS!
tap
tap
wha-?!
0 minutes, 48 seconds
THEY'RE WALKING CLOSER TO THE RIVER THAN WE ANTICIPATED...
nod... nod...
Oh.
PRINCESS?
slap
slap
...AND...
wha-?!
ZZZ
ZZZ
0 minutes, 34 seconds

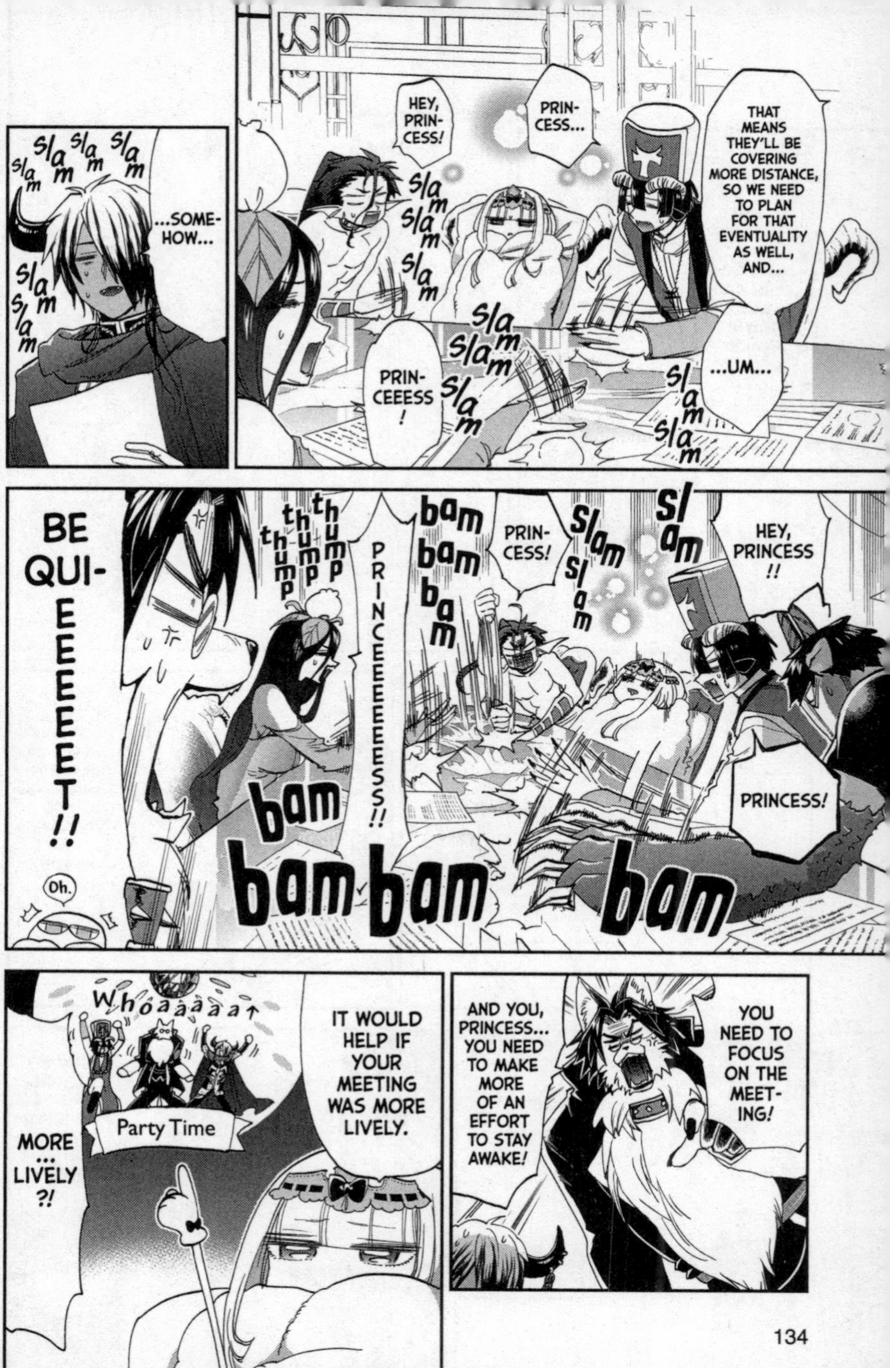
THAT MEANS THEY'LL BE COVERING MORE DISTANCE, SO WE NEED TO PLAN FOR THAT EVENTUALITY AS WELL, AND...
PRIN-CESS...
HEY, PRIN-CESS!
slam slam slam
slam slam slam
...UM...
slam slam
PRIN-CEEESS!
...SOME-HOW...
slam slam slam slam
slam slam
HEY, PRINCESS!!
slam slam slam slam
PRIN-CESS!
bam bam bam
PRINCESS!
PRINCEEEEEEESS!!
thump thump thump
BE QUI-EEEEEEET!!
Oh.
bam bam bam bam
YOU NEED TO FOCUS ON THE MEET-ING!
AND YOU, PRINCESS... YOU NEED TO MAKE MORE OF AN EFFORT TO STAY AWAKE!
IT WOULD HELP IF YOUR MEETING WAS MORE LIVELY.
Whoaaaaaa↑
Party Time
MORE... LIVELY?!

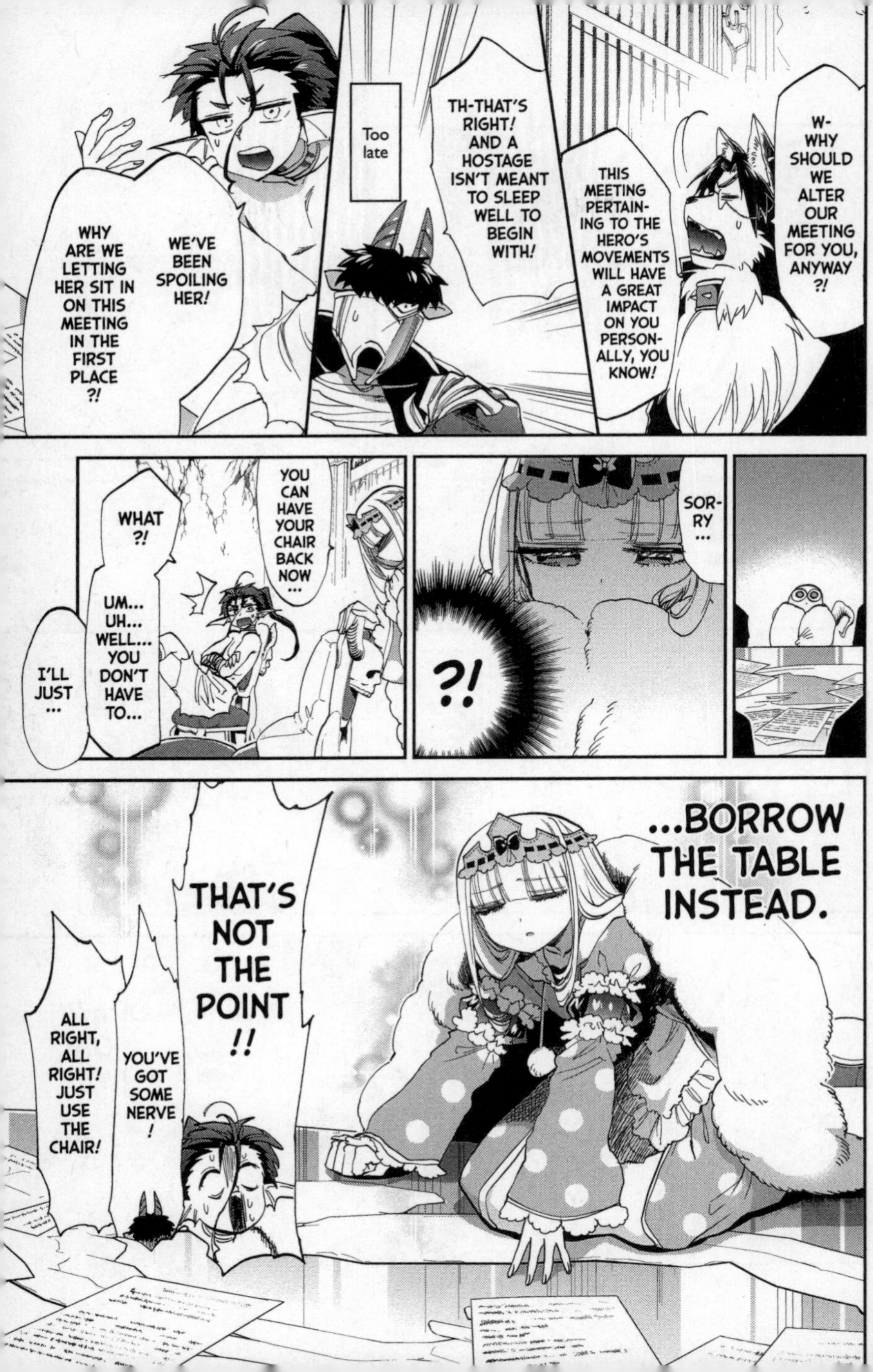
W-WHY SHOULD WE ALTER OUR MEETING FOR YOU, ANYWAY?!
THIS MEETING PERTAINING TO THE HERO'S MOVEMENTS WILL HAVE A GREAT IMPACT ON YOU PERSONALLY, YOU KNOW!
TH-THAT'S RIGHT! AND A HOSTAGE ISN'T MEANT TO SLEEP WELL TO BEGIN WITH!
Too late
WE'VE BEEN SPOILING HER!
WHY ARE WE LETTING HER SIT IN ON THIS MEETING IN THE FIRST PLACE?!
SORRY...
?!
YOU CAN HAVE YOUR CHAIR BACK NOW...
WHAT?!
UM... UH... WELL... YOU DON'T HAVE TO...
I'LL JUST...
...BORROW THE TABLE INSTEAD.
THAT'S NOT THE POINT!!
YOU'VE GOT SOME NERVE!
ALL RIGHT, ALL RIGHT! JUST USE THE CHAIR!

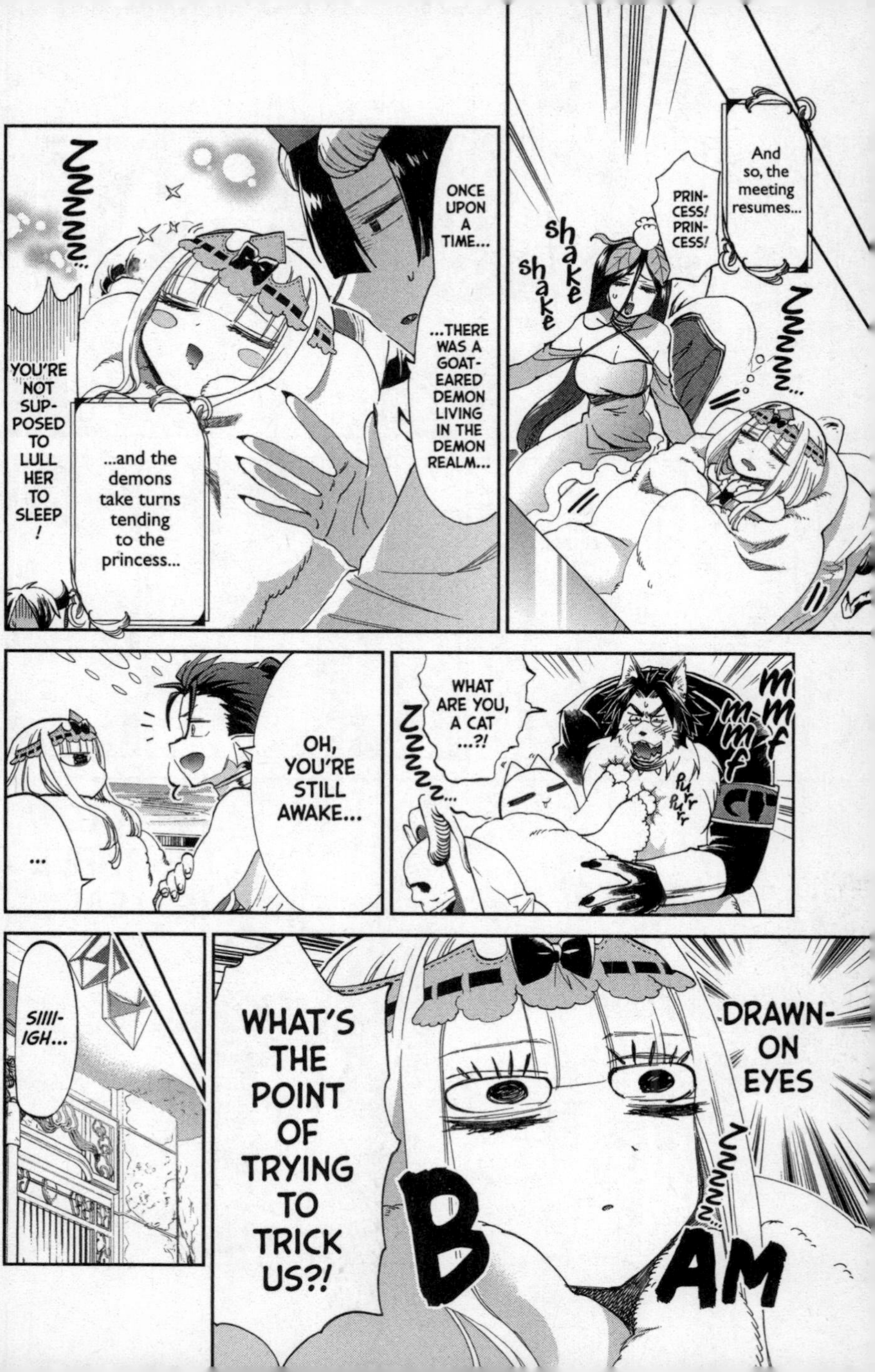
And so, the meeting resumes...
PRIN-CESS! PRIN-CESS!
shake shake
ZZZZZZ...
ONCE UPON A TIME...
...THERE WAS A GOAT-EARED DEMON LIVING IN THE DEMON REALM...
ZZZZZZ...
...and the demons take turns tending to the princess...
YOU'RE NOT SUP-POSED TO LULL HER TO SLEEP!
mmf mmf
WHAT ARE YOU, A CAT ...?!
Purr Purr
ZZZZZ...
OH, YOU'RE STILL AWAKE...
...
DRAWN-ON EYES
WHAT'S THE POINT OF TRYING TO TRICK US?!
BAM
ZZZZZ...
SIIII-IGH...

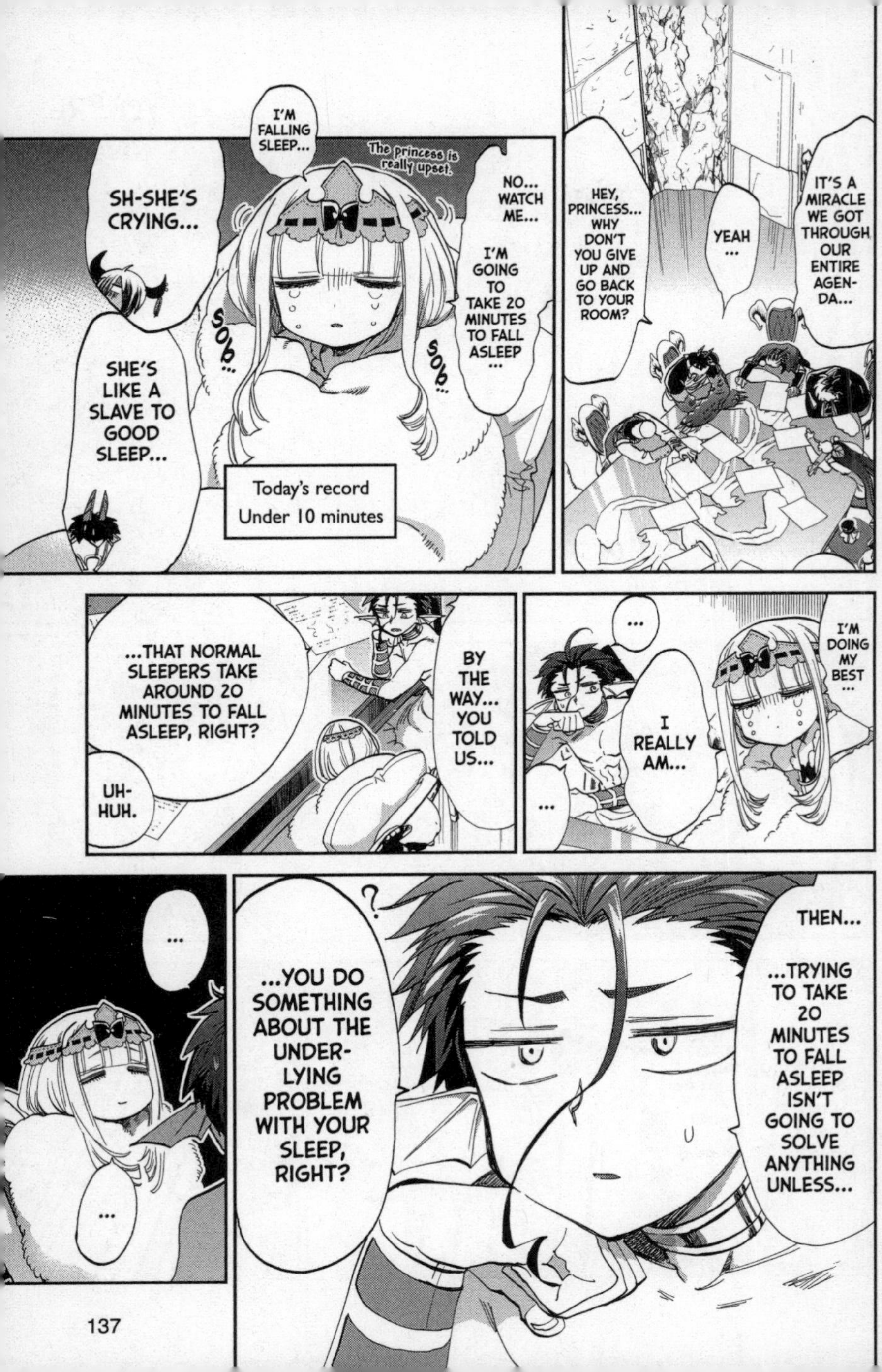
IT'S A MIRACLE WE GOT THROUGH OUR ENTIRE AGENDA...
YEAH...
HEY, PRINCESS... WHY DON'T YOU GIVE UP AND GO BACK TO YOUR ROOM?
NO... WATCH ME...
I'M GOING TO TAKE 20 MINUTES TO FALL ASLEEP...
SOB...
The princess is really upset.
I'M FALLING SLEEP...
SOB...
SH-SHE'S CRYING...
SHE'S LIKE A SLAVE TO GOOD SLEEP...
Today's record Under 10 minutes
I'M DOING MY BEST...
...
I REALLY AM...
...
BY THE WAY... YOU TOLD US...
...THAT NORMAL SLEEPERS TAKE AROUND 20 MINUTES TO FALL ASLEEP, RIGHT?
UH-HUH.
THEN...
...TRYING TO TAKE 20 MINUTES TO FALL ASLEEP ISN'T GOING TO SOLVE ANYTHING UNLESS...
?
...YOU DO SOMETHING ABOUT THE UNDERLYING PROBLEM WITH YOUR SLEEP, RIGHT?
...
...

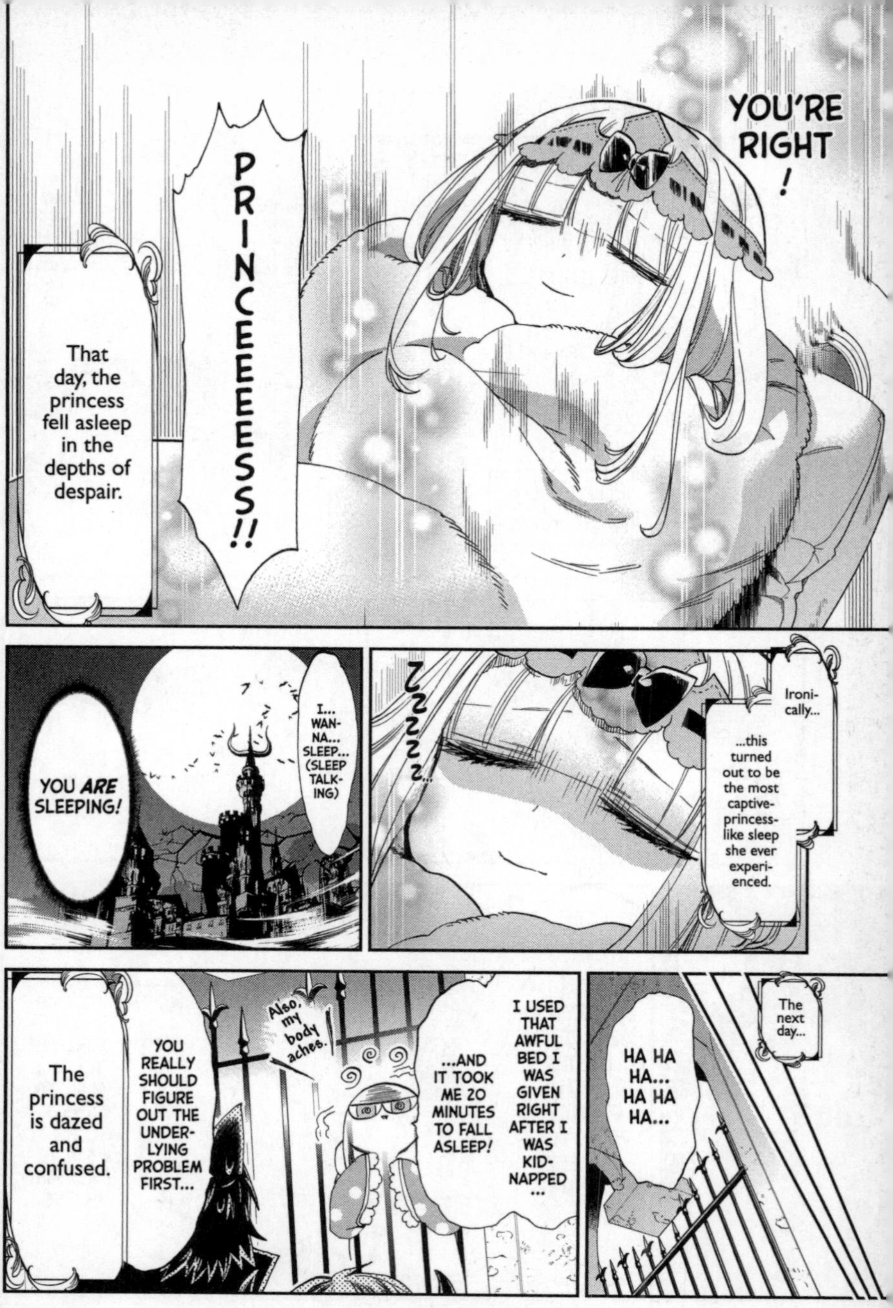
YOU'RE RIGHT!
PRINCEEEEESS!!
That day, the princess fell asleep in the depths of despair.
Ironically...
...this turned out to be the most captive-princess-like sleep she ever experienced.
ZZZZZ...
I... WANNA... SLEEP... (SLEEP TALKING)
YOU *ARE* SLEEPING!
The next day...
HA HA HA... HA HA HA...
I USED THAT AWFUL BED I WAS GIVEN RIGHT AFTER I WAS KIDNAPPED...
...AND IT TOOK ME 20 MINUTES TO FALL ASLEEP!
Also, my body aches.
YOU REALLY SHOULD FIGURE OUT THE UNDERLYING PROBLEM FIRST...
The princess is dazed and confused.

Memory Notes: Complete Version

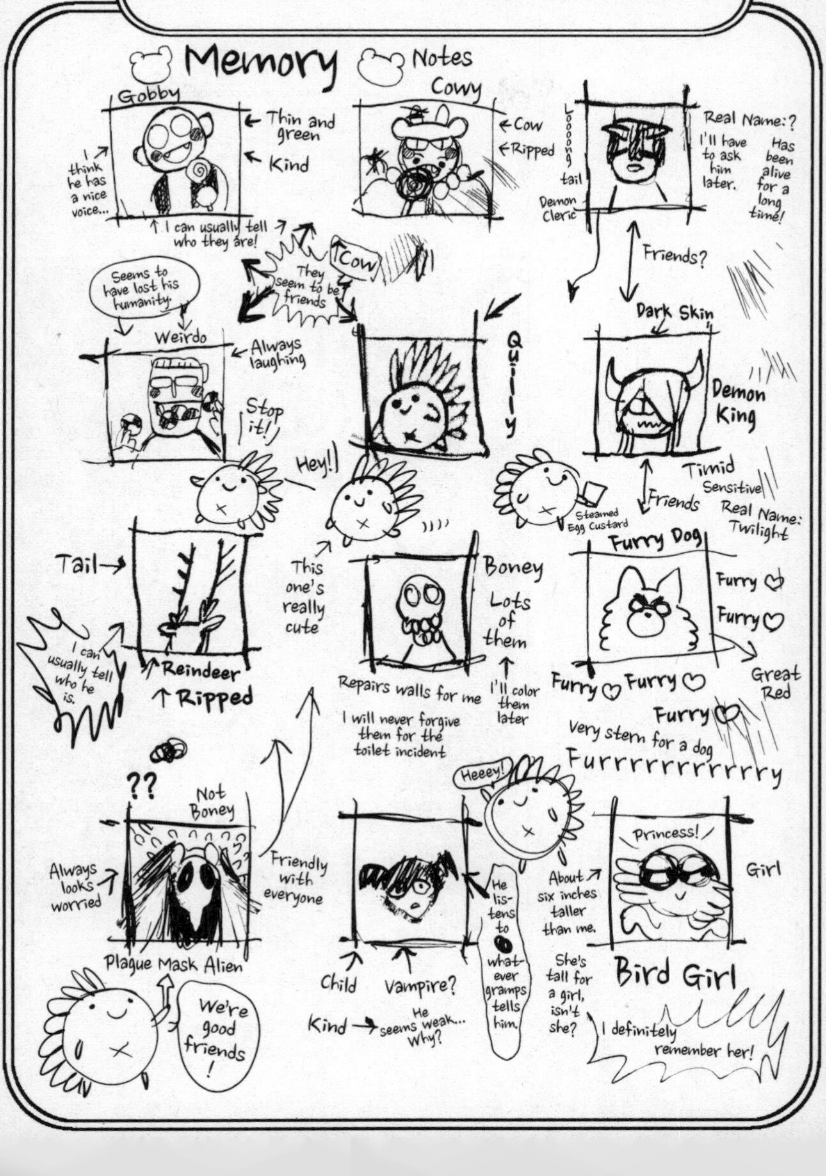

Memory Notes
Real Name:?
I'll have to ask him later.
Has been alive for a long time!
Looooong tail
Demon Cleric
Cowy
←Cow
←Ripped
Gobby
← Thin and green
← Kind
I think he has a nice voice...
↑ I can usually tell who they are!
Friends?
Cow
They seem to be friends
Dark Skin
Demon King
Timid
Sensitive
Friends
Real Name: Twilight
Steamed Egg Custard
Quilly
Hey!)
Weirdo
Seems to have lost his humanity.
← Always laughing
Stop it!
Furry Dog
Furry ♡
Furry ♡
Great Red
Furry ♡ Furry ♡
Furry ♡
Very stern for a dog
Furrrrrrrrrrry
Boney
Lots of them
I'll color them later
Repairs walls for me
I will never forgive them for the toilet incident
This one's really cute
Tail→
Reindeer
↑ Ripped
I can usually tell who he is.
Princess!
Girl
About six inches taller than me.
Bird Girl
She's tall for a girl, isn't she?
I definitely remember her!
Heeey!
He listens to whatever gramps tells him.
Child
Vampire?
Kind → He seems weak... Why?
??
Not Boney
Always looks worried
Friendly with everyone
Plague Mask Alien
We're good friends!

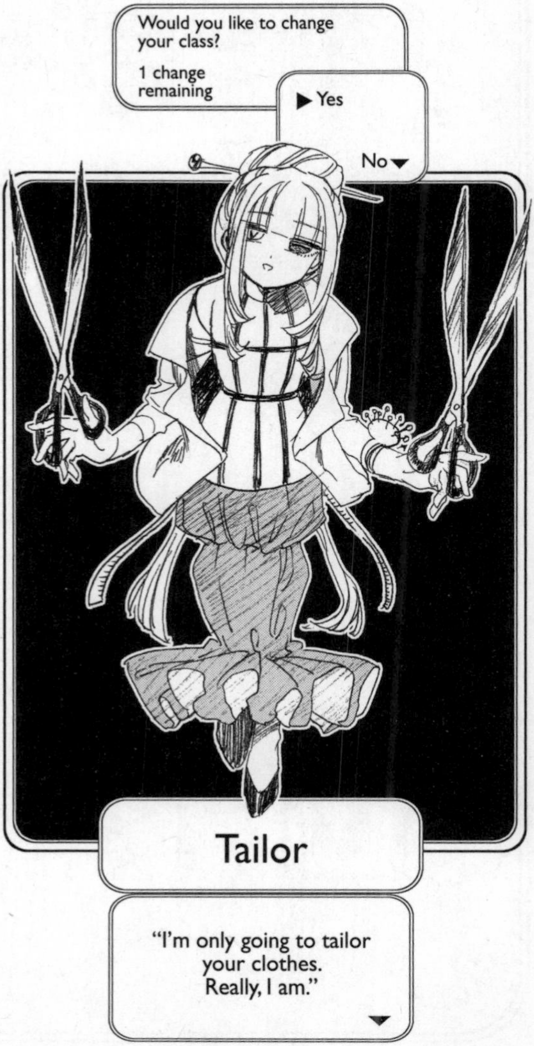
Would you like to change your class?
1 change remaining
▶Yes
No
Tailor
"I'm only going to tailor your clothes. Really, I am."

77th Night: I See You In My Dreams♡

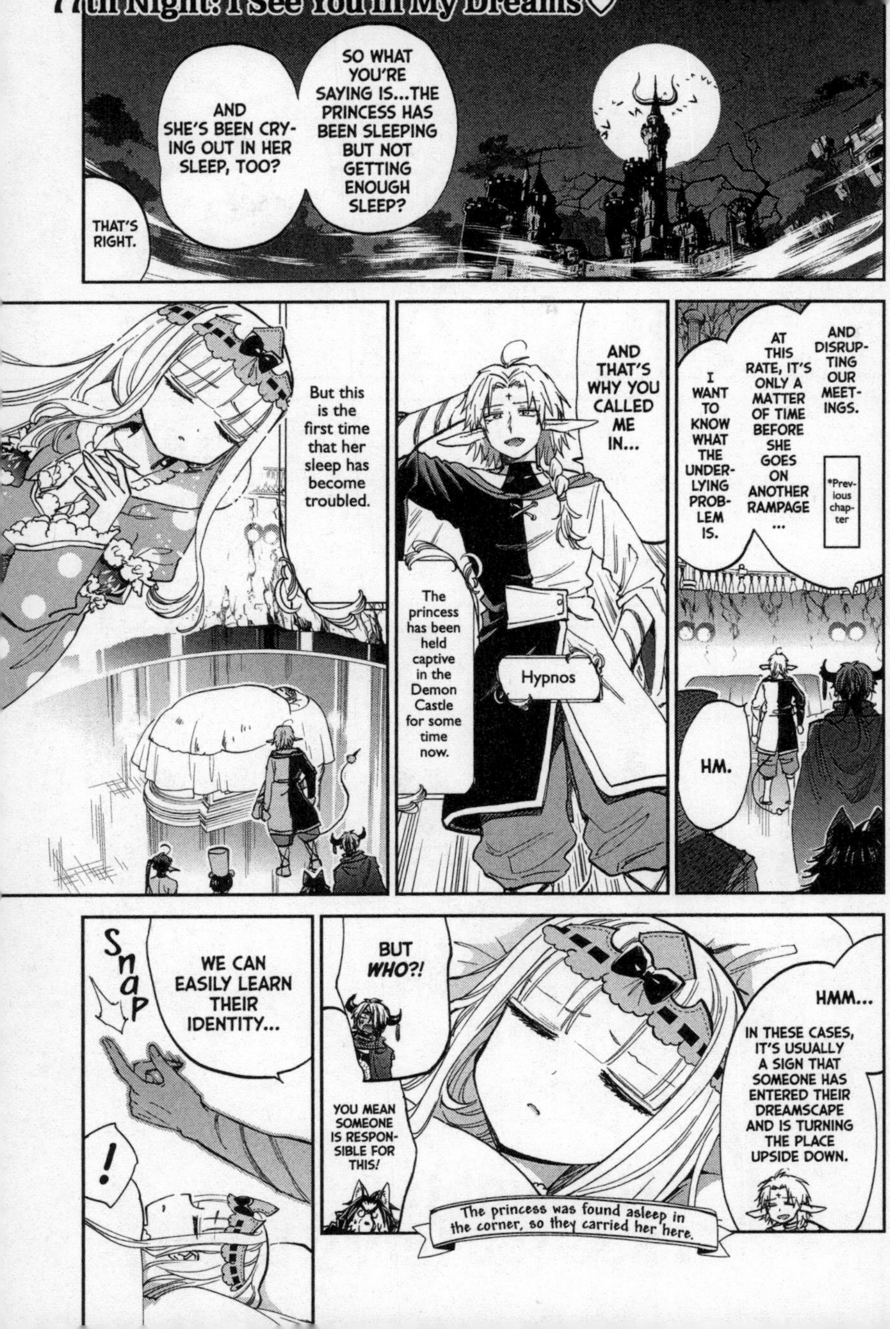

SO WHAT YOU'RE SAYING IS...THE PRINCESS HAS BEEN SLEEPING BUT NOT GETTING ENOUGH SLEEP?
AND SHE'S BEEN CRYING OUT IN HER SLEEP, TOO?
THAT'S RIGHT.
AND DISRUPTING OUR MEETINGS.
*Previous chapter
AT THIS RATE, IT'S ONLY A MATTER OF TIME BEFORE SHE GOES ON ANOTHER RAMPAGE...
I WANT TO KNOW WHAT THE UNDERLYING PROBLEM IS.
HM.
AND THAT'S WHY YOU CALLED ME IN...
Hypnos
The princess has been held captive in the Demon Castle for some time now.
But this is the first time that her sleep has become troubled.
HMM...
IN THESE CASES, IT'S USUALLY A SIGN THAT SOMEONE HAS ENTERED THEIR DREAMSCAPE AND IS TURNING THE PLACE UPSIDE DOWN.
BUT *WHO?!*
YOU MEAN SOMEONE IS RESPONSIBLE FOR THIS!
The princess was found asleep in the corner, so they carried her here.
WE CAN EASILY LEARN THEIR IDENTITY...
Snap
!

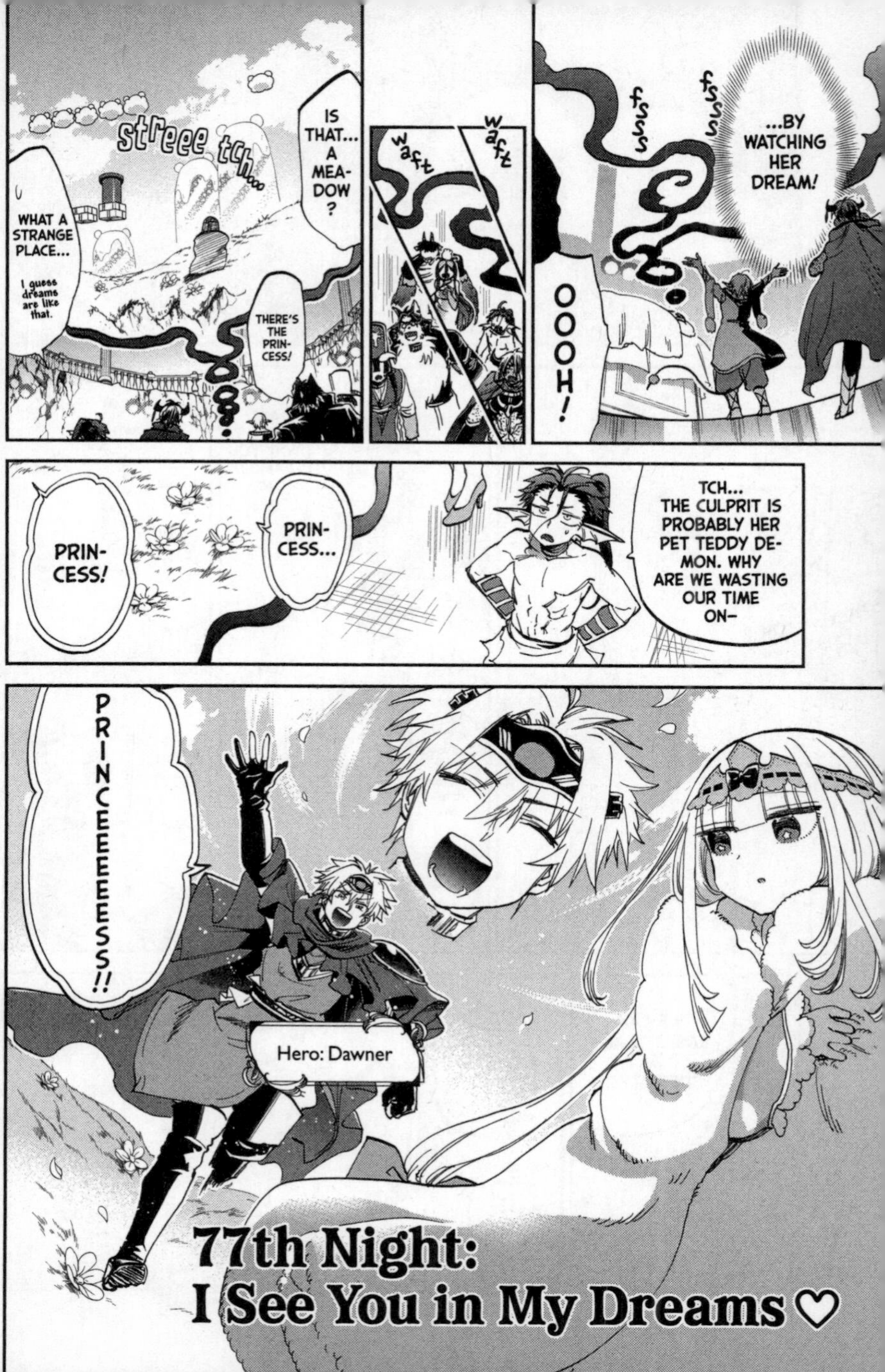
fsss
fsss
...BY WATCHING HER DREAM!
OOOOH!
waft
waft
IS THAT... A MEADOW?
streeee tch...
WHAT A STRANGE PLACE...
I guess dreams are like that.
THERE'S THE PRINCESS!
TCH... THE CULPRIT IS PROBABLY HER PET TEDDY DEMON. WHY ARE WE WASTING OUR TIME ON–
PRINCESS...
PRINCESS!
PRINCEEEEEESS!!
Hero: Dawner
77th Night: I See You in My Dreams ♡

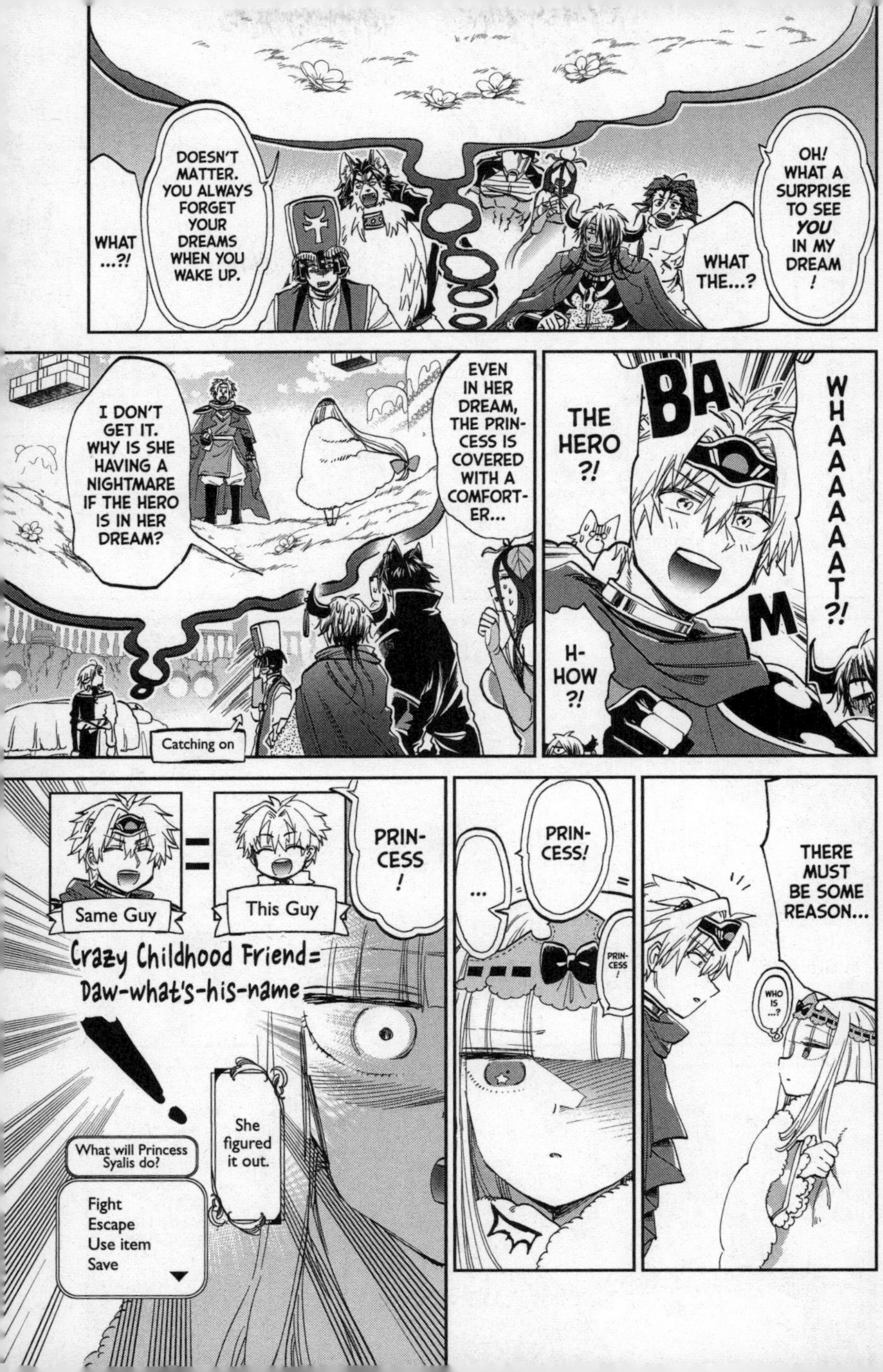
OH! WHAT A SURPRISE TO SEE YOU IN MY DREAM!
WHAT THE...?
DOESN'T MATTER. YOU ALWAYS FORGET YOUR DREAMS WHEN YOU WAKE UP.
WHAT...?!
WHAAAAAAAT?!
BAM
THE HERO?!
H-HOW?!
EVEN IN HER DREAM, THE PRIN-CESS IS COVERED WITH A COMFORT-ER...
I DON'T GET IT. WHY IS SHE HAVING A NIGHTMARE IF THE HERO IS IN HER DREAM?
Catching on
THERE MUST BE SOME REASON...
PRIN-CESS!
WHO IS ...?
PRIN-CESS!
...
PRIN-CESS!
This Guy
Same Guy
Crazy Childhood Friend=
Daw-what's-his-name
She figured it out.
What will Princess Syalis do?
Fight
Escape
Use item
Save

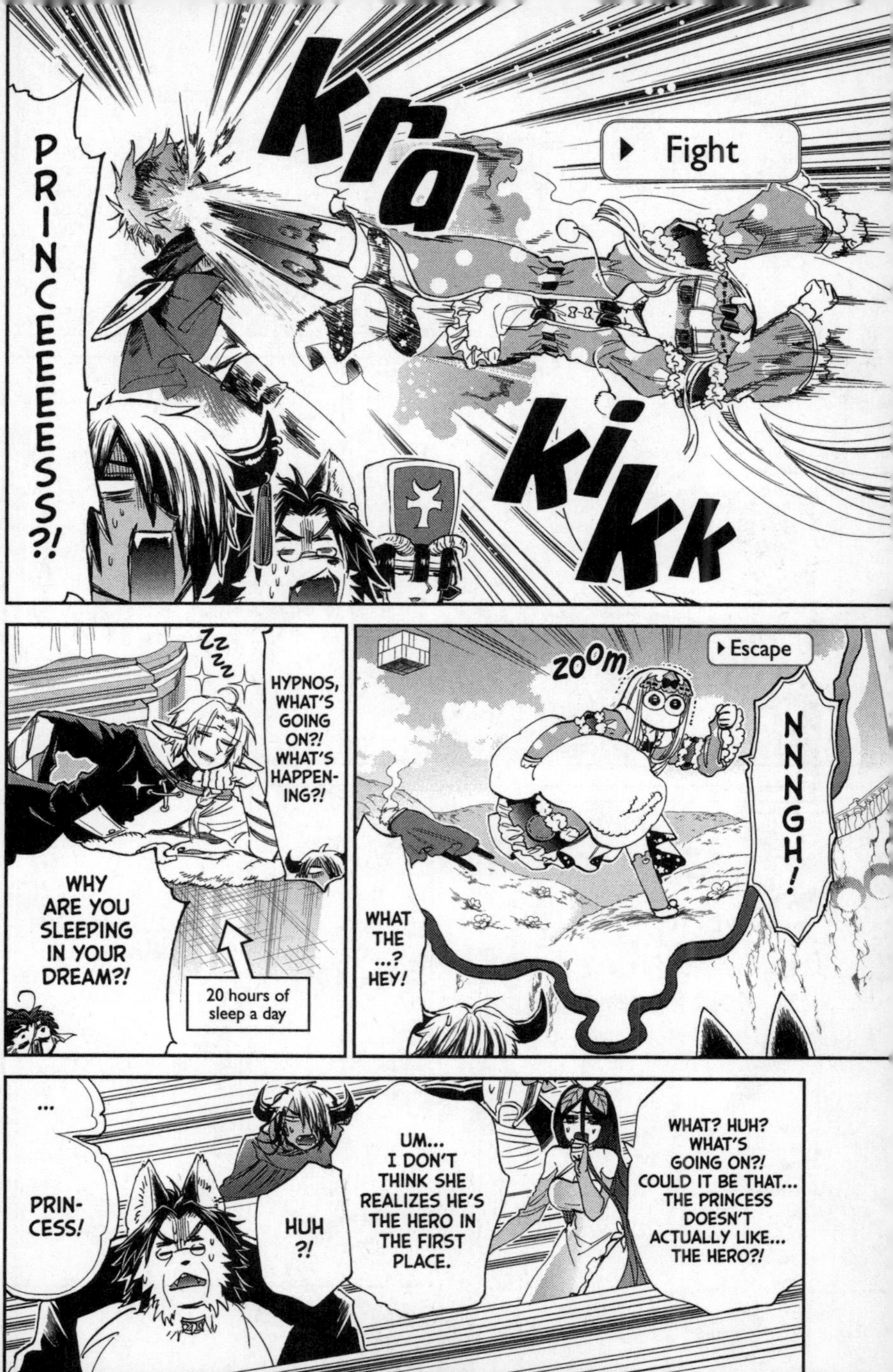
▶ Fight
kra
kikk
PRINCEEEEESS?!
▶ Escape
zoom
NNNGH!
WHAT THE ...? HEY!
HYPNOS, WHAT'S GOING ON?! WHAT'S HAPPEN-ING?!
ZZZ
WHY ARE YOU SLEEPING IN YOUR DREAM?!
20 hours of sleep a day
WHAT? HUH? WHAT'S GOING ON?! COULD IT BE THAT... THE PRINCESS DOESN'T ACTUALLY LIKE... THE HERO?!
UM... I DON'T THINK SHE REALIZES HE'S THE HERO IN THE FIRST PLACE.
HUH?!
...
PRIN-CESS!

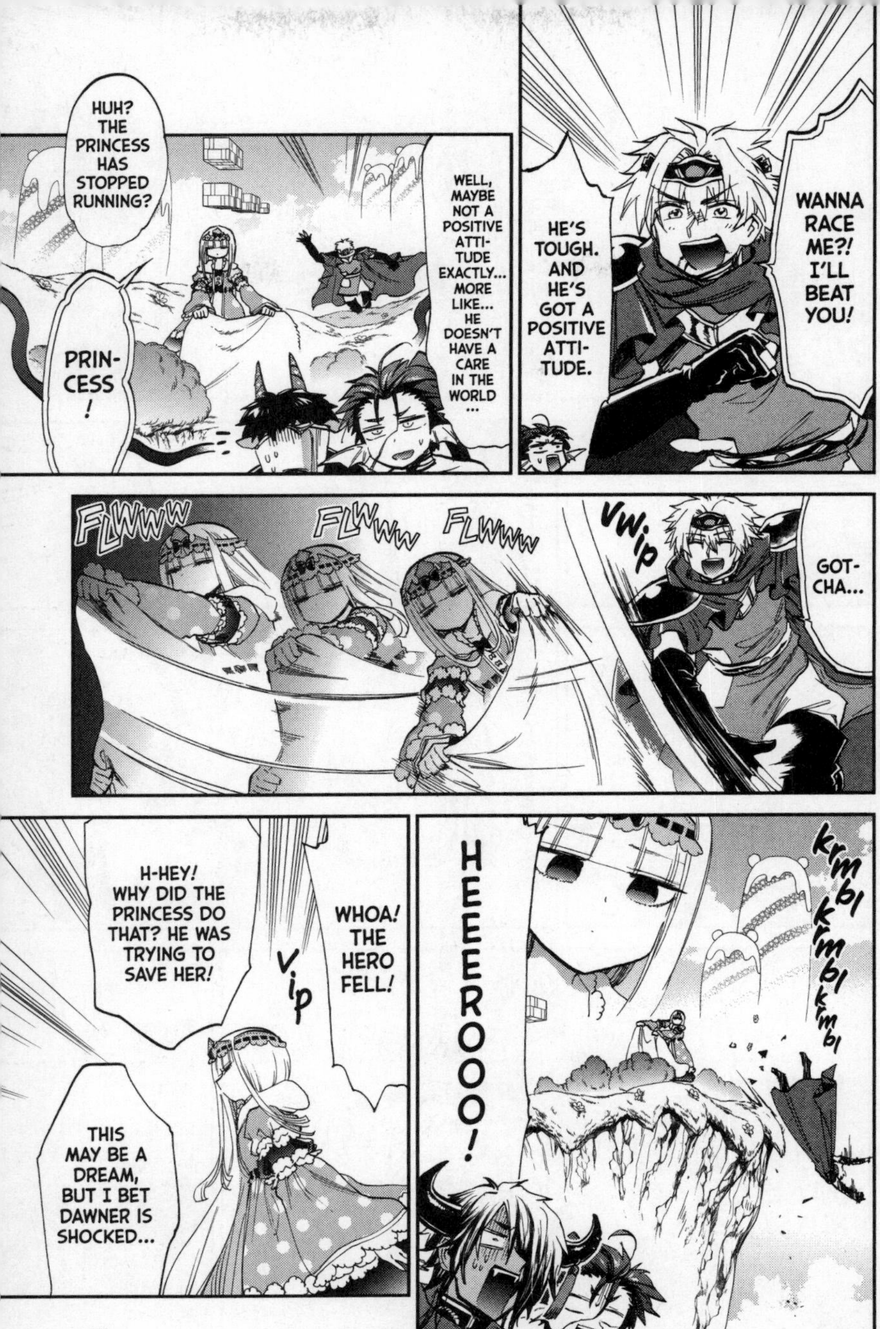
WANNA RACE ME?! I'LL BEAT YOU!
HE'S TOUGH. AND HE'S GOT A POSITIVE ATTI-TUDE.
WELL, MAYBE NOT A POSITIVE ATTI-TUDE EXACTLY... MORE LIKE... HE DOESN'T HAVE A CARE IN THE WORLD...
HUH? THE PRINCESS HAS STOPPED RUNNING?
PRIN-CESS!
GOT-CHA...
VWip
FLWWWW
FLWWWW
FLWWWW
krmbl krmbl krmbl krmbl
HEEEROOOO!
WHOA! THE HERO FELL!
Vip
H-HEY! WHY DID THE PRINCESS DO THAT? HE WAS TRYING TO SAVE HER!
THIS MAY BE A DREAM, BUT I BET DAWNER IS SHOCKED...

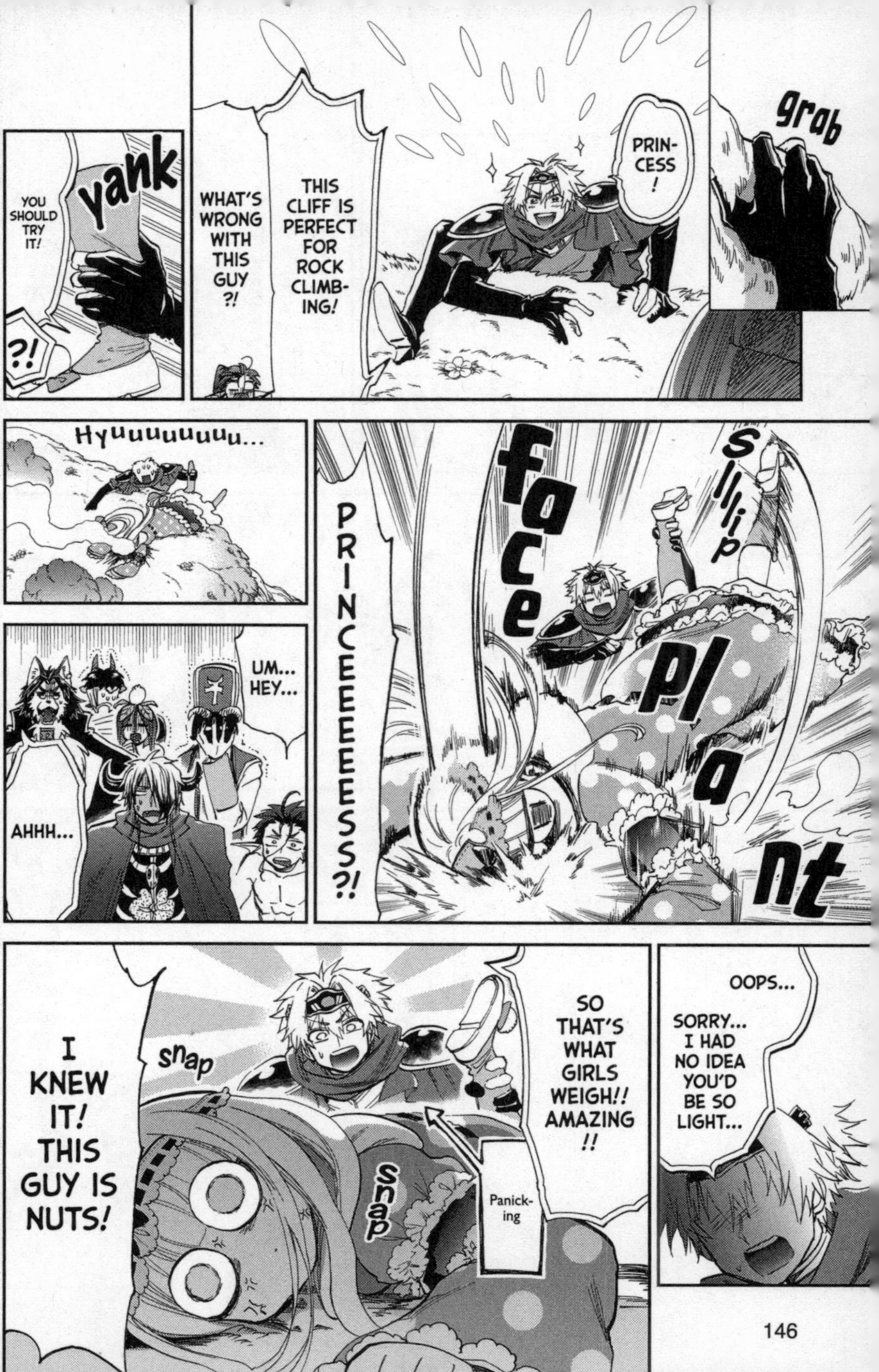
grab
PRIN-CESS!
THIS CLIFF IS PERFECT FOR ROCK CLIMB-ING!
WHAT'S WRONG WITH THIS GUY?!
yank
YOU SHOULD TRY IT!
?!
slllip
face plant
PRINCEEEEEESS?!
Hyuuuuuuuu...
UM... HEY...
AHHH...
OOPS...
SORRY... I HAD NO IDEA YOU'D BE SO LIGHT...
SO THAT'S WHAT GIRLS WEIGH!! AMAZING!!
Panick-ing
snap
snap
I KNEW IT! THIS GUY IS NUTS!

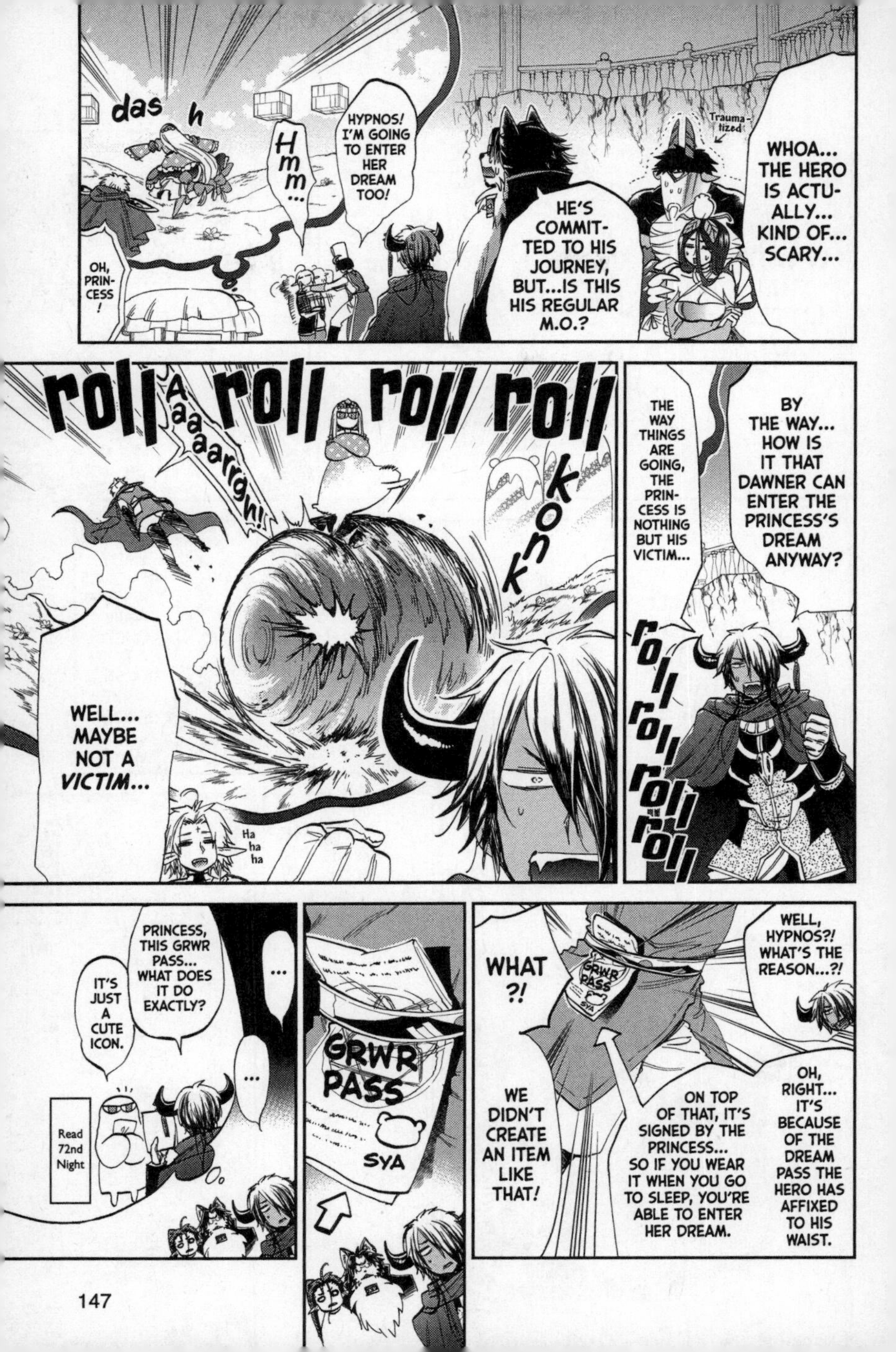
WHOA... THE HERO IS ACTUALLY... KIND OF... SCARY...
Traumatized
HE'S COMMITTED TO HIS JOURNEY, BUT...IS THIS HIS REGULAR M.O.?
HYPNOS! I'M GOING TO ENTER HER DREAM TOO!
Hmm...
dash
OH, PRINCESS!
BY THE WAY... HOW IS IT THAT DAWNER CAN ENTER THE PRINCESS'S DREAM ANYWAY?
THE WAY THINGS ARE GOING, THE PRINCESS IS NOTHING BUT HIS VICTIM...
roll roll roll roll
roll roll roll roll
konk
Aaaaarrgh!!
WELL... MAYBE NOT A VICTIM...
Ha ha ha
WELL, HYPNOS?! WHAT'S THE REASON...?!
OH, RIGHT... IT'S BECAUSE OF THE DREAM PASS THE HERO HAS AFFIXED TO HIS WAIST.
ON TOP OF THAT, IT'S SIGNED BY THE PRINCESS... SO IF YOU WEAR IT WHEN YOU GO TO SLEEP, YOU'RE ABLE TO ENTER HER DREAM.
WHAT?!
WE DIDN'T CREATE AN ITEM LIKE THAT!
GRWR PASS
SYA
GRWR PASS
SYA
...
...
PRINCESS, THIS GRWR PASS... WHAT DOES IT DO EXACTLY?
IT'S JUST A CUTE ICON.
Read 72nd Night

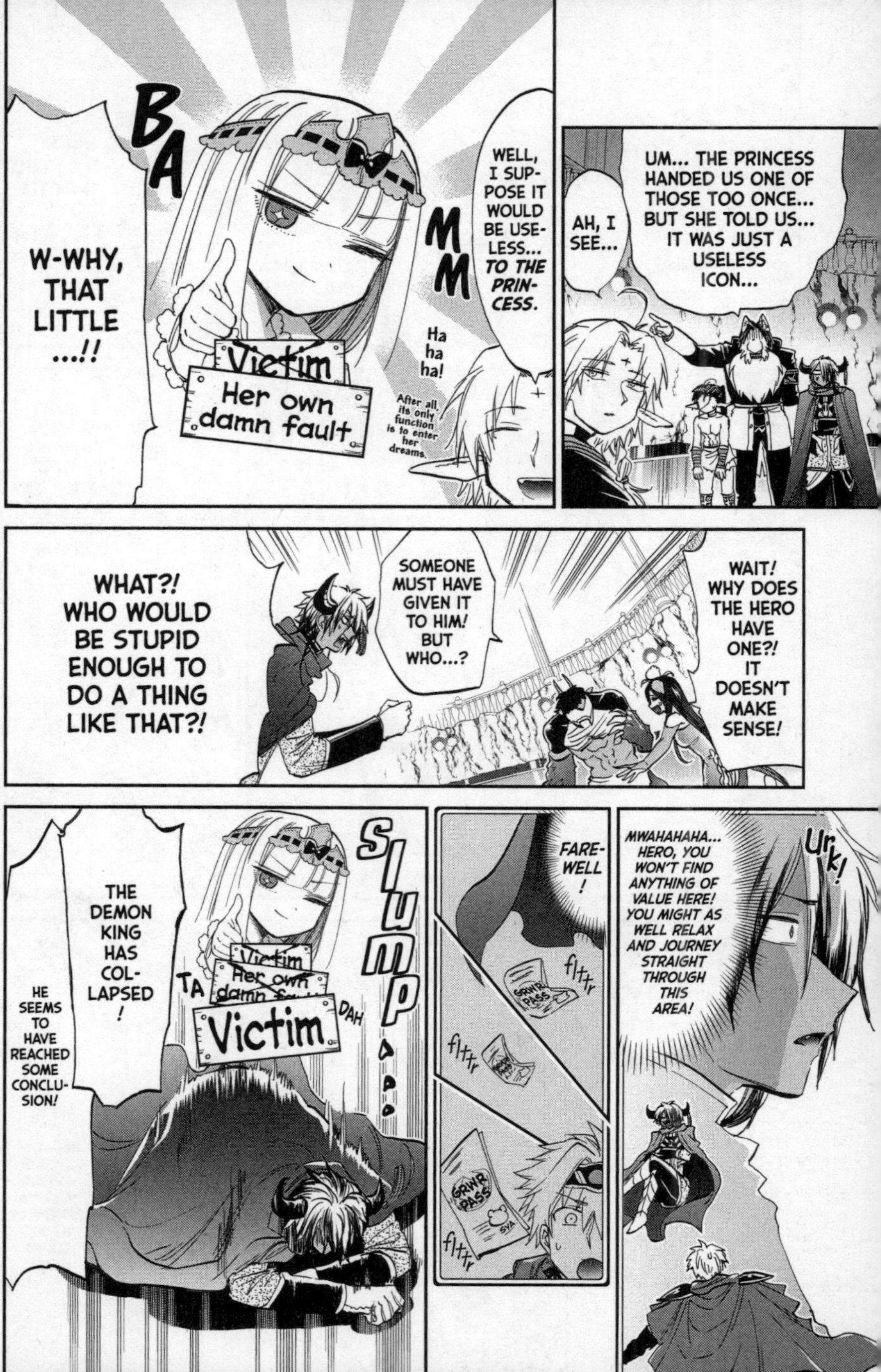
UM... THE PRINCESS HANDED US ONE OF THOSE TOO ONCE... BUT SHE TOLD US... IT WAS JUST A USELESS ICON...
AH, I SEE...
WELL, I SUPPOSE IT WOULD BE USELESS... TO THE PRINCESS.
Ha ha ha!
After all, its only function is to enter her dreams.
MM
BA
W-WHY, THAT LITTLE ...!!
Victim
Her own damn fault
WAIT! WHY DOES THE HERO HAVE ONE?! IT DOESN'T MAKE SENSE!
SOMEONE MUST HAVE GIVEN IT TO HIM! BUT WHO...?
WHAT?! WHO WOULD BE STUPID ENOUGH TO DO A THING LIKE THAT?!
Urk!
MWAHAHAHA... HERO, YOU WON'T FIND ANYTHING OF VALUE HERE! YOU MIGHT AS WELL RELAX AND JOURNEY STRAIGHT THROUGH THIS AREA!
FARE-WELL!
flxxr
GRWR PASS
flxxr
flxxr
GRWR PASS
SYA
SLUMP
THE DEMON KING HAS COL-LAPSED!
HE SEEMS TO HAVE REACHED SOME CONCLU-SION!
TA
DAH
Victim
Her own damn fault
Victim

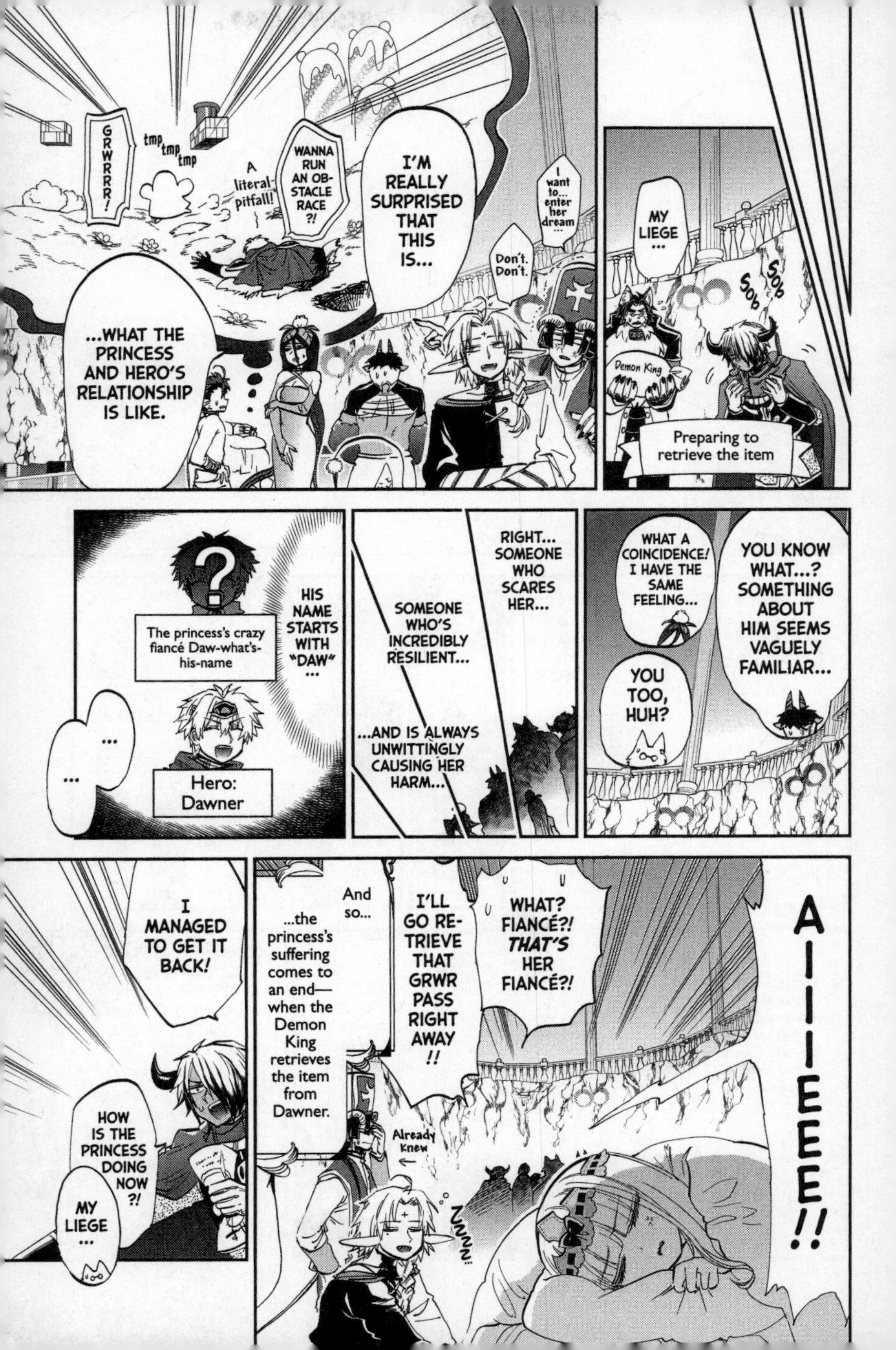
MY LIEGE...
Sob Sob
Demon King
Preparing to retrieve the item
I want to... enter her dream...
Don't. Don't.
I'M REALLY SURPRISED THAT THIS IS...
...WHAT THE PRINCESS AND HERO'S RELATIONSHIP IS LIKE.
WANNA RUN AN OBSTACLE RACE?!
A literal-pitfall!
tmp tmp tmp
GRWRRR!
YOU KNOW WHAT...? SOMETHING ABOUT HIM SEEMS VAGUELY FAMILIAR...
WHAT A COINCIDENCE! I HAVE THE SAME FEELING...
YOU TOO, HUH?
RIGHT... SOMEONE WHO SCARES HER...
SOMEONE WHO'S INCREDIBLY RESILIENT...
...AND IS ALWAYS UNWITTINGLY CAUSING HER HARM...
HIS NAME STARTS WITH "DAW"...
The princess's crazy fiancé Daw-what's-his-name
Hero: Dawner
...
...
AIIIEEE!!
WHAT? FIANCÉ?! *THAT'S* HER FIANCÉ?!
I'LL GO RETRIEVE THAT GRWR PASS RIGHT AWAY!!
And so...
...the princess's suffering comes to an end—when the Demon King retrieves the item from Dawner.
Already knew
ZZZZ
I MANAGED TO GET IT BACK!
HOW IS THE PRINCESS DOING NOW?!
MY LIEGE...

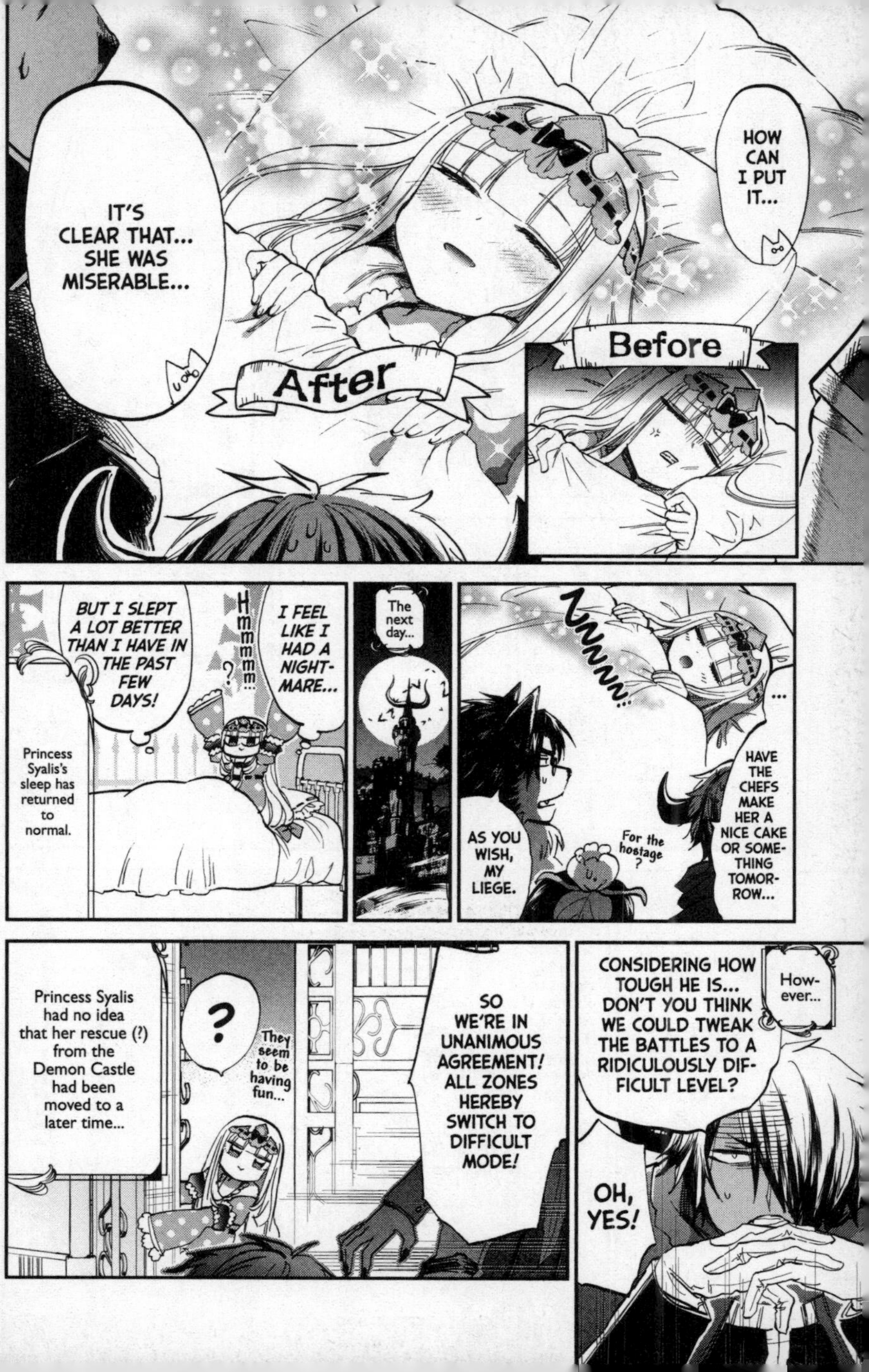
HOW CAN I PUT IT...
Before
After
IT'S CLEAR THAT... SHE WAS MISERABLE...
...
HAVE THE CHEFS MAKE HER A NICE CAKE OR SOMETHING TOMORROW...
For the hostage?
AS YOU WISH, MY LIEGE.
The next day...
I FEEL LIKE I HAD A NIGHTMARE...
Hmmmm...?
BUT I SLEPT A LOT BETTER THAN I HAVE IN THE PAST FEW DAYS!
Princess Syalis's sleep has returned to normal.
However...
CONSIDERING HOW TOUGH HE IS... DON'T YOU THINK WE COULD TWEAK THE BATTLES TO A RIDICULOUSLY DIFFICULT LEVEL?
OH, YES!
SO WE'RE IN UNANIMOUS AGREEMENT! ALL ZONES HEREBY SWITCH TO DIFFICULT MODE!
They seem to be having fun...
?
Princess Syalis had no idea that her rescue (?) from the Demon Castle had been moved to a later time...

GRWR Pass

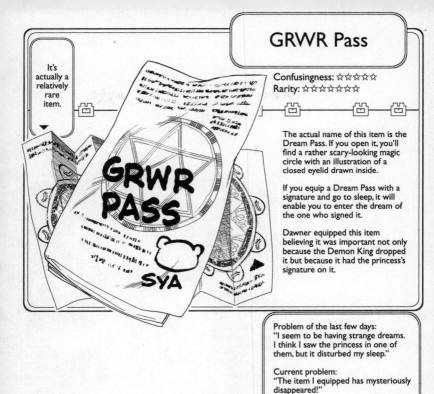

It's actually a relatively rare item.

GRWR PASS
SYA

Confusingness: ☆☆☆☆☆
Rarity: ☆☆☆☆☆☆☆☆

The actual name of this item is the Dream Pass. If you open it, you'll find a rather scary-looking magic circle with an illustration of a closed eyelid drawn inside.

If you equip a Dream Pass with a signature and go to sleep, it will enable you to enter the dream of the one who signed it.

Dawner equipped this item believing it was important not only because the Demon King dropped it but because it had the princess's signature on it.

Problem of the last few days:
"I seem to be having strange dreams. I think I saw the princess in one of them, but it disturbed my sleep."

Current problem:
"The item I equipped has mysteriously disappeared!"

THE DEMON KING SAID TO SWITCH TO DIFFICULT MODE, BUT...
HOW DIFFER-ENT IS IT REALLY?
AC-CORD-ING TO THE DE-MON KING...
THERE'S THE EGGPLANT SEAL AND THEN THERE'S THE GIANT EGGPLANT SEAL.
IT'S LIKE THAT.
I... SEE...
Cuddly...
Furry...
IT'S PROBABLY NOT LIKE WHAT YOU'RE PICTURING.

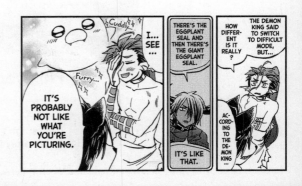

Would you like to change your class?

0 changes remaining

Philosopher

"Please don't use me as a prop."

▼

78th Night: Princess Runnings

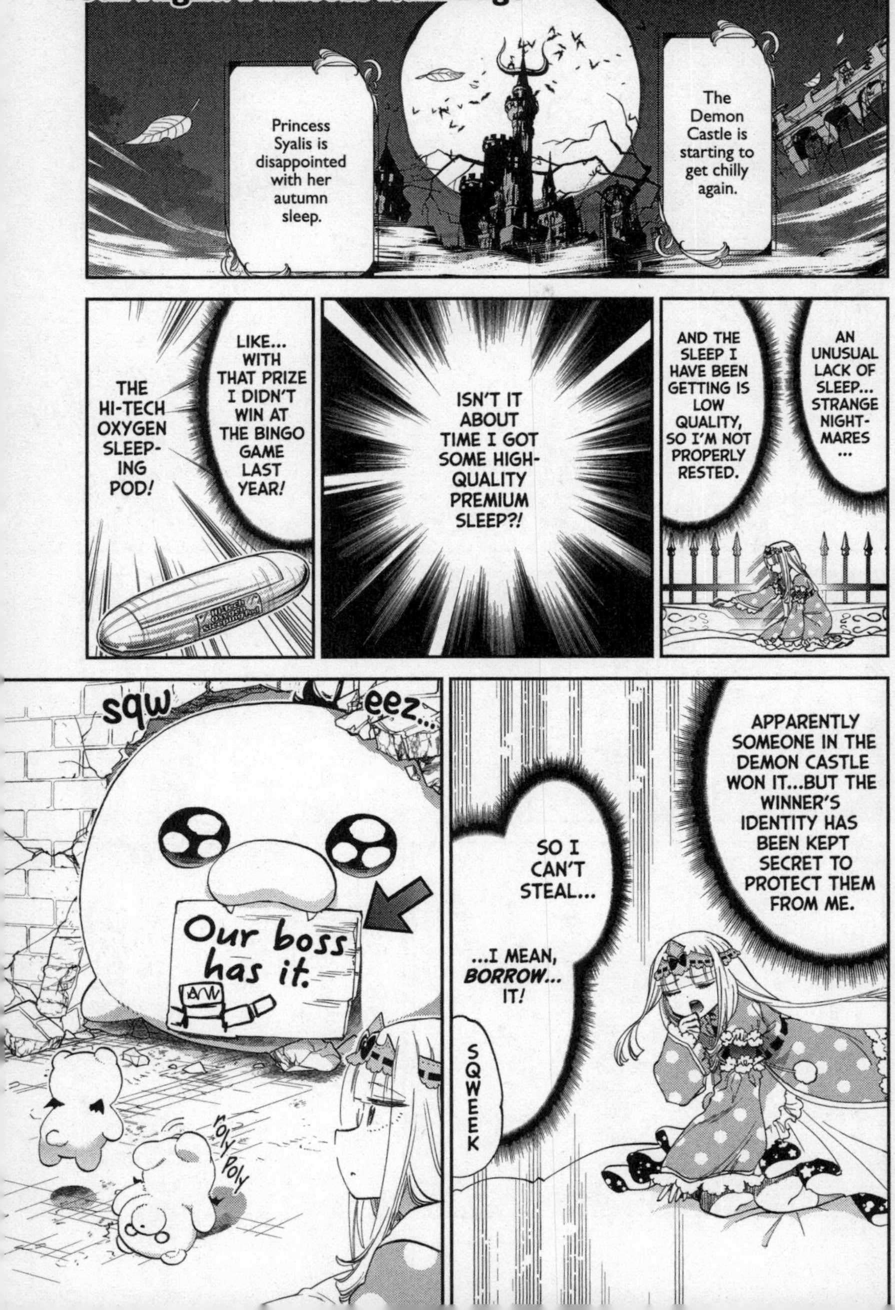

The Demon Castle is starting to get chilly again.
Princess Syalis is disappointed with her autumn sleep.
AN UNUSUAL LACK OF SLEEP... STRANGE NIGHTMARES...
AND THE SLEEP I HAVE BEEN GETTING IS LOW QUALITY, SO I'M NOT PROPERLY RESTED.
ISN'T IT ABOUT TIME I GOT SOME HIGH-QUALITY PREMIUM SLEEP?!
LIKE... WITH THAT PRIZE I DIDN'T WIN AT THE BINGO GAME LAST YEAR!
THE HI-TECH OXYGEN SLEEPING POD!
Hi-Tech Oxygen Sleeping Pod
APPARENTLY SOMEONE IN THE DEMON CASTLE WON IT...BUT THE WINNER'S IDENTITY HAS BEEN KEPT SECRET TO PROTECT THEM FROM ME.
SO I CAN'T STEAL...
...I MEAN, *BORROW*... IT!
SQWEEK
sqw
eez...
Our boss has it.
roly poly

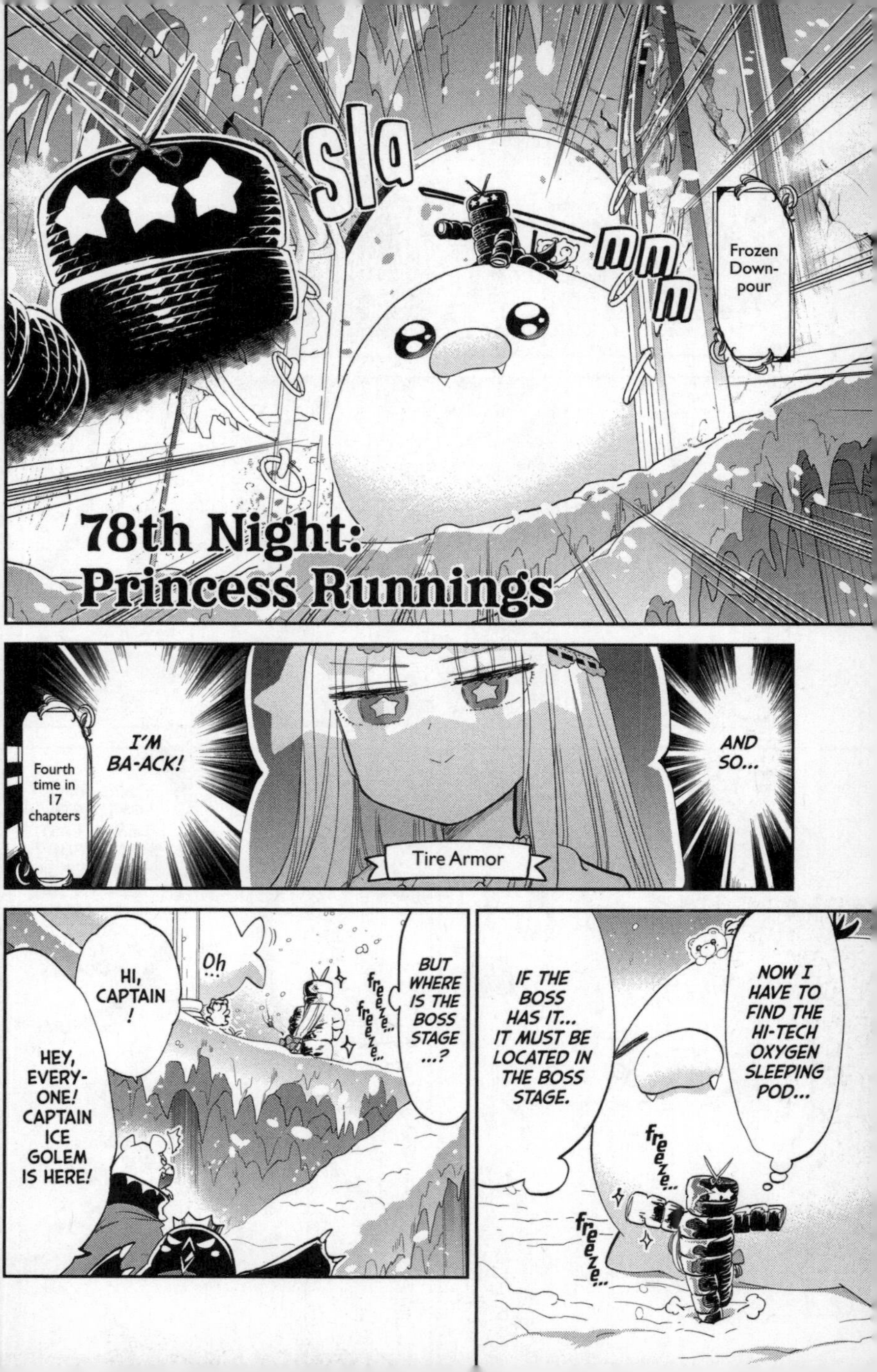
Slammm
Frozen Down-pour
78th Night: Princess Runnings
AND SO...
I'M BA-ACK!
Fourth time in 17 chapters
Tire Armor
NOW I HAVE TO FIND THE HI-TECH OXYGEN SLEEPING POD...
IF THE BOSS HAS IT... IT MUST BE LOCATED IN THE BOSS STAGE.
freeze...
freeze...
BUT WHERE IS THE BOSS STAGE ...?
freeze... freeze...
Oh ...
HI, CAPTAIN!
HEY, EVERYONE! CAPTAIN ICE GOLEM IS HERE!

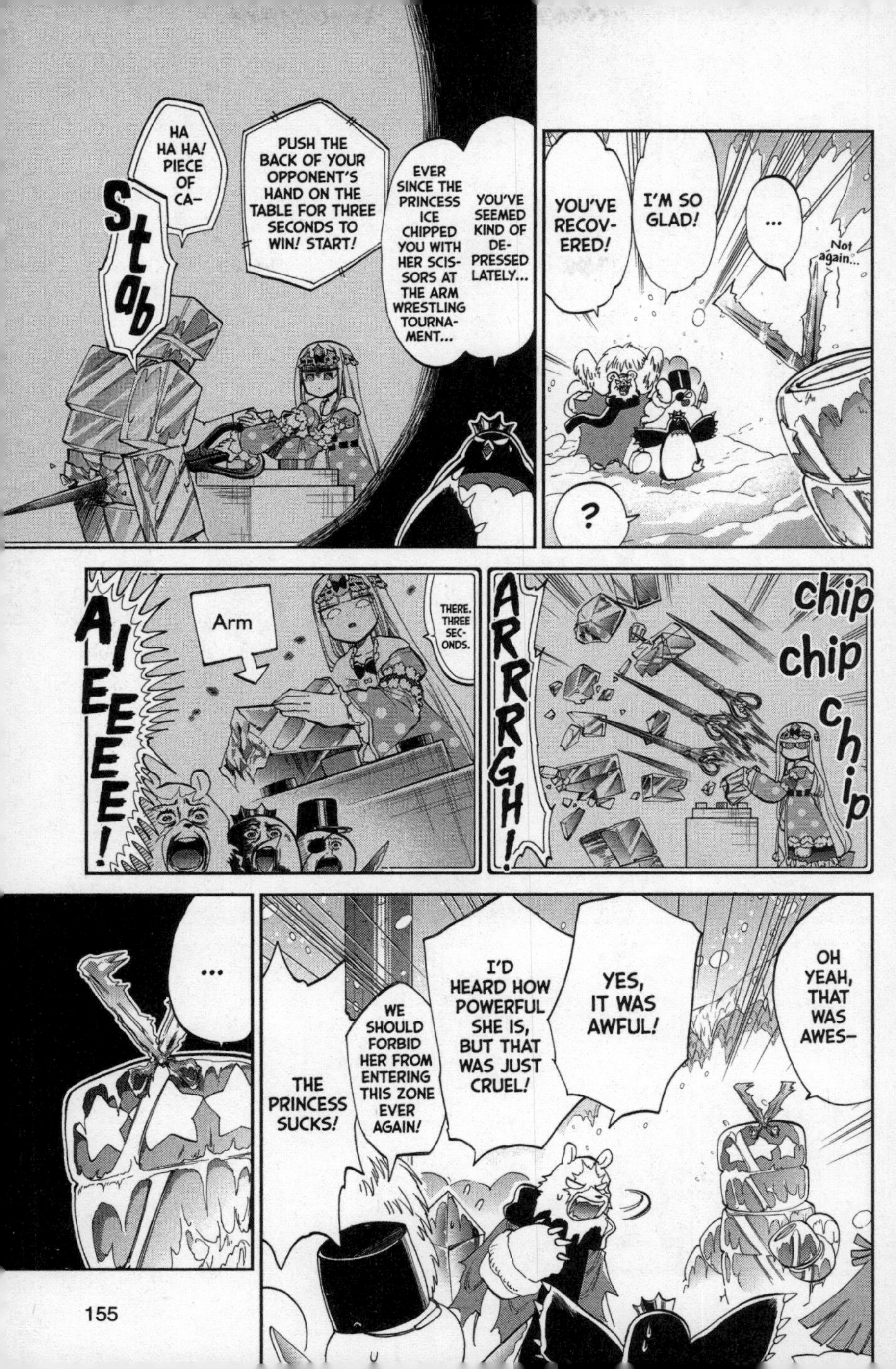
...
Not again...
I'M SO GLAD!
YOU'VE RECOVERED!
?
YOU'VE SEEMED KIND OF DEPRESSED LATELY...
EVER SINCE THE PRINCESS ICE CHIPPED YOU WITH HER SCISSORS AT THE ARM WRESTLING TOURNAMENT...
PUSH THE BACK OF YOUR OPPONENT'S HAND ON THE TABLE FOR THREE SECONDS TO WIN! START!
HA HA HA! PIECE OF CA-
Stab
chip chip chip chip
ARRRGH!
THERE. THREE SECONDS.
Arm
AIEEEEEE!
OH YEAH, THAT WAS AWES—
YES, IT WAS AWFUL!
I'D HEARD HOW POWERFUL SHE IS, BUT THAT WAS JUST CRUEL!
WE SHOULD FORBID HER FROM ENTERING THIS ZONE EVER AGAIN!
THE PRINCESS SUCKS!
...

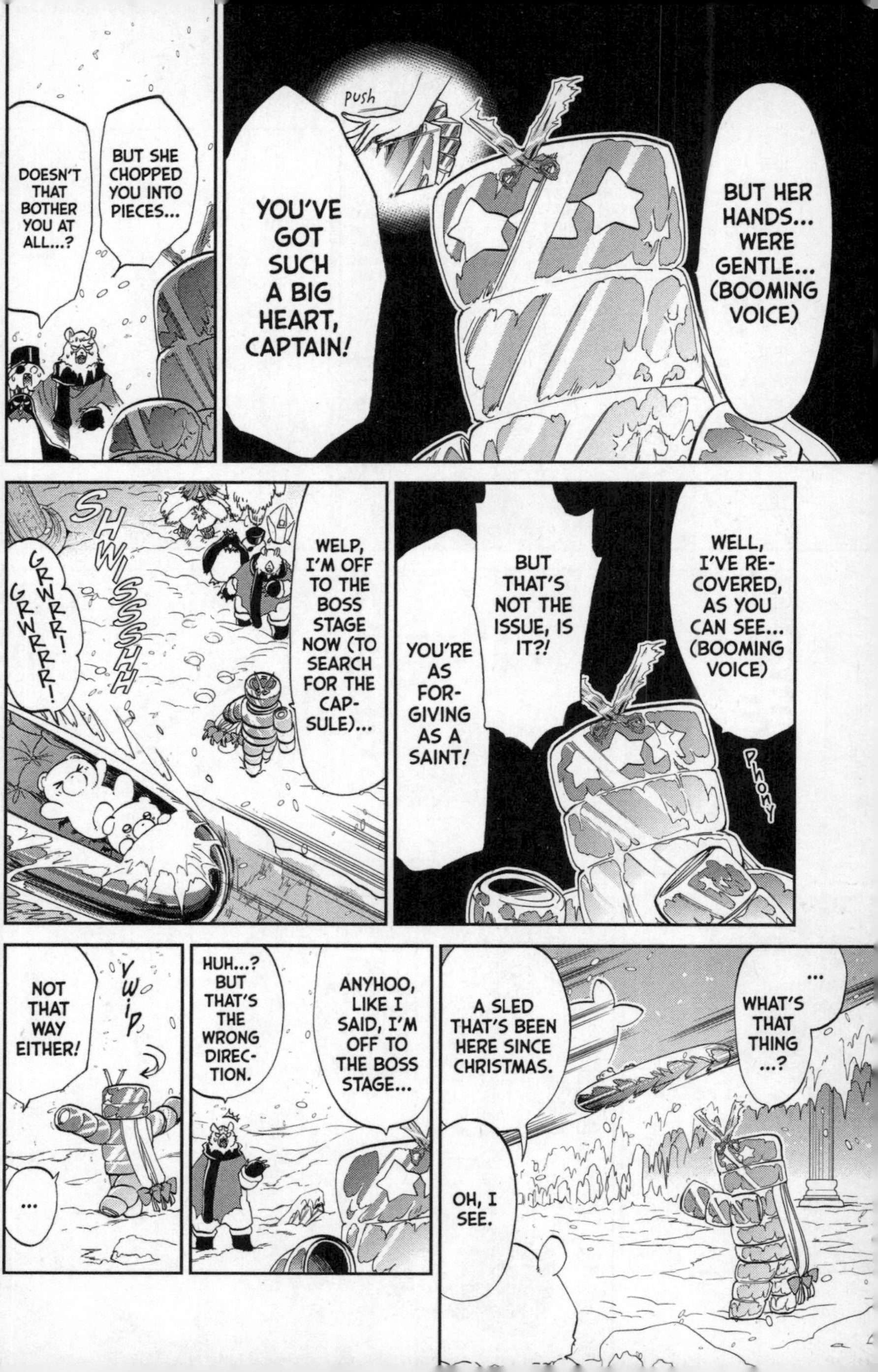
push
BUT HER HANDS... WERE GENTLE... (BOOMING VOICE)
YOU'VE GOT SUCH A BIG HEART, CAPTAIN!
BUT SHE CHOPPED YOU INTO PIECES...
DOESN'T THAT BOTHER YOU AT ALL...?
WELL, I'VE RE-COVERED, AS YOU CAN SEE... (BOOMING VOICE)
BUT THAT'S NOT THE ISSUE, IS IT?!
YOU'RE AS FOR-GIVING AS A SAINT!
Phony
WELP, I'M OFF TO THE BOSS STAGE NOW (TO SEARCH FOR THE CAP-SULE)...
SHWISSSHH
GRWRR!
GRWRRR!
... WHAT'S THAT THING ...?
A SLED THAT'S BEEN HERE SINCE CHRISTMAS.
OH, I SEE.
ANYHOO, LIKE I SAID, I'M OFF TO THE BOSS STAGE...
HUH...? BUT THAT'S THE WRONG DIREC-TION.
VWIP
NOT THAT WAY EITHER!
...

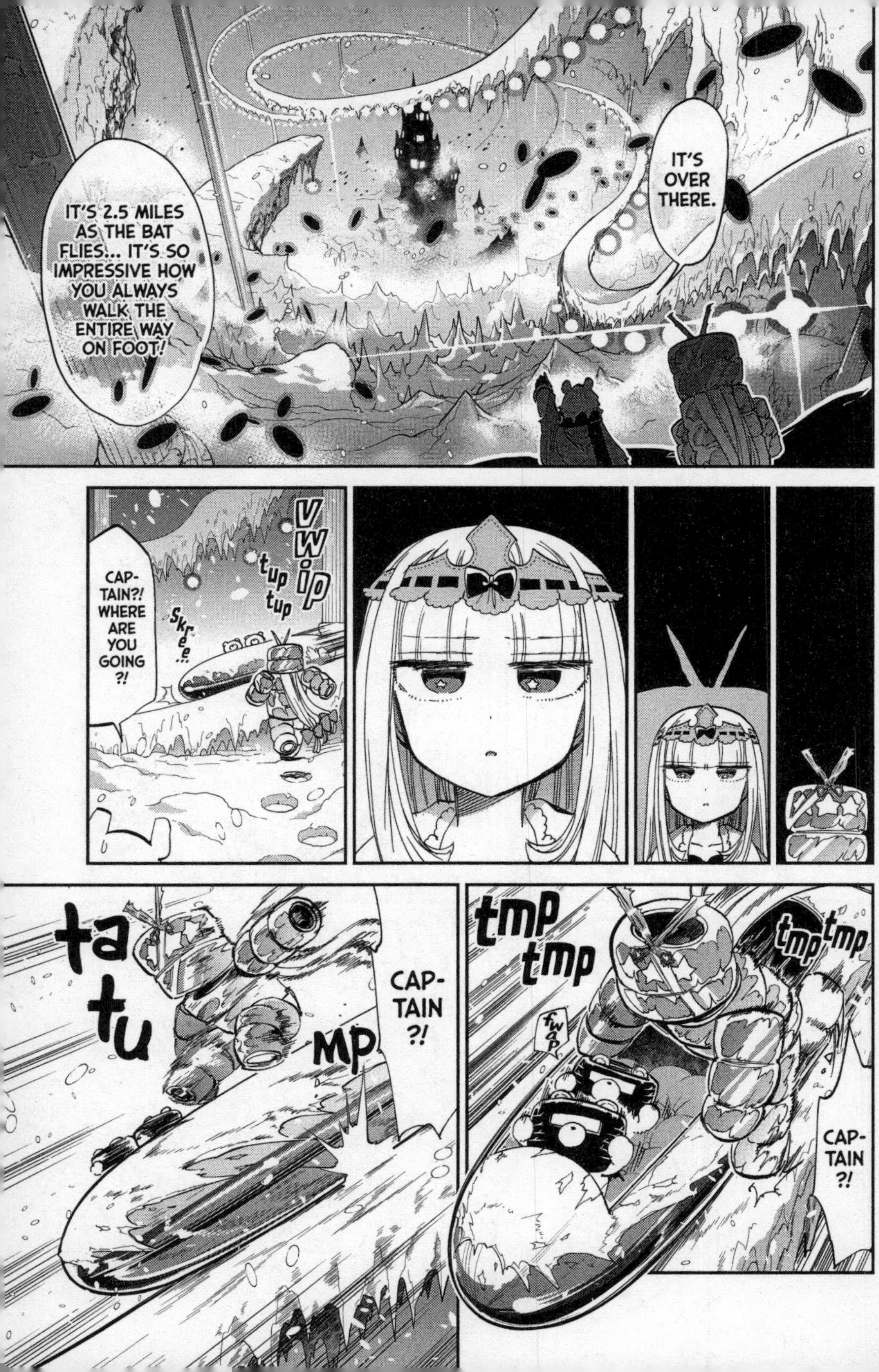
IT'S OVER THERE.
IT'S 2.5 MILES AS THE BAT FLIES... IT'S SO IMPRESSIVE HOW YOU ALWAYS WALK THE ENTIRE WAY ON FOOT!
VWIP
tup tup
Skree...
CAP-TAIN?! WHERE ARE YOU GOING?!
tmp tmp
tmp tmp
fwap
CAP-TAIN?!
ta tu MP
CAP-TAIN?!

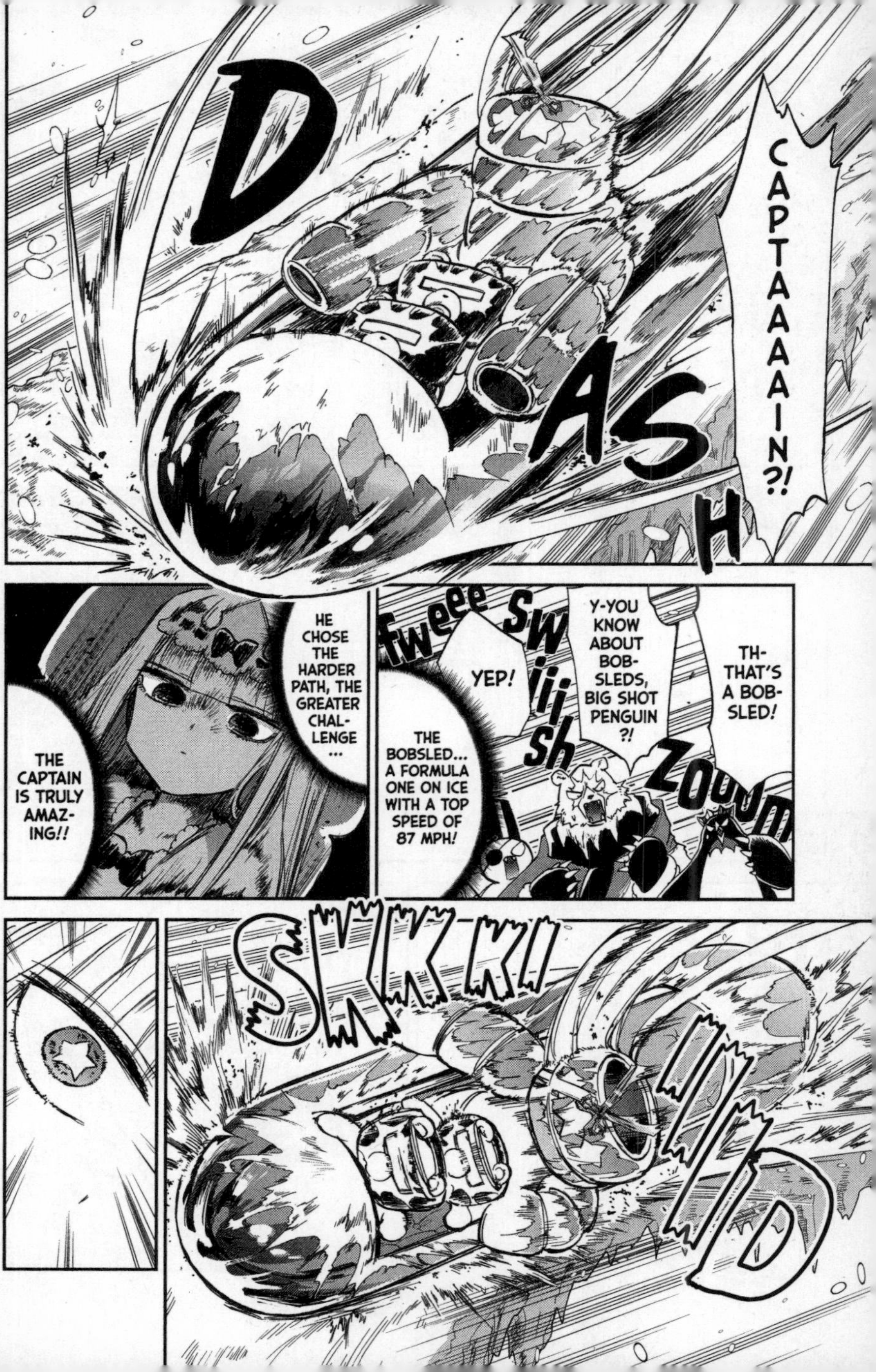
DASH
CAPTAAAAIN?!
TH-THAT'S A BOB-SLED!
Y-YOU KNOW ABOUT BOB-SLEDS, BIG SHOT PENGUIN?!
YEP!
THE BOBSLED... A FORMULA ONE ON ICE WITH A TOP SPEED OF 87 MPH!
fweee
SWiiiish
ZOUUM
HE CHOSE THE HARDER PATH, THE GREATER CHAL-LENGE ...
THE CAPTAIN IS TRULY AMAZ-ING!!
SKKKIIID

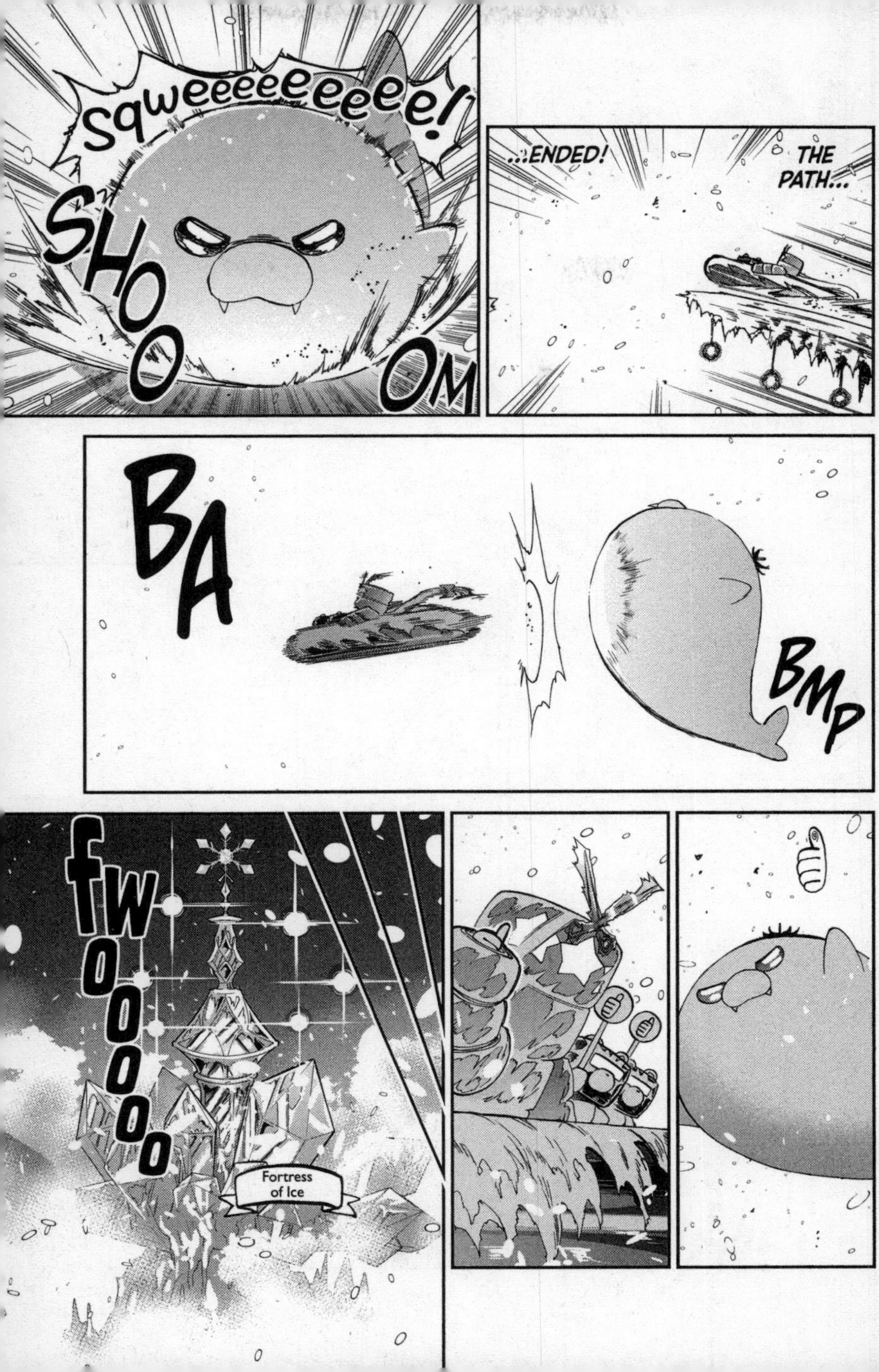
THE PATH...
...ENDED!
Sqweeeeeeeee!
SHOOOM
BA
BMP
fwoooooo
Fortress of Ice

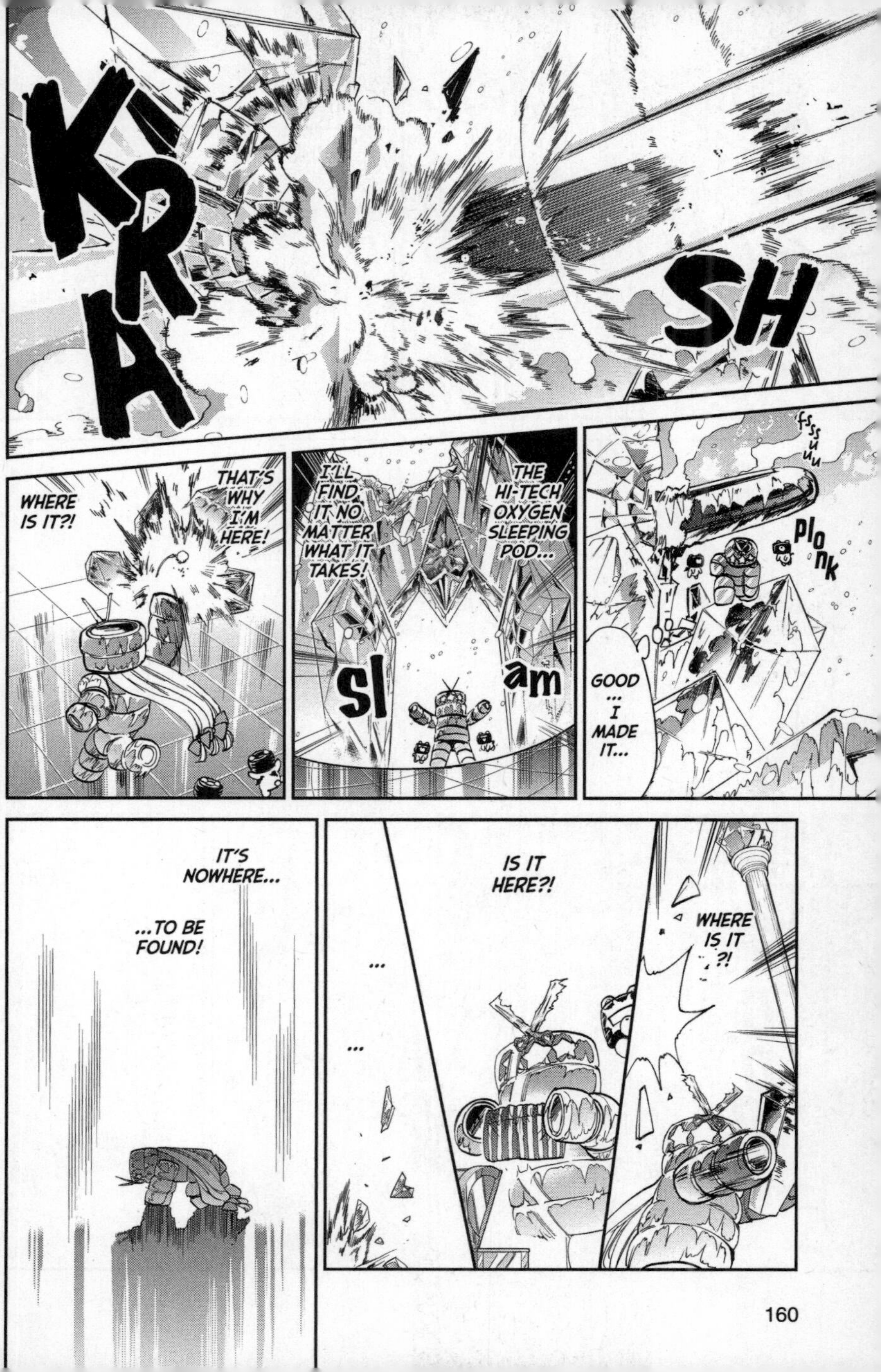
KRASH
fsssuuu
plonk
GOOD... I MADE IT...
THE HI-TECH OXYGEN SLEEPING POD...
I'LL FIND IT NO MATTER WHAT IT TAKES!
slam
THAT'S WHY I'M HERE!
WHERE IS IT?!
WHERE IS IT?!
IS IT HERE?!
...
...
IT'S NOWHERE...
...TO BE FOUND!

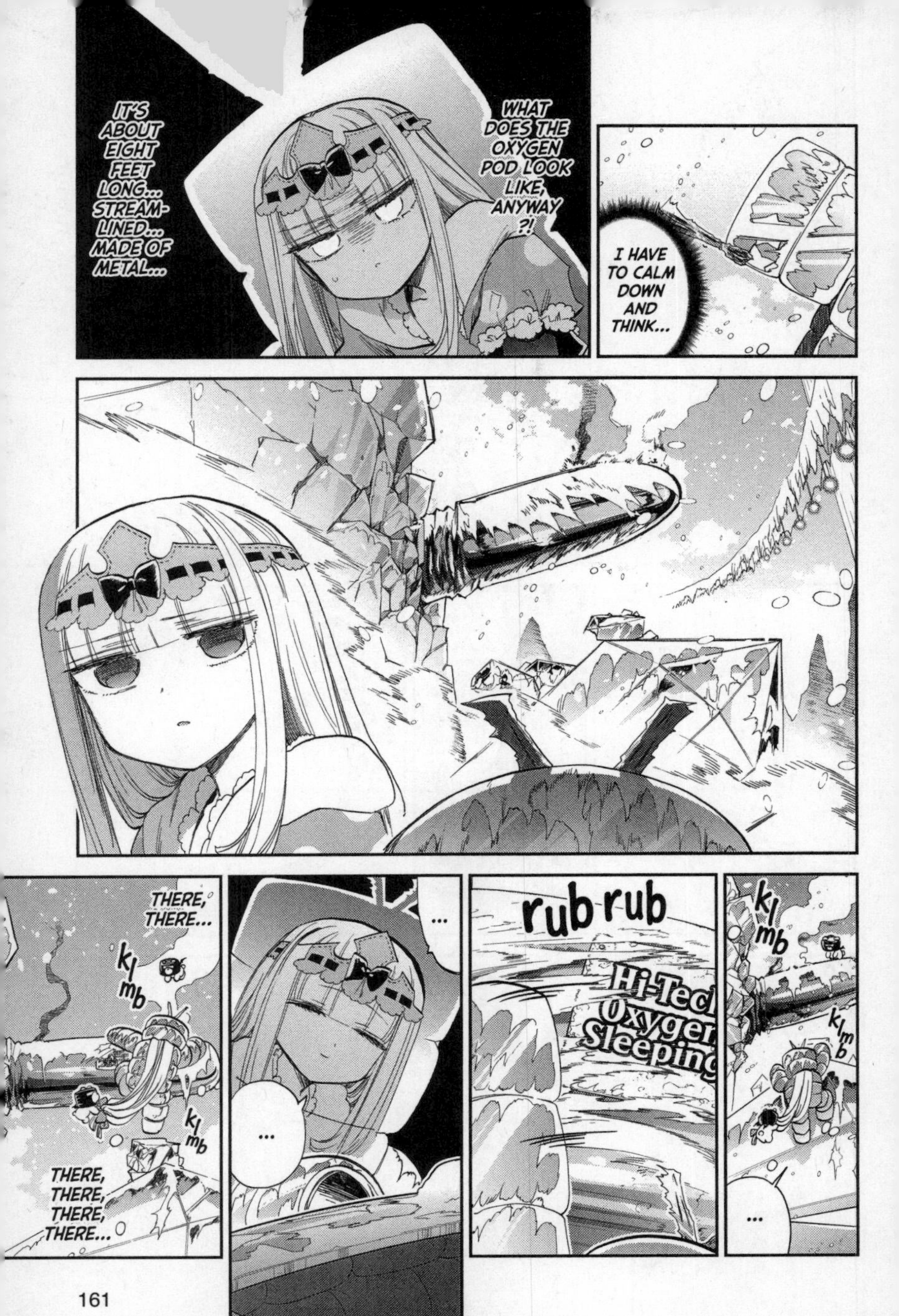
I HAVE TO CALM DOWN AND THINK...
WHAT DOES THE OXYGEN POD LOOK LIKE, ANYWAY?!
IT'S ABOUT EIGHT FEET LONG... STREAMLINED... MADE OF METAL...
klmb
klmb
...
rub rub
Hi-Tech Oxygen Sleeping
...
...
THERE, THERE...
klmb
klmb
THERE, THERE, THERE, THERE...

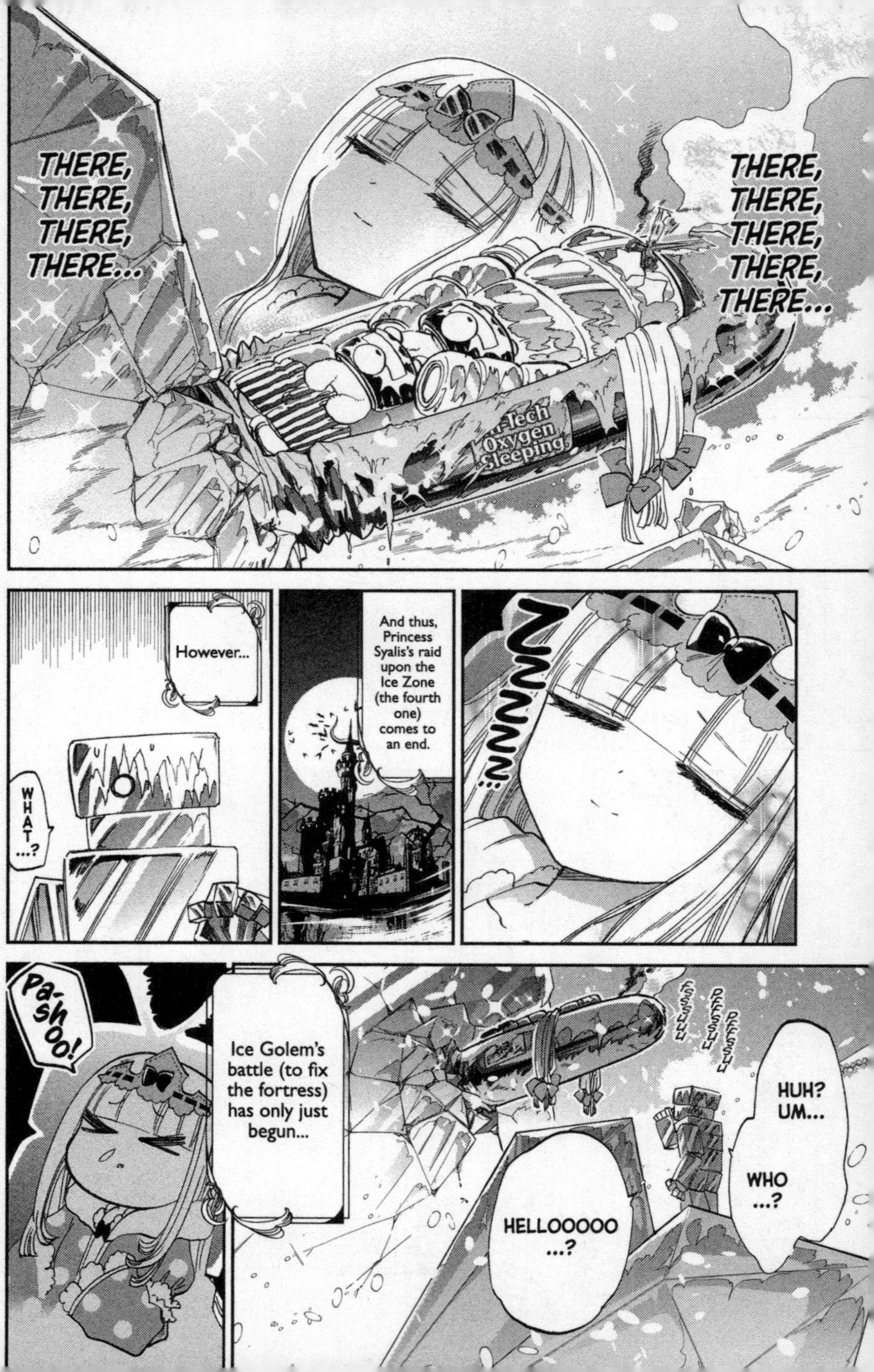
THERE, THERE, THERE, THERE, THERE...
THERE, THERE, THERE, THERE...
Oxygen Sleeping
ZZZZZZ...
And thus, Princess Syalis's raid upon the Ice Zone (the fourth one) comes to an end.
However...
WHAT ...?
HUH? UM...
WHO ...?
HELLOOOOO ...?
Ice Golem's battle (to fix the fortress) has only just begun...
Pa-shoo!

Bonus Page 78.1st Night

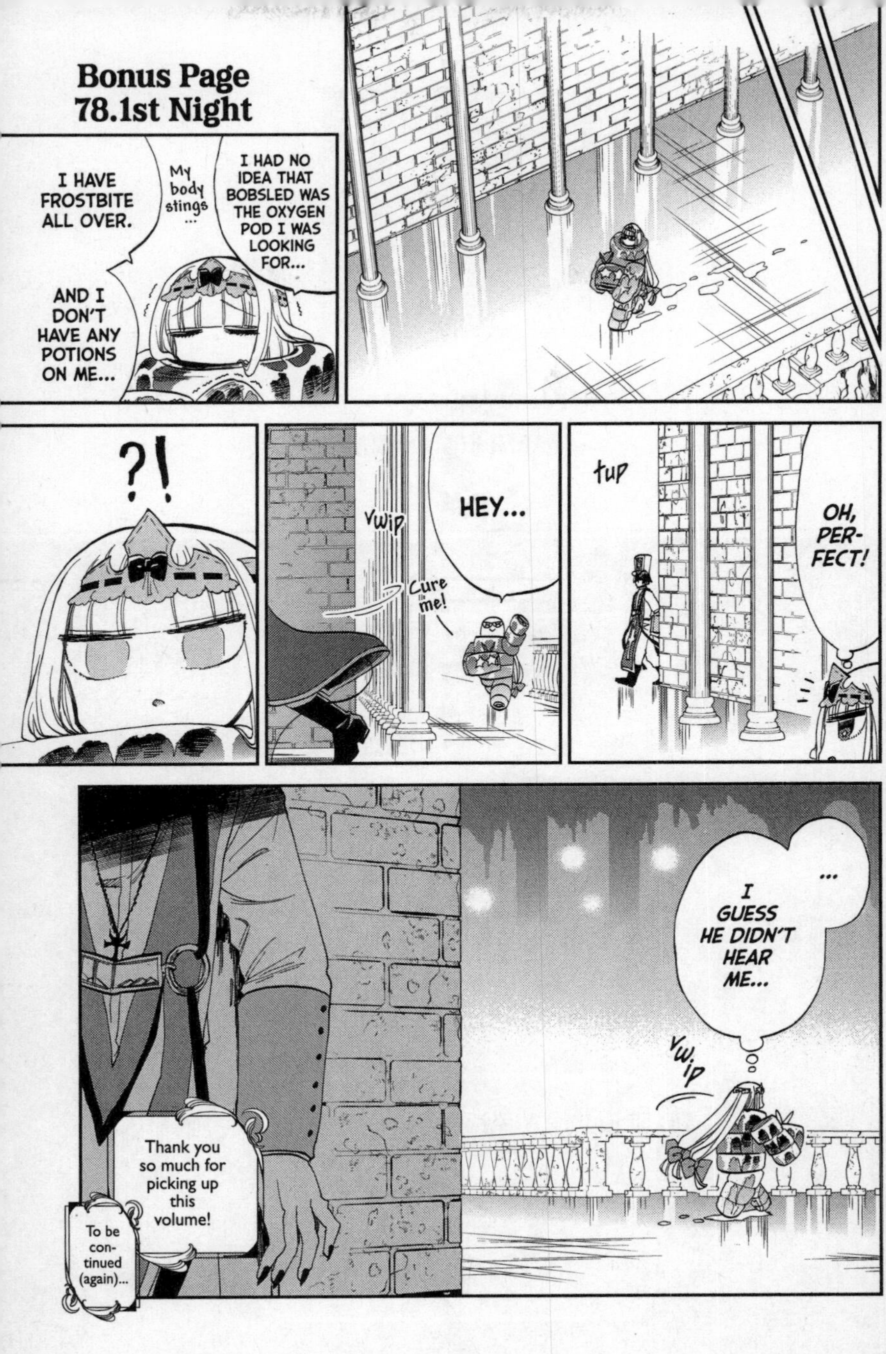
I HAD NO IDEA THAT BOBSLED WAS THE OXYGEN POD I WAS LOOKING FOR...
My body stings...
I HAVE FROSTBITE ALL OVER.
AND I DON'T HAVE ANY POTIONS ON ME...
OH, PER-FECT!
tup
HEY...
vwip
Cure me!
?!
... I GUESS HE DIDN'T HEAR ME...
vwip
Thank you so much for picking up this volume!
To be con-tinued (again)...

Teddy bear butts are so cute!

— KAGIJI KUMANOMATA

Monster Bird Pudding
à la Mode

INGREDIENTS

Monster Bird Egg
Sugar
Spices
Lovely Things

Those who lurk beneath the cover...

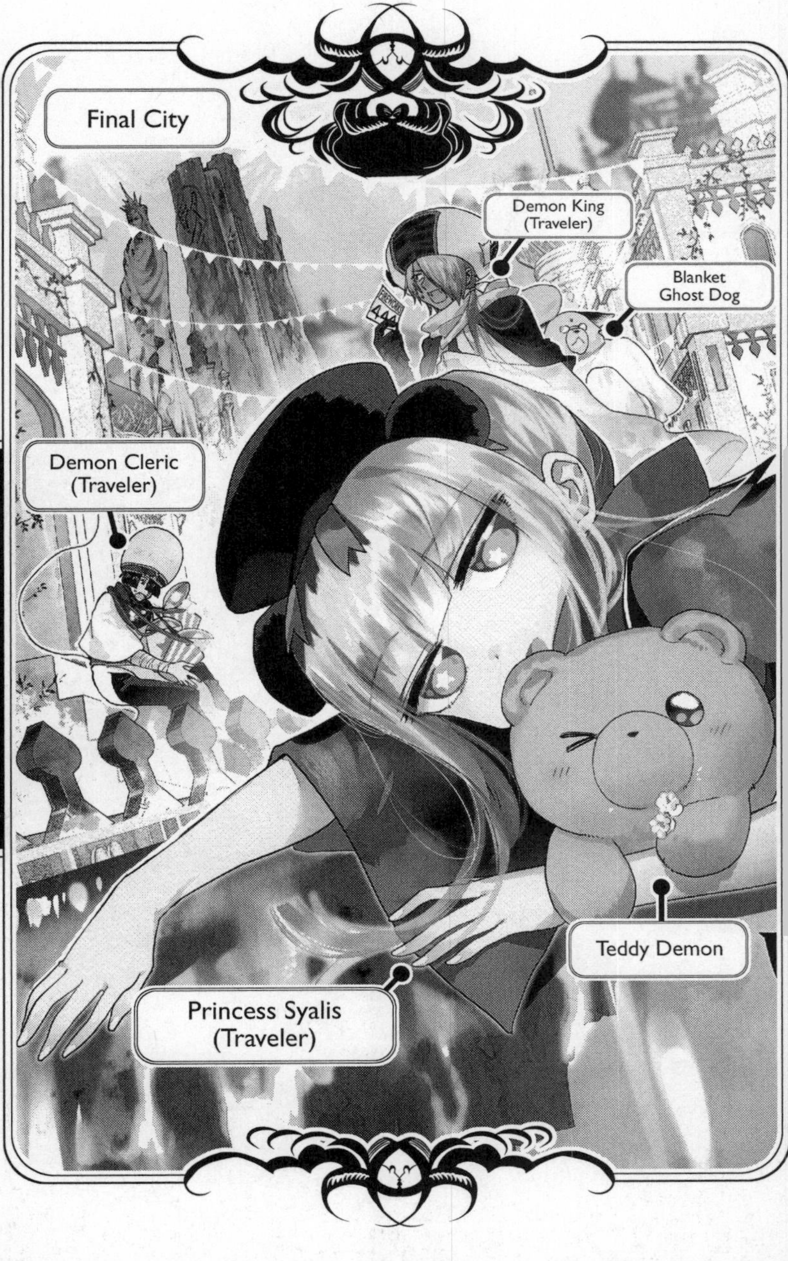
Final City
Demon King
(Traveler)
Blanket
Ghost Dog
Demon Cleric
(Traveler)
Teddy Demon
Princess Syalis
(Traveler)

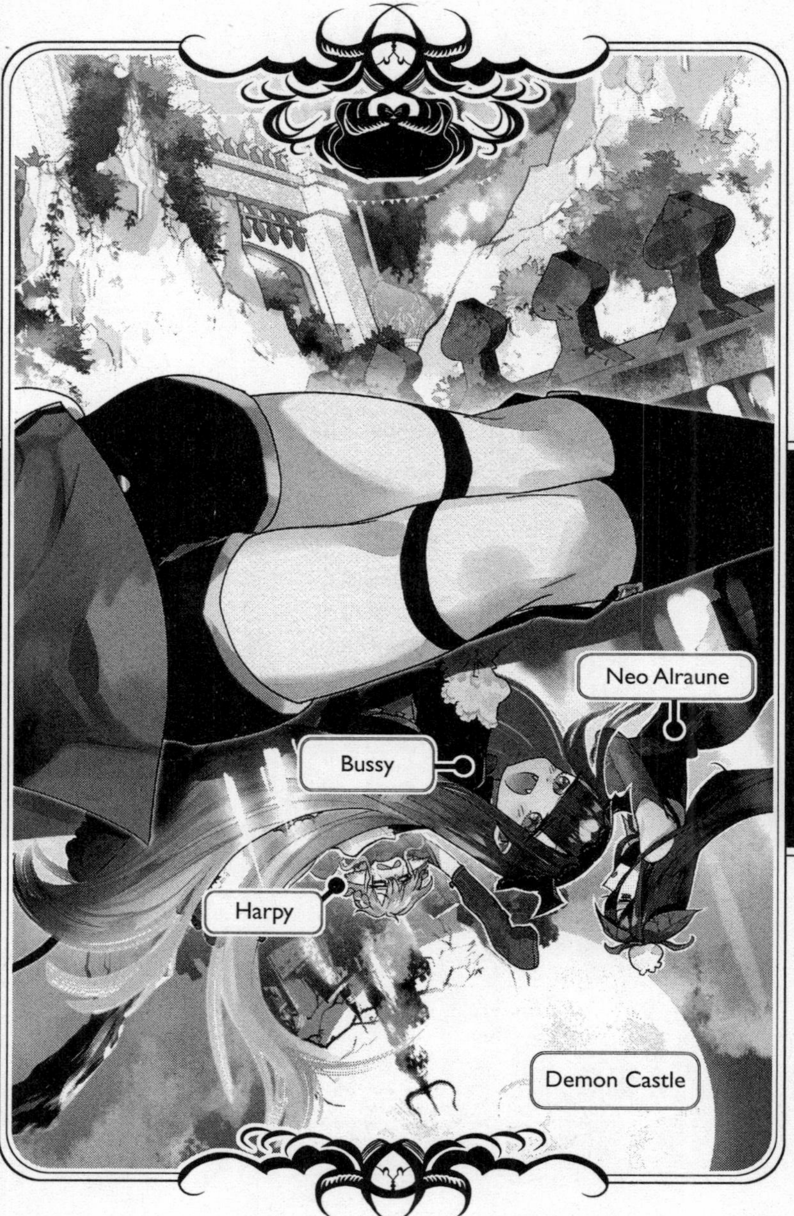
Neo Alraune
Bussy
Harpy
Demon Castle

SLEEPY PRINCESS IN THE DEMON CASTLE

6

Shonen Sunday Edition

STORY AND ART BY

KAGIJI KUMANOMATA

MAOUJO DE OYASUMI Vol. 6
by Kagiji KUMANOMATA
© 2016 Kagiji KUMANOMATA
All rights reserved.
Original Japanese edition published by SHOGAKUKAN.
English translation rights in the United States of America, Canada,
the United Kingdom, Ireland, Australia and New Zealand arranged
with SHOGAKUKAN.

TRANSLATION **TETSUICHIRO MIYAKI**

ENGLISH ADAPTATION **ANNETTE ROMAN**

TOUCH-UP ART & LETTERING **SUSAN DAIGLE-LEACH**

COVER & INTERIOR DESIGN **ALICE LEWIS**

EDITOR **ANNETTE ROMAN**

Printed in the U.S.A.

Published by VIZ Media, LLC
P.O. Box 77010
San Francisco, CA 94107

10 9 8 7 6 5 4 3 2 1
First printing, April 2019

VIZ MEDIA

viz.com

SHONEN SUNDAY

shonensunday.com

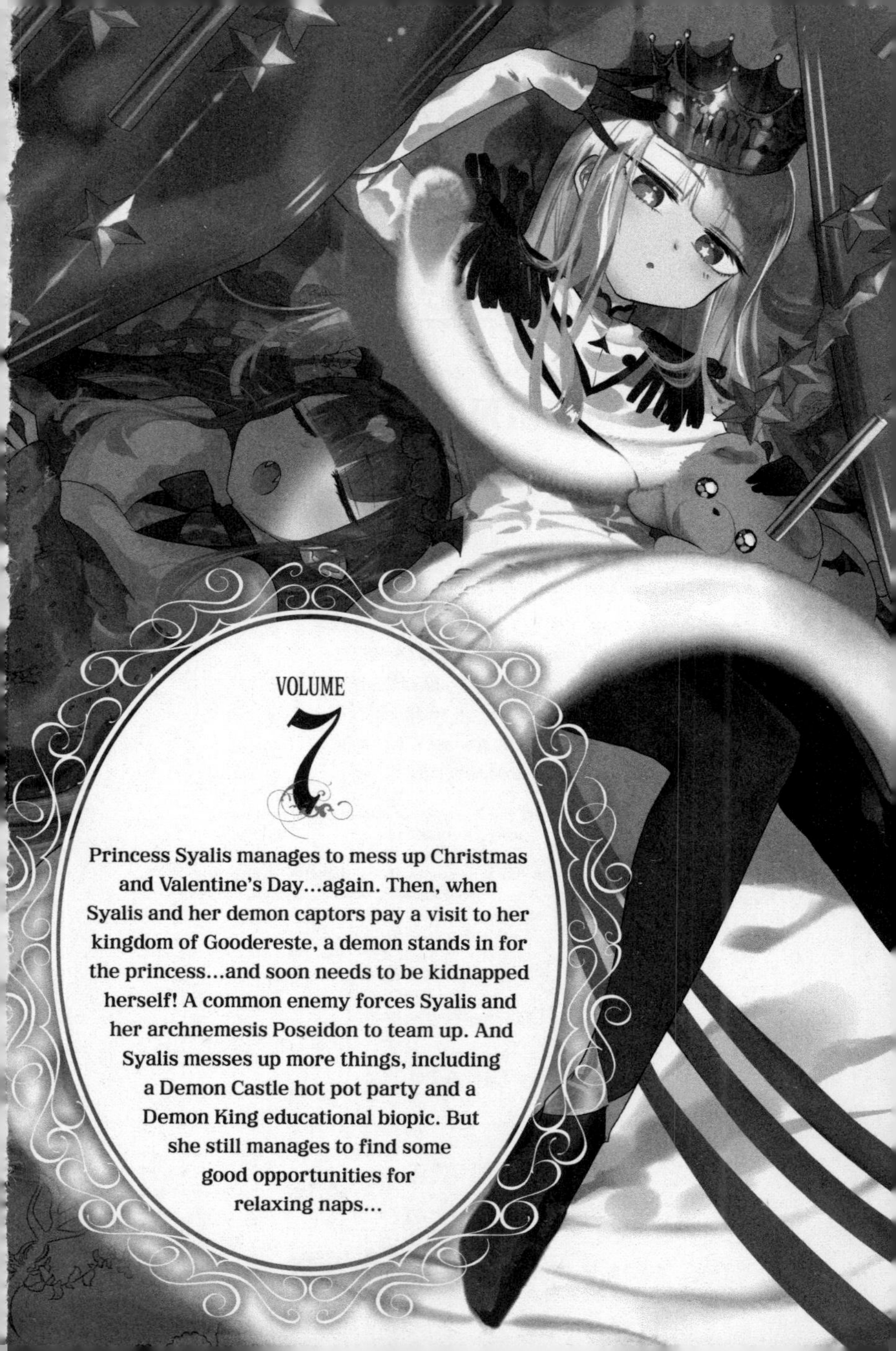
VOLUME
7
Princess Syalis manages to mess up Christmas and Valentine's Day...again. Then, when Syalis and her demon captors pay a visit to her kingdom of Goodereste, a demon stands in for the princess...and soon needs to be kidnapped herself! A common enemy forces Syalis and her archnemesis Poseidon to team up. And Syalis messes up more things, including a Demon Castle hot pot party and a Demon King educational biopic. But she still manages to find some good opportunities for relaxing naps...